THE PSYCHOLOGY OF S

This volume brings together the full range of modalities of social influence – from crowding, leadership and norm formation to resistance and mass mediation and designed objects – to set out a challenge-and-response 'cyclone' model. The authors use real-world examples to ground this model and review each modality of social influence in depth. A 'periodic table of social influence' is constructed that characterises and compares exercises of influence in practical terms. The wider implications of social influence are considered, such as how each exercise of a single modality stimulates responses from other modalities and how any everyday process is likely to arise from a mix of influences. The book demonstrates that different modalities of social influence are tactics that defend, question and develop 'common sense' over time and offers advice to those studying political and social movements, social change and management.

GORDON SAMMUT is Associate Professor of Social Psychology at the University of Malta. He has served as chief editor for *Methods of Psychological Intervention*, *The Cambridge Handbook of Social Representations* and *Understanding Self and Others: Explorations in Intersubjectivity and Interobjectivity*.

MARTIN W. BAUER is Professor of Social Psychology at the London School of Economics and Political Science and a member of acatech (German Academy of Technical Sciences). He is the former editor of *Public Understanding of Science* and investigates common sense, public opinion and attitudes towards novel technological developments.

THE PSYCHOLOGY OF SOCIAL INFLUENCE

Modes and Modalities of Shifting Common Sense

GORDON SAMMUT

University of Malta

MARTIN W. BAUER

London School of Economics and Political Science

CAMBRIDGE
UNIVERSITY PRESS

CAMBRIDGE
UNIVERSITY PRESS

University Printing House, Cambridge CB2 8BS, United Kingdom

One Liberty Plaza, 20th Floor, New York, NY 10006, USA

477 Williamstown Road, Port Melbourne, VIC 3207, Australia

314–321, 3rd Floor, Plot 3, Splendor Forum, Jasola District Centre, New Delhi – 110025, India

79 Anson Road, #06-04/06, Singapore 079906

Cambridge University Press is part of the University of Cambridge.

It furthers the University's mission by disseminating knowledge in the pursuit of
education, learning, and research at the highest international levels of excellence.

www.cambridge.org
Information on this title: www.cambridge.org/9781108416375
DOI: 10.1017/9781108236423

© Gordon Sammut and Martin W. Bauer 2021

First published 2021

A catalogue record for this publication is available from the British Library.

Library of Congress Cataloging-in-Publication Data
NAMES: Sammut, Gordon, author. | Bauer, Martin W., author.
TITLE: The psychology of social influence : modes and modalities of shifting common sense /
Gordon Sammut, University of Malta, Martin W. Bauer, London School of Economics and
Political Science.
DESCRIPTION: Cambridge, United Kingdom ; New York, NY : Cambridge University Press, 2020. |
Includes bibliographical references and index.
IDENTIFIERS: LCCN 2020025520 (print) | LCCN 2020025521 (ebook) | ISBN 9781108416375
(hardback) | ISBN 9781108402897 (paperback) | ISBN 9781108236423 (epub)
SUBJECTS: LCSH: Social influence.
CLASSIFICATION: LCC HM1176 .S26 2020 (print) | LCC HM1176 (ebook) | DDC 302/.13–dc23
LC record available at https://lccn.loc.gov/2020025520
LC ebook record available at https://lccn.loc.gov/2020025521

ISBN 978-1-108-41637-5 Hardback
ISBN 978-1-108-40289-7 Paperback

*We write this book in the memory of our late teachers
and their lasting inspirations; those still
among us are too many to list:*

*Rob Farr (1936–2013, LSE, London)
Serge Moscovici (1925–2014, EHESS, Paris)
Rom Harré (1927–2019, University of Oxford)*

Contents

Figures

ix

Tables

Boxes

Foreword 1

Of the plethora of topics that social psychology addresses, none is more fundamental and ubiquitous than that of social influence. It forms the very essence of human interaction, the way we impact others and they impact us in return. It underlies the phenomenon of human sociality, and illuminates the processes of group formation, intergroup interaction, and the creation of culture. Small wonder then, that the theme of social influence reverberated across a broad spectrum of social science disciplines (including psychology, political science, economics, sociology, and anthropology among others) and was approached on multiple levels of analysis. A great achievement of Sammut and Bauer's *The Psychology of Social Influence: Modes and Modalities of Shifting Common Sense* is its ability to discuss in a coherent fashion the panoply of phenomena, approaches, and methodologies that populate the sprawling universe of concepts and effects known as the domain of social influence. The book weaves its narrative smoothly among epochs, paradigms, and findings, without taking sides and manages to pay equal respect and appreciation to the work of scholars of diametrically opposed methodological persuasions and contrasting philosophical predilections: Social representations are given equal consideration as the conceptions of social experimentalists; Freud's dynamic speculations are treated on par with models of quantitative economists; the observational work of developmentalists; and so on.

In that regard, this book is a distinctly postmodern, and constructivist work. It allows a "thousand flowers to bloom" and implicitly suggests that the different insights and results are but "ways of talking." There is no one Truth to be revealed but rather different narratives to be constructed, each with its own illuminations and insights. It is that perspective that allows the book to succeed in its mission, and spread before its readers the rich smorgasbord of concepts, findings, and observations that it manages to offer: The realization that the science of social influence isn't progressing linearly, nor is it necessarily getting "better and better" as the work goes on. Hence, any insight or perspective merits a respectful consideration no matter when it was articulated, from what disciplinary vantage point, or at what level of analysis. In that regard, too, *The Psychology of Social Influence* contrasts starkly with mainstream social psychological research in that its implicit assumption of scientific progress pays scant attention to the history of ideas and limits its researchers' attention to a relatively narrow band of findings and concepts defining the "here and now." In contrast, the book is wonderfully erudite and scholarly allowing the reader to appreciate the variety of perspectives and intellectual traditions that over time were brought to bear on social influence as a realm of phenomena.

The Psychology of Social Influence has an appealing organizing structure encompassed in the authors *cyclone model* and including its components of normalization, assimilation, and adaptation. Like pieces in a kaleidoscope, individual opinions and attitudes coalesce into broader patterns of beliefs forming normalized social representations, belief systems, and worldviews. These too may change under the impact of innovations often introduced by opinion minorities, if not by lone thinkers who defy the received views and convince the majorities to follow. Concepts of intersubjectivity and inter-objectivity elucidate the crucial importance of shared reality and culture as frameworks from which intelligible behaviours can be launched that afford actors meaning and significance. The concept of public sphere defines the arena where societal debate and discussion embody the shaping of social representations and collective worldviews. Coherence of the book is further imposed by the authors' helpful distinctions between modalities and modes of social influence and by partitioning of the book into self-contained sections that package together approaches and contents that share elements in common.

An aspect of the work that I found particularly valuable is its consistent ties to real-world examples and events. Figures like Adolf Hitler and Julius Caesar are invoked to illustrate leadership styles; Brexit is brought up to show how public debate is the platform for peaceful deliberation as are the examples from entirely different times and places such as ancient India and China. The *Charlie Hebdo* offices in Paris is brought up to argue that material violence should not be classed together with social influence phenomena. Above all, the diverse references to known situations and characters demonstrate the relevance of social influence research to occurrences of broad public interest, and demonstrate the utility of the social sciences in advancing a deeper understanding of history as well as politics.

The Psychology of Social Influence is a work with a definite point of view. In this sense it is often intriguing and thought-provoking. Though

Professors Sammut and Bauer accept the utility of the experimental method in illuminating specific effects, they eschew the controlled experiment as a paradigm for social influence phenomena writ large. As they put it plainly: "In everyday life, social influence attempts do not follow the serial and mechanistic conceptions of the laboratory experiment." In fact, it appears that Sammut and Bauer shun the very possibility of a unified theory of social influence that would treat it as a general phenomenon (X) with knowable antecedents and consequences. Instead, they propose to recognize the inherent variability of influence instances and to parse them according to their sources, modes, and modalities. Whether one ultimately resonates to the "splitter" philosophy of science implicit in this recommendation or believes, instead, that our task is to "lump" surface diversity and reveal its unifying deep structure, *The Psychology of Social Influence* does a wonderful job of characterizing the heterogeneity that, this way or that, must be taken into account. I can't think of a more comprehensive introduction to this fundamental topic of crucial importance to science and society.

Arie W. Kruglanski
Distinguished University Professor
Department of Psychology
University of Maryland, USA

Foreword 2

We have entered a new era – it is not 'business as usual' in the realm of social influence. In this new era, traditional beliefs such as 'the truth matters', 'facts should guide decisions', and 'might does not make right' have been seriously undermined. Of course, such beliefs have always been attacked by small numbers of critics, but now they are openly dismissed by populist, authoritarian national leaders in major societies, as well as the massive crowds that follow them. On climate change, human rights, sexism, minority–majority relations, wealth inequality, and some other enormously important issues, the influence of science and facts have diminished. Moreover, this trend is not limited to any one or a few countries, but sweeps across the populations of numerous societies. Those who look in amusement at Donald Trump in the United States and assume that it is only in America that social influence has been transformed are making a profound mistake. This change is global, associated with rising insecurity and uncertainty, and represents the most serious threat to democracy since the Second World War (Moghaddam, 2019). Nor will this change and its consequences disappear in the next decade or two, if Trump is defeated in the 2020 US presidential elections.

Sammut and Bauer have written a book that is at the forefront of efforts by social psychologists to respond to the foundational global transformations taking place in social influence in all its different manifestations. Their very well-structured book is broad and to some degree multidisciplinary, but its main contribution is to social psychology. Social influence has been a central topic of research throughout the history of social psychology. Sammut and Bauer provide a critical discussion of this history, with insightful coverage of research on conformity, leadership, obedience, and other key topics, but they also provide provocative new ideas for pushing research forward to grapple with social influence in the twenty-first century.

Changes in social influence have to be understood in the context of enormous shifts across the globe: the rise of populist movements, the emergence of 'strongman' authoritarian leaders, and the increasing threat to democracy underway in our age of uncertainty. Research evidence suggests that when people experience uncertainty and threat, they are less inclined to support human rights and more inclined to support authoritarian leadership and punitive measures against minorities (Moghaddam, 2019). Of course, historical case studies also demonstrate the same trend, in an even more concrete fashion. For example, consider the forced relocation and internment in 'camps' of about 120,000 Japanese Americans during World War II, through an executive order issued in 1942 by President Franklin Roosevelt. Most of those interned were United States citizens. In 2008 the US government apologized for this action, which clearly had been based on racist motives. How could President Roosevelt, known for his progressive social policies, have ordered the mass internment of more than 100,000 US citizens without trial and without evidence of wrongdoing? Research evidence suggests that the serious threats experienced by Americans, particularly after the Japanese attack at Pearl Harbor (1941), resulted in lower support for human rights and increased attacks on minorities.

Globalization in the twenty-first century is leading to increased perceived threat because of a number of large-scale changes, the most visible being massive and rapid migrations of human populations across national borders and entire regions. In addition to formal migration, hundreds of thousands of refugees (often deemed 'illegals') are on the move around the world at any one time. These population movements now take place rapidly, so that, for example, in a single year millions of people from Syria and other parts of the Near and Middle East move to Germany and other European countries. The resulting 'sudden contact' between incoming 'invaders' and host communities leads to a perceived threat among the populations of host societies, with a resulting backlash from extremist and sometimes violent nationalists. Consequently, anti-immigrant and anti-refugee populist movements are on the rise in societies as diverse as the United States, South Africa, Germany, and Poland, and attempts are made to construct stronger walls, including Brexit and 'Donald's wall,' to keep out the 'invaders'. In this new climate of rising ethnocentrism, some of the established tenets of social influence have been trodden underfoot.

For example, consider the principle that the influence a bit of information has on people is determined by the status and legitimacy of the information source. This principle has come to acquire the status of 'fact' in the post–World War II period. However, what is the validity of this 'established fact' now? Consider the case of climate change. The vast majority of legitimate scientists report that human activity is a major contributor to climate change and global warming. Second, scientific models of climate change predict that unless we alter our use of fossil fuels and adopt more green technology, human-induced global warming will result in rising sea levels and other changes that will bring catastrophic damage to planet earth and human societies. Our traditional models of social influence tell us that as the legitimate source of scientific information, scientists should have enormous social influence and our attitudes and behavior should be changing as a result of messages from scientists. But Donald Trump and other populist leaders, who have no scientific training, status, or legitimacy, have dismissed the message of thousands of scientists on climate change as 'fake news'. They have decided that in the domain of climate change, scientific facts do not matter.

In response to clear evidence that Donald Trump repeatedly lies and has behaved in racist and sexist ways, one group of his followers stood behind a placard announcing 'We Don't Care!' The same pattern of behaviour has been witnessed in other societies with populist 'strongman' leadership (Moghaddam, 2019). This is the new reality of social influence in the twenty-first century, and this is what social psychologists must confront and try to explain (and find solutions for!). How can we be moving into an anti-science, anti-fact era when electronic communications and the World Wide Web provide us with vast access to information? In answering such questions, we find that in some respects we have entered a new and different world, but in other respects some of the basic principles of social psychology continue to be valid.

Consider the vast and complex role of the Internet in social influence around the world. On the one hand, supporters of democracy have been disappointed in the development of 'echo chambers', with the strong tendency for internet users to communicate mainly with others who hold the same values and opinions as themselves, and to almost exclusively take notice of information that endorses their own perspectives. In practice, instead of seeking new information and opinions that we might learn from but that might challenge our own worldviews, we tend to interact with people and sources that endorse our worldviews and legitimize our biases. This trend in internet communications is new in as far as the technology is concerned, but it is 'old' in the sense that it is based on the principles of similarity–attraction well known to social psychologists. We prefer to interact with similar others, both at individual and collective levels.

Our patterns of internet use follow the same similarity-attraction paths as found in friendships, marriage choices, and inter–group relations.

Sammut and Bauer have rightly called for a new generation of social psychologists to give priority to research in social influence; the urgency and timeliness of this call is most evident in the domain of leadership. Advances in electronic communications mean that decision-making could become more bottom-up, with the general population more involved in deciding policies. Research on social influence among animals clearly shows that collective decision-making does work effectively among some life forms (e.g., honey-bee democracy). However, the rise of authoritarian 'strongmen' around the world, backed by populist, ethnocentric populations intent on building walls around their societies, suggests that human groups are moving in a different direction, one that reflects the values of fascism in the 1930s. There is an urgent need for social psychologists to refocus efforts to better understand social influence processes, and to help strengthen and preserve open societies. Sammut and Bauer have provided a highly timely work that in important ways contributes to this historic effort.[1]

Fathali M. Moghaddam
Professor
Department of Psychology
Georgetown University, USA

[1] Moghaddam, F. M. (2019). *Threat to Democracy: The Appeal of Authoritarianism in an Age of Uncertainty*. Washington, DC: American Psychological Association Press.

Acknowledgements

This book arose from the authors teaching two course modules on 'social influence' for several years (PS464, later PB430, at the London School of Economics and Political Science; PSY2635 at the University of Malta). We thank our students for their enthusiasm and incredulity regarding the unfolding conceptualisation and arguments over the years. Not everything we discussed and learned made it to the end. We hope you will enjoy the final version.

Our thanks go to Janka Romero and Emily Watton at Cambridge University Press for their guidance and patience in negotiating the progress of the manuscript. Many thanks to Sue Howard for her help in editing the final manuscript and to Penny Hilton and Piero Zagami for discussing and redesigning our graphics. And we are very grateful to Arie W. Kruglanski and Fathali M. Moghaddam for their appreciative introductory commentaries (forewords) on the book project.

Special thanks to our significant others, Claire, Aanah and Nina (GS), and Sandra and Ana (MB), for their unwavering support and tolerance of recurrent absent-mindedness, without which this project would not have been possible.

CHAPTER I

Modalities of Social Influence
Preconditions (Public Sphere) and Demarcations (Non-violence)

In January 2007, Apple Inc. launched the iPhone, and it seems that the world was never the same again. A gadget was devised to do away with stylus pens and keyboards that dominated the design of the earlier Personal Digital Assistant [PDA] aimed at the business market. The iPhone, brain child of Apple tech guru Steve Jobs, was the first device of its kind to target the mass market. Smartphones quickly proliferated and ushered in an era of mobile connectivity over social media platforms. Riding the tech tide, social media became the new way of being in touch. Facebook, originally conceived as a digital book of Harvard University students, quickly expanded to become the world's most used social networking website and was valued at $15 billion just four years after its launch in 2004 – a hefty return on the original $2,000 invested by its start-up founders. Google, Yandex, Facebook, WeChat, Twitter, Weibo and Baidu's impact, on the back of attention-grabbing affordances, enabled by the global proliferation of smartphones, seems unparalleled in history. Social networking ushered in an era of citizen journalism and rapid collective action. Social media is implicated in the mass uprisings that took place against long-standing dictatorships in North African countries in 2010. Citizens coordinated public protests against prevalent regimes over social media. On the other hand, privacy has been jeopardised. In 2016, Facebook data was misused by Cambridge Analytica, a small United Kingdom–based consultancy that became an eponymous scandal: the company had harvested personal data from millions of Facebook users' accounts to fine-tune political propaganda, linking their likes/dislikes to a volunteered personality inventory in order to create more effective micro-targeting of messages. Social media became a new platform for exercising social influence by manipulation in everyday life and globally.

Yet, despite the hyperbole, while many things are different with this new technology, much also stays the same. In this book we take a closer look at nine different modalities of social influence, from crowd behaviour to persuasion, not least to clarify how these social influences are affected by new technology. For instance, we will ask: how did social networking affect crowd behaviour or leadership; how do we conform to peer pressure or obey authorities in everyday life, or how are we persuaded or resistant to these influences in everyday life?

The study of social influence has waxed and waned across the social sciences over the years. Many readers will no doubt be familiar with landmark studies, such as LeBon's crowd psychology, Asch's conformity experiments or Milgram's obedience demonstrations. Whilst scandalously insightful at the time, the focus of social influence research has largely ebbed towards more neutral and less controversial paradigms such as dual-track persuasion. However, the turmoil instigated by a new cycle of political populism worldwide and issues of 'fake news' and cyber-propaganda, brings renewed public interest to the dynamics of social influence in a wider sense. When faced with Mr Trump's presidential election success and the UK Brexit referendum in 2016; the earlier Arab Spring and Russia's meddling in Ukraine and the Baltics; the looming United States–China trade war; and nuclear proliferation in Asia and the Middle East, we seek to answer the question: who influences whom and in what way? For a while, it seemed as if history had set the world on course towards a peaceful and prosperous global village. But once more, this utopian hope has retreated, not least because of the effects of nefarious social influence.

Our aim in this volume is to take stock of the disparate literature on 'social influence' with a programmatic focus on different modes and modalities. We will proceed in three conceptual steps: first, we review different **modalities** of social influence in separate chapters, on crowds, leadership, norm formation, conformity, conversion, obedience and persuasion. Secondly, we examine face-to-face interactions, and amplifications of social influence via mass mediations and designed arte-facts as three different **modes**. Thirdly, we examine the contributions of social influence to three functions: to build, to defend or to shift common sense in the face of challenges. We will call these three functions 'normalisation', 'assimilation' and 'accommodation'. Finally, we bring this mode-modality-functions matrix into our **Periodic Table of Social Influence** (in Chapter 10). We hope that this integrative framework will revive the impetus for social influence research by suggesting new research questions, identifying gaps in traditional paradigms and opening the way to recognise and 'discover' novel modalities (as periodic tables often do).

However, before we delve into discussing the modes and modalities, we want to address some key assumptions of this field of inquiry: for this we need a short history of ideas of social influence which highlights the need to address the question of violence and the constitution of a public sphere. Here we inherit ideas of the Greek Polis: 'among ourselves we debate, with barbarians we fight'. Among themselves the Greeks practised civic rhetoric, across borders they practised warfare; competitive strife being the common theme. We start by elaborating these necessary assumptions of our model.

A Very Schematic History of Social Influence Ideas

A world in turmoil needs a better understanding of social influence as part of an array of conflict resolution strategies. And yet, the academic study of social influence is stagnating while public and popular references are widespread and growing. A cursory review of a number of popular social psychology textbooks (e.g., Aronson et al., 2017; Hogg & Vaughan, 2018) reveals that the treatment of social influence is limited to a rehearsal of classical experiments and no attempts to integrate processes operating at the individual level with those operating at the group level. The diversity of social influence as different modalities is presented disparately in separate chapters neither bridging concepts nor offering integrative theorising.

We can easily recognise that this state of affairs is the legacy of a series of historical 'flavours of the time'; in any period 'social influence is X', and over time the many Xs simply accumulate and gather dust without any systematic comparison nor coherent theoretical ordering of the phenomenon. The past 150 years thus reveal the fashion cycles of social influence (see Figure 1.1). These cycles can be notionally reconstructed by using N-gram keyword searches, a useful Google service. And indeed, past episodes show a recurrent rise and fall of particular paradigms as referenced by specific keywords. This coming and going would clearly call for some in-depth historical investigations (see Paicheler, 1988) which is however beyond our present purpose. We simply note how the history of the past 150 years has accumulated different ways of naming, analysing and talking about social influence see also Box 1.1. We need to sift through these discursive resources and secure the 'truth' of each cycle of what remains insightful for the understanding of social influence at present.

We confess to harbouring a degree of dissatisfaction with this 'empiricist' treatment of social influence and our efforts to write this book are motivated by an aspiration to redress this 'butterfly collection' with a theoretical integration of different modalities. A further aim of the present

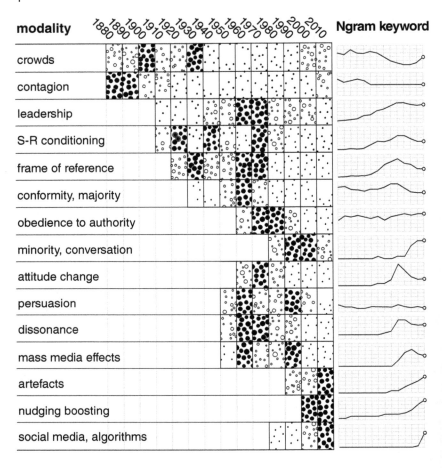

Figure 1.1   'Social influence' has the flavour of time; the word means different things at different times

book is to take stock of the rich scholarship in the field of social psychology, and avoid exaggerated claims to a new theory of 'social influence is X' which would be little more than presenting 'old wine in new bottles', as the claim to innovation so often is. What are seemingly novel insights into human behaviour may be rehearsals of old facts in new language. In summary, we tackle three overarching concerns in this volume: the processes, the structure and the context of social influence, and for this we need to address some key assumptions first.

Power: Hard or Soft – Violence or Non-violence

Nye (1991) famously distinguished between 'hard' and 'soft' power. Hard power refers to the use of force, such as military interventions and law-and-order police forces. Hard power does not demand conversion, only compliance and submission; it observes the overarching rule of 'Might Is Right'. Soft power, on the other hand, refers to a range of strategies and tactics that increase conformity or precipitate conversion, and thus changes minds; it constitutes the 'Politics of Persuasion' or diplomacy. The two combine in strategic thinking although they are conceptually distinct and indeed serve different functions.

It seems that historically the process of 'civilisation' is tied to the containment of violent force in favour of **non-violent forms of life**; the reduction of hard power is compensated by the elevation of soft power, whilst their sum total might be a constant in any society [Power$_{const}$ = Hard + Soft]. Elias (2000 [1939]) reconstructs this process of 'civilisation' as the progressive control of affect and violent behaviour, which required the centralisation of violent force, initially at the King's Court and later in the state authorities. The psychological and the social sphere interlink in this process of 'taking control', so that the diffusion of manners of hygiene, napkin use and eating with implements such as forks and spoons correlate with this monopolising of power (at least in European history). Violence as a form of life is progressively sectioned and relegated to the preserve of professionals in the armed forces and police services – and this state monopoly for the use of violence is strictly regulated (Howard, 2001).

As a form of life (Reemtsma, 2016), violence is an immediate relation between bodies. Violence treats other bodies as mere obstacle-objects; it is harmful to bodies for sexual motives; or it gratuitously kills because a body is a nuisance; or it is fun to demonstrate that you simply can (exercise absolute power): 'I am God', says the torturer, 'no salvation from anybody ... I call the shots here'. This communicative potential of gratuitous violence, indeed a natural capacity, is progressively reduced and contained in the process of civilisation by *delegitimating*. For civic communication violence is the exception, and this is buttressed by recorded memories of survivors of violence, who speak with authority of

Box 1.1 'Social influence' beyond social psychology

Clearly, social psychology has no monopoly over the phenomenon or the term 'social influence'. The term is also popular in other fields of the social sciences. A brief glance into neighbouring fields reveals different vocabulary and foci of analysis.

Political science recognises social influence as constraints on public opinion and on voting behaviour (e.g., Kinder, 1998; Zaller, 1992). The processes of public opinion and of voting are seen to be variously constrained and the research examines and seeks to control these constraints. Generally, public opinion is defined as those streams of beliefs, ideas and preferences which governments might be prudent to heed in order to avoid the risk of losing support; hence public opinion itself is a lever of influencing governments.

According to the **strategic theory** of international relations, military force is the 'continuation of politics by other means' (Clausewitz); hence politics includes violent force as a form of influence and thus distinguishes between hard and soft powers. Military strategy is the logic of imposing one's will on an opponent, therefore influencing them by mobilising military means of conflict engagement.

Sociological theory considers social influence arising mainly from authority and prestige, thereby distinguishing different sources of authority: traditional, charismatic or rule-based (Weber, 1922). Authoritative influence defines a middle way between violence on the one hand and argumentative deliberation on the other. Social influence becomes one of several GSCM (generalised symbolic communication media) which disambiguate social situations and make the acceptance of claims more likely (Luhmann, 1990; Parsons, 1963); language, technology and GSCM are crutches to turn communication from a highly improbable to a more probable event. Influence is the general medium of persuasion, leading to actions for good reasons, which are based neither on deontic obligation (ethics), sanction (power) nor incentive (economic). GSCM are modelled on the legal system which operates on a binary code (legal–illegal; an action is concordant with the code of law or not) and regulates all matters accordingly; this is guaranteed by an institutional backstop (the constitution of the country). Social influence is similarly coded as persuasion based on prestige and reputation (high/low–good/bad) and supposedly guaranteed by a prestige hierarchy in society (social influence needs A-lists of celebrities). However, whether social influence can be guaranteed by a unique hierarchy is challenged by Habermas in his theory of communicative action (1994). Systems guarantee the playing field of strategic communication on a specific code. By contrast, social influence is tied to the sphere of communicative action oriented towards a common understanding. Communicative action serves multiple functions and not just one single code, 'famous or not'.

what has happened; but also buttressed by collective denial of the violent origins of 'civilisation' (Girard, 2008) and the sublimation of aggression into more acceptable activities such as sports or cinema (Lorenz, 2005).

On the other hand, soft power is permissible by rules of engagement within a secured field: *among ourselves we talk, with the Barbarians we fight.* History traces the ways in which humans have tried to extend this secured playing field of rules. For instance, in the United Nations General Assembly (since 1946), national representatives meet to discuss issues and forge solutions with the explicit intention of setting a global common ground that avoids or reduces armed conflict. Literally speaking, the guns are left at the door and do not feature at the negotiating table. In this way, soft power may curb the need for hard power; it becomes part of the effort of civilising even warfare in the context of an international search for stability or eternal peace (Howard, 2001). That said, allusions to the ability to use force may also mean that some actors strive to combine soft power *with* hard power in a dual strategy, leaving interlocutors with the sole option of learning who is 'ultimately' right: the soft way and/or the hard way.

In modern societies, hard power is relegated to a resting state, kept in reserve. In other words, it can be revived and utilised if needed but unless actively resorted to, its potential remains at rest when interacting agents commit to resolve discordances through soft power alone. Contemporary modern societies have centralised the use of force and the 'rule of law' designates the aspiration to make violence an exception, not a norm of the game. In most modern societies, only the armed forces and police services carry arms, under extensive training and close regulation. Any use of force requires justification in line with rules and regulations. 'Wild West' gun slinging is a characteristic of only war-torn societies dominated by armed militias in 'failing states'.

Thus, we need to address how we can neatly categorise any strategy of influence as either a soft or hard power exercise (see Box 1.2). For the purpose of this book, we equate soft power with the exercise of a mix of modalities of social influence at the expense of violence, but with the inclusion of authority.

Needless to say, establishing an agreement to relinquish hard power does not mean that discordances will not arise. It only means that when they do, the parties are committed to restraining from using violence to resolve discordances in an effort to reconcile disparate perspectives and concerns in communication. In doing so, different parties engage social influence that convinces other parties about the legitimacy of their own issues. Social influence furthers the cause without bloodshed.

Box 1.2 *Charlie Hebdo* **and the question of terrorist propaganda**

On the 7th January 2015, masked gunmen attacked the offices of Charlie Hebdo, a weekly newspaper in Paris, killing twelve people and injuring eleven others. The gunmen singled out editor Stephane Charbonnier and his crew in the attack. Charbonnier was held responsible for publishing controversial cartoons of the Prophet Muhammad. Reports claim that upon leaving the scene, the gunmen declared they had avenged the Prophet. Both gunmen were killed in a stand-off with police officers two days after the Charlie Hebdo attack.

Whilst the attack itself seems to be a direct retaliation to the newspaper's provocative cartoons, terrorist attacks have an intended target beyond punishing the perpetrators themselves. Terrorist attacks involve the use of hard power to achieve material outcomes in eliminating a specific target, such as editor Charbonnier. They are also intended as a warning to others who are similarly inclined as the victim. The message imparted by a terrorist act is 'if you do the same thing, you will suffer the same fate'. The fear associated with the outcome is intended to alter hearts and minds in a determined direction. Consequently, terrorism can be argued to be a hard power tactic with social influence ramifications, otherwise known as the 'propaganda of the act'. However, we contend that terrorism cannot be treated as a modality of social influence, due to the fact that it has a clear violence dimension. As we argue in this chapter, hard power may serve to secure the playing field. In this way, actors may go on to negotiate the playing field with those commanding the might. Terrorism is however 'outlawed' when parties have committed to 'leave guns at the door'. Social influence proper starts when political actors have put hard power aside.

On the other hand, social influence is part of competitive scenarios where alternatives are appraised and preferable options selected over others. In other words, social influence is competitive and serves for some perspectives to prevail at the expense of others. Social influence settles the competition score by securing collaboration from like-minded others that, in itself, becomes the mechanism to compete. There would be no need for social influence in a gathering of 'perfectly enlightened' Buddhas as no work is needed to achieve common sense; the common mindset is already in place.

Grey Areas of Social Influence – Manipulation and Symbolic Violence

If soft power makes exclusive use of social influence, this does not mean that all social influence is always soft power. The exercise of social influence often involves some dubious strategies that raise questions regarding their morality and how their usage may 'corrupt' the playing field. For instance, in trying to be persuasive, one may opt for a positive self-presentation to stimulate agreeableness (see Cialdini, 1984). This practice is quite common, for instance, when dressing up for an important meeting or for a job interview. In such a managed situation, an individual may present a somewhat different version of their true self, one that they think a prospective employer might prefer. Similarly, presenting one's operational results during a 'business breakfast' helps put critics in a positive mood that should help them accept one's output more readily.

These anecdotal examples may be multiplied along a sliding scale of ever more dubious strategies that may involve 'dinners' with complimentary wine and entertainment. If this is still licit social influence, then how about spiking an opponent's drink to amplify the powers of the wine? Or what about having a vicious dog showing teeth, while 'suading' some behaviour? Our sliding scale is anchored on convincing by unending conversation on the one hand and by use of the gun on the other extreme, with a grey area for the middle ground (see Figure 1.2). The question we want to pose is: at which point does an attempt to influence become illicit, that is, become equivalent to a threat of violence? We contend that this depends on the established rules of engagement, but it also involves perception and

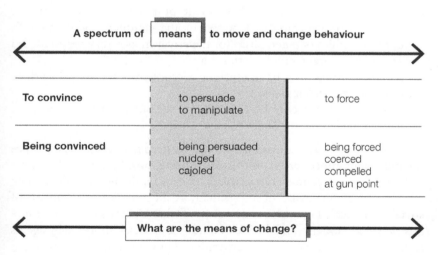

Figure 1.2   The continuum of 'means of influence' with a grey area between licit methods to persuade another person and illicit methods of forcing their will

judgement. In other words, it is part of local norms of acceptability. For instance, whilst racial 'symbolic violence' is explicitly outlawed as 'violence' in many countries, questions remain as to whether freedom of expression can be invoked to 'incite hate' and whether such incitement is 'violence', therefore something outside freedom of expression. This became the downfall of the famous international PR firm *Bell-Pottinger* in 2017 when it became public notice that, far from being illegal, they suggested 'inciting racism' in Africa as their client advice on how to campaign. Other clients distanced themselves wanting to avoid being associated with such 'illicit tactics'.

The *dubiousness of social influence* lies in its fuzzy demarcation from manipulation and symbolic violence. This calls for ethical considerations of licit and illicit social influence. Indeed, Fischer (2017) analyses the **ethics of manipulation** which recently is highlighted with the wide propagation of 'nudges', 'decision-preserving decision architectures' or 'non-fiscal policy interventions' (see Chapter 9). Because manipulation can have long-term collateral consequences affecting the self-respect and sense of agency of the manipulated persons, Fischer develops four criteria to justify such grey-area interventions in social life:

- the persons manipulated need to be respected as persons; the manipulation must be confined to and focussed on a particular aspect of their lives;
- manipulation must be for benevolent purposes; it must be in the interest of the manipulated person or the common good; this calls upon the ethics of paternalism (or maternalism as it may be) modelled on a caring parent–child relationship;
- the intervention must be transparent, recognisable and stoppable; there must be an opt-out clause;
- manipulation can only be a temporary measure, never a permanent installation.

These ethical concerns make it clear that we need to assess social influence not only on its **effectiveness**, but also on it being **morally sound**. The latter is, however, not a primary characteristic of social influence, but depending on the context and its rules of engagement, we might call this the **'culture of social influence'**. These boundary norms of what is admissible into the tool box of 'social influence' might itself be subject to social influence by agents seeking to secure influence opportunities. Thus, in understanding social influence, we need to consider each tool but also the tool box: what is included, and what's better left out.

Modes and Modalities of Social Influence and the Cyclone Model

Our particular take on social influence in this book rests on *four basic propositions* (P): social influence is many things, rests in the quest for the modern public sphere, unfolds in three basic functions and converges on common sense.

P1: Social Influence Is Many Things; It Comes in Modalities and Modes

In this book we unfold social influence as a set of different modalities. Social influence is many things. In the applied literature, social influence is often defined in terms of persuasion (e.g., Cialdini, 1984), or simply the latest fashion concept such as 'nudging', as we argued previously (see Figure 1.1). This leads to a limited understanding of the phenomenon. We offer a more comprehensive vision. Social influence is not just X (e.g., persuading or nudging); it is also leading, crowding, pressuring peers, converting opponents, agenda setting, barricades, installations of all sorts and so on and so forth. Our first thesis, therefore, is that influence needs to be analysed across a range of **modes and modalities**. Indeed, we have structured the present book into different chapters which introduce and review these manifestations of social influence in distinct modalities and also across the three modes of face-to-face interaction, mass mediation and extensions into designed artefacts, which is unusual considering the existing literature.

P2: Social Influence Is Pre-conditioned by a Public Sphere and a Rhetoric That Shuns Violence

The second point concerns what one might call historical preconditions for social influence. We have introduced the notion of a non-violent lifestyle as a marker of civic society and civilisation. Indeed, one historic correlate of a non-violent life is the public sphere of collective decision-making (Habermas, 1989). Social influence happens within **public spheres** that permit mutual engagement on exclusion of violence. Rhetoric, that is, fighting with words, arguments and images, is deployed in an effort to build and sway opinion in the community, whilst striving at all times to avoid violence. The idea of a public sphere and the practice of rhetoric are homologous, that is, both share common origin in ancient European history; though there are non-European equivalent sources (see shortly).

This is put succinctly by the person who was instrumental in reviving this rhetorical tradition after 1945:

> we can obtain results either by use of violence or speech ... Use of argumentation implies that one refuses to resort to violence; one is not regarding the other as an object, but appealing to his or her judgement through the establishment of a community of minds excluding violence (Perelman, 1982).

The public sphere and rhetoric provide a context of interaction where all assume that violence is no longer part of the game. We concede that if one wanted to get somebody to do X, wielding a gun might be the most effective way of getting there. We are, however, considering this to be outside that remit of social influence. The public sphere and the cultivation of civic discourse are a historical reality, but at the same time a continued aspiration towards ideals. The conditions of public life can always be improved, and the ideal shows us how. Thus, any analysis of social influence requires mapping the characteristics of actual public spheres and the existing rules of engagement, that is, the culture of social influence. In this way, the US PEW foundation has started to ask questions on how people evaluate the tone of the political debate (see www.pewresearch.org/fact-tank/2019/08/26/how-we-examined-public-attitudes-about-the-tone-of-u-s-political-debate), and political scientists seek to measure the quality of debate in terms of level of 'cognitive complexity' (Wyss et al., 2015).

P3: Social Influence Operates on Three Functions – Normalisation, Assimilation and Accommodation of a Frame of Reference Form a Whirling Cyclone

Thirdly, our ordering of social influence hinges on *three functions*, that of *normalisation*, *assimilation* and *accommodation*. Modalities of social influence can be associated with one or several of these contributions to sociality and common sense. These three achievements form three interlocked loops of establishing a frame of reference for future collaboration (normalising order out of chaos); defending this structure against challenges arising from newcomers within, or from strangers without (maintenance, assimilating detractors); and finally adjusting the frame in response to continued challenges (structure shifting in concessions). We model this threefold looping not on a 'law of eternal return' (nothing new under the sun, only repetition under different names), but as a whirling cyclone that moves along a 'path of landfall' (the course of history) (see Figure 1.3).

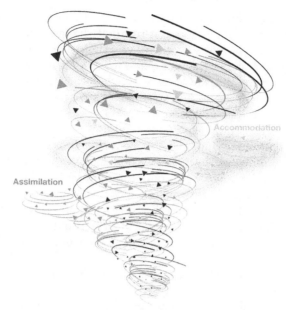

Accommodation

Assimilation

Normalisation

Figure 1.3   The cyclone model of social influence, showing the confluence of three functions of normalisation [N], assimilation [AS] and accommodation [AC]

This metaphor imports several ideas. Where the landfall happens can only be determined in hindsight. We recognise 'Progress' or 'Decline or Decadence' as the case may be on a map of the larger landscape of history. In the whirlwind any notion of 'progress' is discursive and part of the social influence attempt by way of self-fulfilling prophecy. Also, simply looping does not guarantee 'progress', sometimes no change can mean progress, or change can be decadent. More is needed to achieve progress than mere 'changing'. The question will be: which direction is taken, where is the 'landfall' going to be? Such equivocation is nothing new for historians (LeGoff, 2015), but it may be more difficult to handle for social engineers with a bias for change.

P4: Social Influence Builds, Supports and Shifts Common Sense

Last but not least, we consider the outcome of social influence and what this achieves for social life. In other words, we seek to understand: when some form of social influence has been successfully exercised, what changes would this have precipitated? Commonly, social influence is understood to be the dynamic that brings about **attitudinal change**. Somebody who is negatively inclined towards something, say purchasing a new smartphone, or supporting nuclear energy, finds their inclination has changed following a social influence attempt. However, we argue that attitudes themselves are part of a larger rhetorical context (Billig, 1987, 1991) in which these inclinations are deemed common-sensical and some others non-sensical. Common sense here means 'sensus communis', the conditions of community and of community building. We argue, therefore, that the toing and froing of social influence, over time, is able to shift the common ground; for instance, from one where it is only common-sensical for women to be exclusive housewives to one where it is at least equally common-sensical for women to have their own career. The question here is: what does public opinion prescribe in each specific epoch. One could well find that in a particular society, public opinion tends towards women serving the home. Yet what might differ from one epoch to the next is the fact that a woman choosing her own career becomes a legitimate (if unpopular) choice. The move from one common sense (typical of a particular epoch) to another (atypical, but possible in the next epoch) requires processes of social influence that change individual attitudes from one point of view to another. Social influence, therefore, is not limited to changing individual inclinations. Rather, it shifts the common ground, which in its turn justifies individual attitudes. To elucidate this shifting calibration of common sense and individual attitudes, we raise the following three questions in this volume:

1   *What are the **processes** that mark the manifestations of social influence?* We call these the different modalities of social influence. We will deal with seven basic modalities one by one in this volume – crowds, leadership, norm formation, conformity, conversion, obedience and persuasion – and we unusually broaden the perspective to include the modes of mass media and technological installations by which these modalities are enhanced and extended beyond face-to-face interactions. This opens the eyes to an eighth modality of influence, that of 'resistance': what appears to work against change reveals itself as an instigator of change.

2   *What are the **structures** that social influence targets for change?* The basic target of social influence is common sense (CS) in which social representations are anchored at any moment in the time relative to some direction of projected movement. Common sense (CS) is all

those structures of belief, judgement and inclinations which are taken for granted at any moment in time, established in the past as 'the way we do things around here', defended if challenged, and challenged because they offend. Common sense comprises different forms of mentality such as attitudes, opinions, mindsets and stereotypes, and prejudices.

3   *What are the **constraints** on the exercise of social influence?*
We will be dealing with three constraints on the psychology of social influence. These are often more implicit than explicit in models of influence. First we consider **intersubjectivity** and **inter-objectivity**, two fundamental constraints on human interactions that arise at the transition from simians to humans; what is characteristic of the human ape are **conditions of possibility of common sense**. We must further examine, as we have already mentioned, the **public sphere** for collective decision-making at the exclusion of violence. We must finally consider **individual differences** in our responses to influence. Models of influence are probabilistic, advancing effect claims to a certain degree, rather than 'magic bullets' that are fail safe.

Constraint 1: Intersubjectivity and Inter-objectivity

The first constraint on social influence arises in the transition of humans from simians. The human ape has much in common with other apes, not least large parts of the genetic code, but the small difference that there is between humans and other animals bears on social influence. Latour (1996) has argued that a specific difference between humans and other primates might be that the social life of the latter is complex, while for the former it is complicated. Complex means that it always could be otherwise, so much so that animals live in a permanent present where stability is sustained by a fragile dominance hierarchy within the roaming group. This hierarchy requires permanent vigilance as it is threatened at any moment either from within the group or from outsiders. Animals might work together, focus attention jointly and collectively hunt for prey, but they do so as a pack, each one individually contributing and seeking immediate gratification from a share of the spoils.

The human side is less complex, but complicated by more enduring arrangements and installations. Human relations are structured by settings that have a certain persistence and give both a sense of past and of future, an experience of time. Joint attention and following the gaze of another, that is, taking the perspective of another mind in a different spatial position, is partially shared among apes, humans and non-humans, but only human children seem to reach the *capacity for joint intentionality* as a precondition of intersubjectivity (Tomasello & Carpenter, 2007; see Chapter 4). Under these conditions, humans calibrate individual minds and feelings to common standards of some longevity: humans operate on shared goals rooted in values which are mutually shared. Mutual means I know that you know X, that I also know X, so X is a **common ground** between us that we can take for granted. Taking a way of life for granted makes life less complex, but maybe not uncomplicated. Also such arrangements are not above challenges, but challenges are episodic rather than a permanently lurking danger of revolution.

This permanence is further buttressed by **inter-objectivity**, the fact that humans, much in contrast to apes, accumulate artefacts in a built environment. For sure, apes use tools occasionally, at times even safe keeping them. However, they do not systematically build and stock tools and construct environments as humans do. Monkeys do not build irrigation systems to produce excess food, nor vehicles on highways for locomotion faster than on foot. It is also unheard of that chimps should use a mobile phone to link up with other conspecifics in faraway herds.

Thus, humans are able to make arrangements permanent by setting frames in intersubjectivity and inter-objectivity and defining the moral community on a dual constitution. With this complicated arrangement of norms and artefacts humans can achieve large feats of collective projects, often celebrated as miracles of humanity, such as large bridges, cathedrals, nuclear power parks, pyramids and space satellites connecting the earth. Human sociality is thus constituted in normative beliefs, opinions and attitudes, but also, and this might be less obvious, in walls and buildings, small gadgets and installations of grand infrastructure.

For our purposes, it is important to recognise that modalities of social influence operate in three different modes, which cut across this dual constitution as shown in Figure 1.4. Much research on social influence involves *face-to-face* interactions (mode 1), as demonstrated in laboratory experiments on norm formation, peer pressure, obedience and persuasion (see Chapters 4, 5, 6 and 7). But social influence extends, changes character and amplifies in *mass mediation* (mode 2: symbolic). Modern

Figure 1.4   The modes of social influence cutting across intersubjective
and inter-objective arrangements of human social life

leaders made ample use of radio or TV to address the nation, or tweet their stream of thoughts to supporters and thus massively spread symbols in word and image. Finally, social influence is amplified by artefacts that remind people how to behave and think. A wall is often more effective to instruct people where not to tread, or to separate those who are allowed from those who are not allowed to enter or to leave. Let us recall that these structures are set to last, but only in permanence relative to the volatile arrangements in ape groups. Human arrangements are flexible and open to change, but in historical times moving from the past, via the present into the future. What is up for grabs is subject to social influence. In this book we seek to clarify and to order how different modes and modalities influence and elucidate how the frames of social life are established, maintained in the face of challenges and ultimately shift if these challenges persist.

Constraint 2: The Public Sphere – A More or Less Perfect Context

The public sphere is a pertinent notion for the study of social influence. The public sphere is an interrelational space with certain characteristics. For instance, people in the public sphere are not all cousins. It is a social arrangement not based on *kinship*. In the public sphere, the rules of engagement give advantage to argumentation over *hierarchy and authority* (Jovchelovitch, 2007). The public sphere is also no *marketplace*, where the logic of price, balancing supply and demand, settles all encounters. Classical criteria for the functioning of a public sphere are: inclusivity, force of the argument, bracketing of social hierarchy and no self-delusion (in the sense that speakers at least are committed to 'mean what they say and say what they mean'; Habermas, 1994). This is to ensure that what carries the day are arguments based on purely reasonable, neither loyal nor marketable, criteria.

Thus, an argument may carry force on reasonable grounds even if it involves costly implications. Some have argued that the UK Brexit referendum of 2016 (52 per cent of voters opted to leave the EU on an unqualified majority vote) favours self-governance over economic prosperity (i.e., taking back control at all costs), something very much out of character with traditional British common sense. This also illustrates that what constitutes 'reasonable' grounds for justification is a moving goal post, contentious and itself amenable to social influence. But this outlines the precise merits of the public sphere. It provides the fourth way for aligning preference next to voice of authority, kinship, loyalty and market utility. To examine arguments for a specific course of action, the public sphere is the 'battleground' for peaceful public opinion.

The notion of a 'public sphere' defines the conditions of possibility, in ideal form, of reaching decisions by rhetoric in deliberation. This idea has its origins in ancient European history (Billig, 1987; Gross & Walzer, 2000; Habermas, 1989; Kennedy, 1998) but can also be recognised in non-European sources, for example in Ashoka's Buddhist Council of ancient India (Sen, 2006). Historians now trace such ideals to the axial age (800–200 BCA) and its mysterious synchronicity of seeking non-violent reasoned debate in China (Confu-zi, Lao-zi, Mo-zi), India (Buddha), Persia (Zoroaster), the Middle East (Jewish prophets) and ancient Greece (Heraclitus, Plato, Aristotle). Here one can find a common ground for an ethical *'encouragement of limitless communication'* (Assmann, 2018; Jaspers, 1955, 31;). Therefore, modalities of social influence constrained by a public sphere are not restricted to a European context, to the contrary, the historical preconditions are given worldwide but may be hidden under the rubble of several revolutions.

Social influence provides mechanisms for controlling public opinion, for pushing and nudging it in a certain direction. Propaganda through mass media campaigns can control opinions. Charismatic leadership moulds public opinion. The public sphere provides the platform for public opinion to form. This manifests itself in the social media, in mass meetings, protest marches and petitions. Marginal opinions can gain traction and go on to challenge a dominant worldview. It is where 'uncommon nonsense' becomes uncommon sense and eventually, with critical mass, turns into common sense; or vice versa, common sense becomes nonsense.

As Figure 1.5 illustrates, in the public sphere we can observe how over historical time gender stereotypes shift from 'women belong at home' to 'women in careers', views of 'gay life' as an 'abomination' to an 'everyday normality', attitudes towards nuclear power as 'an imperative of Nation building' to a 'poisonous legacy of the past'. Common sense shifts, but so does how we might understand common sense itself, from 'science trumps common sense' to 'common sense informed by science'. Finally, in modern society few people maintain that 'innovation' is undesirable and an evil heresy; rather, innovation is the imperative, desirable and necessary.

We contend that social influence targets this common sense and we proceed to outline some variable features of it in this book. With our 'cyclone model' we suggest that common sense changes over time by normalising, assimilating and accommodating new ideas; this involves challenging the dominant order. In this way, uncommon ideas may go on to become

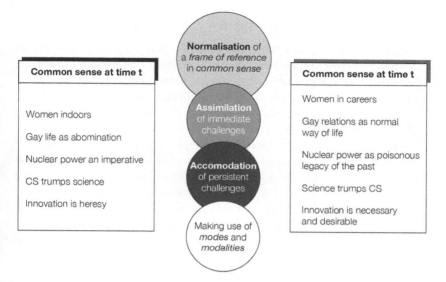

Figure 1.5 Illustrating the transition of commonly accepted state of affairs from one common sense to another state of common sense on gender stereotypes, gay lifestyle, nuclear power, the relation between science and common sense and on the idea of innovation

prevalent social norms (think of communication via smartphone apps). We contend that common sense is best conceived of as work-in-progress, rather than a fixed set of prescriptions. Think about what may have been common-sensical in social relations a mere fifty years ago – in a world without internet connectivity. This new infrastructure has led to changes in what we carry in our pockets (we essentially all go around carrying a personal computer), and it has redefined the taken-for-granted norms of social interaction.

For this dynamic to concretise, the public sphere must retain a sense of ideal, such as inclusivity, equality, absence of deception and of violence (Habermas, 1987) by way of self-fulfilling prophecy. Different public spheres are able to secure some or all of these constraints to different degrees. Being able to refer back to 'common sense' as a set of fixed prescriptions is part of this flexible stabilisation of common ground (Lindenberg, 1987; Markova, 2016). But often, the public sphere is unable to guarantee its own preconditions of successful operation. Mostly, it will require the use of hard power to police the boundaries, liked running mental hospitals to confine the 'deluded' or prisons to confine the 'cheats'.

Constraint 3: Individual Psychological Differences and Citizen Competences

Finally, we need to consider the psychological notion of **individual differences**. Naturally, human beings differ from one another. Some are taller than others, some fairer than others, some more intelligent or more aggressive than others, and so on. This might seem like a simplistic notion. Yet, it is of critical import when considering the exercise of social influence and its effective outcomes.

Much empirical research on social influence is searching for controllable conditions that increase marginal effectiveness or 'increased risk' of hitting a target against a comparator or prior benchmark (i.e., odds changes in a logistic regression model). And such conditions of interest arise from individual differences in responding to social influence.

The notion of individual differences has roots in evolutionary psychology and describes how individuals vary from one another due to two factors: (a) nature, that is, biology, and (b) nurture, that is, the environment in which individuals are reared. The former sees individuals differ from one another due to inherited genetics as well as random mutation. The latter sees individuals differ due to variable environmental resources to which individuals may have access to over their lifespan. In essence, human apes demonstrate variability, which is in itself adaptive as it ensures that whatever challenges might arise for the species, some will be well placed to cope, to survive and to pass on their genes to the next generation. In this way, the species lives on (Dawkins, 1976).

All of this means to say that we must expect that individuals, however constituted in nature–nurture, react to social influence attempts in variable ways. Because people are different, what influences one person may well fail to influence, or even dissuade, somebody else. We contend that there is no silver bullet to social influence and however effective some strategies claim to be, they cannot be expected to work invariably. To return to our former example, a prospective employer interviewing a job candidate may well appreciate the candidate's effort to dress up for the occasion and take it to be a sign of motivation. A different employer may well reward a candidate who fails to dress up, interpreting the act as a more authentic self-portrayal.

Essentially, human beings cannot be treated all alike and social influence cannot, and should not, be standardised according to what prevails in a single public sphere on the assumption that this is representative of the entire species. The only thing that is universal, in natural terms, is human variability itself. The implication of this is that no influence strategy in itself nor any expected outcome deserves the status of being 'the one best way'. On the other hand, from a naturalistic perspective, we need also concede that as human beings, we are subject to influence in many different ways and just like we are able to, on occasion, influence some others to do our bidding, we are also amenable to social influence ourselves in one way or another.

The constraint of individual differences also includes variable **competences** demonstrated by individual citizens. The notion of individual differences suggests that people will demonstrate different sets of competences that foster dialogical engagement. These, as we have argued, serve to settle the competition score without recourse to violence. Moghaddam (2016) outlines ten such competences which enable citizens to observe the 'rules of the game':

(i) to understand that I could be wrong,
(ii) to critically question everything, including sacred beliefs,
(iii) to revise my opinion in light of emerging evidence,
(iv) to understand those who are different,
(v) to learn from different others,
(vi) to seek information and opinions from different sources,
(vii) to be open to new experiences,
(viii) to create new experiences for others,
(ix) to infer principles of right and wrong,
(x) to seek experiences of higher value.

Certainly, human beings differ in the extent to which they partake in these competencies. However, societies are also able to nurture these competencies in citizens through education. The more they do, the better able citizens will be to observe the rules of the game and to settle the competition score without violence. The test of any public sphere lies in its ability to absorb social influence without recourse to hard power, even when this means that some will gain and some others will lose out. Consequently, dialogical engagement in any public sphere takes place under a spectre of violence. Yet, insofar as the playing field is secured and the guns are left at the door, with everybody's acceptance, social influence remains the social–psychological mechanism to settle the scores.

Overview of the Book

Given the introductory considerations, it should be clear that research programmes on social influence are far from being the 'dust of history', as contemporary textbooks seem to suggest. These phenomena are timely and deserve full scholarly attention. Through this volume, we hope to reboot research on social influence, and to do this from a coherent and integrative perspective. We believe that this is achievable once interlinkages between different social influence modalities are fleshed out. We pave the way towards an integrative portrayal of social influence phenomena by visiting them discretely in eight chapters grouped into four parts. To use an image, we might say that this book is like a 'concept album' in pop or a classical 'sonata'. It is constructed in four movements of different tonality, rhythm and texture; kept together by a fixed 'melodic' concern for how common sense is built, maintained or challenged and the dissonant 'tritone' of **normalisation, assimilation and accommodation** is a key building block.

We open our discussions by looking at mass gatherings and **crowds** in Chapter 2. In this chapter we revisit some classical theories that have furnished critical insights that remain pertinent today; indeed crowds exist in dual form, as real crowds and through discourse of 'crowds'. In Chapter 3, we proceed to deal with the other side of the coin of crowd research, that is, **leadership**. Leaders require followers, and followers appoint representatives to lead. Recurrent populist leaders successfully appeal to the crowd, and claim to represent them in a direct and exclusive way. Crowds and leadership are the perennial modalities of populism rehearsing the doctrine of irrational suggestion.

We deal with norm formation explicitly in Chapter 4, where we visit a number of experiments that demonstrate the human urge to create order, to fabricate **norms** for framing and regulating social conduct. In interaction, norms are intended or unintended products that stabilise standards for anyone who participates in future efforts. This poses problems for strangers who need to be framed. In Chapter 5, we revisit peer pressure research on **conformity,** a mechanism by which a dominant order is defended and preserved, and **conversion** by which that order is developed. This pair is also known as majority and minority influence. Chapter 6 provides a vertical extension to this by looking at hierarchy and the phenomenon of **obedience**. Popular experiments and recent replications provide insights on the paradox logic of authority in anti-authoritarian modern society. In Chapter 7, we address the popular topic of **persuasion**, which has become the current prototype of social influence across the social sciences, much under the spell of dual-process models and sitting in tension with classical rhetoric which considers the optimisation of logos, ethos and pathos. All of these eight modalities have their focus, at least in research, on **real-time face-to-face interactions** of what we call mode 1.

They also represent the post–WWII experimental paradigms of social influence which, by overcoming the doctrine of suggestion, went in search of the rational individual in all circumstances.

In the remaining chapters, we advance our vision of social influence into less common research territories, at least in social psychology. In Chapter 8, we examine different modalities of social influence under conditions of **mass mediation,** or what we call **mode 2:** the broadcasting of symbols and images which became a pervasive reality of modern life during the twentieth century. Here we bring to bear a parallel research tradition of media effect studies, as developed by psychologists in communication science, and link these to modalities of social influence. A key modality added here is **agenda setting,** or modality number 8. Chapter 9 takes this ambition even a step further, and considers modalities of social influence also under conditions of **inter-objectivity**. Here we examine how influence is exerted and amplified by designed installations and technological gadgets and infrastructure; in this context we 'discover' the effect that resistance against such machinations has. In the light of this extension, **resistance** becomes our ninth modality of influence; paradoxically, by being obstructed, innovation becomes sustainable. For this we refer to our **mode 3: artefacts.**

In Chapter 10, we attempt to sum up the key tenets of our conceptualisation by outlining a **Periodic Table of Social Influence**. We propose that social influence can be considered in terms of several modalities, as detailed in the various chapters, and three modes including face-to-face, mass mediated symbols and artefacts. Arising from this all is our **cyclone model of social influence** that takes shape in the combination of three functions: normalisation, assimilation and accommodation of challenges. With this model we offer a more comprehensive treatment of the phenomenon of social influence than is typically the case. This will provide the researcher with novel questions, and the general reader with new insights into practical actions and events that are witnessed in everyday life. Finally, in Chapter 11, we address by way of excursions four theoretical issues of our model, each of which would have been unduly burdened in the various chapters. These four issues are: the challenges of common sense arising inside and outside the moral community; the controversy over dual or single processes models; the problem of hardware 'objects' in psychology; and finally the question of authority in modern society.

Two final remarks, we believe, will enable readers to develop the implications of this volume further. Firstly, it is worth bearing in mind that as human beings we are not immune, but prone to influence; we are both capable of influencing others as well as being influenced ourselves. It is incorrect to claim that social influence is only effective on 'unthinking dupes and cognitive misers who do not have cognitive capacity to recognise nefarious interventions and who, consequently, fall for it', as the stereotype might go. We reject a general model of the human sucker. For example, we find it hard to concede that we might be influenced in purchasing a new car by browsing advertisements of scantily dressed women in motor car magazines. We might think this strategy works with the average bloody-minded chauvinist, but we ourselves know better. Similarly, we might find it hard to believe how someone who takes issue with the USA relocating its embassy from Tel Aviv to Jerusalem was not indoctrinated. However, we believe it is reasonable to admit that as human beings we are subject to influence, and not necessarily in obvious ways.

There is also the exact inverse to consider: being familiar with the dynamics of social influence could potentially shield us from its effectiveness. Similarly, for centuries the teaching of rhetoric was thought to immunise its student to the devious tricks of the trade (see Schopenhauer, 2004 [1830]). In analogy, an *enlightenment effect* of 'knowledge liberates' could arise from reading the 'social psychology of the time', as claimed by Gergen (1973). Knowing the tactics of social influence could liberate us from getting entangled in them.

We hope that this book will provide readers with useable old and new insights that facilitate their own reflections on modern social relations and, in times of uncertainty, ambiguity and confusion, will enable them to persist with dialogical engagement rather than resorting to violent alternatives.

In Essence

> *Social influence is a social–psychological dynamic that achieves soft power at the expense of violence, with sometimes fuzzy boundaries to manipulative tactics akin to hard power.*
>
> *Social influence manifests across three modes: face-to-face, mass media and artefactual designs.*
>
> *Social influence manifests in different modalities: crowding, leading, norming, conforming, converting, obeying, persuading and resisting.*
>
> *Social influence functions to build, support or challenge common sense.*

PART I

Recurrent Sources of Populism

This part is looking at mass gatherings and **crowds**. In Chapter 2 we revisit some classical theories that have furnished critical insights and that remain pertinent today; indeed crowds exist in dual form, as real crowds in the street and through discourse of 'crowds'. In Chapter 3, we proceed with the other side of the coin of crowd research, that is, **leadership**. Leaders require followers, and followers appoint representatives to lead. And recurrent populist leaders successfully appeal to the crowd, and claim to represent them in a direct and exclusive way. Crowds and leadership are the perennial modalities of populism rehearsing the doctrine of irrational suggestion.

Over time, human beings acting in coordinated unison have brought about the events recited in history textbooks worldwide. Social change requires, as a matter of course, collective action that challenges the status quo and ushers in a new order. Scholars have argued that collective action in the human species is different from other forms of animal collaboration and hinges on the evolved capability of sharing intentions – the catalyst for pursuing shared interests. An individual expresses an intent in such a way as to catalyse like-minded others to join the effort and act towards the achievement of a collective project.

There are two parts to this equation. Firstly, the collective – in which common sense and collective norms emerge and stabilise. There is no common sense without a collective for whom certain tenets are common sensical. There is no English language without a community speaking English in sufficiently similar grammatical ways that enable comprehension amongst the multitude. Private language or meaning has no currency in the collective.

On the other hand, for the achievement of communal projects, crowds need to be coordinated and not simply aggregated. A crowd waiting at a bus stop achieves no social change – it is limited to pursuits fulfilled at the individual level, like a hungry wolf pack. Social movements bring about change when coordinated in the pursuit of common projects. For this to happen, crowds require leaders; followers need to know whom to follow if the group's aspirations are to gain sufficient traction to achieve social movement. This part is concerned with these minimal ingredients that constitute the two sides of the coin of social movements everywhere they materialise: crowds and their leaders.

CHAPTER 2

Crowding
Contagion and Imitation

phase	modality	function for CS	outcome	Mode 1 face-to-face inter-subjective	Mode 2 symbolic	Mode 3 artefact inter-objective
				Order created 'out of Chaos' of interaction: social representations, common sense, joint intentionality		
Phase 1	crowds	**Normalisation**	echo chambers	contagion virality/rumor	joint attention imitation	barricades

Figure 2.1   A challenge and response model I: crowding

The weekly *Economist* (30 March, 2019, p. 73) carried a piece entitled 'the madness of crowds' on the cryptocurrency Bitcoin which increased its value from $1,000 in mid-2016 to $20,000 by the end of 2017, ending up at $4,025 in March 2019. It argued that this boom–bust cycle involved exaggerated reporting, technological difficulties and endemic fraud. **Market bubbles** of exaggerated profit on investment hopes have been observed over 400 years of shares and stocks in the capitalist system. The recent crashes of 2000 (the Millennium bubble) and of 2008 (the Lehman sub-prime crash) attracted new attention to irrational 'animal spirits'. Ferguson (2009, 121ff) refers to three conditions that bloat markets: asymmetry between insiders in the know and ignorant outsiders; cross-border capital flow without controls; and easy availability of credit at low interest rates. On these conditions, stock markets are more likely to bubble as shown in the light periods since 1895 in Figure 2.2. Ferguson also refers to characteristic phases of this mass behaviour: from an initial displacement where new profitable opportunities arise we move fast to euphoria and overtrading; this is followed by a mania 'bubble' where the news of prospects attracts novices and swindlers alike. Signs of distress lead the insiders to start selling which discredits the proposition; now also the lesser informed outsiders start panicking and stampede for the exit, selling as fast as possible, and the share price index tumbles as it did massively in 1929 from 400 to 40 and in 2008 from 16,000 back to 6,000.

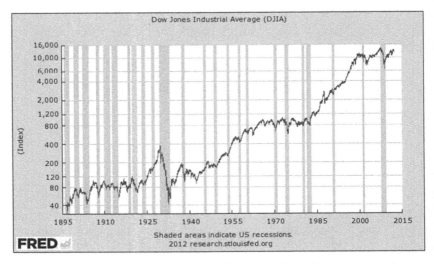

Figure 2.2   New York Dow Jones Industrial Average stock market index since 1895 on a log scale. Shaded periods indicate US economic recessions which are often related to rapid stock-market retractions or so called 'bear markets'; light periods are periods of expansions with 'bull markets' or 'market bubbles'.

Source: 2012 research.stlouisefed.org; Federal Reserve Bank of St Louis, created and cropped from FRED App using free access economic data.

Observers have for centuries worried about threats of unrest and disorder related to religious enthusiasms and the machinations of witches, devils and demons. The Enlightenment tradition produced a curiosity cabinet of such mass behaviour, trying to secularise explanation away from demons and miracles onto social conditions in need of medical therapy and state policing. Still popular are the ironic comments of a nineteenth-century Scottish lawyer working in London, observing such strange behaviours (Mackay, 1980 [1841]):

> In reading the history of nations, we find that, like individuals, they have their whims and their peculiarities; their seasons of excitement and recklessness. We find that whole communities suddenly fix their minds upon one object, and go mad in its pursuit; that millions of people become simultaneously impressed with one delusion, and run after it . . . Some delusions, though notorious to all the world, have subsisted for ages . . . omens and divinations . . . Money . . . has often been a cause of the delusion of multitudes.

Over 700 pages never out of print, Mackay (1980 [1841]) examines popular delusions including dubious investment schemes (money bubbles of Mississippi and in the South-Sea in 1729, and tulips in Holland in 1636), alchemy, prophecies and fortune-telling, animal magnetism, fashions in hair and beard, crusades, witch hunts, poisonings, haunted houses, admirations of outlaws and the veneration of relics. Mackay offers infotainment, mixing information and entertainment, with no ambition to classify and to theorise beyond the call to common sense; he simply appeals to his readers that such aberrations are to be avoided by prudence. He states:

> the object ... has been to collect the most remarkable instances of those moral epidemics which have been ... To show how easily the masses have been led astray and how imitative and gregarious men are, even in their infatuations and crimes ... a miscellany of delusions more than a history, – a chapter only in the great and awful book of human folly ... *Men, it has been well said, think in herds* ... they go mad in herds, while they only recover their senses slowly, one by one (1980 [1841], preface).

Mackay is 'debunking' popular delusions by appeal to the common sense of like-minded readers, couched in an entertaining tableau of human folly and weakness. We could easily update these observations into the twenty-first century with UFOs sightings, fake news or abstruse conspiracy theories. However, debunking does not do justice to their sinister role in society (Butter, 2018). We need to appreciate their discursive functions.

In this chapter, we will review still vivid ideas of nineteenth-century **mass psychology**. In that context, social influence means *suggestion* and *crowding* create perfect conditions of susceptibility to mental **contagion**. We position **crowds** and **crowding** as a force of *normalisation*, establishing a new standard for viewing and dealing with the world. Crowds offer *new beginnings* announced often with the force of historical revolution, but also peacefully as tactics of collective action. Fear of disorderly energy gave the analysis of crowds a particularly resentful undertone.

This nineteenth-century crowd has been superseded by modern views of crowding as self-regulating systems, as tactics of social movements, as the 'wisdom of the crowd' and 'crowd sourcing' in markets and as crowd management at sports and music events. Most modern views of crowds are thus positively connoted, yet old concepts of regressive **animal magnetism** persist, not least for the attribution of responsibility in disasters, stock market crashes and protests, but more recently also in dealing with the new social media, the new 'virtual crowds'. Talking about modern crowds

Box 2.1 Demographic transition, population density and 'fear of touch'

A social fact of the past centuries is the **demographic transition** on a global scale from high birth and high death rates – large families and likely death from disease – to lower rates on both. But as death rates were falling faster with increasing welfare and better medicine, and higher birth rates persisted, this led to a massive population increase; in different countries at different times and on different dynamics, as shown in Figure 2.3. This growth, seemingly out of control, raised alarm in the mid-twentieth century; the book 'Population Bomb' (Ehrlich, 1968) kick-started the modern environmental movement. What began in the eighteenth century turned into a social problem: crowding became an object of social–psychological observations. Canetti (1973/1960) refers here to an anthropological constant as shown in Figure 2.3: with rising population levels, human fear of touch is accentuated at medium population density, phobias about being caught up in the crowd is a syndrome of suburbia, it seems. At low density, privacy prevails and physical contact is an unlikely event, at high density, the body warms and a sense of safety and security prevail; it is the mid-range population density that gives rise to high anxiety.

World population growth
1750–2100*

Model of 'fear of touch' as inverted
U-shape function of population density

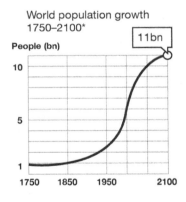

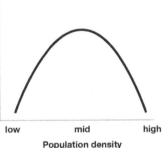

* estimated.
Source: United Nations (adapted)

Source: Canetti (adapted)

Figure 2.3   On the left, a model fit for the development of world population growth since 1750 from a standard of below 1 billion, to high plateau between 11 and 12 billion at the end of the current century (others say it will level out at 8–9 billion). On the right, Canetti's (1973/1960) implied model of 'fear of touch' as an inverted U-shape function of population density

requires us to juggle several issues: (a) to understand how 'crowds' work, (b) to be aware of old and new concepts of 'the crowd' and (c) to be mindful of the ideological investment in such concepts. In talking about crowds it is difficult to remain value-free. The BBC (March 2018) recently referred to a 'secret' science of crowds: www.bbc.com/future/story/20180312-the-secret-science-that-rules-crowds.

We will be tackling these issues in turn, starting with beginnings in the nineteenth century, followed by ways of going beyond the 'doctrine of suggestion', and finally how we face continued ambivalent meaning of the crowd. Several discourses of mass behaviour are available to us: are collectives a mad and bad moment of regressive animal magnetism or are they forces for good in society? Crowd events continue to pose a problem of identification and perspective taking: how do the few think about the many? *I was there, part of it and inside; it felt differently from when observing from the outside.* Let us trace this fear of 'being caught up in the crowd' (see Box 2.1) and understand how to cope with it. Crowd psychology is the foundation of modern social psychology (the nature of crowds, how they work) and of political psychology (what can crowds achieve and how to lead them), and crowd psychology periodically revitalises as a resource of 'populism' to the present day.

Beginning: 'Men, It Has Been Well Said, Think in Herds'

This **doctrine of suggestion** (Asch, 1952) arises from pop science. The model is microbial *disease propagation* and hysteric *hypnosis* as publicly demonstrated at the time. In the late nineteenth century, microbiological research was breakthrough science, as was the study of hypnosis. And fear of contagion correlates with worries about hygiene in conditions of growing urban centres. Being in a crowd, it was argued, induces a 'group mind' of pure potential energy that is incapable of resisting influence. The crowd is a super-organism without agency of itself, in a hypnotic state highly susceptible to suggestion of ideas. This makes for a fundamental ambivalence among observers: the nineteenth-century political crowds in the streets of Paris and elsewhere are a source of deep worries and anxieties about revolutionary fervour; on the other hand they offer a historical opportunity for decisive elite leadership.

LeBon and Freud on the Crowd

The founding fathers of crowd psychology, and indeed they were significantly all male, are considered to be Gustave LeBon, Gabriel Tarde and

Sigmund Freud. They all shared an interest in hysteric hypnosis. In three widely circulating books, *The Laws of Imitation* (Tarde, 1890), *Age of the Crowd – A Study of the Popular Mind* (LeBon, 1895) and *Group Psychology and the Analysis of the Ego* (Freud, 1921), they set the tone for thinking about crowds in what later would be defined as the 'doctrine of the suggestion' (Asch, 1952, 398). LeBon (1982 [1895]) formulated the famous law of mental unity of crowds:

> under certain circumstances ... an agglomeration of men presents new characteristics very different from those of the individuals composing it (p. 2).

And what are the circumstances for these characteristics to arise? During particular events involving strong emotions

> thousands of isolated individuals may acquire at certain moments, and under the influence of certain violent emotions – such as for example, as a great national event – the characteristics of a psychological crowd (p. 2).

In these crowd moments, irrespective of numbers, the newly constituted 'collective mind' becomes an entity amenable to classification. What are the characteristics of crowd mentality? They can be ordered into three: the state of the crowd, the features of crowd rhetoric and crowd behaviour.

The state of the crowd is characterised by de-individuation: 'a collective mind makes them feel, think, and act in a manner quite different from that in which each individual of them would feel, think and act were he in a state of isolation' (p. 6); lesser intelligence: 'the intellectual aptitudes of the individual ... are weakened ... That is why they can never accomplish acts demanding a high degree of intelligence' (p. 8); stupidity: 'In crowds it is stupidity and not mother-wit that is accumulated' (p. 9); absolute equality: 'the heterogeneous is swamped by the homogeneous' (p. 8); return of the repressed: the normally repressed, unconscious qualities obtain the upper hand (p. 8); impulsiveness, mobility and irritability of crowds (p. 16); suggestable: crowds are credulous and readily suggested; images evoked are accepted and taken as realities; imagination: the crowd thinks in images, not in analogies or inferences from premises.

The rhetoric recruited by crowds accentuate the archaic, spell-binding power of words: in the crowd, individuals are subject to the magical power of words and formulas; affirmation by repetition is common: making use of the rhetorical figure of repetition, instead of reasoning and proof, to induce contagion and imitation among crowd members; images and legends: crowds are influenced by images and storytelling as in marvellous legends, not by reasoning. Popular imagination is a basis of power: 'to know the art of impressing the imagination of crowds is to know at the same time the art of governing them' (58); exaggeration prevails: crowds are prone to hyperbole and always given to extreme responses: 'like women, [the crowd] goes at once to extremes' (33); intolerance: crowds are dictatorial and conservative, 'an individual may accept contradiction and discussion; a crowd will never do' (37); 'crowds exhibit a docile respect for force, and are but slightly impressed by kindness, which for them is scarcely other than a form of weakness' (38); lofty morality is possible: the standards of crowds are transitory and display abnegation, self-sacrifice, disinterestedness, devotion and equity. These are quite contrary to what we consider normal respect for social convention and self-control of impulses; but crowds act unconsciously on such exceptional values (40f).

Crowd behaviour shows characteristic manifestations of personality cult and tribal leadership: convictions of the crowd approximate that of religious fervour, including obedience and submission of willpower, fanaticism at the service of a cause or leader and intolerance in the pursuit of the secrets of happiness and salvation (61). 'Crowds demand gods before everything else' (63); leadership: 'as soon as ... living beings are gathered together ... they place themselves instinctively under the authority of a chief (112) ... men gathered in a crowd lose all force of will, and turn instinctively to the person who possesses the quality they lack' (114); prestige 'is a sort of domination exercised on our mind by an individual, a work or an idea. This domination paralyses our crucial faculty, and fills our soul with astonishment and respect' (127). Prestige is the mainspring of authority; it is artificially acquired and accumulated or naturally personal as in 'charisma' (129ff).

LeBon mentions three 'causes' for these characteristics: (1) the dissolution of individual responsibility occurs in the safety of numbers, which induces

> a sentiment of invincible power which allows him to yield to instincts, which, had he been alone, he would perforce have kept under restraint (p. 9).

In the crowd, under protection of anonymity, the individual relinquishes self-control and normal levels of responsibility; (2) individuals abdicate their self-interests so that

> every sentiment and act is contagious, and contagious to such a degree that an individual readily sacrifices his personal interest to the collective interest. This is an aptitude very contrary to his nature (p. 10).

Note that the collective pursuit of a common good is considered to be unnatural. And finally (3) hypnotic suggestion determines

> in individuals of a crowd special characteristics which are quite contrary at times to those presented by the isolated individual' (p. 10) ... He see ... the disappearance of conscious personality, the predominance of the unconscious personality, the turning by means of suggestion and contagion of feelings and ideas into an identical direction, the tendency to immediately transform the suggested ideas into acts ... He is no longer himself, but has become an automaton who has ceased to be guided by his will', and we see 'the disappearance of brain activity and the predominance of medulla activity' (p. 11).

Gustave LeBon (1841–1931) was a medical doctor diagnosing the 'social body' and making a successful living from popular writings outside academia (VanGinneken, 1992, 134ff). In his *Age of the Crowd* (1895), which was reproduced in forty-five editions by 1939 and translated into numerous languages, he argued that in the company of others, individuals lose all resistance against peer contagion of ideas and feelings, and against hypnotic suggestion by a leader's voice. Crowding induces a *crowd effect* that shuts down critical faculties and opens one to the will of a hypnotising leader. While the crowd is pathological and often criminal, its preconditions are not. We all live a daytime somnambulance and are mass material by the pure fact of our sociality. When modern commentators explain stock market crashes by 'mad crowds' they pick up these ideas.

Sigmund Freud (1856–1939; 1921) adds to this account two further notions: the *return of the repressed* and the erotic significance of the *leader*. Both are ironically immortalised in two children's stories and set to animated song lines by the Disney Corporation: 'I Wanna Be Like You' in *The Jungle Book* (1967) and 'Following the Leader, the Leader, the Leader ...' in *Peter Pan* (1953). For Freud de-individuated impulsivity means the liberation of repressed desires giving to a sense of omnipotence, abdication of self-interests and counter-characteristic behaviour. Crowds are guided by images and imagination, not truth and evidence. While for Tarde the crowd is a kind of *social epilepsy*, a social network out of control, for Freud the crowd effect is a *collective neurosis* given to fantasy, compulsive behaviours and guilt-ridden hysterical projections. In identifying with the leader as ego-ideal (I wanna be like you), and in hypnotic suggestion we channel libidinous energy from a peer sexual object vertically to the leader (wanna be like him to have what he has); the idealisation of the leader (being in love) is hysterical, asexual and unlimited because not subject to homeostatic satisfaction. The crowd imitates horizontally this projected ego-ideal by contagion. It is difficult not to think of present day North Korea and its crowds paraded on TV and in reality, adulating its past and present leaders.

Tarde on Crowds, Opinions and Conversations Technically Mediated

Gabriel Tarde (1843–1904), an established academic, adds to all this his distinction between crowd and opinion (see Chapter 8 on mass mediation). Like most commentators at the time, Tarde was engaged in the Dreyfus Affair (after 1894), a miscarriage of justice with anti-Semitic motives: a French officer of Jewish decent was wrongfully condemned for high treason, later acquitted after a long public controversy. The affair turned into a culture war between political milieus and gave birth to the public intellectual (Gildea, 2010). Tarde observed that most people paid attention to this home-made scandal while ignoring the war in North Africa. Why this distribution of attention? Tarde pointed to a novel phenomenon: the joint attention created by reading the daily press.

The nineteenth-century press had created a new information environment, similar to social media creating a novel news environment 100 years later. The French public was by now mostly literate, and ever larger numbers informed themselves by daily reading of the press. This created joint attention distributed de facto in very different locations. Tarde called this phenomenon 'opinion' in contrast to the 'crowd'. The distributed focus of attention was powerful; because governments could not ignore it, it set the agenda: 'we must act on the Dreyfus scandal, and the war can take its course'. Like all attention, collective attention is selective and limited. Tarde agreed with LeBon on the character of the crowd, but not on its significance: 'I cannot agree with the vigorous writer Dr LeBon that we live in an age of the crowd; we live in an age of the public, or publics, which is very different' (Tarde, 2006; p. 15). The crowd was not the only public; there was also 'opinion' distributed by printing technology. People who have never met, can join anti-Semitic opinion as they read the press. The psychology of the crowd needs to be complemented by a psychology of public opinion. In a crowd, participants are co-present here and now; in public opinion they are in different locations and in asynchrony. You can be part of only one crowd, but partake in many streams of opinion.

Opinion publics are not exclusive and therefore more tolerant. Crowds are hypnotically dependent on a leader and thus stable; opinions are mutual and fluid; opinion does not rhyme on the rhetoric of truth or justice, but on the news value of utility and what needs to be done. Crowds are forces of nature, while opinions are part of civilisation (ibidem, p. 8). Tarde found more homogeneity in opinion than in crowds where bystanders and spectators partake in its madness only by degrees, while opinions are more defined streams of conversations, in politics as well as in religion and culture. With origins in letter writing, and the salons of the eighteenth century, news attention is the real novelty: individual minds in ever larger quantity fuse to 'inter-minds'; joint attention, as we will see in Chapter 3, being a precondition for joint intentionality. Tarde's hypnotic contagion, nowadays referred to as virality (see Chapter 8), focuses on horizontal peer imitation, rather than LeBon's vertical contagion induced by the leader. While shifting from contagion to *imitation*, both notions are modelled on hypnotic somnambulance as everyday condition. Logical imitation is persuasive to conscious belief and desire; extra-logical imitation is unconscious (ibidem, 199ff). But this duality is more analytical than empirical 'but it remains rare that logical imitation manifests itself in purity' (my translation, p. 200).

People imitate each other, assimilate and thereby distance themselves from third parties; this 'inter-psychology' has its laws of imitations (Tarde, 2001): according to *the first law* imitation proceeds from the inner to the outer man (ibidem, 252ff); first we change ideas and attitudes, then behaviour: literary fashions precede changes in dress code. *The second law* states that imitation follows the prestige hierarchy (ibidem, 271ff). If the Queen changes her hat, everybody follows suit. The scene is set top-down not by dictate but by imitation. This prestige hierarchy is still with us, commercialised in the A-list persons of the advertising industry; famous faces with wide recognition can be used for product association. The Internet did not invent the virtual world, it's Tarde who spotted distributed opinion over 100 years ago – what we nowadays refer to as 'echo-chambers' (see Box 2.2). Tarde recognised the media effect, and called for a social psychology to study it. We will return to this on mode 2 of influence by mass mediation (see Chapter 8).

Box 2.2 *Charlie Hebdo* in Paris or 'Boko Haram' in Nigeria

Tarde had observed the virtual reality of opinion which complemented the crowd to exert public pressure at the end of the nineteenth century. The same observation occurred again recently in the new context of social media and the Internet. *Charlie Hebdo* stands for the Paris terrorist attack of early January 2015 in Paris. A group of Islamists entered the offices of the satirical magazine and shot seventeen editorial staff and shoppers in the vicinity. Zuckerman (2015) compared the coverage of twenty-five mainstream US news sources on *Charlie Hebdo* and the massive terrorist attack in Baga, Northern Nigeria, by Boko Harmam during the very same week. Joint attention was not on Africa, but on Paris; even Nigerian news was on Paris and less on the northern province. However, different to Tarde, commentators no longer recognise 'the logic of opinion' but diagnose an operational news bias (Malsin, 2015) due to cultural distance, racism, lack of foreign correspondents, difficult access, etc. The assumption is that the news must be balanced, but how can that be defined on any day if we consider that the entire world is the scenery?

Tarde had already observed that opinion did not primarily reference truth or justice, but individual utility and public actuality of something needs to be done! Our modern take on public opinion has recently entered a massive agitation over 'fake news' and the distinctions between fact and 'fake', legitimate and illegitimate news and agreeable and disagreeable coverage. Figure 2.4 shows a map of news values that offers orientation for a psychology of public opinion in the new millennium (See Freelon, 2018).

		✔ Agreeable	✘ Disagreeable
Claims of fact	True	Facts that support your case	Inconvenient truths
	False	Comforting lies	Libel/slander
Opinions	Legitimate	Opinions you agree with and are compatible with broadly shared values	Opinions you disagree with but are compatible with broadly shared values
	Illegitimate	Opinions you agree with and are incompatible with broadly shared values (e.g., your prejudices)	Opinions you disagree with and are incompatible with broadly shared values (e.g., other people's prejudices that affect you)

Figure 2.4   On news values in the age of social media

Theoretical Assumptions of Crowd Psychology

It has been observed that classical crowd psychology was less a programme of systematic research than a cultural commentary and pop science responding to political anxiety, or as LeBon put it himself

> the entry of the popular classes into political life – this is to say, in reality, their progressive transformation into governing classes – is one of the most striking characteristics of our epoch of transition ... the divine right of the masses is about to replace the divine rights of kings ... Our middle classes display profound alarm at this new power they see growing (1982 [1895], xv–xvii).

The historical context is important: a growing population, the establishment of freedom of expression and voting rights, and middle-class anxieties about street politics were accentuated by the centenary of the French Revolution 1789–1889 (van Ginneken, 1992). This social psychology even absorbs thinking about popular classes of earlier centuries. The literate, leisurely and dominant classes had a traditional habit of describing the common people through lenses of policing and control: the commons have passions that need to be repressed, the rulers have reasons and interests for doing so. This slowly changes into the twentieth century with a recognition of economic interests and different assumptions: citizens are principally equal and economic interests can be reconstructed as 'rational', independent of social position (Groh, 1986).

In mass psychology, we also hear the call for a 'science of new politics' (Moscovici, 1985; p46ff): the grammar of politics was changing, from a politics of elite reason and interests (classical) to the politics of people's passion and imagination, from parliamentary debates to extra- and anti-parliamentary mobilisations of feelings of love and hate, revenge and guilt, memory and commemoration. It involves a change in the main modality of social influence: 'Individuals you persuade, masses you influence' (ibidem, 50) in order to exert power; the pressures of the street become an extra lever to lift the political agenda and force decisions: 'Psychology discovered the energy of the crowd at the same time, when physics discovered the energy of the atom' [ibidem, 381]. Let us examine in more detail the ideas underpinning this doctrine of suggestion.

Hypnosis and Daytime Somnambulance

Hypnosis was a great discovery of late nineteenth-century France. Earlier notions of 'animal magnetism', or Mesmerism, elaborated the idea of the induction of ideas and sentiment between people in analogy to a magnet that binds and orients metals at a distance and without physical contact

(Sloterdijk, 1985). Flourishing at the fringes of science since the eighteenth century, such ideas became increasingly experimented upon with growing interest in spiritism, clairvoyance, occultism and parapsychology (Bensaude-Vincent & Blondel, 2002), and France was a centre of all this. Hysteric hypnosis became a matter of scientific debate between medical researchers in Paris (Charcot) and Nancy (Bernheim). They agreed on the reality of hypnosis, that is, the induction of ideas, sentiment or action tendencies from a hypnotiser to a patient in three steps: lethargy, catalepsy and somnambulism. They disagreed on the nature of the process and its preconditions. The Charcot school argued that hysteric hypnosis involved a neuropathology with an identifiable organic cause. The Nancy school, however, maintained that hypnosis was an everyday condition that could be induced to anybody who was prepared to let go; its precondition was moral and psychological rather than organic. For Nancy, hypnosis implied consent; for Paris it was an illness.

In this context LeBon and Tarde elaborated their model of the crowd by freely concocting their own thinking from available ideas. LeBon adopted the language of pathology; Tarde tended towards criminality to denigrate the crowd, but both leaned towards the Nancy school on its everyday potential: human sociability makes us daytime somnambulant. They modelled on the doctor–patient hierarchy; the crowd leader was the hypnotist of the multitude. The fusion of analogy into theory was ideological: these arm chair authors confused criminal behaviour and the new politics of the street; for social–psychological theory, it was a missed opportunity at a cross-roads of politics and ideas (Apfelbaum & McGuire, 1986, 47). This language entirely sidelined any glimpse of the crowd as a positive force in society. However, there existed a third stream of thought. Political radicals saw in 'animal magnetism' and its off-shoots a pathway to revolution. Spiritism was at the time part of a secular and anti-clerical activism that aligned itself with social reform. In the United Kingdom, Annie Besant was a famous spiritist, Fabian socialist and founding member of the London School of Economics in 1895 (MacKenzie & MacKenzie, 1977).

Irrationality Induced by Mere Sociability

The second point to explore is the 'irrationality' of the crowd. It seems this can only be understood against the background of a notion of what 'rationality' is at the time, clearly a big question beyond this chapter. We highlight here three assumptions about rationality. First, the individual loses self-control in the crowd which unleashes unconscious impulses normally well contained by the individual in splendid isolation. It seems that rationality is pitted against impulses from below. A dualist, even Platonic, model is invoked which pitches rationality against passionate emotions. Crowd psychology elaborates a 'pressure pot' model of rationality; unless the lid of reason keeps the underbelly of unruly impulses at bay, the whole thing explodes.

Secondly, rationality seems to be a faculty of the isolated individual. The crowd effect is defined by 'what the isolated individual would not do'. Taylor (2007) has reconstructed the history of this model of the super-buffered agent. The rational agent of secular society is buffered and disenchanted,

> he is not only not 'got at' by demons and spirits; he is utterly unmoved by the aura of desire. In a mechanistic universe ... there is nothing it could correspond to. It is just a disturbing, supercharged feeling, which somehow grips us until we can come to our sense, and take on our full, buffered identity (ibidem, 136).

The super-buffered self is worried about passions and also outer influences. Inside and outside are equal sceneries of dangerous interference. The civilising process filters human intercourse, sensitises against 'mixing bodily fluids' with strangers and gets rid of demonic and spiritual influences in our everyday ontology. Rationality is vested in this dual clean up, and the fear of the crowd arises from this: the heroic, rational individual is losing ground and under threat. By contrast, Taylor (2007) outlines how modern rationality is increasingly liberated from this dual strait jacket, reincarnated in the body (in reasons of the heart) and in the social world (in communicative reason). The classical authors of crowd psychology could see the influence of the many others only as a threat of their sobriety. The third element involves the assertion that the crowd's disinterested pursuit of a 'common good' is an aberration. LeBon grants that crowds can perform lofty ideals such as 'devotion, sacrifice and disinterestedness' (1982, 42), but he can only acknowledge this as an aberration. The communality of the crowd cannot be a force for good, because it is not based on reason; and reason is the privilege of the isolated individual. Thus, 'good' can only come from outside of the crowd, it is not part of the crowd's inner dynamics. We will come back to this point.

'Effemination' – Gender Stereotype and Misogyny

According to nineteenth-century crowd psychology, to be suggestible and out of control is a particularly female tendency; a vivid male imagination of 'the female' lives in this description of crowd behaviour. The texts are littered with assimilations of crowds and women. The crowd is given to exaggeration 'like women, it goes at once to extremes' (LeBon, 1982, 33); contagion of false testimony is ripe as 'often made by women and children – that is to say precisely among the most impressionable persons' (ibidem, 29); the characteristics of crowds are 'always observed in beings belonging to inferior forms of evolution – in women, savages and children' (p. 16). An otherwise rational individual is turned into an irrational animal and this is called 'effemination', becoming like a woman (see also Moscovici, 1985, 107ff). This reproduces nineteenth-century stereotypes of gender with lesser cognitive capacity of women, but also of children, the mad and non-white races mixed with evolutionary notions of 'animality' and loss of control. Deficits attributed to the crowd use a language that assigns a dominant role to men in society. It is in this context that Tchakhotine (1952) could summarise the political propaganda of Nazism and Communism as 'rape of the masses'. The ideology of crowd psychology reproduces stereotypes of the time, and that leads us to the last of its assumptions.

Chemical Analogies, Hylomorphism and Design

Mass psychology examines the mannerism of the 'crowd', it hardly asks the what-for-question. What do crowds seek to achieve, what are their reasons for gathering? The strategy and agency of the crowd is not to be found within, but only outside of the crowd (Apfelbaum & McGuire, 1986, 47). This kind of metaphysics is known as *hylomorphism* (Aristotle) which originally dealt with body and soul. Juggling dualism we observe the 'hyle' (the stuff) which is the mass, and the designer, the 'morphing' which gives it form as the potter shapes the clay. Stuff has no direction, form is impressed on it. This image dominates the classical analysis of crowds, the leader addresses the crowd and gives it direction, the crowd being pure energy, thus 'informed', is a powerful tool for setting the political agenda.

Crowd psychology is also shot through with chemical analogies, the crowd effect makes for emergent properties like a 'compound' or a 'fusion': the whole is different from the sum of the elements. Energy is released as in explosive 'combustion', or 'catalysis' lowers the energy threshold of crowd processes. However, these metaphors never go beyond hylomorphism: crowds need a leader to refine, as the marble needs Michelangelo to become 'La Pieta'. Hylomorphism offers a solution to body and soul dualism and gets caught up in the distinction between passive and active parts. The radical counterpoint to hylomorphism are modern notions of self-organisation, order out of chaos, where endogenous processes are sufficient to bring about structure and direction. The auto-poietic system is goal-directed but not impregnated with a telos from the outside (it is teleonomic, not teleological). We recognise such shifting metaphysics in modern notions of groups that produce their own goals and identify in inter-group behaviour (Cranach, 1986). No need for outside leaders to instil a telos, to the contrary the leader is itself an emergent property (see Chapter 3). The notion of self-organising social systems is here the radical alternative, which is indeed elaborated in modern theories of crowding as a social identification process (Stott & Reicher, 1998).

Current notions of crowds avoid the language of denigration and criminalisation, celebrate the crowd experience and its force for good, but retain a residual notion of risk of crowding that needs to be managed. The twenty-first-century multitude has two discursive sides: considered as 'mass' its movements are powerful but random and indiscriminate, as in riots, panics, fads or lynch mobs. On the other side, there is 'collective action', strategically coordinated towards a political goal, arising from legitimate conflicts of interest, defensive of rights and celebrating identity and solidarity in a common fate. This dual discourse poses an identification problem that persists: crowding has happened, was this a random mob or a collective action? We must also ask: who says what, and who is the observer? Let us examine several ways of leaving behind the 'mad and bad' crowd.

Celebrating the Many: Social Movements and Crowd Sourcing

The analysis of 'collective action' became a sociological topic that recruits social–psychology on 'social identity' issues (Kelly & Breinlinger, 1996; Simon & Klandermans, 2001). Social movements fight to bring currents of opinion that are not represented into the political arena. They complement campaigning political parties and lobbying interest groups. There are 'old' social movements such as farmer and trade unions who represent economic interest, and 'new' social movements such as peace movements, environmentalists, Women's Lib or LGBT, with a focus on identity and life-styles (Pakulski, 1993). Four features define a social movement: grievance, action repertoire, organisation and opportunities (Tarrow, 1994). Movement needs a grievance to highlight as a social problem; a Hamlet moment that in the state of Denmark, things are out of joint and need to be put right. However, there are many grievances and few mobilise the wider public. Here, the social movement organisation (SMO) with a leadership and a core membership recruits a larger pool of sympathisers into a repertoire of action that creates visibility and marks a presence in society. The leadership is forward leading and not fronting the crowd; crowds are part of the repertoire of tactics. Finally, movements need historical timing and seek seasonal opportunities where the political agenda is more likely reached. These elements are held together by *resource mobilisation* to lower the costs of participation; collective action requires buses and train fares to get to places, and there are costs of lawyers needed when challenged in court. Symbolic framing mobilises the language of what this is all about, names the problem, identifies the causes and culprits and suggests actions to set things right (see Chapter 4). Symbols celebrate a shared identity with powerful narratives of common fate. Music, poetry and dance energise the movement. We can see that this 'crowd' is a far cry from the 'bad and mad crowd' of LeBon, Freud & Tarde, except maybe in the calculated political energy that comes with the physical crowd (Moscovici, 1985). It is in this context that we recognise that social media are neither a crowd nor a social movement; the platforms help to bring people out into the street, where the political pressure builds up and the political agenda is shaped (Sanders, 2007). However, the networked multitude beyond nation and class has become the latest 'revolutionary subject', open-source action scripting, self-organising and powerfully performing the global resistance against the liberal empire of privatisation of what has hitherto been common land, air, water and the internet space (Hardt & Negri, 2005).

Social psychology has reformulated the 'crowd effect' in terms of social movement, **social identity theory**, inter-group behaviour and conflict escalations between protesters and police forces (Drury & Stott, 2011; Zomeren et al., 2008). Field work observing crowd events from within rather than anxiously from a window onto the street, highlights the spontaneous creation of order and directionality in crowds. The social identity of a crowd member is triggered by the physical presence of friends and foes; the crowd forms in an inter-group context of 'us and them'. Rather than mindless bodies enacting the return of the repressed, researchers find thoughtful people guided by emerging norms and identities. Self-categorisation as 'one of us' limits appropriate behaviour (we don't do that), and shares the meaning of events with a sense of solidarity (Reicher, 2011 and 1984). Crowd behaviour is not only a mannerism, but an active display of purpose and allows us to understand marginalised groups in society.

Recent research also rediscovers the energy arising from coordinated interaction with an evolutionary argument on 'synchronised behaviour'

(Fessler & Holbrook, 2016). Synchronised behaviour as in dancing rituals, music making and military parading affects both the participants and the bystanders. Participants experience increased social bonding, conformity pressure and social support, and observers are impressed by this signal of coalition strength: coordinated movement affords perceptions of an entity with formidable potential (increased size, height and muscles to fight, if needed). Such behaviour is able to attract allies and intimidate rivals in agonistic contexts whether you are friend or foe.

Another way of leaving behind the 'mad and bad', comes with the appreciation of the many by the few in market behaviour. Similar to the style of LeBon, this story forms in popular books and airport literature. The crowd has become a cherished resource. In the wisdom of the crowd (Surowiecki, 2004) the many are smarter than the few. Forecasting by the many will be more accurate than the estimates of any one person, echoing ancient Greek wisdom that the many cannot always be wrong (Aristotle). Average markets such as stock prices, point spreads, bets and future contracts all do better forecasting than any individual if certain conditions are met: there has to be diversity, independence and decentralisation of actors. Outsiders lack vested interests and carefully assess information and thus compensate for group bias.

Equally, the many are a resource in crowdsourcing, 'the mechanism by which talent and knowledge is matched to those in need of it' (Howe, 2008; p. 19). Enabled by network technology and low transaction costs, credit can be assembled from many creditors. Getting a little from many is equal to getting a lot from one, and the risk is widely spread. By turning fans into believers, harnessing the community, musicians and movie makers can get going with their projects without the difficult middle man. Not entirely new, as churches and politics worked on volunteer donations for years, and the cooperative movement has been around since the nineteenth century or earlier, but the Internet gives new clothes to a good old idea.

Crowd Management: Civil Engineering, Public Safety and the Blame Game

The image of a 'dangerous crowding' persists in crowd management, urban planning and civil engineering. Civil engineers are interested in underground trains, traffic jams, mass demonstrations, festivals and football stadiums as an issue of public safety. Crowding is here an issue of environmental psychology (Kruse, 1986) and recognised as an aspect of urbanisation and city life: too many people in too little space. Urban density is threefold: social, physical and temporal. Many people living in one place; the physical space for any one person is cramped; and the day has only twenty-four hours which are already full with commitments. Experiments with rats, breeding freely in confinement with ample food and water, dramatically demonstrated the breakdown of normal species behaviour into a **'behavioural sink'** with increasing population density (Calhoun, 1962).

Crowding is a stressor affording physiological and psychological alarm reactions which, if persisting, lead to adverse consequences. But contrary to rats in a cage, while human crowding strains with stimulus overload and spatial constraint, the adverse effects are mediated by a sense of control and efficacy that comes with effort, skill and social support. Retrospective accounts of crowd experiences in confined places reveal how they build up suddenly or slowly over time. During the events, contrary to stereotype, there is evidence of courtesy and politeness, self-policing and discipline, mutual help and support. Even under strain, we-feelings, groupiness and an embryonic social identity emerge. In the aftermath of events, the recovery needs assistance and brings additional stress. However, disasters demonstrate community resilience, and in subsequent 'disaster commemoration' the social identity and we-feeling is further strengthened. There is a growing historical literature on disasters and their importance for nation-building (Kempe et al., 2003).

Civil engineers simulate what happens when people panic in confined places (Berlonghi, 1995; Helbling et al., 2000). They have traditionally modelled the crowd on fluid dynamics in a funnelling tube, that is, a homogenous mass with viscosity, speed and friction. They noticed that this might be somewhat unrealistic as a drop of water does not think nor emote. Recent models therefore allow for thinking, wilful directions and interaction between persons, thus they bring heterogeneity into the picture. Panicking people try to move faster, pushing towards the exit; normal movement flow disorganises as *arching clog up* at the bottleneck. People *herd*, imitating what others are doing. With the pushing, the jam builds up physical pressure and walls or fences can crumble; people fall and are crushed as they stampede over each other. As people are trampled, hurt, injured or even killed, they become obstacles to further movement in uncoordinated, faster-is-slower mass behaviour. In this build up, what is a good strategy: individual or herding? Apparently a mixture of herding and everyone for themselves: keep away from the arching clog up; look around and look for any opening, then rush for the escape in a small herd.

Crowd control has three basic possibilities: First, you appeal to self-control, keep calm and carry on, and stick to the advice given. That goes well, if the advice is adequate in the circumstances. It was not, at the tragic Grenfell Tower fire in London (14 June 2017): people were told to stay in their flats and keep the twenty-four-storey stair case free for the fire fighters until the fire was under control. However, the fire got out of control torching the entire edifice and 72 of 293 inhabitants were horrendously death-trapped in their flats. Second, you line up policemen, bodies against bodies, to push and confine street protest to a side street; this was called 'kettling' during the London student protests of 2010. Maybe add a bit of equipment, armoured police forming a phalanx. And thirdly, one can build an actual wall as the Romans and the Chinese did to keep the 'barbarians' out; the GDR built one in 1960 to keep people from leaving. We will come back to these artefactual modes of social influence (see Chapter 9).

But, whatever happens in the streets or in the confined space, after the events there is often an identification and liability issue: the damage and injuries are either due to 'mad crowd behaviour' or facility management. How to **apportion blame** in public if it comes to it? If crowding is a mad force, it cannot be blamed, which frames the facility management. 'Crowd' is a forensic category and we can account in several ways (perceived or real; crowd or action): First, the event was an 'anomic mob', and we call a spade a spade, hence the mob is the culprit. Second, there was collective action and we recognise a legitimate grievance. Thirdly, there was crowd action, but defamed as 'anomic mob' by law enforcement. Usually, event organisers talk of 100,000 participants, the critical media counted 35,000 and the police speak of 5,000. The *Financial Times* (30 March 2019) had a piece on this matter of divisive politics. How many people took part in the anti-Brexit march on 23 March 2019 to London's Parliament Square? They intimated two methods to settle estimates: common sense to avoid the blatantly absurd, or the Jacob's method of dividing the area into sections and counting the average number of people across some sections multiplied by the total number of sections. Finally, there has been indeed an anomic mob, but somebody claims it as their action for a cause. A random event is claimed for purposes of visibility and propaganda. So, with 'crowds' we face an identification and an attribution problem: what happened, and who can be blamed? Thus, crowds have a dual life: they really happen and they are performed and accounted for in public discourse.

Lasting Ambivalences of a Mass Society

In a recent newspaper essay, the German philosopher Hermann Luebbe (2013) reviewed three secular predictions of the early twentieth century. The first predicted the globalisation and centralisation of power in a few totalitarian states. For a while, at least, it looked like Fascism and Communism were winning the day. But, many states emerged from the decolonisation process after WWII, so that the United Nations now have 193 members rather than a handful of empires. Secondly, secularisation was irreversible and religion was to be a thing of the past. However, since the resurgence of Islam this no longer seems so clear. And finally, modern society was to be a **mass society**. The dominance of a mass character would bring cultural decline and culminate in the cult of the mediocre clamouring for leadership. But modern mass culture is highly diverse and gave rise to new elites, such as the rock stars of the Rolling Stones or Beatles.

Our focus here is on this third failed prediction, the mainstreaming of a homogenous 'mass character' in a mass culture. Indeed, manifestations of human crowds have indeed proliferated and not stalled. We find them in military parading, not only North Korean style, in the Hajj to Mecca or at processions Catholic style; there is mass excitement in music and dance at the Love Parades of Berlin or Zurich, and certainly in sports with football of both kinds, but also in politics, as when Martin Luther King famously announced in Washington DC, 'I have a dream', or when President Trump declared that his inauguration crowd was the biggest ever. We not only have many crowds, but globally mediated crowds. Should these all be indicators of a mass society coming true? Maybe yes, but not in the manner it was anticipated.

The legacy of the historical discourse of crowds has two dimensions: talking about crowds with or without resentment, and exploring crowds as subjective experience from within, or observing it objectively from without (Kruse, 1986). The language of resentment keeps referring to madness, herding, animal spirits, hypnosis, contagion, loss of self-control and responsibility, irrationality, criminality, barbarity and a state of effemination destined to be raped by a forceful demagogue. The opposite language stresses the movement, mobilisation, force for good, the experience of empowerment, group dynamics, inter-group behaviour, social identity, streams of opinion, distributed cognition, wisdom of the crowd, resource, control of bias and **self-organisation** and creativity.

The resentment of masses was amplified in Culture Critique (Kulturkritik, in German). Ortega y Gasset (1956 [1930]) lamented the cultural decline and the entry of barbarism into history; the heroic, high-cultured and rational individual is displaced by the mediocrity of mass entertainment hinging on the irrational. Later authors distanced them-selves from such critique. Carey (1992) offers two literary archetypes of dealing with social masses. On the one hand, he positions *Sherlock Holmes* (author Arthur Canon Doyle), who may not be a man of the people, but he gives the common man his due. In his search for cues and signs to solve crimes, individuality is denied to nobody, everybody can be a potential witness or give off cues to trace the murder. This is a far cry from *Zarathustra* (author Nietzsche) who expresses utter rejection of common spirits. The titanic 'Ubermensch' (not a taxi driver), is remote from and above the masses. The Nietzschean celebrates a low-to-higher revolution and cultivates the vanguard as a beacon of the future. Modernist art celebrates unintelligibility and inaccessibility as a trademark; popular cul-ture is rejected and held in contempt as false consciousness.

For the sociologist T. W. Adorno, jazz was little more than escapism of the masses with no intrinsic cultural value. These expressions of elitism echo a much older Gnosis (Jonas, 2001), the most radical form of elite dualism between the knowing few and the ignorant crowd. In the gnostic temptation, the concrete world is devalued by a mood of being homeless in a dark and sinking world, and with reference to another world that is full of light but totally alien (see Chapter 11). This alien but 'real' reality is only accessible to the elected few, while the ignorant many are condemned to live 'in the noise of the world' (ibidem, 73f). For the elected few it is given to know; they have only contempt for those who are left behind on this journey. The Gnostic world is full of symbols, the meaning of which is transmitted in esoteric initiation. A spoof version of this landed the bestselling *Da Vinci Code* (2003) about a world of symbols, hidden truths and conspiracies over the blood line of Christ.

Conclusion

The project of modernity is still thinking about masses. The mass has not gone away, how could it with still rising world populations and resurgent populism in politics? Moscovici (1985) and Graumann & Moscovici (1986) reconsidered the reality of masses, and Sloterdijk (2000) recognised in the discourse of masses the great culture war of the past 200 years that ended in the emancipation of the many. For thousands of years, societies were ruled by the few – the few being families, oligarchs or aristocrats – in the twentieth century the masses staked their claim to widen this rule, to gain access and impose accountability. The masses of common people had really become the subject of history so fearfully evidenced by LeBon, Tarde and Freud. In nationalist movements, masses mobilised for independence from imperialist powers; in social–democratic movements, masses mobilised for economic interest; in populist movements they clamour for denied representation for the 'real people' (Chiantera-Stutte, 2018; Mueller, 2016). In that vein, the search for the historically critical mass continues under the heading of 'multitudes' (Hardt & Negri, 2005).

Sloterdijk (2000) identifies in the *contempt for the masses* a key dispute of modernity; elites are responding to the emancipation of the masses and the *normalisation of new beginnings*. The vertical identification towards the 'Uber' (not the car hailing service, though the name is indicative), the striving on a low-to-higher pipeline, finds salvation in the foundational critique of Nietzsche and Heidegger. The other response is LeBon's and horizontal, and celebrates the revolutionary alliance between mob and elite, culminating in exclusive party rule and personality cults with examples in Hitler, Mussolini, Stalin, Mao and to the present day Kim dynasty in North Korea; maybe even recently Trump (United States), Salvini (Italy) and Bolsonaro (Brazil). The golden middle way between these extremes is given by the path of seduction, seeking alliance with the issue crowd, domesticating its energy and managing it by recognising the crowd's logic, accepting the 'rule by imagination' and mobilising for punctual collective action rather than a new regime. It seems that Tarde, rather than LeBon or Nietzsche, has won the day in this dispute.

Maybe, on the ambivalence of crowds as normalising social influence in modern society, Canetti (1960) might have a last word. He offered a panoramic phenomenology of masses. Ambivalence arises from our fundamental fear of being touched, of being caught up in it. Touch is necessary in human interaction, not least for sex and procreation. On the other hand, humans fear that interference, the sting of being incorporated, absorbed and assimilated by others, and to lose their distinct individuality. This fear of touch is strongest in medium dense crowding; we enjoy our privacy in isolation, in high density we appreciate the cosiness and warmth of other bodies. Canetti recognises in historical world religions (Catholicism, Islam) a way of containing the natural energy of the crowd by taming its potential violence:

> the crowd they envisage is universal; every single soul counts and every soul shall be theirs ... But the fight they sustain leads gradually to a kind of hidden respect for adversaries, ... the dead weight of institutions, which

have a life of their own, then gradually tames the impetus of the original appeal ... A sense of the treacherousness of the crowd is ... in the blood of all historical world religions ... in the heretical movements which the churches fear and persecute ... What they want in contrast is an obsequious flock (ibidem, 26f).

If crowding and its normalisation effect is an anthropological constant, the only adequate response is surviving. Crowds can neither be avoided nor dictated by a ruler. Charles Taylor (2007) deconstructed the mentality of 'buffered individualism' that inspired the false prospect of crowd psychology: *the idol of an isolated and heroic rationality*. Rather than a real constant, this vision is a last stand against rising masses. The future sources of self are reincarnated, embedded in body, passion and sociality, and thus offer a view of social life that is foundational rather than corrupting. Corruption being secondary, primary is communality in communication, and reason emerges under favourable circumstances.

In this chapter, we looked at crowds through their function of normalisation and creating new beginnings. In the next chapter, we will focus on leaders, closely tied to crowds as we have seen, and equally involved in defining new directions and shifting the standards for common sense.

In Essence

Crowding has long been held to induce a 'crowd effect' that shuts down critical mental faculties in individuals and opens up the will of individuals to influence from the leader.

A corollary of the crowd is 'public opinion', forged amongst distributed individuals through mass mediated communication in moments of passive participation in joint attention. In contemporary times, we find similar ideas in the notion of 'virality' and 'echo-chambers', representing the potential to 'infect' of 'contaminate' minds.

The psychology of social movements is based on a symbiotic identification process involving leadership and membership, as opposed to somnambulant followership. Human beings are agents and rationally engaged in the development and management of their identities and lifestyles. They identify with and join movements that collectively spur social action to defend interests and identities.

CHAPTER 3

Leading

Directors, Dictators and Dudes

				Mode 1 face-to-face	Mode 2 symbolic	Mode 3 artefact
phase	modality	function for CS	outcome	inter-subjective		inter-objective
	Order created 'out of Chaos' of interaction: social representations, common sense, joint intentionality					
Phase 1	leadership	**Normalisation**	atmosphere	social identification	priming	monument

Figure 3.1   A challenge and response model II: leading

Human history is sometimes defined as a chronological narrative of how certain famous individuals achieved inspiring goals during their lifetime and beyond by following a visionary path that led them and their followers to some incredible outcome. Such a definition of history is sufficiently broad to attract little by way of critique, other than that it is not very tangible. The 'great men theory of history', which for historians has little value beyond the popular history bookshelf (Carr, 1961), often takes the form of detailing what certain leaders did and documenting how events turned out. Think, for instance, about Julius Caesar and his March on Rome; Napoleon and the French Revolution; Lenin and the Russian Revolution; Mandela and the overthrow of apartheid in South Africa. What these examples have in common is a powerful figurehead at the helm, who has changed the regular course of events by mobilising a critical enough mass of followers to precipitate social change; although leaders are also held capable of mobilising a critical enough mass to resist change. In essence, leaders are seemingly capable of steering followers to challenge or defend established norms, by transmitting their ideas in a powerful way that energises followers to action. Due to this allure, strong leaders often acquire a cult status. Certain leaders are depersonalised in this sense and portrayed to the masses (or by the masses) in ostensibly supernatural terms. The personality of the leader can be cultivated for propaganda purposes – the cult of the leader. This projects an idealised image of the leader embodying characteristics which the masses follow. Behind the scenes, as in Oz, the wizard may be no more than an imposter. But for as long as the personality cult survives, the faithful will keep lining up to have a go at the wicked witch.

Our fascination with the personality of leaders and the consequences this precipitates for mere mortals everywhere remains very much alive. In a recent volume treating the making and unmaking of presidents and prime ministers in contemporary times, the political scientist David Runciman (2019) explores the personality attributes of modern great leaders like Barack Obama, Tony Blair, Boris Johnson and Donald Trump. He notes how many leaders report, after gaining office, a degree of frustration at their inability to get things done. Leaders in power come to understand the limits of their power more than aspiring candidates motivated by the illusion of unlimited power. For this reason, many question what attributes a leader *really* needs to possess: does a second-class personality make for a first-class leader? Runciman argues that certain personality attributes help shape the rise and fall of leaders. He claims that in an era of populism, the sane lose out to the stamina of ego-driven challengers. When we examine the personality type of leaders, we engage in a compare and contrast exercise to find what one has that another lacks. But as Runciman himself queries – is it the character of our political leaders that determines the character of our democracies, or is it rather the case that, now more than ever, we get the politicians we deserve? This question strikes at the heart of psychological theories of leadership, with which the present chapter is concerned. In Box 3.1, we review an example that illustrates our ongoing fear and fascination with leaders. It exemplifies leadership as a modality of social influence in its own right. Indeed, leadership constitutes an obvious point of discussion in any consideration of social influence. Both leadership and social influence require a minimum of two interacting parties to manifest where one influences, or leads, the other. Social influence is essentially the defining criterion of leadership (Chemers, 2001): a leader who is not able to influence followers is not their leader.

Box 3.1 The fear and fascination of leaders

On the small Mediterranean island of Malta, two parties dominate the political landscape (Briguglio, 2015). The population has historically been divided between supporters of the Labour Party [PL] and supporters of the Nationalist Party [PN]. Over the past decade, however, the Labour Party has recorded the biggest back-to-back electoral successes in the political history of the republic. The PL premier, Dr Joseph Muscat, proved to be a very popular leader throughout his tenure.

One event that took place on the island during Joseph Muscat's term was an abrogative referendum on spring hunting (see Briguglio, 2015). Hunting for wild birds is a relatively popular sport in the Mediterranean region. Since the 1990s, however, it has attracted criticism in Malta due to the inconvenience caused to locals by hunters practicing the sport, as well as for representing the killing of migrating birds from Europe to their breeding grounds in Africa as a 'sport'. The problem with regulating hunting in Malta was that the issue was politicised in the general election of 1996. At the time, the PL agreed to represent hunters' interests should they be returned to power. The PL went on to win the election and hunters have been recognised by the Maltese to be a significant and powerful lobby ever since. The referendum proposing a ban on spring hunting was posed to the Maltese population on the 11th of April 2015, following a successful petition that gathered the requisite number of signatures.

*In the lead-up to the referendum, both political parties abstained from the campaign and left the matter entirely up to the Maltese people. Two rival groups emerged, fronted by NGOs representing hunters for the YES campaign (i.e., yes to introducing a ban), and NGOs representing wildlife conservation for the NO campaign (i.e., no to the ban). The question posed to the electorate was whether spring hunting should be banned. Throughout the campaign, the NO camp had a clear edge and up to a week before the referendum they seemed to be cruising to a victory that would keep hunters away from their sport during the spring months, when birds migrate to Africa to breed. Hunters were told that they would then be able to practice their sport in Autumn, when migrating birds return from Africa to Europe in greater numbers that include offspring. A couple of days before the referendum, however, Dr Muscat made some casual remarks about the issue whilst campaigning for local council elections being held on the same day. Dr Muscat remarked that whilst he considered the matter purely personal, he would himself be voting 'yes' as he supported minority rights. In this way, the PL leader is argued to have **primed** his followers to vote YES, by **framing** the issue in a way that appealed to those who had already voted for him for similar reasons in the past. Dr Muscat, as leader of the PL, is credited with* <u>*swinging*</u> *the vote to a YES victory of 50.4 per cent (Briguglio, 2015).*

Leadership can be defined as a situation in which some individual/s, more than others, exercise/s influence over/on behalf of others. This definition of leadership takes into account the fact that individuals are open to plural forms of influence that could emanate from different sources. It also does not preclude the influence obtained by bad or unpopular leaders. Some leaders can be identified as leaders not by virtue of popular support, but by their sheer ability to exercise influence over others. In this chapter, we treat leadership as a modality of social influence. We start by reviewing the classical theories of leadership. We proceed to focus on the role that leaders play in movements that establish or challenge particular norms. As a modality of influence (see The Periodic Table, Chapter 10), leadership aims directly at normalising some particular claims or perspectives. In this way, a certain **leadership atmosphere** is set that attracts followers to variable degrees. Followers who **identify** with the leader sign up to the cause. In essence, a critical mass will be required and successful leaders are capable of mobilising a critical enough mass of individuals who grant allegiance in pursuit of common goals. The leader steers this collective impetus through **priming**, as in the example set out in Box 3.1. Success is achieved through the extent of diffusion a leader's claims acquire in the group. Over the longer term, some leaders acquire **personality cult** status by embodying the cause itself, representing it through their very being. When this happens, leaders are objectified, for example by erecting monuments to remember them, such that the cause may retain influence beyond the leader's own actions and limited lifespan. We conclude the chapter by considering leadership as a group dynamic, embedded in social relations that prioritise some forms of collective action over others.

Leadership Criteria

Our definition of leadership is based on an individual's capacity to exercise influence over others. As detailed, we understand leadership to be a modality of social influence. In our view, leaders are those individuals who command a disproportionate amount of influence in a given group. There are other criteria implied in this definition that will help us to conceive of leadership in a way that serves our analytical purposes, which we proceed to review.

We have seen that some form of groupness is requisite for a leader to emerge; one cannot become a leader if there is no group to lead. This point, however, is far from trivial and needs to be explored further before moving on to review the psychological theories of leadership. In practice, we identify leaders as those individuals vested with authority to exercise power on behalf of the groups they lead. In other words, we understand leadership to manifest whenever a group delegates the management of collective resources or aims to some individual/s. A leader is vested with power to exercise on behalf of the group in managing collective resources and implementing a collective agenda. In this exercise, the group can proceed to achieve its fundamental aims more efficiently than the alternative of doing so without centralising power. One could argue in this line that leadership is a corollary of division of labour. A key criterion for leadership, therefore, is an inequitable distribution of power amongst group members that is meant to be group serving. Groups do not put leaders in place to maximise the leader's individual interests. Rather, leaders are tasked with maximising the interests of the group. This suggests at the outset that leadership is a group, rather than an individual, dynamic. We shall elaborate this point shortly.

The distinction between individual and group interests is also a critical one, as it underlines two dimensions of leadership (Kellerman, 2004), which we visited briefly already. The first dimension refers to the effectiveness of leaders, that is, the extent to which leaders are able to set goals and successfully achieve them. The second dimension of leadership is moral and refers to the extent to which leaders adopt ethical means in achieving group-serving goals. The two dimensions of leadership, therefore, serve to appraise both the *means* and the *ends* of leadership. Good and effective leaders are those who achieve group goals using ethical means. Bad and ineffective leaders are those who prioritise their own goals over those of the group and who pursue their own interests in unethical ways. One could also think of good and ineffective leaders, that is, morally upright leaders who fail to achieve group-serving goals, along with bad and effective leaders who achieve group goals using unethical means (Figure 3.2).

As noted, these two dimensions of leadership serve to appraise particular leaders and address some central concerns: 'Whose goals are being pursued, the leader's or the group's?', 'Is power being used or abused by the leader?'. Answering any of these questions requires a consideration of both leader *and* group. One cannot understand one without understanding the other. The assessment of a leader on these two dimensions, therefore, provides an appraisal of the leader from some particular point of view – that of the group. This point is worth bearing in mind, and we will return

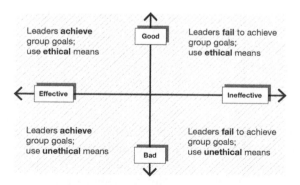

Figure 3.2   Dimensions of leadership

to it again later in this chapter. The effectiveness and morality of a leader are not objective criteria that exist independently of whomever is conducting the appraisal, even though some great leaders in history seem to have been great leaders in an objective sense. However, whether a leader is held to have achieved goals successfully depends on *whose* goals are being considered. Similarly, which means justify which ends depends equally on whose ends are being achieved. One could think of good leaders who lose popularity after being deemed ineffective. Or bad leaders who gain popularity by being effective. The point we wish to make here is that the properties that are valorised or deprecated in leaders do not lie with leaders themselves, but lie in the eye of the beholder. This will be a recurring theme throughout this chapter and one that, as we note in the next section, leadership theories have largely overlooked.

The Personality Trait Approach

Leaders typically enjoy power by virtue of commanding widespread popular support. History, however, is littered with examples of rogue leaders who brought about devastation on their followers. Now ask yourself this question: 'How is it that these particular leaders managed to gain or seize power over the many others who were also around at the time to do the same?' When we think of leaders, we also think of the characteristics they demonstrate that enable their rise to power, as Runciman (2019) claims. What [in the eyes of the Conservative Party] did Boris Johnson have that Theresa May lacked in the ability to deliver Brexit to the people of the United Kingdom? We tend to think that leaders possess some inherent attributes that make them succeed over others – leaders are born not made.

Psychology's answer to the issue of leadership is based primarily on the characterisation of types. That is, psychology has traditionally aimed at identifying which traits (i.e., relatively persistent characteristics inherent to the person that can be measured) make for good leaders. Are 'leaders' generally and consistently different from 'followers' in their personality profiles? This question has recently gained renewed attention in political psychology with focus on the 'Big-Five' and the 'Dark Tetrad' concepts of personality testing (Costa & McCrae, 1992; Paulhus, 2014). The Big-Five profiles people along five dimensions: extraversion, agreeableness, conscientiousness, emotional stability and openness; while the Dark Tetrad assesses the individual's profile on narcissism, psychopathy and Machiavellianism. Personality profiling positions an individual on these dimensions. Whilst there is little reported correspondence between leadership and personality profiles, there is seemingly better covariance between certain personality traits and political style, as expressed in incidences of negative campaigning, character attacks, fear appeals and expressions of enthusiasm (Nai, Coma & Maier, 2019).

One particular focus that has received a lot of scholarly attention over the years is the personality trait that leaders seem to possess that enables them to stand out. Runciman (2019) proposes that this might be stamina. In pre-populist eras, when fascination with leaders presumably tipped fear in the eyes of beholders, scholars focused their efforts on another trait: **charisma** (House, 1977). In the religious tradition, charisma is the 'gift of grace' of a person open to inspiration, enlightenment and revelation, which inspires followers to become 'disciples'. Charisma is how leaders are able to acquire extraordinary prestige and devotion in the eyes of their followers. In sociology, charisma creates an extraordinary regime, often with revolutionary impetus and enthusiastic followers. Charismatic leaders represent their followers directly and exclusively, unmediated by organisation; they are often outsiders by origin and maverick in style (Weber, 1968).

Charismatic leaders are those who are liked and well regarded by their followers by virtue of the traits they possess (House & Howell, 1992). They are perceived as being attractive and competent, and they are able to inspire devotion and commitment in followers. A charismatic individual is someone who is able to inspire confidence in others more than a non-charismatic other. Consequently, in a situation where a leadership position becomes vacant, charismatic individuals are able to garner more popular support and in this way are better able to rise to the top. This research tradition is rooted in the individual differences paradigm in psychology that considers personality traits to be distributed over a population where some have more and some others less of any particular trait. Different traits bear dividends in different situations. In a leadership contest, higher levels of charisma enable some individuals to fare better than others.

The influence of charisma over followers is held to apply to bad leaders as much as it does to good ones. And it applies further to effective and ineffective leaders. In hindsight, we are able to look back on the performance of leaders and appraise them along the two dimensions of leadership detailed. Yet even bad and ineffective leaders were somehow able to rise to the top. We might wonder how it is that leaders like Adolf Hitler, for instance, were able to gain power and how it is that they were not stopped by their fellows long before they had a chance to inflict considerable devastation on others. The personality approach to leadership (House & Howell, 1992) suggests that regardless of their moral intentions, leaders are able to influence others; they are able to be more persuasive; they are able to mobilise group resources; and they are able to sell their vision more than others. In this way, they are better able to seize power given an opportunity.

A more recent extension of the charisma approach to leadership is **transformational leadership** (Avolio & Bass, 1988; Bass, 1985; Shamir, House & Arthur, 1993). This refers to the ability some leaders demonstrate in imagining desirable group objectives and envisioning ways for achieving them. Transformational leaders, unlike *transactional leaders* who pursue cost–benefit exchanges with followers, are able to articulate a more desirable future for the group. On this basis, they are better able than others to inspire followers and lead them to develop higher levels of morale and motivation that ensure adoption of a communal vision. The group itself takes on a different character; followership resembles membership as the group bestows identity so that leader and followers are one – a group. This sets the stage for personality cult. In essence, transformational leaders are better able to *sell* their vision to others, and that vision becomes embodied in the personality of the leader. Transformational leaders generate devotion and are convincing by virtue of their ability to provide followers with a vision and a mission, a strategy for taking things forward whatever the present situation is. In this way, they are perceived as acting in the interests of the group given the lived experiences of the members comprising it. They provide intellectual stimulation and motivate followers to work to make things better. In this way, they acquire popular support and endorsement for their projected version of a desirable future. It was in this way that Apple's Steve Jobs blessed us with a brave new world where most of us can link up via a computerised gadget: the 'smart' phone.

Analysis of managerial discourse over the past 150 years suggests that 'transformational leadership' is no constant, but comes and goes in what Barley & Kunda (1992) call the cycles of 'design and devotion'. Transformational leadership and devotion is correlated with long-term contractions of the world economy: from 1879 to 1900 (contraction1), leaders for 'industrial betterment' are reformers, role models that shoulder social responsibility (p. 337); many of them became famous philanthropists such as Carnegie and Rockefeller. Between 1925 and 1955 (contraction2), leaders under the umbrella rhetoric of 'human relations or welfare capitalism' bridge conflicts and mould cohesive communities by unleashing the actualisation of unconscious potential inspired by psycho-analysis (p. 375). Finally, in the period since 1980 (contraction3), leaders create 'organisational culture'; they are cult gurus and high priests who instil commitment and loyalty and a strong culture in search of excel-lence (p. 382), they became the wacky and wild founding CEOs of the computer and social media industry. Thus, in periods of contraction leaders focus on people whilst cultivating personality and posing norma-tive appeals. By contrast, in periods of economic expansion, 1900–1925 and 1955–1980, leaders focus on rational designs and managing new technology and skills to seek efficient production. It could thus be said that two key functions of leadership, task steering and relationship management, are manifest in a historical sequence oscillating between predominantly designing tasks and otherwise creating devotion.

The Situational Approach

The personality approach to leadership proposes that leaders possess some key virtues over others that enable them to garner increased support when an opportunity for leadership arises in a group. The central objective of this research paradigm is the identification of types suited to the leadership task. Yet, whilst successful leaders may share some common features, such as charisma or stamina, they differ vastly with regards to other traits. An alternative line of inquiry has queried the circumstances under which effective leadership is achieved (Shamir & Howell, 1999). The starting point here is not the characterisation of types but of situations. The situational approach to leadership complements the personality approach in specifying the conditions under which effective leadership may be achieved given different leader types. The general idea in the situational approach is that effective leadership is contingent on circumstances, and some leaders are preferable in certain circumstances than other leaders with different dispositions.

The situational approach to leadership counterbalances the personality approach, inasmuch as it does not specify a particular constellation of objectively desirable leader characteristics that constitute a universally ideal standard. According to the situational approach, unlikely individuals may yet go on to become leaders should different circumstances arise. Conversely, popular leaders may fall out of favour should circumstances change. Perhaps the best historical example of this is Winston Churchill, whose broadcast speeches as prime minister of the United Kingdom inspired British resistance up until victory against Hitler's Nazi regime in the Second World War. Despite this outstanding achievement, Churchill went on to lose the subsequent general election in 1945, although he was returned to power in 1951. Churchill's example demonstrates how different tasks faced by a group over its lifespan may require different leader orientations.

Fiedler's (1965) **Contingency Theory** is probably the best known situational theory of leadership. Fiedler's theory distinguishes between **task-oriented** leaders and **relationship-oriented** leaders (Hogg, 2001). Whether a situation calls for a task-oriented or a relationship-oriented leader is contingent on certain measurable characteristics of the group with respect to the structure of social relations within it. In essence, the quality of leader–member relations, the structural clarity of the task facing the group and the power and authority assigned to the leader determine the level of situational control in descending order. In low instances of situational control, the group benefits by putting in place task-oriented leaders. Relationship-oriented leaders are most effective in high instances of situational control. Fiedler's theory is non-committal regarding how one comes to be task-oriented or relationship-oriented. Presumably, this distinction is dispositional. In this way, the situational approach complements the personality approach to leadership.

Personality and charisma research suggest that leadership offers a unique solution in history: the ONE person fit for the job. The situational approach, however, reformulates leadership as a situational dynamic not an individual trait: if one is not fit for the job, another might be able to step in instead. Equally, charisma is less a trait feature of the leader, but an idea that followers expect and attribute to their leader, and this expectation is often levelled in an extraordinary crisis situation. The historical 'cult of the leader' becomes a self-fulfilling prophecy as the group looks for its next hero – think of the search for the Dalai Lama, or the appointment of a new pope, where the demonstration of characteristic inclinations is not only desirable, but essential. The fate of Pope Benedict XVI, otherwise the largely uncharismatic Cardinal Ratzinger, provides a telling example.

Dictatorship

The personality approach and the situational approach to leadership combined seem to be faithful to Lewin's (1936) equation that human behaviour is a function of the person and the environment. Taken together, these two leadership theories seemingly account for the rise and fall of leaders worldwide. Individuals with particular predispositions are able to court support given an opportunity for leadership, which sees them rise to the top. When circumstances change, their influence may dwindle as their inclinations may not serve the group's best interests over the longer term. Such leaders stand to be displaced by other transformational leaders who promise a more popular outcome. That is to say, if provisions are in place for leaders to be displaced. Arguably, dictatorships do not abide by any such provisions so that when the leader falls out of favour, they are able to retain command and exercise influence through sheer hard power. Moreover, these two approaches also seem to cater for long-term leader popularity. To the extent that a leader is able to change their dispositions over time to match changes in circumstances, they stand to retain popularity and influence over the longer term. One of the best examples of changing leadership styles corresponding to changing societal circumstances and long-term popularity is that of Nelson Mandela, whose leadership credentials spanned a period of active armed resistance, long-term incarceration and presidency, along with a period of active retirement. Mandela remained an influential leader for the native South African population throughout. Unlike Mandela, many other dictators are subject to a rise and fall in popularity over the years they serve as leaders and many of them do not relinquish power easily when their popularity dwindles (see Box 3.2).

Moghaddam's (2013) work on the psychology of dictatorship suggests that the personality approach combined with the situational approach may nevertheless be too simplistic in accounting for the phenomenon. Moghaddam notes that ousting a dictator who seizes power is no mean feat and more often than not requires nothing short of armed revolution. The common explanation for this recurrence is that dictators wield hard power, so followers are forced to carry out the dictator's commands under fear of execution. Yet, clearly, this explanation cannot apply to *all* followers. A dictator is rarely the executioner. More commonly, it is someone else's finger that pulls the trigger or presses the red button. We argue that the personality and the situational approaches to leadership overlook a critical ingredient – that of the specific role of *followers* who bestow upon the leader legitimate authority. Let us consider the illustrative case of Julius Caesar. Caesar was at his time the most powerful person in the longest-standing empire in history. Following victories in the Gallic wars, he refused the Roman Senate's order to step down from military command and return to Rome. Rather, he marched a legion to Rome and precipitated civil war. Victory once again ensued for Caesar, and he went on to assume control of government and establish himself dictator in perpetuity,

Box 3.2 The rise and fall of dictators

Colonel Muammar Gaddafi was Libya's leader from 1969 up until his death in 2011. Gaddafi seized power from King Idris of Libya in a bloodless coup d'état in 1969, leading a military operation that lasted a mere two hours whilst King Idris was on holiday abroad. Following the coup, Gaddafi established himself chairman of the Revolutionary Command Council. He went on to abolish the monarchy and proclaim Libya a Republic, which he ruled by decree. In 1977, he dissolved the Republic and established the Jamahiriya, which means the state of the masses (the official title for the Libyan nation during this time was Great Socialist People's Libyan Arab Jamahiriya). He presided over the Jamahiriya as brotherly leader of the revolution, a position he occupied on a permanent basis that saw him retain control of the government and the armed forces. The tide turned in the early months of 2011. Civil unrest that had started in Tunisia spilled over into Libya as Arabs rose up in protest against their dictators. At the time this became known as the Arab Spring, suggesting the imminent ushering of a new era for the Arab world, free from dictatorial tyranny. Gaddafi's relations with Western powers at the time remained strained. In the months following the uprising, NATO proceeded to enforce a no-fly zone targeting Gaddafi's facilities. This enabled the rebel uprising to push forward and defeat Gaddafi's armies. Colonel Gaddafi was killed on the 20th October 2011 in the course of being captured by rebel forces. A decade after his execution, Libya remains torn by civil war and democratic governance in the country remains a far-flung ideal.

Not all dictatorships necessarily follow a similar trajectory, as the case of Ghana makes clear. Jerry John Rawlings seized power in Ghana following a coup in 1979. He went on to oversee general elections, which were won by Hilla Limann. In 1981, Rawlings once again overthrew the government and seized power anew, setting himself up as chairman of the governing council. In the years that followed, Rawlings set up political parties and organised presidential and parliamentary elections, which he himself contested and won. He served two terms in office then stepped down as per constitutional requirements. Following his departure, he was succeeded by John Agyekum Kufuor – Rawlings' primary adversary. In gaining power, Kufuor saw off John Atta Mills, Rawlings's own vice president. Kufuor, like Rawlings, went on to win a second and final term.

only to be assassinated less than two months later by a group of rebellious senators. The ousting of numerous other dictators since has taken a lot more than literal back-stabbing and oftentimes has only been achievable through technological military edge. It is rather surprising that the removal of despots also requires the removal of plenty of others willing to fight and die for the leader and for the cause (see Box 3.2).

Moghaddam (2013) proposes a normative model over the causal model underlining both personality and situational approaches to leadership. This focuses on collectively constructed and collaboratively upheld social values, norms and rules for behaviour. According to Moghaddam, behaviour is regulated by normative systems, rather than caused by independent variables (such as traits or particular situational circumstances). Individuals go on to become leaders, or dictators, by following local norms and local rules of good conduct. Leaders thus emerge by following particular norms that make sense in a particular society. Given these norms, and given the right background factors as well as a set of opportunities, an individual may find themselves legitimately *springing* to power.

Moghaddam's argument turns the psychological notion of leadership on its head. For a dictator to emerge, according to Moghaddam, one might not need recourse to hard power at all, even though we might mistakenly assume that dictators necessarily fight their way to the top. In a context where members of a group expect the leader to assume absolute authority, the leader *will* assume absolute authority. Moghaddam's point is that psychology needs to look further than the traits of the leader and extend its restrictive individualistic focus. His argument is reminiscent of Arendt's (1963) banality of evil notion. Arendt, reporting on the trial of Adolf Eichmann in Jerusalem who was executed for crimes committed as a Nazi officer, claimed that Eichmann appeared to be a dull, ordinary bureaucrat who was seemingly simply doing his job.

Moghaddam argues that it is naive to think that removing one, seemingly evil individual from power will liberate a nation and everything will go back to 'normal'. In practice, this exercise creates a situation vacant and could go all the way to ordinary people who are not outrightly affiliated with the dictator. This is also essentially Arendt's argument. She claims that the most shocking aspect of Eichmann's trial was not the atrocities committed but that there were so many like Eichmann who were, themselves, neither perverted nor sadistic but 'terribly and terrifyingly normal' (1963, p. 276). In other words, reverting back to 'normal' refers to local practices that are normative in some particular context, not the normative standards we are ourselves accustomed to. In recent years, we have witnessed a number of military interventions by various countries in Arab states justified in the name of liberation and democracy. Following the displacement of many a dictator in the process, democratic governance has remained largely elusive. We argue that it is the context that is particular for a dictator to emerge, not the particular individual herself. The example of Julius Caesar and the Roman Empire is again illustrative. Following Caesar's assassination, Mark Anthony was able to spring to power and serve as dictator in his stead. The Roman Senate subjugated to this dictatorship due to the fact that its own supreme authority was no longer popularly supported. In other words, the normative context at the time had shifted and dictatorial authority became the 'new normal' with Mark Anthony, despite the Senate's extreme act of resistance in assassinating Julius Caesar.

The Social Identity Approach

Moghaddam's account of the psychology of dictatorship relies on an understanding of the role of followers, who subscribe to certain normative practices which characterise their own culture. We have seen how this understanding of the role of followers is unaccounted for in both personality and situational approaches to leadership. On the other hand, **social identity** theories of leadership have examined leadership by looking at the leading process.

Building on social identity theory, Hogg (2001) argues that leadership entails an element of identification within a group that grants members self-esteem in comparisons undertaken relative to other social groups. Social identity theory (Tajfel & Turner, 1979) proposes that individuals negotiate an identity that enables them to define who they are for others. In other words, identity is not merely an individual concern describing how I define myself. Rather, identity includes a reference to the social in terms of how I define myself *for others*. In fact, an individual may subjectively take issue with how she is identified by others. Howarth, Wagner, Magnusson & Sammut (2014) document how the social categorisation of somebody as 'black' does not depend on the individual but on the reaction of others to that individual on the basis of their skin colour being black. To the black person herself, the colour of her skin is in itself inconsequential. It becomes consequential in social relations that are structured along racial lines. In this manner, insofar as one's identification by others acquires social validation, it goes on to influence one's own identity and the ensuing sense of personal esteem attached to it. This happens as a result of three processes. Firstly, the social world is categorised into different groups. Secondly, a process of identification ensues by which one comes to recognise that one is a member of some group and not another. Thirdly, a process of social comparison follows by which some groups come to be valued more or less than others.

Social comparison thus serves to establish positive distinctiveness for one's own group, relative to other groups. These comparisons form the basis of *stereotypes*, which typify what black people are generally like, or what Catholics are generally like, and so on. There is nothing intrinsic to these stereotypes in and of themselves. Stereotypes are social representations that typify individuals on the basis of some socially salient criteria. They go on to exert an influence on social relations, however, inasmuch as they assign value to some characteristics over others. For instance, in some settings it would pay to be white, or Catholic, or whatever other feature holds value in that particular setting. Membership of a relatively well-regarded group alone may be sufficient to generate a positive social identity for the individual regardless of their own personal dispositions and merits. In this way, intergroup relations transpire as a competitive exercise for generating self-esteem amongst group members. Some white people may be rather unremarkable on a personal level, but their whiteness may be sufficient for them to look down on others around them. This implicit exercise of social categorisation and belonging accentuates prototypical similarities across group members and precipitates a degree of depersonalisation that focuses on group features rather than personal idiosyncrasies marking the individuals involved.

In their efforts to develop positive self-esteem on the basis of membership of a particular social group, individuals thus go on to identify with some typical features that are valued by their group. For instance, some groups may value authoritative dispositions that help maintain a definite hierarchy, whereas other groups may value piety and humility. The former may be the case in the military, for instance, whereas the latter may be valued in a monastic order. These social values (Sammut, Tsirogianni & Moghaddam, 2013) acquire consensual validation within the group and come to represent the group ideal. A colonel is somebody who can give a command; a monk is somebody who can discern the spiritual. This ideal is implied in how leaders come to be chosen.

According to the social identity approach to leadership, there are three processes governing the basis of leadership. The first of these processes is *prototypicality*, which refers to the characteristics marking the ideal group member – in other words, the group prototype. Let's do a mental exercise here: think of the social group that you identify with mostly, and then think about what characteristics are desirable for the average group member. Depending on which group comes to mind, there are certain personal features that will be valued over others. If the social group you have identified is, for instance, a national group, then you can think of certain dispositional attributes that mark what is positive about your own national group. Or, you might have identified with a professional group, in which case the valued attributes will be different from those marking national groups. Amongst psychologists, for instance, one could expect that being empathetic is considered to be a virtuous trait. This is not the case for soldiers, who would be expected to demonstrate quite different traits in their dealings with other human beings. In any case, some particular features are valued amongst members of particular social groups over other features. The social representation (Sammut & Howarth, 2014) of the constellation of valued dispositions marking members of a group defines the prototypical member, that is, it defines what the ideal group member is like and what features they demonstrate. The relevance to leadership here is in terms of the extent to which specific group members approximate this ideal prototype. Some group members will, due to individual differences, be more prototypical than others, as we have seen.

The second process identified in the social identity approach to leadership is *social attraction*. We have seen that group members define themselves relative to prototypical features they value. In this way, they come to be attracted to individuals who embody these prototypical features. In essence, more prototypical members are liked more. Those individuals who best embody these valued features acquire an ability to secure compliance from others to those very same prototypical features that they themselves value. But this compliance is not a function of the social influence leaders are able to exert over others by virtue of some personality disposition that they claim. Rather, this compliance is willingly extended to them by group members who hold leaders in higher prestige than they hold their own selves and less prototypical others. This element of social attraction empowers prototypical members to exercise social influence. They do not need to impose themselves and their features on others as they find themselves, by their group's standards, more naturally normative than others around them. Consequently, they amass greater support for their own inclinations relative to others.

It is worth underlining that prototypical members are conferred prestige by others due to the fact that they embody features that others would typically like for themselves. However, followers proceed to attribute behaviours and features (which they already subjectively endorse) to dispositional traits that they perceive embodied in the leader (rather than to their own subjective ideals). They commit a *fundamental attribution error* (Ross, 1977) relative to their leaders. The fundamental attribution error refers to a bias in social cognition by which individuals attribute the behaviours they see others engage in to dispositional causes, whilst overlooking or minimising situational influences. This process of *attribution* constitutes the third process in the social identity approach. The most prototypical members of a group are regarded as great for who they are, rather than for what they represent for the group. Consequently, given these three processes of social identification, some individuals who by their very nature fit the group prototype better than others find themselves better able to capitalise on opportunities for leadership. They come to be considered as naturally great and capable, and are able to acquire cult status within their group. Leadership itself transpires, therefore, as the consequence of a social representation of the valued attributes of a particular prototype defined and elaborated by the group itself.

Prototypical members may find themselves in a position where they can exercise more power over others due to the fact that this opportunity is granted to them by the group. They do not need to exercise power. Prototypical members do not need to put a gun themselves to anyone's head to acquire the possibility of exercising influence, as some typically understand with regards to dictators. Power is extended to them naturally out of their representing some particular features that others find desirable and look up to. The leader ends up in that position because everyone else is interested in putting them, as opposed to any others, in that position.

In the social identity approach, therefore, the role played by followers is crucial. Leadership is not a function of certain objectively critical traits that enable some to be more influential than others, which is implicit in both personality and situational approaches to leadership, as we have seen. Rather, which traits confer this ability to influence are in themselves contingent on what is socially constructed by followers. In this sense, we can understand that leadership is not a function of some personality traits that necessarily provide some individuals with a clear edge in certain pre-specified situations. Rather, leadership transpires as contingent on how its features are perceived by the beholder.

Paternalistic Leadership

Lewin, Lippitt & White's (1939) study (see Box 3.3) is insightful inasmuch as it treated leadership as a *group dynamic*. We have seen how followers play a critical role in how leadership is manifested in different social groups. Rather than homogenising a particular personality disposition across a diversity of conditions, Lewin, Lippitt and White's study considered the value of different roles that a leader could adopt. Their findings went on to demonstrate that a democratic leadership *style* (as opposed to a democratic leader *type*) led to the best outcomes,

Box 3.3 Classic: Lewin's leadership atmospheres

Lewin, Lippitt & White (1939) conducted a classical study on social climates testing different kinds of leadership. A key insight in their experiment was the treatment of leadership as a 'group dynamic'. The authors wanted to investigate what happened to groups when they changed their leadership style, that is, whether different leaders could precipitate a different group climate (see Lezaun & Calvillo, 2013). Lewin, Lippitt and White recruited children who met for eighteen weeks in an attic equipped with various material objects. They gave respondents the task of fabricating masks out of the items they found in the attic, but left the arrangement and decoration of the room to the groups themselves. The authors appointed leaders who acted out different leadership styles. The leaders switched groups every six weeks and adopted a different leadership style so that performers could trade places with no effect on group dynamics. Originally, the study investigated two atmospheres, but a third was added along the way when one of the performers settled into a different style. In the 'authoritarian' condition, the leader dictated and directed group tasks. In the 'democratic' condition, the leader presented an agenda, explained alternatives and participated in the tasks the group undertook. In the 'laissez-faire' condition, the leader was passive and left the output to the group to determine. The authors reported that in the authoritarian condition, participants experienced higher levels of psychological tension that led to outbursts of violence, whilst the laissez-faire condition led to an anarchic state. The optimal climate was found to be the democratic condition, in which participants adopted a matter-of-fact attitude and demonstrated lower levels of aggression than the other conditions. Leadership, in this study, was investigated as a role rather than a personality attribute, and the leader was deemed no more than an administrative technician.

A key observation of these experiments concerned the sequencing of these atmospheres of leadership. By creating experimental transitions between different leadership styles, the experiments showed the effects of 'regime change'. They showed that moving from laissez-faire to autocratic did not result in much change in child activities. Moving from democratic to autocratic, however, brought about much lower levels of production and a state of apathy. Finally, the move from autocratic to democratic or laissez-faire precipitated in both sequences considerable outbursts of 'aggression release', only to settle later. However, laissez-faire retained much higher levels of post-autocratic aggression than the democratic regime (Lippitt & White, 1947). The researchers noted that the transition seemed to create an opportunity for some 'hell raisers' to raise hell (see Lezaun & Calvillo, 2013). This is similar to Moghaddam's (2013) 'springboard' model. Different regimes of leadership attract different types of follower activities, and 'regime changes' bring additional accents to these profiles. In the light of these demonstrations, is it not surprising that South Koreans might be concerned about the implications of an all too sudden regime change among their northern brothers and sisters from seventy years of autocratic to a laissez-faire market regime? We surmise that the expected level of initial disruption from 'bottled up aggression and discontent' could be considerable.

and much research into leadership has proceeded along this assumption with the result that contemporary leadership styles that resonate with particular cultures, such as transformational leadership, are granted a pre-eminent value over others. It is worth bearing in mind, however, that Lewin, Lippitt and White's study investigated a particular set of leadership styles in a specific cultural setting, that is, in the USA. As we have seen, the outcome of leadership is contingent on the responses of followers, and it seems that those in Lewin, Lippitt and White's study favoured a democratic style. This is not to say that democratic leadership is the only leadership style that is effective and that it is necessarily superior to other styles across different cultural conditions and situational circumstances.

Another leadership style that has received scholarly attention is **paternalistic leadership**. This refers to a father-like leadership style that combines authority with benevolent care and concern for the well-being of followers. Paternalistic leadership traces its origins to Weber (1968) and has been extensively studied in the management literature (see Pellegrini & Scandura, 2008 for a review). Paternalistic leaders provide followers with protection in return for loyalty and deference. The literature suggests that this is an effective leadership style in cultures that tend towards collectivism. Individualistic cultures do not respond well to paternalistic leadership as members tend to be sceptical of benevolence and treat it with suspicion. Our point here is that in the scholarly consideration of leadership, a restricted focus on personality dispositions based on the individual differences paradigm in psychology, will not do. Essentially, understanding the social influence implications of leadership requires an expansion of scope to (a) sociocultural conditions that determine which features are charismatic for whom – what is charisma to one is mere stamina to another; (b) social representations of the group and its raison d'être that define the cult – deference aspiring at achieving mass unity requires a different kind of leadership style than assertion aspiring at preservation of status, depending on the collective projects implied (e.g., think of a Xi Jinping versus a Donald Trump to further American versus Chinese collective interests); and (c) dynamic sociohistorical conditions that determine the ecological challenges for the group's activities at different points in time (e.g., think Mao Zedong, and later Xi Jinping in leading China; Abraham Lincoln, and later Donald Trump in leading the USA). What this means to say is that the social influence that stems from leadership accrues as a function of how a group adapts to accommodate the challenges it faces to its own normative and self-interested ways over the longer term. Advancing a particular group's project over time may require dynamic transitions from one leadership style to another in ways that ensure the survival of the group's project given changing ecological circumstances, in ways that fulfil social identification processes of membership. Changing from one to the other is no whimsical matter, it is a *process* by which participating individuals value and uphold particular characteristics in the leaders they select that serve the purpose of furthering collective interests. The ties that bind leaders and followers are none other than those discernible in any division of labour, including the exercise of disproportionately distributed social influence amongst the group's members over time.

Conclusion

We have seen that there is no one-size-fits-all to leadership. Whilst certain cultural climates clearly favour a democratic approach and place high value on charismatic or transformational elements demonstrated by their leaders, we have also seen how different social groups may value different attributes and may put in place leaders who demonstrate different qualities to the ones we ourselves hold in high regard. In this way, leaders across the world gain opportunities to exercise influence on masses of followers. Transformational leadership may be a salient social representation in Western democracies at present, but different people may well desire something different from the traits we ourselves value. Some may want their leaders to demonstrate a personal interest in their affairs rather than an exclusively professional one. Inasmuch as they do, they will favour paternalistic leaders or servant-leaders over others. In the right circumstances, however, different leadership styles could be equally effective. Additionally, changes in leadership styles may be precipitated by changing ecological circumstances that help mobilise the group further over the long term and beyond the span of activity of its individual members. What this argument makes clear is that Lewin, Lippitt & White's (1939) original insight was correct: leadership is indeed a group dynamic and as such a neglected property of the group or group action (Graumann & Moscovici, 1986). Its effectiveness hinges on what particular people desire, what the particular situation they face is, and what normative elements are in place in their particular setting. In this way, we can understand some self-evident issues that are present both in the psychological literature on leadership as well as in social reality at large. That is, what is charismatic to some may well be despicable to others. Leaders do not necessarily have to wield a gun to gain an opportunity for influence.

Conscious of this insight, we would like to highlight the fact that leadership remains a modality of influence in its own right. Leadership is not an epiphenomenon of the influence of crowds. A leader who rises to power is indeed able to exert a normative influence on followers. Leaders present ideas that are more likely to resonate than those presented by others, by virtue of the fact that others identify with the leader already. The leader is the person that approximates the desirable group prototype best. Their calls to action, therefore, are more likely be heeded and to spread than similar calls made by others. This is due to the fact that leaders are better able to tap into followers' sentiments than others, by virtue of their being naturally more prototypical. As we have seen in the opening example of this chapter, leaders are capable of priming and framing issues in ways that are palatable to their followers. For this reason, they are held in high enough esteem to acquire a depersonalised cult status and to thus serve as a referent for the group in quasi-objective terms. In certain institutions, leaders are accorded an omniscient status that transcends their own personhood. The voice of the judge is the voice of the court; the voice of the president is the voice of the nation; the voice of the Pope is the voice of God. In this way, leaders are depersonalised, whilst at the same time, they themselves personalise what they represent. Mandela personified the anti-apartheid struggle. Putin personifies the new Russia. In this way, leaders are associated and intertwined with social movements that usher in new normative orders. Jesus Christ marks the New Testament. Chairman Mao marks the Chinese revolution. Only changes in the normative system supporting the leader could precipitate a fall from grace. This is the reason why displacing dictators rarely brings about genuine democratic transitions (Moghaddam, 2013). Rather, new dictators typically emerge to take the project forward. Paradoxically, as per the Ghana example reviewed in Box 3.2, it may take an autocratic and dictatorial leadership style to bring about the necessary changes in the normative order for transitioning to democracy. In the final chapter of this book, we will consider how the interplay of modalities of social influence serves to support or usurp a background of normativity.

We would like to end this chapter by drawing attention to three issues that remain critical to developing a full understanding of leadership as a modality of social influence. Firstly, any consideration of leadership requires a consideration of followers. We have treated this topic in the previous chapter as well as the present one, and will return to it again in the final chapter. Crucially, to understand how particular leaders come to exercise the degree of social influence that they do, one needs to understand the cultural climate that sees leaders with particular inclinations rise to the top. In other words, to understand the effectiveness of leaders one needs to understand the social representation of effective leaders in a given social and political milieu. In our periodic table of social influence, we position leadership in the function of normalisation and setting standards; though clearly leadership plays into other modalities as well.

Secondly, as we have seen, leadership plays a crucial role in the establishment of a personality cult that elevates particular aspirations and inclinations to a quasi-sacred status. Think of the immortalisation of particular tendencies in the conferral of sainthood. The immortalisation of the saint's inclinations serves as inspiration for entire monastic orders. The leader herself, as an individual, might well feel trapped in the role on a subjective level, particularly if personal characteristics do not entirely correspond with the valued attributes. This is the case in King Edward VIII's abdication of the British throne in 1936, which paved the way for King George VI's (King Edward VIII's brother) accession. King George VI is father to Queen Elizabeth II, current sovereign and longest-serving monarch in history. As such, she has successfully personified the attributes of a monarch better than any other individual in history – her portrait has graced banknotes longer than anyone else's and a lot more so than her uncle King Edward VIII's portrait, natural heir to the British throne following her grandfather King George V's passing. However, had things followed their natural course, that is, had King George VI never abdicated, the longest-serving monarch in history might have never sat on the throne. In Chapter 9 we discuss artefacts that serve to objectify personality cults for intergenerational transmission, as per the paradoxical monarchic dictum: 'The King is dead, long live the King!', signifying the trans-generational permanence of monarchy beyond the human lifespan.

Thirdly, our consideration of leaders needs to extend beyond the study of individuals who manifestly occupy the specific role of identified leader, such as presidents and prime ministers. It is equally relevant to extend inquiry into public opinion, specifically into the role played by opinion leaders and social media influencers. We treat this subject more fully in Chapter 8 when we consider mass media influences. For the moment, we simply note that official leaders exercise authority to manage and administer resources on behalf of a certain group, and their ability to do so hinges on the support they are able to garner from followers who are able to sway power their way. Whilst they do not enjoy official executive authority, opinion leaders play a critical role in this sway that marks the rise and fall of formal leaders. Like the famous example of comedian Beppe Grillo and the role he played in the rise of M5S (Movimento Cinque Stelle, or the Five-Star Movement) in Italy, opinion leaders are critical in mobilising the populist impetus leaders need to rise to the top. As Franks, Bangerter & Bauer (2013) note, opinion leaders disseminate representations by framing them into action, which itself provides the context for the emergence of a leader. It is in this spirit that we argue in our final chapter that leadership is part of relational dynamics alongside other modalities of social influence. Before considering this further, we proceed to discuss the role of social influence amongst followers in more detail in the two chapters that follow, which deal with conforming and obeying respectively.

In Essence

> *Leadership is a corollary of division of labour. A leader is vested with power to exercise on behalf of a group in managing collective resources and implementing a collective agenda.*
>
> *Leadership is a situation involving a disproportionate use of power over the management of collective resources. The psychological sciences have traditionally focused on leader types. Social identity theory has redressed the balance through studying the leading process. Both are implicated in leadership situations.*

PART II

Experimental Paradigms

This section reviews the core of experimental social influence research. These studies are commonly treated in a disparate fashion due to two reasons: they have been compartmentalised for experimental research in a laboratory setting to control for other influences, and for pedagogical reasons the separation of paradigms might make sense. In this volume, we aim to challenge the former but nevertheless benefit from the latter.

We deal with norm formation again in Chapter 4, where we revisit experiments that demonstrate the human urge to create order, to fabricate **norms** for framing and regulating social conduct. In interaction, norms are intended or unintended products that stabilise standards for anyone who participates in future efforts. This poses problems for newcomers, strangers and aliens that need to be framed. In Chapter 5, we revisit peer pressure research on **conformity,** a mechanism by which a dominant order is defended and preserved, and **conversion** by which that order is developed. This pair is also known as majority and minority influence. Chapter 6 provides a vertical extension to this by looking at hierarchy and the phenomenon of **obedience**. Popular experiments and recent replications provide insights on the paradox logic of authority persisting in anti-authoritarian modern society. In Chapter 7, we address the popular topic of **persuasion**, which has become the current prototype of social influence across the social sciences, much under the spell of dual-process models and sitting in tension with classical rhetoric which considers the optimisation of logos, ethos and pathos. All of these modalities have their focus, at least in research, on **real-time face-to-face interactions** of what we call mode 1. They also represent the post–WWII experimental paradigms of social influence which, by overcoming the doctrine of suggestion, went in search of the rational individual in all circumstances.

As happens across the sciences, answering one question opens up inquiry into another. Understanding how people converge on norms leads to questions concerning subsequent deviance and conformity. Answering the latter precipitates concerns with obedience and the manner by which authority is exercised amongst modern human beings. In turn, this raises concerns about compliance and persuasion in order to elicit desirable behaviour – in more or less justifiable terms.

CHAPTER 4

Norming and Framing

				Mode 1 face-to-face	Mode 2 symbolic	Mode 3 artefact
phase	modality	function for CS	outcome	inter-subjective		inter-objective
	Order created 'out of Chaos' of interaction: social representations, common sense, joint intentionality					
Phase 1	norm formation	**Normalisation**	frame of reference	deliberation, compromise	debate	installed affordances

Figure 4.1   A challenge and response model III: norming

Think of 'nature'; how has our understanding of it changed? Over the past seventy years, national and international debates – initiated and ushered in by various environmentalist groups – have shifted the conversation globally from 'nature' to 'environment', and with this *reframed* from limitless exploitation to effective stewardship (the limits of growth). We now naturally perceive 'nature' as something to care about (i.e., stewardship), where we in the past had a free resource and a convenient waste dump (i.e., exploitation; see Radkau, 2011). With this shift in common ground, nuclear energy too changed from energy too cheap to meter to a risk to safety, security and global peace (Bauer et al., 2019).

In this chapter, we examine the **normalisation** of a novel frame of reference based on which we see and judge things in the world. The 'frame of reference' moves beyond 'mad and bad' crowds. The doctrine of suggestion (Asch, 1952) still echoes in 'animal spirits', 'contagion' or 'viral memes' against which we have little resistance as our mind is compromised by sociality. However, we must now choose between framing human crowding as corruption of rationality or a springboard for novelty. The idea of a frame of reference also shows that we are judging under dual constraints, the thing judged and the frame applied, and the latter is rarely an individual affair.

In social interaction, humans establish common ground, a shared intentionality that also secures social identity: 'We see things not as they are, but as WE are' (a saying often attributed to Talmudic-Biblical wisdom). Basic human capacities of sharing minds scale up into rituals of religion, scientific objectivity as well as of democratic deliberation, culminating in 'discursive reason' and cultural diversity. Sociality is the very basis of human life. Social isolation is no good place to be; it constitutes a form of painful torture (see Chapter 5).

The social psychologist Muzafer Sherif (1906–1988) is our key witness for this shift. To understand this new thinking beyond irrational crowding let us highlight two points. Firstly, social interaction creates social products of two kinds, recognised by Sherif (1936) and Solomon Asch (1952; see Rock, 1990), but lost on future readings: humans share mindsets and accumulate clutter. We put in place soft stuff such as **'intersubjective'** norms on opinions, beliefs, attitudes, attributions and knowledge which we share in mutuality 'I know that you know that I know that he knows that you know'. We also put in place the harder stuff of **'inter-objective'** gadgets, tools and architecture around which we synchronise our bodies; we travel in the streets like water in a riverbed. We will come back to these artefacts in Chapter 9. Secondly, the results of past interactions become 'common ground' for further interactions: 'we both know that you know that I know, so we can work together' and 'we both know to ride a bicycle, thus we can go on a tour together' is partly taken for granted below the threshold of awareness and partly an explicit 'identity' marker (us and them; we-intention).

Gestalt Experience and Sherif's Experiments

In order to reach new insights on sociality (see Box 4.1), Sherif (1936) sought a new attitude: 'we must first gain the necessary distance from [our] own roles as members of privileged groups ... of which [we] may be beneficiaries' (ibidem, 2003). Social researchers must avoid reproducing social stereotypes. LeBon, Tarde and Freud translated their anxieties into a resentment against the masses (see Chapter 2). Instead, social psychologists need to understand 'whatever we experience is a **psychological reality**. If we wish to study ... any phenomenon we have to accept psychological realities without imposing our prejudices ... We perceive objects and situations relationally ... Thus the stimulation, external and internal, of a given moment forms a functional system' (ibidem, p. 80). Sherif conceptualises psychological reality in news ways. Firstly, individuals in crowds/groups have positive as well as negative effects. Without denying a lynch mob or the thin veneer of civilisation, Sherif focuses on positive potential of sociality: generosity, heroism and self-sacrifice in war and disaster. Secondly, crowds

---

Box 4.1 Experimenting with the autokinetic phenomenon

We tend to judge things or events not by themselves only, but within a normalised framework, which is a social product as demonstrated in a series of experiments (Sherif, 1935, 1936 and 1937).

Autokinetic movement (Schiffman, 1976, p. 266) arises when a stationary light point is projected in a dark room; the light point, though physically fixed, moves in phenomenal experience. This also arises when gazing into a starry night; the stars seem to oscillate irregularly. Sherif showed that when asked to judge this movement, people do this by establishing a benchmark. When people are put in a group situation they establish an **intersubjective frame of reference**, *compromising on individual judgements, and thus* **reduce complexity** *for future intents and purposes.*

In the experiments, participants in groups of two or three were presented with light points projected into a dark and featureless room. The dependent variable is the median and range of light movement across 100 judgements each. Judgements were taken either (a) in individual isolation or in groups, and (b) in session sequences, with isolated judgements followed by three group situations or vice versa; (c) in groups first, with judgements induced either in peer conversations, or by a prestigious or authoritative leader voice. When in initial isolation, persons established their own 'benchmark' widely differing from each other (between 1 and 10 inches); introspective reports revealed individual clamouring for standards of judgement (1936, 96f); however, these judgements converged into a common baseline when people were put together in subsequent sessions; Sherif found the 'funnelling' of initially wide divergence into a common baseline. And importantly, after three group sessions, individuals stuck to the established standards depending on their group (between 1 and 5 inches). This demonstrated, on ambiguous visual stimuli, the **emergence of a framework for judgements under uncertainty**. *The group sessions created an intersubjective basis, established social meaning of a situation, and this common ground persisted beyond the immediate co-presence of others. Variants of the experiment showed that this judgement can indeed be induced by a prestigious or by an authoritative source; but equally peer, prestige and authority voices were constraints in future judgements by the new frame of reference. Leaders who later change their mind were no longer followed (1936, 105).*

---

are a transition from an old to a new order. Any impression of 'decline' is due to temporary confusion. Thirdly, crowds establish a new **frame of reference**. 'Liberty, Equality, Fraternity' (French Revolution, 1789) or 'Life, Liberty and the Pursuit of Happiness' (American Revolution, 1776) are well-known value references that started with historic crowd events.

Sherif experimented with social meaning on autokinetic movements (see Box 4.1 and epilogue). Earlier Gestalt Psychologists (Kohler, Koffka, Wertheimer) had conducted perception experiments without being vested in atomism and the psychophysical 'constancy hypothesis' (see Chapter 11: excursions). Identical physical stimuli, as in ambiguous Rubin figures, can flip between entirely different perceptions of profiled faces or a drinking vessel, either/or, without blend or confusion. Can this stabilise? In perceiving X, we relate to X in two ways: directly to X, but also with people as the background. Perception P of X is an attitude that is doubly relative, to X and to a frame of reference F shared with others; perception is a conditional judgement $P = f (X / F)$. If we stabilise the frame, we can stabilise the perception. Our judgement is not dominated by the 'stimulus'; take the case of noise alarming us independently of whether we recognise a signal or not; our biological range of hearing defines the 'noise' as alarmingly loud and relative to audible ambient background noise, thus grabbing immediate attention. X is alarming in relation to a body frame of reference. Sherif demonstrated how ambiguous uncertainties can stabilise in common ground for future action.

Later, research into norm formation investigated uncertainties in decision-making: the stabilisation of person perception (intelligence of people); also colour after-images are tested against social influence (see Chapter 5); and researchers asked how lasting are experimentally established judgement frames; one month or up to one year with enhanced training (Abrams & Levine, 2012), in real life they seem to have an even longer life cycle. The uncertain utility of investments (stock market betting) received much attention under *prospect theory* which, contrary to expected utility theory, highlights framing effects: a gain frame creates different decisions than a loss frame, and the loss frame is stronger (Kahneman & Tversky, 1979). Similarly, risk perception (of climate change, nuclear energy, vaccination or genetically modified food, see Chapter 8) depends on the hazards but also on the set of boundary anxieties of the moral community (Douglas, 1990). And most negotiations start with establishing a common ground on how to disagree (e.g., a Pareto space to identify give-and-take and win-without-loss situations); moderating this process means teasing out steps on this common ground among protagonists.

Sherif had demonstrated the positive *social product* of group interaction in several points: first, there are no initial 'empty minds', but priors meet to converge in compromise (*convergence*). Second, common ground once established persists in subsequent judgements (*robustness*). Third, different groups converge into different standards (*group relative*). Fourth, group judgement can be primed, but the primer is also framed and loses autonomy in future interactions (*binding constraint*). Fifth, reduction of complexity is real for individuals in isolation as well as in the crowd (need for closure, see Chapter 7). Experience is organised in a frame that reduces uncertainty (things could well be different, but not for us nor for now), and this intersubjectivity arising from communicative interaction (*inter-subjectivity*). Six, frames have a temporal life cycle, some are short-lived (opinions), others persist for longer (attitudes), others inform generations (mentalities, myths and historical narratives). Sherif noticed that the auto-kinetic movement was an innocuous uncertainty, with little ego-involvement, prior need, investment and interest; the formation of the norm was largely uncontested. This is indeed an *idealisation of new beginnings*. The streams of social life are mostly already running, new beginnings rarely come from nothing as in *order out of chaos*. However, in moments of crisis or catastrophe when common ground collapses, new beginnings are possible. This however, is also the condition of possibility for a cunning stratagem: creating ambiguity and uncertainty in order to foster an artificial need for closure and longings for a new beginning. Thus spreading conspiracy theories and 'fake news' create confusion, destabilises order and creates a 'revolutionary' situation, hastening crowds and populist leaders to force a new order (insurgency or terrorism tend to follow this logic). The ushering of a new frame to disambiguate uncertainty is both used and abused in history (Sherif, 1936, 74), thus the manner in which it is brought about determines its subsequent legitimacy and stability.

Normalising What: The New Frame or Mind Set

With Sherif, the 'frame of reference' became a core idea of (social) psychological reasoning, but its reach is far wider. Let us examine some other notions of 'frame' and the inevitable flexibility of any normative standard of judgement.

A 'frame' is originally a painters' metaphor. The frame stabilises the painting and separates it, figure on ground, from the wall where it hangs; thick or a mere contour, ornamented or plain, heavy gold or colourless. The frame gives aura; the painting is different in a different frame. Frames are peeping windows, a hole in the wall opening to wider imagination (Arnheim, 1974, p. 239). In photography, the 'frame' selects context and thus defines content. In cinema it is 'mise en scene', with narrow or wide camera angle, which makes the composition (Monaco, 1981, p. 149).

Cinema mounts a sequence of frames into a movie experience. Shakespeare intimated the framing of aesthetic judgement in Sonnet 24 when he describes the experience of beauty being framed by a body-in-love:

> Mine eye hath played the painter and hath steeled
> Thy beauty's form in table of my heart;
> My body is the frame wherein 'tis held.

The moving body, coordinated and synchronised by social life, frames all perception (Merleau-Ponty, 1962) insofar as 'external perceptions and the perception of one's own body vary in conjunction because they are the two facets of one and the same act . . . the body is a natural self . . . the subject of perception' (ibidem, p. 206). During action it becomes clear that 'my body is the fabric into which all objects are woven, and it is . . . the general instrument of my comprehension' (ibidem, 235), or 'the thing is correlative . . . to my existence, of which my body is merely the stabilised structure' (p. 320). We move in space collectively and this gives meaning to our physical surroundings; we become aware of this only on occasion. To stabilise our perceptions we need to fix our bodily movements. Lately, this is called 'embodied cognition', cognition arising in a brain-in-a-socially moving-body (Prinz, 2012) which amounts to the *reincarnation of rationality*, reason is no longer separated from bodily passions nor is it socially contaminated (Taylor, 2005). Intersubjectivity is constituted in communication and synchronised movement; dancing or eating together establishes common ground.

Classical rhetoric was aware of the framing problem. An issue (exigency) can be variously presented using non-literal speech (tropes) and commonplaces (doxa) from a repertoire of accepted arguments (topics). The purpose of rhetorical composition and delivery is to manage the distance between speaker and audience on a particular topic with logos (argument), ethos (trust) and pathos (sentiment; Mayer, 2008). Effective frames (tropes of logos, ethos and pathos) must resonate. From here arise modern mass media effects within the duality of themes and frames on audiences (see Chapter 8).

Another influential idea is **frame analysis** (Goffman, 1974) which assumes that 'the common-sense world has a paramount position among the various provinces of reality, since only within it does communication with our fellow-men become possible. But the **common-sense world** is from the outset a socio-cultural world' (ibidem, p. 4). Goffman analyses social role playing and the giving of account in terms of 'frames' (or 'keys' as in musical tonalities). When we are explaining ourselves, we can focus either on make-belief and play (it was just a joke for fun), contest and rule-following (gaming to win), ceremonials and ritual (procedures), technical and skilful redoubling of effort (efficiency), or regrounding of our deeds (as in raising chicken as a hobby rather than for a living). All the world's a stage, and we are performing and explaining ourselves as role models or to dupe an audience (p. 83). For Goffman 'frames' offer an account repertoire available to society like its language, both specific and changeable. From here the cognitive science of artificial intelligence derives notions of **mindsets** as the taken-for-granted background knowledge necessary to orient and act in a real-life situation and which robotics struggles to model: 'A frame is a data-structure for representing a stereotyped situation, like being in a certain kind of living room, or going to a child's birthday party. Attached to each frame are several kinds of information. Some of this information is about how to use the frame. Some is about what one can expect to happen next. Some is about what to do if these expectations are not confirmed' (Minsky, 1974).

The notion of 'framing' is also prominent in new social movement research. The term 'action framing' links a grievance to actions to put it right. Benford & Snow (2000, p. 614) define a frame as 'action-oriented sets of beliefs and meanings that inspire and legitimate the activities and campaigns of a social movement organization'. Frames mobilise members, garner support from bystanders and demobilise antagonists. *Diagnostic framing* turns grievances into a well-defined social problem with attributed causes and responsibilities. Troubles are a matter of 'terrorism' or of 'defending of human rights'. *Prognostic framing* asks 'what is to be done?' and offers solutions and means to ends. Finally, *motivational framing* calls to arms and offers a rational. Gamson & Modigliani (1989) find shifting 'meaning packages' that inform public opinion on an issue; we are for or against with shifting arguments over time. Frames are sponsored by interested actors, often have a visual–metaphorical image core that captures the imagination, and constitute an agreement on how to disagree. Thus we might disagree on nuclear power over 'progress', 'public accountability' or 'clean energy', or on abortion in terms of women's choice or compassion for women in difficulties. Frames are selected to resonate with an audience; they are rhetorical.

Finally, the idea of **social representation** (SR) is the most generic elaboration of a frame of reference. SRs allow us to orient ourselves, communicate and to act in an uncertain world by familiarising the unfamiliar, by anchoring events in existing common ground and objectify and make concrete what is abstract in familiar metaphors. SRs are the basis of sense-making as well as a pragmatic guidance of action. The term arises from the study of public understanding of science in a particular society, of how different social milieus adopt and transform the science of the unconscious (Moscovici, 2008 [1961]) or of 'mental illness' (Jodelet, 1991), or of genetics (Bauer & Gaskell, 2002) and of many other matters (Sammut et al. 2015). SRs are socially shared mindsets, akin to 'world-views' linked to competing social milieus (Farr, 1987, Kracauer, 1977). SRs mediate between stimulus and behaviour, giving meaning to both. They are sampled from individual minds (conversational data) and from circulating symbols (mass media data). They allow us to opine, to take attitudes and to stereotype depending on our resistance and to set us apart from other milieus. Social representations overlap with common sense, at times indistinguishably (Lindenberg, 1987), they are epistemic (lay epistemology) about the world, but also expressive of a self-other community (Jovchelovitch, 2007); they defend the autonomy of contending milieus. What is normalised in communication is the way subjects (S, the group, the milieu) think, value and opine about an object (O) arising from their future project (P), in the context of intergroup relations. The unit of analysis is the conversation, the triangle (SOP) in the 'toblerone' and 'windrose' models (Bauer & Gaskell, 2008). In times of controversy, the SR refers to a 'boundary object', where the label denotes different things. The common signifier allows the conversation to unfold with constructive ambiguity.

In this long excursion we tried to show how the notion of a frame, judging [X ~ Y, considering framework F], developed in many different ways, but demonstrating the dual dependence of experience on a variable exogenous (world) and relatively stable endogenous conditions (framework). Let us now return to one of Sherif's original concerns: the robustness of a novel frame of reference.

Kurt Lewin's Field Experiments: Group Decisions Last Longer

Lewin (1890–1947), a contemporary of Sherif with a similar theoretical outlook, conducted field experiments on leadership (see Chapter 3), food habits and industrial productivity as *group dynamics* in a frame of reference (Lewin, 1952). Lewin conceptualised a temporary equilibrium of a field of forces. Interventions change this equilibrium in three steps – unfreezing, moving and refreezing; by increasing and decreasing some 'forces' (vectors), we can tweak the force field into a resulting direction (i.e., a vector combination in space). With psychological field theory, Lewin set out to demonstrate that group discussions make for lasting norms by strengthening the forces 'interest', 'ego involvement' and 'commitment' to a group norm. We will focus here on the normalisation or re-freezing phase of the change process.

During WWII, eating habits were out of line with food supply. Much food was destined for fighting solders and offal meat, for example, was underused on the family table and left over in the abattoirs. In 1942/1943 Lewin and his team took on the project to find ways of changing food habits. They analysed the food practices, how channels linked farm to fork and store to table in families of different economic situations. The **gate-keepers**, mainly women and housewives, did the shopping and decided the menu. Conclusion: food habits are stabilised by multiple 'forces'.

Then, women were invited to take part in nutritional workshops to hear about novel recipes using offal meat, introduced as part of the war effort and for a healthy family. Six Red Cross groups of 13–17 volunteers were formed. Three groups got a sales pitch and new recipes on how to prepare beef heart, sweetbread and kidneys; side issues of smell and disgust were addressed upfront. Each individual was left to make of it what they wanted. The three other groups were treated differently: after a short introduction, discussions opened; the women discovered and elaborated cooking issues around offal. The same nutritional advice was available as to other groups, but only after issues were discussed and interest in offal recipes was expressed. At the end, a show of hands declared the commit-ment to try the recipes. The experimental effect was striking: after one week, 3 per cent of the 'lecture group' had taken up a new recipe, while with 'group decision' 32 per cent had done so. A further experiment to encourage consumption of milk (fresh and evaporated) showed similar gains: after two weeks, uptake was stronger for 'discussion' at 50 per cent than for 'lecture' at 15–30 per cent, and over four weeks, this gain differential further increased. A third set of studies compared 'group decision' with 'personal instructions' for uptake of cod liver oil and orange juice. Although person-to-person instruction increased uptake, it did not reach the level of group decisions. Later, the team varied how group decisions were taken: anonymously, partially in public and in public commitment with show of hands.

Lewin and colleagues saw group decisions as part of democracy, dem-onstrating the self-organisation of social system: deciding, in the group and in public, contributes to the normalisation of a frame of reference that persisted after the workshops. Group decisions are more robust than person-to-person decisions, and both are superior to a mere sales pitch (Lewin, 1943). Similar conclusions were reached on resistance to change in industry: redesigning work activities in a textile factory showed that resistance among workers was a function of the degree of participation: all-member participation led to fewer 'difficulties' than discussions with delegates, and this to less resistance than mere information prior to change (Coch & French, 1948). Thus, the instrumental logic of participation arrived at social engineering: besides being morally virtuous, participant involvement in decision-making motivates and commits to a new standard that is set to last. Later, observers noticed that resistance also produces content and input for the process itself (Bauer, 1991; Lawrence, 1959). The logic of participatory change entered business management, social policy, urban planning and science and technology policy, harnessing robust commitments through 'democratic' procedures (Arnstein, 1969; Einsiedel, 2014; Escobar, 2011).

Interpenetration of Views – Working towards Intersubjectivity

Social interaction also creates intersubjectivity. Let us understand better what is involved and how people get entangled in it. We see the world from a perspective. I stand in one point in space and my gaze is directed; my ears open into the soundscape from where I stand. You standing over there, how is it possible that we can ever reach a common understanding, intersubjectivity, of how things are or ought to be in the world? This involves three steps: (a) recognising one's perspective at any time; (b) decentring in the face of others; and (c) and establishing common ground in a frame of reference. This moment is also known as the **'fusion of horizons'** after possibilities have been worked through (Gadamer, 1960). In any particular position and perspective, our take on the world is necessarily limited, literally by our angle of vision and location in space, but also metaphorically by the narrowness of our 'world-view'. As celebrated in 'crowd sourcing', this limitation can be overcome by consulting others. I broaden my perceptual field by asking my fellows, 'how it is for you?' This means consideration of others becomes part of our thoughts. We henceforth navigate our world by referring to knowledge of others (I know that you know ... that she knows, therefore ...). This requires that we step into the shoes of other people and relativise ourselves. Asch (1952, 162) speaks here of the **'interpenetration of viewpoints'** which separates an acting group from the acts of individuals:

> in full interaction each participant refers his action to the other and the other's actions to himself. When two people, A and B, work jointly ...

Each includes in his view, simultaneously and in their relation, the follow-ing acts: (1) A perceives the surroundings, which includes B and himself; (2) A perceives that B is also oriented to the surroundings, that B includes himself and A in the surroundings; (3) A acts towards B and notes that B is responding to his action; (4) A notes that B in responding to him sets up the expectation that A will grasp the response as an action of B directed toward A. The same ordering must exist in B (ibidem, 161f).

This transcendence of the individual viewpoint takes place in the individ-ual, but we 'objectify' it in action as 'action in the social field is steered via phenomenal fields which are structurally similar' (ibidem, 162). This assimilation does not define the actual relation between A and B, they can cooperate or compete in rivalry or identity of interests. This phenom-enal field allows for common ground, the joint frame of reference of self with others (Gurwitch, 1964; Sammut, Daanen & Moghaddam, 2013).

Berger & Luckmann (1967) elaborate on intersubjectivity in the 'social construction of reality'. Society is constituted by routines, rituals and habits of behaviour, hearts and minds. These routines are performed as 'objectified' institutions, rule-based, predictable and legitimised functional necessities; some are even 'reified' as natural and unchangeable. Newcomers internalise these rules by taking up position and roles; they do this however, incompletely; role-taking is never perfect and shows resistance, freedom and deviance. Society thus unfolds on normalised and objectified knowledge, rules and routines.

Intersubjectivity arises in interaction and is defined as the 'variety of relations between perspectives' (Gillespie & Cornish, 2009, 19) where parties orient in the orientations of others. It is recognised through writing, talking and behaviour, it can be subconscious with only partial overlap between these aspects. I may not be aware of it, but common ground is visible to an observer in body sways, motor mimicry, activity of 'mirror neuron' in the motor context and imitated behaviour (ibidem, 27f). We perceive disagreement between orientations, we feel (mis)understood, and we point to (mis)understandings. The coordinated movements of a military formation marching in step are impressive to an observer (see Chapter 2 on crowding). Thus, intersubjectivity is often implicit, taken for granted, unquestioned and tends to reach the threshold of awareness only when breached, when participants seek to repair and return to common ground by taking turns. Thus, stabilising intersubjectivity with non-verbal feed-back (nodding or yeah-yeah interjections) and frequent turn-taking is a mundane activity, constantly putting at stake, breaching, repairing and 'normalising'. Much of this is often tied up with use of nomenclature.

We know a 'terrorist' act, but we also know that for some people the act is a 'fight for freedom'. And there is often conflict over naming a behaviour, because the acting terrorist or freedom fighter can be named as terrorist or a freedom fighter.

This normalisation of a common ground by inter-penetration of perspectives might indeed be a matter of time. Simply growing older together can create communality. Tuckman (1965) has suggested that any group formation goes through a sequence of phases of building communality that is needed for its operations: forming, storming, norming and performing (see Box 4.2). However, the playing of music together suggests that accumulating joint practice might not be sufficient, albeit a necessary condition for *collective flow*. This peak experience in joined-up performance that sustains itself and gives all-round pleasure, improvising jazz musicians aptly call 'to swing': 'you want to dance, clap your hands, or tap your feet, it is what many people call swinging music ... the feeling that the group sound is getting off the ground. Music that keeps a relatively steady beat, is performed well and with great spirit, seem buoyant' (Gridley, 1978, 14ff). Improvising jazz musicians get there, but with no guarantee, by working on a common frame of reference that includes beat, tempo and tonality, a tune and the chord sequence, maybe the sequence of solos: let's do 'Take-five' in Db ... 3, 4, 5 go ...! (Pras et al., 2017). In groove, the music is played with constant tempo, cohesively, and with rhythmic lilt and much spirit. Reaching the 'swing' is a momentary confluence of factors on an underdetermined outcome; the ingredients can be normalised, but not the moment of performance.

Stabilising a Fact: Working towards Inter-objectivity

Sherif and Asch had recognised that social interaction produces, besides social norms, opinions and attitudes, also inter-objective formal institutions such as laws, money and technology infrastructure (the stuff hardware of social life). Inter-objectivity is equally significant for the coordination of social life, not least as both norms and stuff are a zone of conflict over what is set for duration (Bauer, 2013). But 'objectivity' is neither given in the environment nor in human cognition; instead, it offers another condition of robustness (next to deliberation). It is an orientation towards the world guiding the process of 'objectification'. In common sense, it is the virtue of passing judgement 'sine ire et studio' (Latin 'without anger and much eagerness'). This concept has two slightly different uses.

Box 4.2 Discontents over models of group formation

In group formation, the problem of normalising a frame of reference merges into **group dynamics**: *how does a group become a performing entity? Crowding people into a place does not make them a functional team. More than mere assembly is necessary. On the basis of Bales (1950) interaction process analysis, Tuckman (1965) summarised the evidence into a famous rhyming scheme:* **forming, storming, norming and performing***. Interaction analysis classified contributions to group activity in two functions:* **task-orientation** *and* **social-orientation***. Tuckman's phases are defined by the preponderance of communicative contribution. At the beginning, 'socio-emotive' contributions (i.e., decision, tension reduction, integration) dominate, while later 'task-orientation' (i.e., defining problems, evaluating, controlling and regulating feedback) takes over. Transition phases are 'storming' and 'norming'. After initial friendly exchanges, things get heated and people more task-oriented, debating head-on, haggling and struggling about what is to be done and how to get there (defining the situation, the ends and the means); in 'norming', these debates are calmed by socio-emotive contributions; suitable ends and means are established so that one can get on with the job. The 'performance' phase indicates that the group turns into a settled 'team'. Task and socio-emotion orientation show characteristics presence across these four phases. Simple schemes are practical and liked, and they persist. Tuckman & Jensen (1977) reviewed the evidence and recognised that 'teams' are temporary structures, and added an ending 'mourning-adjourning', recognising the life cycle of structures. Hingst (2006) reviewed things again, and noted that stable membership is rare over the life cycle of teams; there is much new coming which requires* **setting things in writing and for duration in collective memory** *away from informal and implicit practice. Thus the focus shifts from normalisation to assimilation processes such as conformity (see Chapter 5).*

However, critical discussions about group development argues against a fixed phase sequence unfolding a blueprint. Such a teleological model assumes a 'natural end state' (as in 'adulthood' for human development). Developmental models are open and more varied. Gersick (1988) is interested in sudden and non-linear shifts where group performance demonstrates a sudden taking off (maybe modelled on improvising jazz combos). Cranach (1996) unfolds the self-acting group based on self-organisation with an open future; this is called 'teleonomic' because it is goal-oriented, but the goal arises in the group's own discourse. Arrow et al. (2000) and Smith (2001) focus on the relations of groups and context, and stress the fluid and adapting structures rather than fixed changes. Whatever model of group formation, all agree that a 'joint mindset' is normalised for robust permanence and thus build on the legacy of Sherif, Lewin and Asch.

Moghaddam (2003) uses 'inter-objectivity' metaphorically in the context of conflict: objective is a judgement when it exists factually, person-independent and widely recognised. It is 'taken-for-granted', a common ground across communities where, in the absence of questioning, peaceful cooperation is possible. Such an 'inter-object' has acquired status and legitimately so; it is a token of hope in confusing times. As a boundary-object, its ambiguous features unite rather divide. The inter-cultural is characterised by a matrix of what enjoys 'inter-objective' status, be it a person of repute and aura, a sacred thing of shock and awe or a procedure of proven efficiency. Anything dignified and beyond questioning is a bridge across conflicting communities.

Latour (1996) is more literal. Humans accumulate much clutter, not so simians. Monkeys or indeed other animals grab the odd stone to crack a nut and show it to others, but they do not accumulate tool boxes, specialise in tool making, trade and store tools beyond a little hiding place. Homo Faber makes things to 'enframe' interactions with fellow humans, turning *complex* situations – be alert, everything can change at any time – into *complicated* arrangements for interactions – be careful as you navigate a fixed design; it should make life easier. We use objects that in-script us into what a designer wants us to do or think. The medium becomes the message. Objects substitute for spoken commands. What for Latour is a misunderstood human condition (e.g., the social sciences have no 'real objects'), is for Heidegger (1977) an overbearing bias (Gestell) towards a technical logic. In this set-up, thinking is trapped by operating on a framework, and this makes it desirable, however difficult this may be, to think outside the box. Such observations justify making artefacts, innocuous or nefarious, a mode of social influence across modalities. We will return to this point vigorously in Chapter 9. This brings us to the '**fact making**', which is curiously absent from textbooks of social psychology. The canon focuses on social objects (rather that objects are social), that is, other people as the referent of attributions, attitudes, stereotypes and opinions, and hardly at all on facts as 'social objects' (objects are of social origin, e.g., attitudes to nuclear power), and then only as fait accompli. We need to turn to the self-identified tribes of the social construction of knowledge who observe how lab experiments are disambiguated, and follow engineers around to find out how bicycles get their shape (Sociology of Scientific Knowledge [SSK] and Social Construction of Technology [SCOT]: see Bucchi, 2002).

On stabilising facts, our key witness is Ludvik Fleck (1896–1961), a Polish microbiologist with a social-psychological hobby, and a contemporary of Sherif. In studying current debates over syphilis (see also Box 4.3 on climate change), he observed that 'theoretical and practical elements, the a priori and the purely empirical, mingled with one another according to the rules not of logic but of psychology' (Fleck, 1979, p. 5). Different ideas about venereal diseases circulated among doctors, and in public, an ethical-mystical entity of 'carnal scourge' and 'bad blood' attracting blame, and an empirical-therapeutic entity seeking a cure. Are there one or many venereal diseases, inherited or acquired? Fleck showed in much detail how syphilis became fixed as a 'microbial infection' traceable by serological testing, that is, the Wasserman reaction. Normalising this fact was far from straightforward; it involved twists and turns, false starts, unreproducible experiments and people with contradictory ideas (p. 76). Four processes stabilised the fact: the figure 'microbial syphilis' recruited a thinking style, a thought collective, communication genres and popular science (see Figure 4.2).

A **thought collective** is a network of researchers, a 'community of persons mutually exchanging ideas or maintaining intellectual interaction ... The thought collective supplies the missing components' (p. 39). The thought collective is the carrier of a 'thinking style' that produces 'forms of thinking'.

The **thinking style** involves a historical lineage of ideas that gives context: 'this is how a fact arises: At first there is a signal of resistance in the chaotic initial thinking, then a definite thought constraint, and finally a form to be directly perceived ... a fact always occurs in the context of ... a definite thought style' (p. 95). Resistance is a reality marker; but only a thought collective with a thought style can notice this resistance, because it is triggered by their network of ideas: 'the signal of resistance opposing free, arbitrary thinking is called a fact' (p. 101). A thought style is a disposition for feelings and actions, and socially reinforced in the tribal community. It is defined as 'readiness for directed perception, with corresponding mental and objective assimilation of what has been so perceived' (p. 99). Syphilis is microbial, in the blood and acquired, *only if* the notion of an 'infecting microbe' is firmly in place and 'running in the blood' is also thinkable but no longer the key to inheritance. The historical linage reveals twisted ties to common sense and mythical thinking of the past.

The fact needs to be communicated and this occurs in concentric genres on a gradient of **popularisation**, from the esoteric to the exoteric (105). The esoteric core is made up of lab talks, conference papers and journal publications to a peer audience. Further afield are textbooks for education, and further afield are the popular science articles to a wider or mass audience (p. 111ff). These genres operate with different rules of excellence. The wider public encounters the theories of syphilis through the

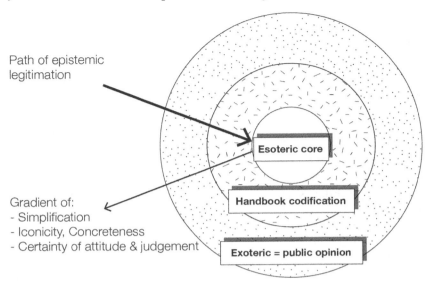

Figure 4.2   The esoteric and exoteric circles of science communication
Source: Fleck 1936/1979: Jurdant 1993

mass media, or maybe textbooks, and informing the public is not for fun. Downstream engagement with exoteric circles introduces language of ever more 'certainty, simplicity, vividness [and] that is where the expert obtains his faith in this triad as the ideal of knowledge. Therein lies the general epistemological significance of popular science' (115). Popular science not only informs, educates and entertains the public, but reassures and raises the self-confidence of the experts themselves (Jurdant, 1993). Popular science stabilises the very episteme. Down the esoteric–exoteric gradient the fact gets accepted: a conditional proposition [X is A, conditional C] is now a simple predicate [X is A]; the spade is a spade and nothing but a spade. Sounding awfully relativistic, Fleck took pains to argue that factual 'truth' is not an arbitrary convention where only the powerful get their way, 'but rather (1) in historical perspective, an event in the history of thought, (2) in its contemporary context, a stylised thought constraint' (p. 100). Scientists fix the facts according to the world and in accordance with their fellow scientists.

Indeed, with Fleck's account and later philosophical insights of no-theory-free fact and empirical observations as a way of life (Feyerabend, 1981), we have the basic ingredients of Kuhn's account of scientific revolutions. Kuhn (1962) coined the term **'paradigm'** for the shifting

Box 4.3 Current troubles with stabilising a fact: climate change

'Climate change' and 'global warming' demonstrate the difficulties of stabilising facts. Not everybody agrees on the facts, nor on what should be done about them. We live in the 'age of ecology' (Radkau, 2011), and this debate reveals the 'frame of reference' that has been established over many years and on the basis of which issues are discussed and acted upon. Since the global alarm over the environment has been sounded (Mazur & Lee, 1993), ever more people have taken notice of unstable weather conditions and human responsibility, and not only in the United States (Nisbet & Myers, 2007). Climate scientists have visualised the long-term data on global surface temperature as shown in Figure 4.3. Initially shown as a J-curve since the 1950s, the time-series have been extended backwards, which allows assessment of the human footprint.

Three points of controversy have arisen over 'climate change': (a) is the climate getting warmer and how much (there are different models and scenarios), (b) is the human footprint leading into a new geological era, the 'Anthropocene' (Steffen et al., 2011) and (c) what shall be done about it: geo-engineering or carbon capturing; carbon trading and international commitments to close the fossil fuel age? But these facts are socially endorsed and challenged. Climate scepticism is particularly vociferous in the USA (also in Australia). PEW data shows that views about climate change are strongly aligned with party loyalties in the United States: Republican voters are less inclined to believe in climate change irrespective of science culture; Democrat voters believe in climate change in proportion of their scientific knowledge (Funk & Kennedy, 2016). The validity of an old saying 'we do not see the world as it is, but the way we are' is emphatically demonstrated at the beginning of the twenty-first century. Inter-objectivity is no automatic process, it is tied to social interaction and its frame of reference.

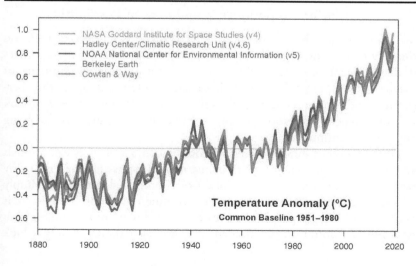

Figure 4.3   Different measures of global temperature anomalies since 1880

background assumptions of scientific knowledge: 'all knowledge of nature emerges from prior knowledge, usually extending, but sometimes by partially replacing it' (Kuhn, 1987). Normal science is puzzle-solving (1962, 35ff), and the current set of puzzle pieces are the current paradigms. This normality is punctuated by occasional revolutionary science, when the puzzle changes and new problems take over; new questions arise from different frameworks. Kuhn explicitly refers to Piaget's assimilation and accommodation and Gestaltists frame of reference as basis for this theory of *epistemic change*. Subsequent historians recognised the transition from a Ptolemaic, the Earth at the centre of the universe, to a heliocentric model with the Sun at the centre, to a cosmology without any centre at all. This shift is no sudden process, but one that takes centuries, and involves a shift in the 'frame of reference', relocating the 'centre' and finally extirpating any centre of the universe in relativity. In the struggles between 'normal' and 'revolutionary' science, the development of scientific knowledge involves social-psychological processes of storming, forming and norming the frame; but moving from paradigm A to paradigm B is no necessary pathway of civilisation; notions of 'Progress' are tied to the new paradigm by telling its history in hindsight (Kuhn, 1987). The tumultuous reception of Kuhn (Masterman, 1970) makes epistemology into a 'social epistemology', and gives rise to a (social) psychology of science beyond its traditional biases (Bauer, 2013; Fuller, 2013).

Conclusion: Evolutionary Conditions of Possibilities

We want to close this chapter with a few comments on development, on the very conditions of possibility for sharing a frame of reference. Studies of development examine conditions of how is it possible that humans, or maybe animals, are capable of fixing a fact, understanding another perspective and thus entertaining intersubjectivity. For this we need to look into the biological evolution of joint attention, pointing and gaze following and joint intentionality.

Let us consider different ways of coordinated action between animals and among people. Firstly, there is *swarming*. It starts raining and many people open umbrellas. What looks like coordinated action are simply simultaneous individual responses to a common situation such as 'it is raining'. This is aggregated behaviour of a crowd without a common goal; no sense of communality is needed; it is no ballet though it might look like one. Secondly, let us consider a *hunting wolf pack*. Here, animals show coordination in movements. The wolves operate together in circling and driving the deer to the final kill, which they share according to hierarchy. Humans, monkeys and wolves exhibit joined-up behaviour focussed on outcomes. In the behavioural phenotype 'hunting' each contributor individually satisfies their needs responding to what everybody else is doing; the logic can be modelled on tit-for-tat exchanges, I scratch your back, you scratch mine; and satisfaction makes collaboration next time more likely (following a consequentialist logic). Every hunt is a new round in a free-rider game, can I profit without contributing? One hunt does not settle norms for future hunts beyond emulation of individual behaviours; this type of interaction is 'complex', it can totally change at any moment. Finally, we know of collaborations, mainly among humans, which are based on *joint attention* and *joint intentionality* (Tomasello, 2009). Humans develop we-feelings, engage common we-intentions, focus on procedures, develop role structures and institutions and collaborate 'because it is right to do so' (for its own sake) and they can make sacrifices for 'higher goals' (deontological ethics). Humans are capable of all three types of cooperation, while 'shared intentionality' (Tomasello & Carpenter, 2007) might be a uniquely human capacity; it includes stuff and technical hardware that complicate collaborations, but make them less complex; this will concern us in Chapter 9.

Establishing a norm for judgement and behaviour fixes a common frame of referencing the world, the self and others (intersubjectivity) and this creates stable circumstances for future interaction. Thus, humans act in part under circumstances of their own making and this includes hard stuff (inter-objectivity). Our key witnesses for these normalising processes were from social psychology (Sherif, Lewin, Asch et al.), history of science (Fleck and Kuhn) and developmental anthropology (Tomasello). These authors stand for key new ideas of sociality in strongest possible contrast to pejorative views of 'mad and bad crowds' (see Chapter 2). It has also been shown that the manner in which a frame of reference is established bears on its robustness. But what do people do when an established frame is challenged? For this, let us turn our attention to conformity pressures. In the following parts of this book we will examine how shared intentionality, once established and normalised, is defended against its detractors (assimilation), but also open to further development (accommodation).

In Essence

Human interaction brings about common ground, and common sense, which achieves shared intentionality and coordinated action. In this way, social interactions secure social identities framed by norms, rituals and artefacts; we call this 'culture'. Interaction establishes order out of chaos by framing coordinated action.

Social representations orient people to one another enabling communication and guiding action in line with a collective project. They make the unfamiliar familiar by locating novelty within an established frame that has already mobilised a social group in a certain action direction. In the process, unfamiliar novelty is normalised.

Over time, social rituals and routines are objectified as legitimate, rule-based and reified institutions that acquire 'objective' properties. The social construction of institutions defines social reality and the possibilities for action that are open to individuals when participating in social life. In this way, enduring inter-objective infrastructure frames intersubjective exchanges in everyday life.

CHAPTER 5

Conforming and Converting

phase	modality	function for CS	outcome	Mode 1 face-to-face inter-subjective	Mode 2 symbolic	Mode 3 artefact inter-objective
				Challenge from conflict, dissonance, controversy arising from newcomers, homecomers, strangers or 'aliens'		
Phase 1	majority	Assimilation	conformity	peer pressure, ostracising	diffusion	acceptance

Figure 5.1   A challenge and response model IV: conforming

Imagine you are meeting your friends in a pub for a discussion on this chapter. You walk in, you find a table, you sit down and you turn to your friends – shall we start? Somebody asks: *are we ordering food?* There was no prior agreement on this before, so menus are circulated and checked out. Somebody else queries: *what are we eating?* Now think about what you would typically do in such a situation. Would you typically consult your gut to see whether you're hungry and if you are you order some food that you fancy and if not you give it a pass? Or do you also check what the others are doing? Maybe you settle on sharing some nibbles, just for the sake of the social climate. Or maybe everyone else is ordering a full meal. Would you be inclined to think that you could also eat, if everyone else is? Or would you go along simply and exclusively with your own physiological inclinations? Snyder (1987) suggests that individuals vary in terms of a **self-monitoring** personality trait. High self-monitors check the world around them for clues regarding socially acceptable behaviour and tailor their own responses to these external demands. By contrast, low self-monitors rely on their own inclinations, disregard social demands and maintain a stable self-presentation across different situations. In *Zelig* (1983), Woody Allen has offered a mocking version of the socially anxious self-monitor: Leonard Zelig changes even his physical appearance to adapt to the personalities surrounding him.

The eating out example we have just reviewed may or may not be trivial in reality. It illustrates a bias in social cognition that sees individuals look around to check what others typically do in similar situations and act in line with these expectations rather than what they themselves privately think is right in the circumstances. Our main thesis here is: individual rational choice, with a focus on nutritional value and price, is not a realistic model of social interaction in such situations. The reason why what everyone else is thinking or doing matters is because the human mind is set towards considering what everyone else seems to be thinking or doing as right and proper, when judging one's own inclinations. The tendency is represented in the common aphorism: 'When in Rome, do as the Romans'. Boyd & Richerson (1985) claim that this tendency represents the **conformity bias** in human cognition, which is adaptive in evolutionary terms and serves to avoid the cost of individual learning. In other words, individuals are prone to think that widespread behaviours are successful-because-tested behaviours. This is why peer pressure works. After all, deviant behaviours that are not successful do not spread. To the extent that individuals adopt widespread behaviours for themselves, they expect them to be effective.

But this begs the question of how human subjects cope in situations where the mainstream behaviours they draw on are themselves challenged by alternatives. In such instances, we commonly assume that as human beings, we are all endowed with a rational mind that is capable of weighing options, and that we choose to act in the ways we do for good reason. To the extent that others choose different courses of action than the commonly accepted ones, we assume that this must indicate that their reasoning is at fault. We typically say that they are 'biased' in their reasoning, misinformed, prejudiced or indoctrinated. This tendency has been identified as the **naive realism bias** by Ross and Ward (1996), which sees individuals considering their own point of view as realistic, objective and correct, and discrepant points of view as necessarily faulty.

In this chapter, we will trace the implications of these socio-cognitive biases on human behaviour. We will review a number of experiments that demonstrate how sociality is a fundamental condition for human development and how from an early age human children are predisposed to utilise norms competing with evidence to guide their own behaviours. We will proceed to review a number of studies that demonstrate that the natural tendency to conform serves in maintaining norms that regulate collective human conduct. We thus see conformity mainly in the function of social *assimilation*, the defence of the current standards of behaviour, attitudes and beliefs against challenges from detractors, such as naive and ignorant newcomers, disoriented strangers or imaginary nefarious aliens. We will conclude by arguing that conformity is not nearly as surprising as the early scholars investigating it presumed. We argue that whilst serving the purpose of group cohesion, our natural inclination to conform to prevalent social norms may also be at the core of misunderstandings and disagreements in intergroup and intercultural encounters.

Sociality and Over-Imitation

Back in the 1950s, Harlow's groundbreaking experiments, if unethical according to current regulations on animal research (Box 5.1), demonstrated that primate behaviour that was seemingly instinctive was actually contingent on early socialisation experiences. Artificially inseminated rhesus monkeys who were reared apart from their group grew up to be incapable of providing for their offspring. Some years later, Bowlby & Ainsworth (Box 5.1) showed that human infants use the relational patterns they engage in during a critical period in their early development as a template for their future adult behaviour. Both of these classical experiments have powerfully demonstrated the role that sociality plays in ontogenetic processes, that is, the psychological processes guiding human development. In other words, for human beings to grow up and become well-functioning adults, they require guidance in human affairs (including seemingly instinctual behaviours) that is provided to them in childhood through socialisation. Social needs open up to social experiences in the family and peer group, and this cultivates a style of interaction that persists in later life.

Box 5.1 The need for affiliation and belonging

Harlow (Harlow & Zimmerman, 1958) conducted a series of experiments with rhesus monkeys that were designed to explore instinctive needs. Harlow started by isolating baby rhesus monkeys from their parents and rearing them in a setting that provided two dummies that the baby monkeys were at liberty to explore. One was a mesh dummy with a baby bottle that provided nutrition. The other dummy was covered by a cloth that provided warmth. The baby monkeys spent their time on the cloth dummy and only climbed the mesh dummy when hungry. This first

---

experiment demonstrated the primacy of the need for affiliation over mere nutrition in primate species that live in social groups. Subsequent experiments proved even more insightful. When reintroduced back to the group after a period of social deprivation in infancy, the monkeys were incapable of reintegration. They demonstrated difficulties making and holding relationships, were fearful and aggressive and they were incapable of engaging in sexual relations with peers. In a further experiment, monkeys were artificially inseminated in the hope that they would bond with their offspring through a 'motherly instinct'. Monkeys reared in social deprivation proved themselves incapable of tending to their infants' needs and neglected them. Harlow's various experiments suggest that sociality is a fundamental condition for species that have evolved to establish social groups and that in these species, including humankind, much seemingly instinctive behavior is down to socialisation.

Bowlby (1969, 1979) proposed that attachment in human infants developed as a function of the response of an attachment figure to perceived distress by the infant. Bowlby argued that attachment for humans served survival needs. According to Bowlby's attachment theory, infants become attached to adults who are responsive to their survival needs between the ages of six months to about two years' of age. The infant uses the attachment patterns experienced during this critical period as a template for subsequent relationships in adulthood. According to Bowlby, human infants have a need for a 'secure base', that is, a secure relationship with an adult caregiver who provides certainty of care, without which social development for the child may be impaired. Bowlby's attachment theory was famously tested by Ainsworth using the Strange Situation experimental method (Ainsworth, Blehar, Waters & Wall, 1978). This involves a mother and infant placed in an unfamiliar playroom and a series of episodes in which (a) a stranger is introduced in the environment; (b) the mother leaves the environment; and (c) the mother is reintroduced to the environment. The infant's responses to reunion with the mother are held to be revealing of the infant's attachment 'style', that is, the attachment pattern that sets in during the critical period and that will typically serve the infant as a template for future relationships. Ainsworth proposed that infant behavioural patterns varied along three types: (i) secure attachment; (ii) anxious–ambivalent or resistant attachment; and (iii) anxious–avoidant attachment. Bowlby and Ainsworth's studies of attachment theory have proven highly influential and inspired, amongst others, Harlow's exploration of the consequences of maternal and social deprivation. Evolutionary psychologists have argued that variable attachment styles are adaptive as they enable the child to tailor their responses to the degree of risk they experience in their environment in terms of the level and quality of care they are provided with during the critical period (Buss, 2008). Attachment theory demonstrates that certain human characteristics are not merely intuitive but develop as a function of the social relations we experience during our early development and during our later life. In turn, attachment styles colour how we experience other situations, for example chronic pain (Romeo et al., 2017).

A more recent study has similarly demonstrated how human children are naturally attuned to socialisation. Whiten, Horner & de Waal (2005) conducted an experiment comparing human children with wild-born chimpanzees. They gave children and chimpanzees a puzzle box that provided a treat once a certain hatch was opened. Before the children and chimpanzees got to handle the puzzle box, they were provided with a demonstration by the experimenter that included a sequence of actions, some of which helped obtain the treat and some of which were redundant to this task. In the first condition, the puzzle box itself was opaque. Subjects, both children and chimpanzees, had no way of discerning which of the sequence of actions performed by the experimenter was relevant to releasing the treat. In the first condition, both children and chimpanzees successfully imitated the experimenter and were able to perform the entire sequence of actions on the box to obtain the reward.

The experiment was then repeated, this time using a clear box made of transparent material. In this condition, users could see inside the box – they could see the actual layout of different compartments that the box was made of. Subjects could therefore see which actions were relevant to opening the hatch that released the reward and which were irrelevant to this specific task. It was here that marked differences emerged between human children and chimpanzees. In this condition, chimpanzees opted for discarding irrelevant actions and performing only those actions that were causally needed to gain the treat. Human children, on the other hand, proceeded to perform the entire sequence of actions as demonstrated by the experimenter, even if they could see that some of the actions in the sequence were irrelevant to the task of obtaining the food reward. In other words, chimpanzees *emulated* the behaviours and successfully reached the end point in obtaining the reward, whilst human children *imitated* the action sequence faithfully at the expense of efficiency.

At first glance, these findings might be surprising as they suggest that chimpanzees demonstrate more efficient and therefore superior problem-solving skills to human children. Chimpanzees appear to be more intelligent than children. Yet, as the authors aptly note, the difference in performance may be due to a greater susceptibility of human children to follow social scripts than chimpanzees. What we see here is the inception of a dilemma between efficiency and ritual which plagues many adults in later life. Rituals guarantee social life by rule-following for open ends, while efficiency seeks immediate ends at minimal effort. Recent research has demonstrated that this mysterious 'over-imitation of causally irrelevant action' observed among children compared to chimps is the basis for distinguishing causal from social constraints on behaviour, and flexibly learning the meaning of actions by parsing and embedding them in different act–action hierarchies (Keupp et al., 2018).

Whiten, Horner & de Waal's (2005) experiment tapped into the human tendency to conform to convention of rule-based sequencing of actions (to get X, you have to do A, B and C in that order), which we argue is highly consequential. Conforming to convention, over a period of time, enables the stabilisation of cultural rules, traditions, rituals, habits and collective behaviours on a grand scale, the implications of which may not be fully known to any one particular individual (Harré & Sammut, 2013). Humans are indeed engulfed in massive set-ups of joint intentionality where very few, if any, have a full understanding of its future direction (see Chapter 9 on designed artefacts). And yet, despite this contrast to efficient rationality, human subjects conform. Let us illustrate with an example. Think about the last time you went through security clearance at an airport. You would have approached the security area and been instructed to line up, after which you would have been instructed to put liquids in a transparent bag and put certain belongings, such as your laptop, aside from the rest of the luggage you were planning to take on board. But aside from these actions with clear security implications – we know that liquids and laptop computers have been used as explosive devices – you might have had to engage in smaller behaviours, the security implications of which may not be quite as evident. For instance, you might have been instructed as to whether your passport and boarding card should go with your luggage, or whether your belt and coat needed a separate tray, and so on. Both of us can recount numerous such experiences during our travels, and we both have only ever simply conformed. Imagine if only a small proportion of travellers adopted a chimpanzee-style emulation strategy at airport security and followed procedure only for that portion of the overall behavioural sequence that they themselves understood to be a security issue, disregarding everything else. Chaos would ensue. And for sure, the security forces would not tolerate such rationality. The chimpanzees in the Whiten et al. (2005) experiment followed only that part of the action sequence that they could see led causally to the food reward. When action steps seemed irrelevant to the task, they trusted their perceptions over the demonstration provided to them by the researchers, and proceeded to discard a portion of the action sequence. Unlike chimpanzees, human children executed the full sequence, even if they could recognise, as did the chimpanzees, that some actions were causally inconsequential. Faced with the dilemma of acting efficiently on their individual understanding, or following all the steps, children conformed. In other words, their manifest public behaviour was not consonant with what one could construe as 'chimp rationality' of private perceptions and faced with this discrepancy, they prioritised convention over private inclinations. In adult life, they will sometimes prioritise ritual over efficiency. In evolutionary terms, we would say that human beings have evolved a predisposition for cultural norms, which by way of a tendency to conform helps to galvanise social groups into coordinated action.

For this to happen, the individual needs to be critical of their own private thoughts and to consult the thoughts and actions of others before acting individually. This is a critical insight with regards to the psychology of conformity. Asch (1952) has described this tendency as the **social check**, that is, the tendency to consult the thoughts of others that helps correct potential errors in one's own thinking. He argued that the social check is possible because human cognition permits the *interpenetration of views*. In other words, by evolving communication, humans became capable of using another person's cognitive abilities as ancillary to their own. In a social group, the interpenetration of views gives rise to what cognitive scientists call **distributed cognition** (Salomon, 1993). This is how groups are able to act as a single system, made up of gatherings of individuals enacting collective events in unison (Harré & Sammut, 2013). The discrepancy between private beliefs and public orientations in conformity was highlighted in one of the best known experiments in psychology – Solomon Asch's line experiments. It is to these that we now turn.

Asch's Line Experiments on Peer Pressure

Following the Second World War, psychologists grappled with numerous questions concerning the atrocities uncovered in the war's aftermath. We will revisit this historical context again in the following chapter on obedience. One question that Solomon Asch (1951, 1956) sought to address in his experimental demonstrations was how human beings could go along with what they witnessed happening around them. Asch set out to prove that human beings, as individuals, were capable of rational thinking and that they were able to stand up for their beliefs and jettison conformity in light of their direct experience. His hypothesis was in line with the American individualist ethos that human beings are sovereign and capable of thinking and acting for themselves. Consequently, they should be protected to do so by law. Deviant behaviours are attributable to particular individuals who do what they do on the basis of their own rational choice.

The findings of Asch's experiments are probably the best known and most influential negative findings in the history of psychology.

Asch established a setting that involved recruiting subjects to participate in an experiment on perception. Perception was a favoured topic of inquiry for the Gestaltists, a group of psychologists who studied the laws of 'self-organising perception' and who had a profound influence on Asch (see also Chapter 11). In fact, Asch's experiments responded to Sherif's autokinetic experiments, which we reviewed in Chapter 4. Asch thought that a problem with Sherif's experiments was that they did not have a single correct response. Asch was convinced that had the situation permitted a correct answer, respondents would have converged on this rather than subjugate to an arbitrary group norm. Asch proceeded thus to undertake his experiments on the visual perception of lines.

On the day of the experiment, subjects were directed to a room where they sat behind a desk with fellow experimental subjects. The experimenter introduced a chart with three lines of different lengths marked on it. This chart was to be used for reference purposes. Subjects were then presented with a series of cards showing single lines that had equal length to one of the three lines displayed on the reference chart. The reference chart was visible to the experimental subjects at all times. The task for the subjects involved looking at the single line presented by the experimenter, matching it with one of the three lines presented in the reference chart, then calling out their answer to the experimenter. Subjects did this in sequence, one after the other. What the experimental subjects did not know was that the other subjects in the experiment were actually confederates of the researcher and acted on instructions provided to them. The real subjects had been made to sit towards the end of the line at the time when the experiment was being set up. They therefore had been set up to give their answer at the end, following other subjects (really confederates) who were asked to give their answers earlier. The real experiment was not concerned with perceptual ability; rather the real subjects' answers following the responses of those who preceded them was the genuine topic of study. Subjects did not know this, so they were faced with a situation where on certain trials their answers would turn out to be at odds with what the others were claiming.

On the first few trials, confederates were instructed to select and call out the corresponding line from the reference chart. There was no issue during this preliminary phase as the lines were clearly distinguishable. At a certain point, confederates were instructed to call out an agreed upon wrong answer. On these trials, by the time the real subject got their turn, a number of other subjects would have openly opted for a mismatching line. This was essentially the true experimental condition. The real subject would have found herself in a minority facing a wrong majority made up of secret confederates giving an agreed upon wrong, but consistent, answer. The question was would the experimental subjects stand up for their own perceptions, which were real and incontrovertible to them, or would they go along with the majority and purposely choose a wrong answer and conform?

The findings were as remarkable as they were surprising. Of the experimental subjects, 76 per cent bowed to majority influence and gave a wrong answer at least once. Overall, in 37 per cent of trials, subjects agreed with the wrong response. Asch repeated the experiments modifying the experimental conditions, but the findings remained unchanged. In effect, without any overt pressure exercised upon them during the course of the experiment, human subjects proceeded to go along with the incorrect majority view in over one third of cases. Large individual differences were noted. During debriefing, some said that they knowingly gave false responses and that they simply went along with what the others were saying to maintain consensus. Others claimed that faced with a majority consensus, they distrusted their own judgement and acted accordingly. Others yet claimed that they never gave a knowingly incorrect response even if this had been recorded as such; they had 'perceived' the incorrect majority choice as the right one.

Asch's explanation for these findings, as noted, was that his experiments had tapped a socio-cognitive process by which individuals question their own thoughts and perceptions in light of evidence provided by similar others in their environment. Asch termed this the social check (see also Box 5.2), which he suggested has evolved as a mechanism to correct epistemic errors in one's own thinking. But the fact that Asch had chosen a physical stimulus for the sake of the experiment leaves little basis for personal doubt – when subjects were asked to write answers anonymously and in private on a piece of paper, there was no evidence of perceptual difficulties. The findings of the line experiments demonstrate that human beings are susceptible to conforming to a majority view. In fact, in subsequent experiments, Asch found that conformity dropped whenever another fellow subject was instructed to disagree with the signed-up majority. For Moscovici, this additional finding was the starting point of a series of other experiments investigating minority influence.

Box 5.2 Fear of ostracism as social pain

Asch offered the social check as a natural mechanism to explain why people conformed to the majority view: they overcome doubts about their own judgements by sourcing the crowd (see Chapter 2), thus valuing the majority view as tried and tested. However, another motive of conformity has recently attracted much attention: fear of isolation in response to threats of exclusion or ostracism. Ostracism refers to a group strategy widely observed across many species including humans: to exclude weak or burdensome members which then leads to reduced life chances and even death. Hence, ostracism is called a 'social death' and the co-evolved capacity of responding to this threat is 'social pain' (Williams & Nida, 2011). Fearing ostracism elicits similar brain activity as pain in response to injury, thus forcing attention and re-evaluation of the current situation and preparing an aversive response in the future (Eisenberger et al., 2003). Social exclusion hurts because pain and social exclusion share a common neural alarm system in the dorsal anterior cingulate cortex. However, being excluded from the group not only hurts like injury, but like chronic pain also affects self-esteem, one's sense of control and existential experiences. There is little doubt that with such a massive disposition to respond with aversion to social exclusion, humans are highly motivated to avoid deviance, to stay within the conventions of the majority and to toe the line. Assimilation is not only a function of social influence from the point of view of the group, but also has a strong basis in human motives: be like others and do not stick out. It will need strong cultural buttressing to be able to expect anything to the contrary. Civil disobedience is one flash point where this difficulty arises: it is difficult to bring people into such protest behaviour because it is highly risky in light of the law; and those who seek to justify it rationally find themselves in the paradox of trying to come up with a 'right to resist' that empowers you to break the law (Pottage, 2013).

Minority Influence Leading to Conversion of the Majority

Moscovici (Moscovici, Lage & Naffrechoux, 1969) observed that in Asch's line experiments, subjects were faced with a choice of deviance or conformity regarding a majority view. Taking Asch's experiments one step further, by focussing on dissenting voices, Moscovici investigated the potential of influence exerted by an active minority in presenting a perspective at par with a majority view. By introducing a minority perspective in the experiments, Moscovici ensured that subjects could not dismiss the discrepant alternative by making an attribution regarding the perceptual abilities of others. We have seen how years later, Ross and Ward (1996) proposed a naive realism bias to describe how individuals dismiss alternative perspectives as ignorant (Sammut & Sartawi, 2012).

Moscovici, Lage & Naffrechoux (1969) adopted an experimental procedure similar to Asch's line experiments. Experimental set-ups included a small number of confederates, the minority, who were instructed on their responses by the experimenters. Subjects, recruited for a study on colour perception, were presented with a number of slides and asked to judge their colour and light intensity. A blue photo filter was used in the experiment that changed the colour of the slides, along with neutral filters that changed light intensity. In the experimental trials, confederates were instructed to identify the change in colour of the slides as 'green' and to do this consistently any time the colour was changed by superimposing a blue photo filter. Uninstructed subjects were asked to give their own verbal assessment of the stimulus as in Asch's experiments.

Aside from this, however, Moscovici proceeded to run a second experiment to examine latent effects. After termination of the first experiment, subjects were invited to stay on for another similar experiment. This time, subjects were requested to go through sixteen discs in the blue-green zone of the Farnsworth 100-hue set perception test, and to mark their colour individually on a sheet of paper. Three discs from each end of the blue and green scale were unambiguous, with the remaining ten discs providing an ambiguous stimulus. Subjects' responses were analysed in terms of how early the shift from blue to green appeared in their answers. Results showed that in the first experiment, experimental subjects perceived a higher number of green slides than the control group, with the percentage of subjects who yielded standing at 32 per cent. This is very similar to Asch's own findings. According to Moscovici, Lage and Naffrechoux, this was due not to isolated individuals who followed the one confederate but to a modified judgement within the group – a new reference frame had been established as in Sherif's autokinetic experiments, which we reviewed in Chapter 4.

The discrimination test undertaken in the second experiment provided further insight. Given that the subjects remained the same in both experiments, the key question for the discrimination test was whether those who responded in line with the confederate minority view in the first experiment would also demonstrate latent influence by changing their perceptive code for judging the blue-green discs presented in the second experiment. Three comparisons were undertaken between subjects, comparing their responses with those of others at the 25 per cent, 50 percent and 75 per cent thresholds of blue-green hues out of the sixteen discs. Results demonstrated significant differences between experimental and control subjects at each of the thresholds. In other words, subjects who participated in the first experiment perceived the blue-green transition earlier in the Farnsworth discs than did control group subjects. Once again, this finding is in line with Sherif's demonstration of norm formation. More interestingly, results further demonstrated a significant difference in responses between those who had yielded to minority influence in the first experiment and those who had stuck with the majority view. In the second experiment, those who had *not* yielded reported a greater number of green judgements in the discrimination test than those who had. As the authors note, this is indeed remarkable insofar as it demonstrates that the influence exerted by a consistent minority may occur at a latent perceptive level aside from the social response.

Asch's key finding was that individuals could display public conformity whilst retaining their private reservations. Moscovici and his colleagues showed that minority influence could bring about **conversion**, that is, it might not achieve a manifest change in public attitudes but may nevertheless alter them in private; conversion operates with a **latency effect**. In this way, a consistent minority can influence both public and private responses of a majority – those individuals who resisted a manifest response in the first experiment were more (not less) likely than those who followed the minority view to be influenced in the second experiment. Moscovici termed this process conversion and defined it as: 'a subtle process of perceptual or cognitive modification by which a person gives up his/her usual response in order to adopt another view or response, without necessarily being aware of the change' (Moscovici & Personnaz, 1980, p. 271).

Moscovici concluded that majority influence, or compliance, produced public submission without private acceptance, whereas minority influence produced long-lasting changes in private responses (i.e., conversion). It is worth noting that these changes are intergroup. In other words, consistent minorities bring about conversion in majority group members. More generally, for this to happen, minority group members need to conform to the minority's pitch sufficiently in order to maintain a public profile. The key to success is their **behavioural style:** being rigid but undogmatic in argumentation and consistent across different voices and situations. This helps the minority acquire a public profile and credibility (Maass & Clark, 1984). To be influential, minority group members have to stay on message. The counter-strategies of seeking to break up this group discipline and to pathologise the 'rigidity' of the message can undermine the potential for conversion (Mugny & Papastamou, 1980); the same can be achieved by showing that the dissident minority is beyond the pale, that is, outside what one might possibly consider the moral community. Ethics scholars argue that civil disobedience, involving illegal acts, can be legitimate only if based on shared values (Rawls, 1972). Labels like 'evil', 'mad' or 'terrorist' stand for such disqualification. When these counteractions fail, and the minority is surfing the Zeitgeist (i.e., the long-term trends of opinion, see Paicheler, 1977), a snowball effect sets in, and what was once a 'wacky or wrong' outsider view becomes the new normal; the majority progressively accommodates the minority in shifting attitudes and behaviour. The 'tragedy of the minority' arises from the observation that, although successful in shifting the common ground, the minority will find it difficult to take credit for the conversion unless special efforts go into collective commemoration (see Chapter 9 on monuments). People tend to remember the message not the messenger, and once the new normal is taken for granted, the historic shift is forgotten without any awareness of such amnesia.

This being said, whilst some research has failed to replicate latent influences on colour perception (De Dreu, 2007), meta-analytic findings have concluded that minority influence produces private before public change (Wood, Lundgren, Ouellette, Busceme & Blackstone, 1994). Pérez & Mugny (1987) have further demonstrated that minority influence is more effective in changing related attitudes than focal ones. In a study concerning birth control and abortion attitudes, the authors found that when a **majority** argued for birth control with people who held negative attitudes towards birth control initially, subjects became more favourable to birth control whilst their views on abortion remained unaltered. When a **minority** argued for birth control with people initially holding negative attitudes towards birth control, however, their views on birth control remained negative but their views on abortion became more tolerant. All this shows that despite the social pain of dissenting and its dissuading force, active minorities are capable of shifting the common ground; if style and conditions are right, they find accommodation in a reconstructed majority, their joint intentionality and common sense.

Deviance and Conformity: The Cultural View

We have seen that individuals stand to be influenced by majorities but also by minorities. We have further seen that influence can be manifest as well as latent. And we have seen that certain conditions influence one's public conformity whereas others seemingly exercise a greater influence on private convictions. According to Moscovici & Personnaz (1980), the processes underlying majority influence and minority influence are mutually exclusive processes that result in different outcomes. Bond & Smith (1996) have conducted a meta-analysis of 133 studies from 17 countries that used Asch–type line experiments. They found that conformity rates are far from stable in one context, nor equal across contexts. The authors argue that conformity rates declined in the United States between 1952 and the 1980s, and that conformity rates correlated with the collectivist–individualist dimension of classifying cultural values: more collectivist countries had higher rates of conformity than more individualistic contexts, after controlling for many variables of the experimental set-ups. They concluded that cultural values are an important factor of conformity, and this required closer attention. This was taken up by a set of experiments, which suggest that individual responses treading the conformity/deviance boundary are indeed determined by factors grounded in cultural sociality. Before we proceed further, take a moment to read and complete the task outlined in Box 5.3.

Box 5.3 Uniqueness or harmony

Imagine you are at your local airport queuing up at check-in when you are approached by a young researcher who asks you some questions for the purposes of a study she is doing. After you answer her questions, the researcher puts her hand inside her pockets, takes out five pens in the colour schemes demonstrated in the images hereunder (Figure 5.2), and offers you one to keep in return for answering her questions. Which pen would you pick to keep? And what reasons might you have for doing so? Is this going to be an aesthetic judgement of 'beauty' or a preference for acquisition – the 'need to have it'?

Box 5.3 presents a choice involving an object in a set of similar other objects. Kim and Markus (1999) investigated how cultural values and individual preferences for deviance and conformity influence each other. The starting point of their inquiry is an observation that different cultural contexts place different values on deviance and conformity, that is, depending on one's cultural context *deviance* can be perceived as *uniqueness*, whereas *conformity* can be framed as *harmony*. Both deviance and conformity, therefore, may have positive connotations depending on the cultural setting in which the behaviour takes place. According to Kim and Markus, behaviours in themselves do not carry any inherent valence. Rather, it is the cultural context that provides the connotation and determines whether the specific act is perceived to be good or bad.

Figure 5.2 **Pick a pen**

The authors go on to argue that East Asian cultures seem to emphasise group harmony and cohesion, such that individual members grow up willing to sacrifice their individuality for the benefit of the group. In these cultures, conformity to group norms is valued; individuals socialised into this cultural framework are not shamed or bothered by their conformity and overall, *people follow the norm to follow norms*. By contrast, American cultural values emphasise individual rights and freedoms that are guaranteed by the US Constitution. Conformity is frowned upon as it is perceived as yielding to group pressure and relinquishing one's individuality and autonomy. Individuals socialised in this culture grow up to value charting their own course in life and finding a path for themselves given their own idiosyncrasies. Consequently, people in North America tend to *follow the norm to not follow norms*. According to Kim and Markus, the cultural meaning associated with deviation from norms determines the meaning individuals attribute to being different from others. Where deviation is positively connoted, individuals will strive to be different and seek to evangelise for conversion. On the other hand, if deviation is negatively connoted, people will strive to conform.

Kim and Markus (1999) proceeded to undertake a series of cleverly designed experiments to test their hypotheses concerning differences between European Americans and East Asians in preferences for deviance and conformity. In the first experiment, they measured responses to abstract patterns that included a figure that deviated from the overall pattern (e.g., a triangle in a pattern of circles). Subjects were asked to rate the extent to which they liked the figures. European Americans showed a greater liking for deviant/unique subfigures that broke the pattern than Chinese Americans did. The findings were replicated in a second study with East Asian subjects, reporting the same results. In a third experiment they looked at how preferences for conformity and uniqueness were manifested in action. Participants were asked to choose a pen out of five to test how the appearance of an object as part of a majority or minority would affect individual choices. The pens, as in Box 5.3, were provided following administration of a brief questionnaire. Kim and Markus hypothesised that Americans would prefer minority objects whereas East Asians would prefer majority ones. On every trial, five pens were made available for respondents to choose from, with either a 4:1 or a 3:2 majority: minority ratio.

As hypothesised, Americans more commonly chose a pen that was a minority offering than their East Asian counterparts did. Across both ratios, Americans chose the pen of the more uncommon colour 74 per cent of the time whilst East Asians chose the same option a mere 24 per cent of the time. There was no effect for colour of the pens in the experiment. Kim and Markus (1999) concluded that as expected, individuals' choices were in line with cultural values; most subjects expressed individual preferences that were fully aligned with the prevalent norms of their own cultural setting – whether this was a preference for deviance or a preference for conformity. Their studies demonstrate very powerfully that the actions people engage in and the values guiding their choices serve to reproduce small particles of culture that establish a degree of normative validation for particular forms of action. We thus seem to deal with different cultural mindsets or frames of reference, already established by local history and socialisation: under 'individualism' conformity is foregrounded as the biased judgement, hence we speak liberally of the 'conformity bias' of common reasoning; while under collectivist value orientations, dissent is framed as biased, hence we can talk of the 'dissenter bias' of individual reasoning.

Conclusion

Let us retrace our steps and take stock of the grounds we have charted in this chapter. We have seen how Asch's famous line experiments showed that human beings are subject to a conformity bias by which they consult the thoughts and opinions of others prior to engaging in an act of their own. We have seen that to the extent that their thoughts are in agreement with those of others, they assume them to be right, and that the overt pressure to conform to a majority view is powerful enough to stimulate human subjects to give erroneous responses in a perception task for the sake of going along with what the peer group suggests. This seems quite surprising when starting off with the assumption that human beings are rational beings who make reasoned choices depending on their own inclinations and aspirations. Indeed, this characterisation of human choice has been noted to be a socio-cognitive bias, that is, naive realism. According to Ross & Ward (1996), human beings believe that their own convictions are the product of reasoned, logical and objective thinking processes rather than their own culturally biased orientations. When challenged with an alternative view by newcomers, homecomers (i.e., returning migrants – who have acculturated to a different setting) or strangers, they will hold it as biased or attribute a degree of ignorance to it (Sammut & Sartawi, 2012). Much of the social sciences, outside maybe anthropology, has left these assumptions of ethnocentrism unchallenged. Or as Mercier & Sperber (2017) argue: humans do not reason to solve problems or make better decisions in isolation in front of a computer, or like Robinson Crusoe on his island talking to himself, but to argue with each other within social constraints of what it is possible to argue about.

We would like to suggest that the findings of Asch's line experiments are only surprising if the assumption of 'individual rational choice' is upheld. On the other hand, we have also seen how human beings are predisposed to establish social relations from an early age, driven by needs for attachment and affiliation, to avoid experiencing social pain. We have seen how primates deprived of social contact fail to acquire the necessary instinctive behaviours to achieve functional relations in later life. We have also seen how human infants use the affiliative ties established with a caregiver to navigate uncertain environments. This means that human beings have evolved predispositions to orient themselves towards the group in which they are socialised, and to strive to become fully functional adults by following the norms of their social group. Finally, we have seen how human children are predisposed to follow norms even if these are causally irrelevant to the task at hand. Human children are predisposed to imitate and to not challenge norms that might not make immediate sense to them. Over-imitation leads them to appreciate ritual over immediate efficiency. In other words, if our starting position is a realisation that human beings are socialised in a way that aligns their behaviour with prevalent cultural norms, then we must expect conformity in the face of a challenge to the group norm. Both Asch's and Moscovici's experimental demonstrations can be interpreted along these lines. In fact, we have further seen how human subjects are predisposed to replicate cultural norms in their everyday behaviours including those involving individual choice; and to further distrust discrepant opinions and behaviours (Ross & Ward, 1996; Sammut & Sartawi, 2012; Sammut, Bezzina & Sartawi, 2015).

Now let us take stock of the influence modalities we have charted in this chapter. The human predisposition to sociality seems to be the underlying ingredient for both majority and minority influence. Majority influence serves to defend the status quo and to detract dissenters and rope them in. To the extent that this is successful, the group preserves, even consolidates, social cohesion around an established joint intentionality or project for the future. Majority influence thus assimilates dissenting outsiders (i.e., newcomers, homecomers or strangers) to the prescribed normative code. Peer pressure and the threat of exclusion due to not fitting in ensure that dissent is relegated to the private domain, as per Asch's findings. In combination with mass mediation, this provides fertile grounds for a spiral of silence (Noelle-Neumann, 1974; see Chapter 8) where over time only conforming opinions are expressed, resulting in sustenance of the normative code and its mainstreaming. This status quo dynamic is however challenged with the rise of dissent from an active minority; specifically, when dissenters challenge and oppose the mainstream in unison and with consistent argumentation. Whilst singular dissenters may be relegated to the ranks of the absurd or the ignorant (Asch, 1952; Ross & Ward, 1996; Sammut & Sartawi, 2012; Sammut, Bezzina & Sartawi, 2015), concerted and disciplined dissenting voices may turn the tide. Thus, consistent minorities are capable of influence through conversion of the majority; the majority accommodates them by shifting the common ground. It is worth underlining the *consistency* of argumentation of minorities that succeed in bringing about conversion; consistency requires in turn conformity by minority members. An active minority challenges the normative status quo, itself recruiting conformity. Majority and minority influence transpire as two distinct modalities of influence, functionally nested rather than contradictory, aiming at conformity and conversion respectively. Both are underlined by the human ability to establish communality and coalitions that maximise the fitness of individuals to stay in good health and to attract a partner to pass on genes to the next generation (Lopez, McDermott & Bang Petersen, 2011).

In conclusion, we would argue that human beings have evolved a set of predispositions that orients them to their social peer group and the norms that govern behaviour in **joint intentionality**. These predispositions convey cultural meaning and common-sense to human beings' individual choices. Common sense enables human subjects to make sense of their own behaviour as well as that of others. We would argue that common-sensical behaviour is sensible to the perceiving subject in a way that makes it seem objective and rational to the self (see Chapter 4 on norms). In this way, common sense is seemingly adaptive, as a method by which collective life is achieved. It maximises fitness for individuals in the group. In other words, once we understand each other we are able to live together according to our common understanding, and arguing and reasoning with each other maximises our own individual survival needs. Indeed, this natural predisposition to conform is challenged only by *consistent* active minorities. The consistency aspect documented in Moscovici's colour experiments may be indicative of an alternative *common* sense. Whilst an alternative perspective is distrusted and labelled as biased or ignorant, due to naive realism, an alternative perspective can nevertheless gain a foothold. But minority members need to conform to a favourite alternative themselves, as their potential power lies in presenting a *consistent* alternative, rather than a chaos of alternative choices.

All this suggests, therefore, that our evolved cognition has predisposed us to note and process common-sensical views, not necessarily logical, objective or correct ones. The determining factor in generating influence seems to be the extent to which a view is widespread. Intergroup issues arise in the encounter of different common senses. These instantiate a clash of social representations (Sammut & Howarth, 2014), inasmuch as the good reason one might have for doing something is challenged by outsiders who have seen another course of action justified by equally good reason, or by as yet unconvinced newcomers to the community, a common sense that claims that *that* reason, whatever it might be, is actually not good enough to justify the required behaviour (Sammut, 2015). In these instances, interpersonal discord may mask an intercultural cleavage by which some perspective and not another is denied normative validation. Individual behaviour, which in a different cultural context may be normal routine (eating pork as a delicacy), may thus be challenged by a different normative code (banning pork meat or meat in general from the food chain). Thus far we considered social influence in the horizontal line of peer interactions; establishing, defending or shifting common ground among peers of equal standing. One wonders how social influence is exercised in situations where an individual is commanded by authority, in the vertical dimension of hierarchy, to engage in a behaviour that does not align with the moral values they themselves draw upon. This matter takes us directly to the heart of the next chapter and the phenomenon of obedience to authority.

In Essence

The human disposition for conformity manifests in early childhood and enables the achievement of cultural norms and rituals that serve collective aspirations by means of the distinctively human capacity for joint intentionality.

Consistent minorities are indicative of alternative common sense and thus capable of generating conversion.

After being socialised in a prevalent common sense, human beings become inclined to follow their own culture's norms, whether this is to follow norms (collectivism) or to not follow norms (individualism).

CHAPTER 6

Obeying
Authority and Compliance

phase	modality	function for CS	outcome	Mode 1 face-to-face inter-subjective	Mode 2 symbolic	Mode 3 artefact inter-objective
Phase 2	authority	Assimilation	obedience	command	Hi-Fi signal transfer	monuments

Challenge from conflict, dissonance, controversy arising from newcomers, homecomers, strangers or 'aliens'

Figure 6.1   A challenge and response model V: obeying

In the previous chapter, we saw how social norms influence our individual choices and that human beings are predisposed to follow norms even if they lack a full understanding of the event in which they are participating. We have argued that this serves evolutionary fitness purposes, that is, a social consequence of the act of conforming is the strengthening of ties between group members. This social cohesion helps groups achieve what individuals cannot on their own. In this way, group life strengthens the survival possibilities of individuals, that is, it maximises fitness. It pays human beings to establish strong ties with other group members, and conformity behaviours serve this very purpose (Lachlan, Janik & Slater, 2004).

We can therefore argue, along with Asch (1952), that the social check is adaptive: a single individual in our ancestral environment doubting whether the shadow in front of her is a mere shrub or a lurking predator gains an adaptive advantage in consulting the thoughts, cognitions and perceptions of others. The horizontal triangulation of views that is achieved through communication in such situations extends, as Asch argued, the individual's cognitive capacities beyond their own unaided efforts. The individual becomes able to see much further – by proxy; incorporating another individual's point of view into their own cognitive repertoire and realising thus that the shadow is a mere shrub, or otherwise.

117

Recent research on vicarious perception has confirmed Asch's predictions. Ward, Ganis & Bach (2019) conducted a series of experiments on mental rotation that have provided direct evidence that human beings form proxy mental images of other people's perceptions, and that they use these proxy images to guide their own decisions. In a mental rotation task, subjects who had access to another person during the experimental situation were able to generate mental images according to how the object looks from the other person's point of view (but not from another inanimate object's point of view). In this way, human beings are able to put themselves in another person's shoes and visually perceive the world through the other's eyes. Ward, Ganis & Bach (2019) have provided cognitive evidence, almost seventy years after Asch's (1952) postulation of the *interpenetration of views*, that in perception tasks another person's perspective can stand in for one's own sensorial input.

We have further seen how the collaborative potential that inheres in conformity behaviours can lead to individuals doing something that, to them personally, seems in actual fact to be erroneous or faulty – as in Asch's line experiments where subjects conformed with the wrong view. This demonstrated that human beings distinguish between private and public conformity and whilst they may display a certain characteristic behaviour in public, they might not necessarily endorse this in private. The question that necessarily ensues is: would individuals behave similarly when what is requested of them is manifestly wrong or immoral? Surely human beings might be excused for conforming to a harmless line perception task when put in a difficult position by peers. But what about actions that are not quite 'harmless'? Would regular human beings obey a command to hurt another? This question was picked up for empirical study by Stanley Milgram, a collaborator of both Asch and Moscovici, whose experiments pioneered the **obedience** paradigm in psychology, with which this chapter is concerned. While conformity deals with horizontal influence among peers, obedience focuses on vertical influence along a line of hierarchy.

Obedience in Children

Before we delve into Milgram's experiments and the issues Milgram grappled with, it is worth considering children's responses to **authority**. As in the previous chapter, findings concerning child behaviour are highly pertinent as they provide an indication of what we might consider to be natural inclinations rooted in our evolved genetic makeup. We will then contrast these findings with studies that have focused on adult behaviour.

Aside from natural tendencies, adult behaviour is further influenced by years of socialisation that take place over the individual's lifespan. Consequently, differences between adults and children could indicate how cultural influences steer our natural inclinations in determined directions.

The issue of authority with children is no mean matter for any caregiver who has experienced the 'terrible twos' (Calkins & Williford, 2009). This refers to a developmental tendency in children that takes place at around two years of age (with wide individual differences) and that marks a point in development where children start demonstrating a degree of self-determination. They do this, typically, by being assertive and by striving to make their own choices. At times, these conflict with caregivers' priorities and when they do, the end result is typically a temper tantrum of embarrassing proportions.

What takes place in these situations is very young children resisting or defying authoritative commands issued by caregivers, commands which might very well be in the child's best interests. In mastering the challenge, caregivers necessarily come to understand that authoritative **commands** alone no longer work on a routine basis and that the child's own desires need to be accommodated. In essence, once the terrible twos set in, blind obedience to the caregiver's authority can no longer be assumed and the possibility of defiance on the part of children will need to be factored in. On the other hand, children also display obedience to authority whilst growing up, such as at school. Schools support an authority structure that enables teachers to cater to children in classes rather than individually. This would not be at all possible if children were unable to understand authority and how it works in the real world. So children seem to be widely defiant on one hand, but largely obedient on the other. This is where the issue of authority in children becomes interesting. Do children arbitrarily obey some commands blindly and defy some others in an equally blind fashion? Or are they capable of considering authority in a complex way that caters to the specificity of the situation they find themselves in?

Laupa & Turiel (1986) examined children's conceptions of authority with regards to the age of persons issuing commands, their social position and the type of command given. First, third and fifth grade students were presented with descriptions of two events. The first concerned a turn-taking dispute and the second described a physical fight between children. Descriptions varied between experimental groups. The turn-taking event was resolved with either (a) a peer authority or (b) an adult authority intervening and assigning one child to go first. The physical fight event was resolved with a command to (a) stop fighting or (b) to fight on. Following the presentation of each story, children's responses to (i) an evaluation of the command; (ii) an explanation regarding the legitimacy of the command; and (iii) whether and why the command should or should not be obeyed were gathered. Paired comparisons were also included in the experiment. These involved the presentation of contrasting commands issued by different authorities. Children were asked which authority should be obeyed and why.

Almost all children who participated in the experiment considered the failure to take turns and fighting to be wrong. Both peer authorities and adult authorities were deemed legitimate by the children when issuing commands to take turns and to stop fighting, with the caveat that fifth-graders were less likely to accept peer authority in the turn-taking event, arguing that it was not fair for one child to go first on arbitrary criteria decided upon by peer authority. In the paired comparisons condition for the turn-taking event, children obeyed adult authority over peer authority. However, children of all ages also chose to obey commands issued by a person in an authority position over a non-authority, including peer authority versus adult non-authority. For the fighting event, children only obeyed the command to stop fighting, regardless of variable attributes concerning the source.

Laupa and Turiel argue that children demonstrably take several factors into account in evaluating commands from authority. The weight given to these various factors by children varies according to the situation. Children in the experiment were able to appreciate the values of age, social position and moral criteria in their evaluations. According to the authors, children do not take a unitary orientation towards authority; at all ages they accept some commands and refute others. In certain situations, children were able to accept the *legitimacy* of authority, including that of peers appointed to an authority position. In other situations, they rejected authoritative commands to fight. Rather than a unitary orientation to authority by way of blind obedience or defiant rejection, therefore, children display a complex interplay of cognitive skills in evaluating various dimensions of authority simultaneously, including an assessment of age, social position and moral force in particular circumstances.

It is quite tempting to conclude the chapter here, in celebration of the cognitive powers displayed by the human species from a young age. We have seen how from an early age that children do not just do what they are told. They think about what they are told and they judge whether this is in line with what they themselves think is good or bad. Children are able to distinguish between **power** and authority it seems. One could argue that this assessment of authority is adaptive. Human beings, from an early age, seem to understand that in a social group there is a dominance hierarchy. This serves to grant some people power over others to enforce their will. However, human beings also seem able to understand that it is important for individuals to recognise authority for the group to function, even if they are not able to make sense of the bigger picture on an individual basis, as we have seen in the previous chapter. Even when an individual does not have full understanding of what the social group is enacting, as long as she understands that there are objectives that are common to everyone, and that different people have assumed different roles to make sure that these objectives for the common good are achieved, then division of labour should naturally set in and the rest should follow.

If children are able to understand authority as early as first grade, then when they grow older they are expected to be able to work for a certain industry, assume a certain role and relate to others on the basis of this with a complex understanding of how their own role ties in with that of others. In this way, human beings can be generals in an army, or they can be soldiers; they can be CEOs of a company, or they can be clerks, and so on. In any case, everyone has a role to play and it is important for everyone to play their role if the entire system is to function for everybody's benefit. This would certainly make for a very nice take-home message and we would be justified in feeling good about it. If we have an understanding of power, authority, social roles and morality as early as first grade, then we should be able to get along nicely by obeying commands that facilitate good relations and rejecting ones that do not. So why don't we as adults?

The Banality of Evil

The cognitive complexity that children demonstrate in appraising authoritative commands stands in stark contrast with the actions demonstrated by other human beings who justify heinous acts by recourse to authority. That some human beings are capable of inflicting harm and suffering on others is a fact that any historical account of war or conflict makes abundantly clear. Typically, however, we attribute such behaviours to some abnormal individual who commands an authoritative vantage point that grants him or her the luxury of inflicting evil suffering on others. The Roman Emperor Nero's burning of Christians, for instance, provides an old yet illustrative example. The actions of Roman soldiers who executed

Nero's commands are somewhat excusable if they feared their leader's power and authority. Our lay explanations for such events are that we typically hold leaders themselves as deranged, evil or psychopathic narcissists. We understand there to be something wrong with them and we proceed to lay blame and responsibility directly at their feet. In other words, as we have seen in Chapter 3, we typically commit the *fundamental attribution error* when considering the evil actions of leaders and attribute their behaviours to dispositional causes. This seemingly obvious and natural explanation for behaviour is challenged when we are faced with evidence of more widespread and systematic behaviours of the same kind that, from our point of view, are deemed immoral and therefore objectionable. In these instances, we expect fellow human beings to demonstrate defiance and, like the children in Laupa & Turiel's (1986) experiment, to resist immoral forms of authority as children did when ordered by an adult authority to fight.

Following the Second World War, questions concerning human nature were justifiably raised with regards to the Holocaust. How could human beings justify the systematic murder of 6 million Jews? The genocide that took place during the Second World War is hard to ascribe to a single deranged individual. It had to be bigger than that and it had to involve many others who would readily execute commands to get the genocidal 'job' done. So why did these others not resist authority and defy immoral commands? Hannah Arendt's (1963) analysis of the trial of Adolf Eichmann in Jerusalem (Box 6.1) caused much debate in the social sciences. In particular, her conclusion, that the evil we attribute to deranged leaders is banal, served to pose some critical psychological questions concerning the nature of obedience. Could it really be the case that even ordinary citizens (like us!) could go on to commit heinous crimes just because they are commanded to do so by a higher authority? For Stanley Milgram, there was one way to find out.

Box 6.1 The trial of Adolf Eichmann

Adolf Eichmann was a Nazi SS officer who was later captured, tried and executed for his role in the Holocaust. Eichmann was tasked with managing the logistical operations involved in the deportation and execution of Jews in concentration camps during the Second World War. Following Germany's defeat at the end of the war, Eichmann fled to Austria and later to Argentina where he was captured in a famous undercover operation by the Israeli secret service in May 1960. He stood trial in Israel, where he was indicted on fifteen criminal charges including war crimes and crimes against humanity, in 1961. Eichmann's defence rested on the claim that he was not involved in Nazi decision-making, but was merely executing orders from his superiors which he was not at liberty to disobey. Eichmann claimed that essentially he was doing his job. The judges at the trial disagreed that Eichmann was merely following orders. They held him responsible for subscribing to the Nazi cause and perpetrating genocide and sentenced him to death by hanging.

Eichmann's trial was widely publicised at the time and attracted widespread attention. Hannah Arendt, who reported on the trial for The New Yorker, described Eichmann as a dull and ordinary bureaucrat. He was found to be sane and to demonstrate a normal personality. According to Arendt, this showed that Nazi criminals were no different from normal people. In her book about Eichmann's trial, published in 1963, Arendt introduced the notion of the 'banality of evil'. This referred to the idea that people who are regarded as evil, like Adolf Eichmann, are neither deranged, nor perverted, nor sadistic. Rather, they are simply ordinary people driven by banal motives, such as striving to follow rules, wanting to do a good job or seeking promotion at work. Arendt did not suggest that in the face of authoritative command, individuals do not have moral choice. Neither did she argue that Eichmann was not responsible for his actions. Her contribution, however, was to dispel the idea that individuals commit wrongdoing because there is something 'wrong with them'. On the contrary, Arendt concluded that perpetrators of evil, as individuals, are 'terribly and terrifyingly normal' (1963, p. 276).

The Obedience Experiments

Milgram (1963, 1974) conducted what are amongst the most famous experiments into human nature that have ever taken place (Blass, 1999). The findings of his experiments caused great controversy as well as much surprise, though Milgram's academic career was ironically jeopardised by the controversial attention (Blass, 2004, p. 152). Milgram was influenced by Asch's conformity experiments, in particular the fact that individuals could demonstrate public acceptance to something with which they privately disagreed. He was also traumatised by the magnitude of the Holocaust. The prevalent psychological explanation to the concerns raised by Hannah Arendt and following Asch's conformity experiments was that a deranged leader, or a group of deranged peers, could push for an immoral act that normal individuals would proceed to execute even if they privately disagreed with the command. This private–public persona distinction is what Eichmann's defence claimed (Box 6.1) and what Asch demonstrated experimentally. The question that ensued, which Milgram effectively picked up, was whether normal individuals would obey commands to do something immoral to an innocent participant if they are ordered to do so by a legitimate authority. Would individuals obey, or would they resist?

Milgram recruited participants for a supposed 'learning experiment' with an advertisement in the local newspaper *The New Haven Register*. Participants were screened before the experiment and debriefed at the end. They were called 'teachers' and informed that the experiment was being held to study the effects of punishment on learning, a topical question of behaviourist research at the time. The experimenters had lists of word associations that the learners would need to memorise. The teachers would then read out a stimulus word and the learner would need to respond with the right association. If the response was indeed correct, the teacher would move on to the next word stimulus pair. If the response was incorrect, the teacher would deliver electric shocks of increasing intensity as punishment, starting from 15 volts all the way to 450 volts. These electric shocks were to be delivered using an experimental apparatus designed for purpose, which consisted of a switchbox containing a series of switches of variable intensity marked by corresponding labels from 'Slight Shock' on one end, to 'Danger: Severe Shock' and 'X X X' on the other.

Respondents were paid in advance for participating in the experiment and they were informed of their rights of participation, including their right of withdrawal, prior to the start of the experiment. They also received a mild 15-volt shock during the demonstration process, which was intended to increase believability and realism of the situation. None of the other switches on the electric switchbox actually worked, but the respondents did not know this. They were subjected to a seemingly random draw that would see them assigned to being either learners or teachers. This draw was rigged so that recruited participants were always assigned to the teacher's role. The learner was in-fact a confederate of the experimenters who would act out a pre-determined pain response. Learner and teacher sat in different rooms and communicated with each other using audio equipment. Learners were instructed to proceed regularly for the first few trials but then raise objections when shocks reached a certain intensity. Whenever this happened, and 'teachers' showed hesitation in proceeding with the experiment, an experimenter wearing a full white lab coat would enter the room where the teacher sat beside the electric shock switchbox and order the teacher to go on with the procedure as planned. In essence, in a situation of 'randomly' assigned roles, 'teachers' were ordered to inflict pain of increasing intensity to a 'learner' all the way to electrocution.

Learners were instructed to escalate their protest as the experiment proceeded, including pounding on the dividing wall, calling for the experiment to be terminated, screaming in pain and, finally, to stop responding altogether mimicking loss of consciousness. The question Milgram was looking to answer in this experiment was at which point would respondents stop and actively disobey the experimenter's command?

Sixty-five per cent (65%) of participants in Milgram's experiment proceeded all the way to the end of the 450-volt shock sequence, potentially killing a random subject over failure to memorise random word associations. These were shocking findings indeed. The surprise was intensified because this ratio exceeded any tentative prediction. Whilst no respondent came to any real harm, and whilst they were all debriefed thoroughly after their experimental struggles, the fact that a level of obedience of this magnitude was recorded surprised even the participants themselves. This is all the more noteworthy in view of the fact that participants were screened in advance. Consequently, these findings cannot be attributed to personality or pathology. The fact that 65 per cent of respondents demonstrated complete obedience suggests that the odds, regardless of other criteria, are stacked in favour of obedience. This contrasts very sharply with the findings of Laupa & Turiel's (1983) experiment, which we reviewed previously. If children as young as first grade demonstrate cognitive complexity in their appraisal of authority independent of power that includes a concern with morality, how is it that perfectly normal adults show lesser cognitive prowess?

One possible explanation could be due to a cultural climate at the time Milgram's experiments were carried out in the early 1960s. Arguably, it was the height of the Cold War, the Sputnik Shock (1957) and the Cuban Missile Crisis (1962), and issues to do with national defence, pulling ranks and authority were highly salient. One could further argue that having lived through the earlier hot war, participants in Milgram's study had internalised a tendency towards obedience as this might have been useful in times of crisis.

The question arises whether obedience rates, revealed through the Milgram paradigm similar to a litmus test that shows the acidity of a substance in chemistry, could serve as a cultural indicator of the authoritarian mentality of a society. Blass (1999) compiled fourteen replications of Milgram's experiments in different countries, the latest from 1985, reporting obedience rates between 28 per cent and 91 per cent (Table 6.1). The average rate of obedience overall is 66 per cent and for the subset of US studies slightly lower at 61 per cent. There were no observable differences in obedience rates between men or women, nor was there a shift in the average obedience rate over time (to conduct a systematic comparison across countries, the cases were too few), as Burger later reported.

Burger (2009) sought to replicate Milgram's original study to investigate whether levels of obedience amongst Americans had changed over time as a function of changes in sociopolitical circumstances since Milgram's experiments. In the meantime, the Cold War had ended. Burger's study adopted a 150-volt limit to ensure ethical rigour. Burger noted that 79 per cent of participants in Milgram's study who reached the 150-volt mark proceeded all the way to the end. This was the point at which Milgram's learners screamed out in pain and protested. Accordingly, the shock sequence in Burger's study was terminated at 150-volts. Burger also carried out a modelled refusal condition, where genuine participants witnessed another respondent rebel and disobey the experimenter. Findings, however, showed no statistically significant differences from Milgram's original outcome for both conditions.

Table 6.1 *Obedience rates from different replications studies*

Milgram (1963) Exp 1	USA (New Haven)	65
Exp 2	USA	62.5
Exp 3	USA	40
Exp 5	USA	65
Exp 6	USA	50
Exp 10	USA	47.5
Holland (1967)	USA	75
Ancona & Pareyson (1968)	Italy	85
Rosenhan (1969)	USA	85
Podd (1969)	USA	31
Edwards et al. (1969)	South Africa	87.5
Ring et al. (1969)	USA	91
Mantell (1971)	West Germany	85
Bock (1972)	USA	40
Powers & Green (1972)	USA	83
Rogers (1973)	USA	37
Kilhan & Mann (1974)	Australia	28
Shalala (1973)	USA	30
Costanzo (1976)	USA	81
Shanab & Yahya (1977)	Jordan	73
Shanab & Yahya (1978)	Jordan	62.5
Miranda et al. (1981)	Spain	50
Schurz (1985)	Austria	80
Burger (2006)	USA (California)	<70

Burger thus confirmed the obedience rate which Milgram originally observed in the United States at around two thirds of participants. This cumulative evidence suggests that a tendency to obey is intrinsic to human nature not due to historical conditions, which seems rather worrying in the light of historical evidence of collusion in evil acts. If around 65 per cent of human beings obey a scientist to 'kill' someone over a word association task, one wonders what human beings are capable of when they are asked to demonstrate obedience to transcendental causes, such as religious faiths or political ideologies, or when their own self-interest is at stake. Another replication of Milgram's original study sought to answer these questions. It is to this set of experiments that we now turn.

The Utrecht Studies (1982–1985)

Aside from the ethical concerns Milgram's obedience experiments raised with regards to subjects' participation, a further concern with the experiments was the ecological validity they lacked. **Ecological validity** is the extent to which an experimental setting approximates the real world in terms of tasks and people involved, and is held to have something to do with the extent to which generalisations about real-world phenomena are possible from findings observed in the laboratory. Meeus & Raaijmakers (1995) argued that giving electric shocks to people is not pertinent to our everyday life. In everyday life, normal people do not experience situations where they must decide on whether to electrocute an innocent other. On this criterion, the set-up of Milgram's experiment bears little resemblance to everyday life. The obedience documented in Milgram's experiment could thus be a laboratory artefact. To rule out this possibility, a replication of the experiment testing the ecological validity hypothesis was required.

Meeus & Raaijmakers (1995) conducted a replication of Milgram's experiment with one crucial modification – mediated, or indirect violence. The authors argued that in modern societies violence exercised upon others is mediated, such that perpetrators only indirectly observe the negative consequences of their actions. With **mediated violence**, the relationship between victim and perpetrator is indirect and consequences are not experienced immediately and face-to-face. This is held to be more faithful to our contemporary living conditions. In 'administrative violence', we do our jobs by following the rules without due consideration of what happens to people on the receiving end. The Utrecht studies on obedience – as this set of experiments has come to be known – involved a similar hoax set up to that adopted by Milgram. An experimenter, a confederate and a genuine subject participated in the experiment. The experimenter was armed with a similar range of prods to that used in Milgram's studies, which were used whenever a subject came to hesitate in proceeding with the experimental task. Subject and confederate were sat in different rooms and communicated through audio equipment.

The Utrecht studies did away with electric shocks and punishment, but deployed humiliating remarks as verbal violence instead. Subjects were invited to the laboratory to participate in an experiment on psychological stress and test performance. Subjects were told that in an adjacent room, other people were taking a test that was part of a job selection exercise; and these people had also signed up to the 'experiment'. Subjects were instructed to disturb the applicant (in reality confederates) while she or he was taking the test by making a series of negative and denigrating remarks about their test performance. Applicants were instructed to object and protest against these humiliating remarks and to do so with increasing vehemence as the experiment proceeded, as in Milgram's study. They were instructed to act as if stress disrupted their performance and as if they were very fearful of actually failing the test and of losing the job opportunity.

All this set-up was framed in the light of conducting scientific research on 'the impact of stress on psychological testing'; stress impact studies being a common research topic. Genuine subjects faced the dilemma of refusing to cooperate in humiliating a random person or obeying the experimenter and prodding the applicants on, with a high risk of making them fail the test in the end. They therefore had to weigh the benefits of experimental stress research on the one hand against the costs of stressing an applicant who will consequently fail the test and thus lose a job opportunity on the other. The Utrecht studies further employed a control group of subjects who were not prodded on by the experimenter and who decided themselves whenever to stop making humiliating remarks. This time, the findings were very different from Milgram's.

In the baseline condition, that is, the straight replication of Milgram's experiment, 91 per cent of subjects obeyed the experimenter to the end and proceeded to make all the stress remarks potentially costing an applicant their job. This is notably higher than the constant 65 per cent obedience recorded in Milgram's and follow-up experiments. In the control group, none of the subjects made all the series of stress remarks. In a subsequent variation of the experiment, the authors examined a legal liability condition where subjects were told that they might be held liable for consequences suffered by the humiliated applicants. The latter were instructed to threaten legal action at some point during the course of the experiment in response to ongoing stress remarks. In this condition, obedience dropped to 30 per cent. When, in a further variation, subjects were told that the university would provide legal cover, obedience rates rose once again to baseline level of 91 per cent. The authors concluded that when subjects themselves would have to face responsibility, most of them refused to obey the experimenter's instructions. Self-interest, therefore, seems to break the natural tendency for obedience.

The Utrecht studies did not employ painful electric shocks but their findings are even more shocking than Milgram's. It seems that human beings have few qualms in hurting someone else if the event is in line with the norms and practices that predominate in their social environment. Subjects in the Utrecht studies, unlike Milgram's, found themselves in a situation that was rather understandable. The ails and benefits of stress are a widespread concern and the fact that the sciences are seeking insight into this social problem is lauded as an enterprise that stands to benefit the whole of humankind. Science means progress in a society where science and scientists generally have legitimate cultural authority; in this context the experiment becomes a confirming ritual that cannot be stopped (Meeus & Raaijmakers, 1995, p. 169). Relative to this, a random person performing a social role as 'applicant' failing to get a job seems like a small price to pay. Unless, that is, one is paying out of one's own pocket through legal liability, in which case obedience drops significantly. Remove liability and obedience rises to baseline levels once again. This suggests that human beings are largely obedient to authority when they understand the commanded actions to be legitimate and in line with the common good. Disobedience becomes more likely when personal costs are involved.

The Social Identity Approach

The discrepant findings between the Utrecht studies and Milgram's studies raise further cause for concern when appraised in light of the findings of Laupa & Turiel's (1986) experiment on children's flexible conception of authority, reviewed in the previous section. It seems that whilst children demonstrate circumspection in appraising authority, a prevailing cultural ethos may bypass this appraisal altogether and serve the purpose of harmonising responses across individual differences in adulthood. When 91 per cent of subjects demonstrate obedience regardless of other individual differences, such as personality, one can argue that subjects are demonstrating an ecological affordance of obedience in a predetermined direction.

This does not necessarily mean that human adults are less cognitively adept than children. It merely echoes Kim & Markus's (1999) claim (see Chapter 5) that human beings learn to follow their culture's prevalent norms and when they do, they act accordingly. Consequently, collective life may arise as an emergent phenomenon of individual choice, including obedient or rebellious tendencies.

In Chapter 3, we saw how the social identity approach to leadership suggests that leaders acquire power and authority not through personal traits but through group dynamics and perceived prototypicality. According to this perspective (Haslam & Reicher, 2018; Reicher & Haslam, 2011), people are inclined to obey commands from leaders who would seem to be more prototypical of the social group of which they count themselves as members; they obey because they are in a state of engaged followership. Consequently, in many contemporary societies, university laboratories and scientific research represent an unparalleled epistemic source that itself is granted more authority in society than most other institutions (Jovchelovitch, 2007). Indeed, science is challenged primarily by more and better science; and maybe sometimes over controversial issues such as climate change, vaccination or GM food. Bauer et al. (2019) call this a 'bungee jump' of authority, an occasional, topic-specific fall from an otherwise secure high level of cultural goodwill. In this case, one can expect that expert scientists are considered to be prototypical of a project of progress. Authority and obedience, in such a context, follow from widespread social identification with this quest for progress: experimental subjects identify with the scientific project and engage in an experiment as a ritual confirming this. The scientist, in such a setting, commands a disproportionate level of authority relative to the subject as a function of the social role she occupies. The command of the lab experimenter in a white coat has illocutionary force because it satisfies conventions of who, where and when it can be exercised (Austin, 1976).

The subject both understands and acquiesces to this, such that the scientific project is endorsed at a collective level. In everyday life, one needs to visit specialists for services from time to time. We consult a medical doctor, for instance, for specialist medical expertise and we tend to obey when a medical doctor prescribes medication (though perhaps increasingly less so as in many cases a 'compliance problem' is emerging). We understand that the doctor has access to more scientific knowledge about the issue we're experiencing than we do, so we defer to his or her judgement and happily obey their instructions. This is not an abdication of rationality, but a rational recognition of better judgement. If our automobile breaks down, we similarly resort to a specialist who holds more knowledge in that domain than we do, and again we acquiesce. We do not consult shamans or exorcists to cure a seasonal flu, for the simple reason that the background knowledge that has gained pre-eminence in contemporary Western societies is predominantly science rather than spiritism. It is therefore little surprise, from a social identity perspective, that so many adult subjects readily obey commands from scientists in or outside a scientific institution. Indeed, we would be surprised if it were not so. Science is a key project that our societies seek to advance. Consequently, scientists are held to be more prototypical of this project than others. They thus engender greater admiration, respect and obedience due to the fact that what scientists represent is precisely what we are seeking for ourselves (self-interest, by proxy). In essence, we can expect that the more prototypical the authority (i.e., the stronger the match between projected and endorsed ethos) the higher the expected obedience. Both the findings from Milgram's experiments as well as those from the Utrecht studies are in line with predictions derived from this approach.

Conclusion

In the previous chapter we saw that unlike chimpanzees, children in Whiten, Horner & de Waal's (2005) experiment obeyed the experimenter and copied the entire action sequence fully. They engaged in a ritual, and did this even if they could see (just as well as chimpanzees) that some actions they were executing were completely unnecessary to obtaining the reward. We can argue that just like participants in Asch's (1951, 1956) line experiments, the children in Whiten, Horner & de Waal's (2005) study put their private convictions aside and followed instructions as com-manded. In this way, just like Milgram's (1963, 1974) experimental sub-jects, they obeyed the experimenter in good faith and executed the procedure that was requested of them.

On the other hand, we have seen in this chapter how children do not obey commands blindly. Laupa & Turiel (1986) demonstrated that chil-dren show appraisal of authority including consideration of role, age and morality, thus distinguishing hierarchy of power from that of authority. This seemingly stands in contrast with Whiten, Horner & de Waal's (2005) findings, where children demonstrated obedience in a dilemma with efficiency. We would like to argue that the human capacity for obedience does not contradict, but rather rests on, such cognitive flexibility. This is supported by Kruglanski's (1989; 2010) theory of lay epistemics, which purports that a motivational **need for cognitive closure** obtains the seizing and freezing of an idea that cuts short the search for alternatives and permits the start of action. Were humans incapable or deprived of cognitive closure, cognition would loop in a never-ending search for a better course of action; humans would forever examine better options of what to do next, and never get to doing anything. We argue that experimental observations of obedience have tapped characteristic behavioural outcomes when cognitive closure is outsourced to the epistemic authority of the source of the command.

We contend that cognitive flexibility does not mean that human beings should not be expected to obey. Rather, it means that humans are careful about the authority they choose to obey and when they do, they do so in a manner that aligns their behaviour with the prevalent norm. This explains the higher rates of obedience observed in the Utrecht studies. Human subjects are seemingly inclined to obey commands from authoritative sources they deem legitimate, and to execute actions they deem morally justified. The question of what is legitimate and moral is settled by recourse to prevalent group norms. We have seen in the previous chapter how human beings are inclined to follow group norms in making behavioural decisions (Kim & Markus, 1999). Obeying pertinent commands is part of the story of participating in a social group; it is a way of obtaining cognitive closure by other means. The groups we participate in, whose norms we enact in our own behaviour, confer on us social identities that are prescriptive and that put us in concert with some and against some others (Abrams & Hogg, 1990; Hogg & Reid, 2006). We contend that obedience is a corollary phenomenon of this basic relational tendency (see Box 6.2).

In this chapter, we have seen how authority serves social influence purposes. We can think of authority as a third way for resolving disputes between two extremes. True authority does rely on violence, although the possibility of sanctions against disobedience may be merely implied in commands, in particular when power and competence authority overlap. On the other hand, even without violence, authority is not quite deliberation either. It neither seeks dialogical engagement with an alternative perspective nor does it seek compliance. Authority does not make recourse to a request or some other form of persuasive appeal, which we discuss in the next chapter, but uses commands to ensure conformity with the status quo. Authority means taking someone's word for it, and needs no further argument.

Box 6.2 Obedience in the real world: wearing the veil

The Islamic veil has been a subject of controversy in many Western societies that have debated its public representation and its role in modern secular society. On the one hand, the Islamic veil is associated with freedom of religious worship. On the other hand, many perceive it to be an object of female oppression. Women who cover themselves one way or another are held to do so in obedience of male chauvinist expectations. Wagner, Sen, Permanadeli & Howarth (2012) investigated Muslim women's views on wearing the veil in two countries: Indonesia and India. Their findings reported stark differences between the two countries.

In Indonesia, a Muslim majority country, the veil is not contested in the same way it is in Western societies. Women in Indonesia reported that they wore the veil for convenience, that is, to shield themselves from the weather, to hide embarrassing white hair, for fashion (where the veil is perceived as an accessory) and modesty (in choosing what attire to wear in public). By contrast, in India, which is a Muslim minority country, women reported wearing the veil for religious reasons as well as in opposition to stereotypes and discrimination. In India, the veil was perceived as a symbol of affirmation and resistance to endemic prejudice. Neither in Indonesia nor in India did women report wearing the veil because they were expressly requested or commanded to; respondents did not wear the veil in obedience. In a country where the veil is uncontested, women reported wearing the veil because this was what the norm was and women could behave in normative ways without requiring overt justification. By contrast, in a Muslim minority country, justification was provided in terms of identity concerns and freedom of religious belonging. Rather than a symbol of blind religious obedience, the veil symbolised the opposite – resistance to societal pressure to uncover oneself. Therefore, what seems to be obedience from one point of view is effectively affirmative when viewed from another perspective.

Concerning as it may seem, the use of authority is a feature of any society. In democratic societies, for instance, authority is exercised by the judiciary who apply the country's laws. It is used in turn by the armed forces, who execute judicial commands. Our societies, even democratic ones, could not function if the people appointed to positions of power (Chapter 3) did not also command authority to execute on behalf of the group. In this way functioning societies need a dual hierarchy in partial overlap: that of power and that of special competences. We remind ourselves of Hannah Arendt's (1958/2012) famous dictum: *the absence of authority is not no authority, but tyranny.* Tyrants recognise no authorities beside themselves. Liberal societies need independent authorities to contain the powers that be (see Chapter 11). What this means to say is that authoritative influence is by no means a feature of despotic dictatorships, although despotic dictators certainly resort to authoritarian demands more or less indiscriminately.

It seems thus important to make a distinction between authoritative and authoritarian situations, where the former take legitimacy from sources other than violence (e.g., reputation, expertise, scripture), and the latter exclusively through the threat of violence. Furthermore, it is worth noting that authority is also subject to a fundamental attribution error, as we have seen elsewhere in this volume, by which it is personified in some great and celebrated leaders (see Chapter 3). Authority is perceived as stemming not from a relational position occupied by a person at some point in time, but out of the traits of the particular person who holds office at that time. In this way, iconic monuments are erected in celebration of the cult leader to buttress his or her authority. Many of us will remember the iconoclastic images of Iraqis tearing down Saddam Hussein's statue in Firdos Square following the lost Battle of Baghdad in 2003. The Mount Rushmore national memorial is an equally monumental celebration of presidential authority in the USA. The Mausoleum of Mao Zedong in Tiananmen Square in Beijing is another display of the authoritative legacy of Chairman Mao that still presides over the post–1979 'capitalist' China. These examples of authoritative displays are not limited to leaders in whom authority is personified. They extend to numerous other official roles: the pope sits on a grander chair than the surrounding cardinals in papal festivities; the queen sits on a high throne in opening up the British parliament; at law, the judge commands a central seating position as a function of the higher authority she commands relative to everyone else in the courtroom. In this way, authority is architectured into everyday life, installed to assimilate detractors and challengers (see Chapter 9 on artefacts). This architecture of authority, however, provides scope for iconoclastic intervention and redesign if prevalent norms are to be challenged (Lahlou, 2015).

So how does influence accrue from the exercise of authority? After all, there is also scope for resistance in social life. We address the topic of resistance as a modality of accommodation more fully in Chapter 9. It is worth noting that an increasing body of research highlights and examines the conditions which empowered 35 per cent to defy and resist the authoritative command in Milgram-type experiments, that is, the ordinary qualities of resistance (Rochat & Modigliani, 1996). The 'banality of evil' is juxtaposed with the 'ordinariness of goodness', when small everyday acts of help and little acts of defiance accumulate to resistance, which more or less organised can become a 'weapon of the weak', as demonstrated during wartime prosecutions, or in tax revolts in Malaysia (Scott, 1987). Packer (2008) showed that before the pain of the electroshocks became obvious, at 150-volts, for many 'teachers', a dilemma arose between the demands of the situation and their own right to withdraw, which allowed them to stop. Obedience to authority is conditional on consent. Hollander (2015), following a reanalysis of transcripts of the original Milgram experiments, identified several conversational strategies of resistance, including silent hesitation, imprecation, nervous laughter, addressing the learner directly, prompting the experimenter and attempting to stop. Gibson (2013) examined transcripts of the interactions between Milgram and his 'teacher' subjects, and shows that the experimental ritual far from being scripted was subject to continuous negotiations. Conversation analysis revealed that the situation did not only rely on authoritative command, but involved argumentative persuasion by the experimenter as well as choices on the side of the 'teacher'. And the very final prod that there was 'no choice but to continue' (in the light of science) highlighted the very choice situation which allowed 'teachers' to get out.

At this point, however, it is worth noting that the exercise of authority also relies on the transmission of an uncorrupted and unmediated message, in high fidelity fashion; it tries to undercut interpretation on the side of the receiver of the command message. Messages imparted from a position of authority do not require private conviction, similar to persuasive appeals, which we discuss in the next chapter. Like conformity, authoritative obedience facilities public acceptance and execution of a command. Authority does not seek conversion, it simply seeks compliance. In the previous chapter we have seen how Asch's finding that people could display conformity in public whilst retaining private reservations was highly insightful. The fact that individuals do the same in the face of authority, however, comes as no surprise. Authority functions by assimilation to an existing project or common sense, by defending, upholding and enforcing prevalent social norms in the face of dissent. Another way to deal with dissent in the social domain is to appeal directly to individuals' private convictions. This is the modality of persuasion, to which we now turn.

In Essence

From an early age, human beings are capable of a complex situational appraisal of authority that includes consideration of age, social position and moral criteria when deciding whether to obey a direct command.

Once socialised into their culture's prevalent norms, human beings demonstrate tendencies towards obedience of direct orders that are aligned with prevalent Common sense.

Leaders are able to exercise power and authority through the prestige conferred upon them by followers, who obey the leader to further their own interests as a function of group membership.

CHAPTER 7

Persuading and Convincing

phase	modality	function for CS	outcome	Mode 1 face-to-face inter-subjective	Mode 2 symbolic	Mode 3 artefact inter-objective

	Challege from conflict, dissonance, controversy arising from newcomers, homecomers, strangers or 'aliens'					
Phase 2	persuasion	Assimilation	compliance	request, appeal	micro-target	algorithm

Figure 7.1   A challenge and response model VI: persuading

This volume is concerned with the dynamic phenomenon of social influence. We argue that social influence manifests in different modalities, in circumstances where a social actor strives to influence another to obtain a particular course of events. Conceived in this way, it is easy to note the pervasive nature of social influence and how it permeates much of our routine everyday social interactions. We encounter as well as engage in social influence attempts all the time, simply by virtue of our participating in social life. 'Who will we hang out with this weekend? Who might we like to invite to tag along? Where will we hang out? What shall we do?' Such interactions may be considered trivial in the grand scheme of things and of a completely different order than, for instance, conformity or obedience scenarios. Yet these routine interactions afford us the possibility of persuading others to do our bidding, and vice versa. Persuasion, if successful, achieves social influence without the need for more coercive strategies. For this reason, persuasion has become the privileged modality of social influence research. It achieves certain outcomes without the need for hard power, by co-opting rather than coercing people to behave in desirable ways (Nye, 2004). Consequently, persuasion may be deemed to represent the primary modality by which soft power is exercised.

Persuasion works by getting somebody else to agree with us that our proposal is right and legitimate. It is worth making clear that persuasion is not akin to dialogue. In Habermasian terms (Habermas, 1981) persuasion is a form of **strategic action** for a purpose and measured on success. This contrasts with **communicative action** that seeks dialogue for the sake of outlining and achieving a common understanding and joint intentionality. Persuasion helps in changing an individual's private beliefs to match the desired behaviour the would-be persuader is seeking to obtain. It is also worth making clear that persuasion, as a social influence modality, is open to both majority and minority concerns. For a majority concern, persuasion helps the target *conform* to a normative expectation (its function is assimilation). As an influence modality, it is nevertheless distinguishable from conformity (where an individual displays a certain behaviour in public that contrasts with their private beliefs, see Chapter 5) due to the fact that persuasion serves to align public behaviour with a private belief that is the target of the influence attempt. For a minority concern, persuasion helps *convince* the majority target that an alternative proposition is fair enough (its function is accommodation). As detailed in our periodic table of social influence (see Chapter 10), persuasion is distinguishable between majority and minority concerns in its targeted outcome: to conform or to convince.

In any case, persuasion involves an instance of communication where some agent pitches a designed message to an audience that is intended to alter the audience's behaviour in a determined direction, without recourse to violence. In this chapter, we will examine the study of persuasion in psychology. We start by looking at a research programme that catalysed the search for moderators of persuasion, before delving into the matter of which cognitive processes lead to successful persuasion. We will also consider a range of critiques that have been levelled at the dominant persuasion paradigm. We conclude this chapter by visiting the role persuasion plays as an influence modality regulating normative action both in terms of assimilation (seeking compliance with existing norms) as well as accommodation (to convince about shifting norms and standards).

Needless to say, persuasion is no recent discovery of social psychology. To the contrary, in the 'arts of persuasion' it has been known for over 2,000 years as 'rhetoric', or the skilled practice of gauging for any particular situation the best available means to sway a public audience (Aristotle; fourth century BCE). Textbooks on persuasion make reference to this history, but usually relegate 'rhetoric' to a pre-scientific past that is superseded by the short history of contemporary experimental research into persuasion (e.g., Perloff, 2014, p. 39). We would argue that such a view of the history of persuasion widely undervalues the significance of rhetorical traditions for social influence. We take from classical rhetoric several ideas on persuasion as a modality of social influence: (a) the focus on non-violence in human interaction; (b) the analysis of a three-factor model including 'Logos' or argument, 'Pathos' or emotional appeal and 'Ethos' or character of the speaker, which correspond simultaneously with cognitive, emotional and community-based processes; (c) the recognition of different genres in deliberation of future actions, apportioning blame for past actions and celebrating community building in the present; for present times, we might add advertising for the marketing of products; (d) a sensibility for the use of non-literal and visual language including metaphors and other framing tropes; (e) that persuasion must start from existing attitudes including beliefs, images and values, known as 'Doxa' or common sense; it thus requires local knowledge; (f) inheritance of a polemical tension between dealing with uncertainty under time pressure (true rhetoric) and exploiting the weaknesses of an audience (Sophistry, Eristic, 'fake news'), and finally (g) that rhetoric flourishes in times of freedom of debate and public reasoning (see Barthes, 1988 [1965]; Bauer & Gläveanu, 2011; Billig, 1987; Franzosi & Vicari, 2018; McGuire, 1985; Meyer, 2008). Much current discussion of persuasion either takes too much for granted or falls variously short on these points, and therefore opens itself to justifiable criticism; we will return to this point in the next section with regard to lay epistemology and argumentation.

The Search for Moderators

Each day, every one of us encounters a bewildering array of persuasive appeals. From highly engaging advertisements on television; to posters and billboards that catch our eyes with a hot picture associated with the latest 'must-have' items; to street sellers pouncing on us to provide details of the latest 'special offer' that we cannot afford to miss; to the algorithm-generated Facebook adverts delivered to your screen especially for you based on your personal like-history. In our contemporary societies, persuasive appeals are certainly big business.

Yet, we do not stop and succumb to every persuasive appeal that we encounter. Some of them grab our attention for a short while, some others we engage with and process, and most others we readily ignore. This begs the question of which persuasive appeals are successful and which aren't. Some persuasive appeals seem to work better than others. There are also individual differences in that a persuasive appeal may be persuasive for one person but not for another. In any case, persuasion seems to flow from the source of the persuasive appeal to the receiver, who stands to be persuaded. Framed in this way, the natural question that ensues is how to achieve persuasion to maximum effect. In other words, what features of source, message and audience facilitate successful persuasion? This question takes us to the heart of how persuasion has been empirically investigated in the psychological sciences.

Lasswell's (1948) model of communication served to set the agenda for early persuasion research. Lasswell claimed that a communicative act involves a message that is transmitted from a source to an audience, over some medium, and that achieves some or other effect. This conception updates an age-old medieval analysis of action narratives (*quis, quid, ubi, quibus auxiliis, cur, quomodo, quando*; Latin for 'who, what, where, with whose help, why, how and when'). Lasswell suggested that communicative acts can be captured in the following formula:

Who says what, by which channel, to whom, with what effect?

Carl Hovland, Lasswell's colleague at Yale, led a systematic research programme to identify **moderators** of persuasion structured by Lasswell's formula (Hovland, Janis & Kelley, 1953). This catalysed persuasion research inasmuch as it served to break down a complex concern into a subset of variables, each of which could be investigated experimentally. In other words, variable features of the source (ethos or character), the message (logos or argument) and the audience (pathos or appeal targets) could influence the extent to which a communicative act succeeded in being persuasive – the effect (Box 7.1).

The search for moderators of persuasion has proceeded apace since Hovland's original experiments, sustained by corporate interests seeking a silver bullet to market products. In particular, this research programme has demonstrable utility in advertising, where stringing the right features of an advert together and pitching it to the right audience is held to potentially provide the product with a competitive edge. The moderators of the persuasion programme are often described as a *hypodermic needle model* – like a hypodermic needle that delivers a substance from a syringe to an organism, a persuasive appeal (as per Lasswell's model) proceeds linearly from source to audience with no interaction and no feedback. Through market research, advertisers seek to identify what characteristics of the source, what features of the message and what channel of communication will prove to be persuasive with which particular audience. Market segmentation ensures that persuasive appeals are tailored to particular audiences who have been identified as positively predisposed to yield to the appeal.

> ### Box 7.1 Moderators of persuasion
>
> *The search for moderators of persuasion has generated an extensive list of variable characteristics pertaining to (a) source, (b) message and (c) audience that facilitate persuasion and attitude change.*
>
> *Source characteristics: expert and trustworthy sources are more persuasive than non-experts (Hovland & Weiss, 1951); physically attractive sources are also more persuasive (Chaiken, 1979); sources that are similar to the audience (Brock, 1965) and those who command high status (Lefkowitz, Blake & Mouton, 1955) are more persuasive than their counterparts.*
>
> *Message characteristics: messages that present a clear conclusion (Hovland & Mandell, 1952), that adopt the use of imagery (Gregory, Cialdini & Carpenter, 1982), that link the content of a message to the audience's pre-existing beliefs (Cacioppo, Petty & Sidera, 1982), that present a two-sided argument with a refutation of the opposing position (Hovland, Lumsdaine & Sheffield, 1949), that arouse fear (Leventhal, Singer & Jones, 1965) or that are vivid (Nisbett & Ross, 1980) and messages that are not designed as persuasive appeals (Walster & Festinger, 1962) are generally more persuasive than other forms.*
>
> *Audience characteristics: audiences that are low in self-esteem (Janis, 1954), that perceive some level of self-threat (Kaplan & Krueger, 1999), that are in a state of sensory deprivation (Zubek, 1969) or that are distracted (Allyn & Festinger, 1961) are more easily persuaded.*

And yet, as we have discussed, we do not yield to every persuasive appeal that we encounter. At best, we yield sometimes. Most times we discard persuasive appeals that we encounter altogether; we are simply not persuaded. And at other times yet, we might push the matter aside to return to it later when we have occasion to consider it further. This raises the question whether persuasion may occur depending on the cognitive effort we exert in the process of considering a persuasive appeal; or whether we might be hapless victims in front of a well-designed advert that stands to persuade us unwittingly. The cognitive approach to persuasion, to which we now turn, sought an understanding of *how* persuasion occurs in the human mind.

Information Processing Approach

Rather than questioning what features of an appeal may prove more or less persuasive, the information processing approach to persuasion seeks to understand how persuasion occurs. In this programme, persuasion is not understood to be a function of specific features that typify the appeal, or its source, or its audience, in some objective sense. Persuasion, rather, is understood to occur as a function of how the persuasive appeal is cognitively processed. This approach investigates what happens in the mind once a particular persuasive appeal has been perceived. It seeks to understand how, once a person is exposed to a particular message, cognitive processing leads down a persuasion route in some instances or leads to the individual being left unpersuaded in others.

Two predominant models have been proposed in this tradition that are subsumed under the general rubric of **dual process models**. The **Elaboration Likelihood Model** (ELM), proposed by Petty & Cacioppo (1986), and the **Heuristic-Systematic Model** (HSM), proposed by Eagly & Chaiken (1993, 1998), both posit two routes to persuasion.

The first route is through a deep processing route. This is known as the central route in ELM, or the systematic route in HSM. In this processing mode, a message perceived by an individual is consciously attended to and rationally processed in terms of its core features. Using this mode, the individual attends to the features of the persuasive appeal and to details about the product. This is cognitively appraised and reasons for and reasons against persuasion are mustered by the individual. Persuasion takes place when the balance tips in favour of the appeal after a cognitive evaluation process has taken place. The deep processing route is what comes into play when an individual, for instance, considers the purchase of a product in terms of its salient features and how these may compare to an alternative.

For instance, say you are in the market for a smartphone. You are walking along the street when you see an advert of the latest release that promises twice as fast download speeds, a bigger screen, a longer lasting battery and other features that seemingly surpass competition. You proceed to check these details with those of competing models and you decide that these are indeed valuable and worth the asking price. You make the purchase. In such a situation, you have been persuaded through the deep processing route. You have attended to the relevant information, you have processed it and you have emerged convinced enough to make a purchase. Should you be questioned by somebody else about your choice, you are able to furnish an account (Harré & Secord, 1973) that justifies your decision. At times, however, one processes a persuasive appeal in such detail and remains unconvinced. Perhaps the product is not really better than the competition, perhaps the feature marketed is not as important as it is made out to be, and so on. Even when persuasion fails, if the persuasive appeal has been processed through the central/systematic route, the individual will be able to furnish an account justifying the outcome.

The central/systematic route is one way persuasion can take place. Another way is through a shallow processing route. This is termed the peripheral route in ELM and the heuristic route in HSM. The shallow processing route is used when, for one reason or another, we are not in a position to process a persuasive appeal deeply but somehow the appeal is still attended to and cognitively processed, due to some tangential feature. Again, let us assume that you are in the market for a smartphone. You are walking down the street going somewhere and you see an advert for a newly released smartphone in a shop window. This time the advert presents no particular details for you to consider, which is just as well as you are late for a meeting and have no time to stop and check things out right now. You merely glance at the advert whilst walking briskly on. Actually, the reason you glanced at the advert at all is that it portrays a celebrity you fancy, standing in an exquisite pose with the new smartphone. You are more attuned to the celebrity features of the advert than the smartphone ones. As stated, you are running late and you scurry right past. This does not mean that persuasion did not take place. Rather, it could have happened through the peripheral/heuristic route. This mode of processing is shallow and does not require our full and undivided conscious attention. The peripheral/heuristic route processes information that is picked up sensorially due to some vivid feature, but that is intuitively relegated as not critical to the task at hand. In such instances, persuasion could occur non-consciously.

What happens in these instances is that a tangential feature, whilst irrelevant, is processed by our mind alongside other information in such a way that could generate a pairing between the object of the persuasive appeal and the irrelevant feature. This pairing of information is known as *classical conditioning* and leads to some neutral stimulus, such as a smartphone model, being positively appraised through its pairing with a positive stimulus, such as a celebrity you admire. A cognitive association between the two objects (smartphone and celebrity) is generated in our mind that sees the individual becoming positively inclined to a particular smartphone brand. This inclination, generated in the process of glancing at an advert whilst scampering down a busy road, may yet make all the difference when the individual stops to make a purchase at some later point. The individual might not be able to explain why they like this smartphone over some other; they just do. In such a case, persuasion has ensued through the peripheral/heuristic route.

The reason why some seemingly peripheral features have such power over our cognitive processing is that human cognition is biased in determined directions. Cognition is biased to attend to particular features in our environment over others, and to process such information in characteristic ways that have helped our ancestral survival. This biased cognitive processing is termed **ecological rationality** (Todd & Gigerenzer, 2000). Cognitive biases, 'fast and frugal' and rooted in our evolved genetic baggage, remain active in human cognition today such that certain features of a persuasive appeal may be naturally attended to, even if only nonconsciously, whereas some others are not processed at all. This is precisely what Hovland's programme tapped into, as we have seen, when physically attractive communicators were found to be more persuasive (Box 7.1). Now think of a street seller calling out to you to introduce some product, which you politely decline. Well, their flair may still have done the trick by activating the peripheral/heuristic processing mode. It might have generated enough attitude change, however slight, for you to be positively inclined to persuasion the next time you do have occasion to process the item deeply. In situations where tangential features come into play, persuasion may occur through the peripheral/heuristic route.

To repeat, the information processing models build on the moderators programme we reviewed. Essentially, if the tangential elements of a persuasive appeal are designed effectively, the appeal could still activate the peripheral/heuristic route and persuasion might still occur. Human beings can thus be persuaded in either of two ways. They can be influenced by good solid arguments and adequate information that what is presented to them is what they actually need. Or, they can be influenced through tangential features that are catchy and sweet but that have nothing to do with the product itself. Much advertising relies on the latter.

There are some differences between the ELM and the HSM models (see Eagly & Chaiken, 1993). However, there are also plenty of commonalities. Firstly, both models identify two routes to persuasion. Secondly, both models assume that the central route leads to more persistent and resistant attitude change. Thirdly, both models assume that engagement of the central mode depends on motivation. That is, an individual needs to be sufficiently motivated to expend cognitive effort on the appeal for the central/systematic route to be activated. Fourthly, both models argue that either route can be persuasive and that both routes can be activated simultaneously. Adverts can therefore be designed with this in mind, presenting some detail for central/systematic route processing along with catchy features for activating the peripheral/heuristic route at once.

Alongside the search for moderators programme, the information processing approach has furthered our understanding of when persuasive appeals might succeed as well as when they seemingly fail. An associated strand of work has examined situations of compliance. Rather than being actively persuaded one way or another, individuals may simply be invited to pursue a particular course of events even if this is not in line with their private inclinations. It is to this topic that we now turn.

Compliance

So far, we have seen how aside from more overt influence tactics such as obedience, changing somebody's behaviour could follow a persuasive appeal. This happens when the subject is persuaded to alter their attitude in line with some desirable response. The desired behaviour should then ensue as a function of attitude change. This assumption is rooted in Fritz Heider's (1958) balance of reciprocity model. Heider argues that human relations are essentially systemic and that our individual attitudes form part of a holistic orientation we adopt to the world around us. In the event that our attitudes towards some objects are not aligned with those held by significant others in our environment, we will experience **cognitive dissonance**. This is a state of discomfort that arises when our attitudes are misaligned, either with those of relevant others or with our own behaviours. Cognitive dissonance is a motivating drive; we are motivated to change either our attitudes or our behaviours to reduce the discomfort and restore balance (Figure 7.2).

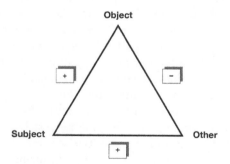

Figure 7.2 Heider's (1958) balance of reciprocity model

In the previous example, the subject is positively orientated towards another individual as well as towards an object of mutual concern. The other, however, is negatively inclined towards the object. Heider's balance theory suggests that both subject and other will experience cognitive dissonance and be motivated to change one of their attitudes to restore balance. This will either involve a change of attitude between the individuals concerned, or a change of attitude by one individual relative to the object. Let us illustrate with an example. Suppose Fred, the subject, has made a new friend, Bret. Fred and Bret get along very well and they both like each other. Fred is also a staunch climate change activist and positively inclined towards climate change measures. In the future, he plans on getting himself an electric vehicle. Bret, on the other hand, is a petrol-head and whilst sensitive to climate change issues, he would never consider an electric vehicle as this, to his mind, would be no fun. At this point, both Fred and Bret will experience cognitive dissonance that will motivate them to change some attitudes to restore balance. This can proceed in one of two ways. Fred or Bret might change their attitudes towards electric vehicles. Fred could decide that he doesn't want an electric vehicle badly enough because, really, they're not much fun. Or, Bret might decide that even though they're no fun, electric vehicles are a good thing. However, if neither of them is able to change their attitude towards the object, for whatever reason (maybe there are third parties bearing more influence on their attitude to the object in question), then Fred and Bret will be motivated to change their attitudes towards each other and they might end up disliking each other after all.

Heider's balance theory has served to advance a research programme concerning compliance. This can be considered as a different form of persuasion inasmuch as it serves to precipitate an attitudinal change that ensures that the right behaviour will follow. Sometimes, all that is needed for this to occur is a simple request. Instead of being forced, commanded or persuaded to engage in some particular behaviour, compliance can also be induced by pitching a *compliance request* in certain characteristic ways. Cialdini (1984) claims that six compliance principles constitute the six weapons of persuasion that maximise the influence of appeals: reciprocity (acting in kind); commitment (inducing an affirmative decision before the final contract); social proof (validating the request by reference to widespread behaviours); liking (inducing positive sentiments); authority (referring to an epistemic source); and scarcity (inducing an impression of declining opportunities) (see Box 7.2).

Box 7.2 Compliance tactics

Just as the search for moderators enables the design of adverts that maximise the potential for a successful persuasive appeal, compliance research seeks to identify ways to maximise the potential for successful persuasion (Cialdini & Goldstein, 2004):

Foot-in-the-door: This procedure involves asking for a small request first that the subject will be inclined to accept, and to then escalate to a larger request once the subject is engaged. The first request is intended simply to engage the subject. The subject having complied to this request already, the probability for full compliance is higher than presenting the second request to the subject on its own (Burger, 1999).

Door-in-the-face: This procedure is the inverse of the foot-in-the-door. A large response that is meant to be refuted is presented first and, when refuted, the subject is offered a more reasonable alternative. Having witnessed the other scale their business down, the subject will be more inclined to comply than had the second offer been presented first (Cialdini et al., 1975).

Low-ball: This involves presenting an unrealistically good deal to induce compliance and to then revise the deal to a less attractive offering. Having already committed, the subject is less likely to reject the new deal than had it been presented faithfully in the first instance (Cialdini, Cacioppo, Bassett & Miller, 1978).

That's-not-all: This tactic is the inverse of the low-ball procedure. It involves presenting a somewhat unattractive deal that is made progressively better by adding 'extras' before the subject commits either way. By the time the real package has been offered in full, the subject is led to perceive better value so that compliance with the genuine full package is increased (Burger, 1986).

Forced Compliance

Heider's balance of reciprocity model laid the groundwork for a very interesting experiment on cognitive dissonance. Festinger & Carlsmith (1959) hypothesised that if an individual is forced to engage in a negatively valenced behaviour, the cognitive dissonance that arises should be settled by the subject changing their attitude spontaneously. Festinger started by inviting subjects to an experiment that attracted a payout at the end. After completing the task set by the experimenter, subjects would receive either (a) $1 or (b) $20 for their services. The task set by the experimenters was for the subject to sit at a table, take spools from a bucket and place them on a tray on the table, then take the tray and empty the spools back into the bucket, and repeat the same procedure for thirty minutes. After that, subjects were instructed to turn a series of pegs a quarter turn each, and again, to repeat the procedure over and over again. The idea behind the experiment was to get subjects to engage in boring tasks that were negatively valenced.

After completing the tasks but before they were free to go, subjects were asked if they could help recruit some other students for the same experiment by pitching a motivational appeal to them, such as telling them that the experiment was fun, that it held scientific merit, and so on. In essence, genuine subjects who had just engaged in highly boring tasks were asked to recruit other subjects to do the same task by framing the experiment in positive terms. Payment was conditional on this attempt. Following their effort at recruiting other subjects, genuine subjects were asked to fill in a questionnaire that measured the extent to which they themselves had actually enjoyed the task, the perceived scientific importance of the experiment and the likelihood that they would participate in a similar experiment in future.

The findings confirmed the experimenters' hypotheses. Relative to the control group and the high-payout condition ($20), subjects in the low-payout condition ($1) reported that they enjoyed the experiment more, that they perceived more scientific merit and that they would participate in a similar experiment in future. The researchers concluded that subjects in the low-payout condition experienced more cognitive dissonance than subjects in the high-payout condition. The latter justified their efforts at tricking fellow subjects to undertake a boring experimental task by the size of the payout – $20 was worth the lie. By contrast, those in the low-payout condition did not get paid enough for this. Consequently, to resolve the dissonance between doing something boring and selling it as something interesting to others, the subjects changed their attitudes towards the task and gave it a positive appraisal. Festinger & Carlsmith (1959) demonstrated that when cognitive dissonance is triggered, individuals are motivated to restore balance and if they cannot change their behaviour, they will change their attitudes accordingly.

Non-forced Compliance (Nudge Theory)

The less leads to more principle that is at work in Festinger and Carlsmith's cognitive dissonance experiment also underlies non-forced compliance, or **nudge theory**. In their experiment, individuals in the low-payout condition reported more positive attitudes towards the task than those in the high-payout condition – less reward leads to more attitudinal change. Similarly, in non-forced compliance, small changes in behaviour are held to have wider implications than radical ones.

Nudge theory received widespread acclaim following Thaler & Sunstein's (2008) publication as choice preserving decision architecture. Thaler's contribution in the domain of behavioural finance earned him the Nobel Prize in Economics in 2017. In essence, nudging involves a process of choice architecture that makes certain options more feasible and easier to pick than other, less desirable options. Nudging can be educational involving information, warning, labels or reminders; or non-educational involving defaults, or ordering of items on a choice menu. Opting for the non-desirable option is not prohibited or punished; it is just made more pragmatically difficult than the socially desired option. Policy makers find this very exciting; they have extended their tool box beyond laws and fiscal incentives to psychological 'tricks'. The behaviours involved may only be slightly shifted; individuals are not invited to make a full-blown commitment to some overarching enterprise. For instance, having a ready selection of fruit around the home helps avoid snacking on unhealthy items by making the choice of fruit an easy option. Another example is the default option offered on websites that makes it easier (by default) to pick the desired response. In making slight choices in determined directions, individuals end up aligning their attitudes with the overarching enterprise by engaging in successive low-cost behaviours along the way. At every step, attitude change is achieved that aligns the individual's attitude with the behavioural option chosen for the sake of simplicity. Relying on cheap and easy interventions ensures that resistance is avoided and that desirable behaviour is achieved in the end, a nudge at a time. In this way, nudge theory bears a striking resemblance to Skinner's (1953) notion of behavioural **shaping**. This involves rewarding successive approximations of a desired behaviour and at every step, rewarding only that behaviour that is in line with the end goal. Nudge theory, however, does not rely on positive reinforcement to achieve behavioural change. Rather, nudging relies on the power of compliance to change discrepant attitudes. However, nudge theory as behavioural shaping dodges the question of who determines the socially desirable behaviour; one would assume that this direction should not itself be nudged or shaped.

Lay Epistemic Theory

The persuasion research paradigm has made great strides in our understanding of how and when a persuasive appeal or a compliance request may prove successful or, more accurately, what characteristics of appeals tend to be more or less persuasive. The fact that human beings differ from one another, that is, that humankind is marked by *individual differences* where not all elements of a species are alike, also means that persuasion and compliance involve a subjective element that does not necessarily correspond to anything objective in any of the elements in persuasion. What we mean here is not only that what might persuade one might dissuade another, but also that what might be peripheral/heuristic to one might be central/systematic to another.

Kruglanski's (1989) **lay epistemic theory** provides an alternative conceptualisation of the dual-process persuasion paradigm based on three criteria: (a) the need for cognitive closure; (b) the unimodel of persuasion; and (c) epistemic authority (Kruglanski, Orehek, Dechesne & Pierro, 2010). Kruglanski's point of departure is that social interactions are always diffused with prior knowledge that interlocutors bring into their communication as background or frame of reference. This knowledge has two dimensions: on the one hand it is a belief that is active in the individual's mind; on the other hand it is part of a broader network of meanings, known as social representations (Sammut & Howarth, 2014). The distinction is analogous to Saussure's (1916) demarcation of language (*langue*) from its individual counterpart, speech (*parole*).

According to Kruglanski, knowledge is represented in the mind as a syllogistic conclusion where evidence (E) warrants a claim (C) considering existing knowledge (if E, then C, considering backing B). In other words, a minor premise supports a conclusion on the basis of a major premise rooted in a background of knowledge. The key here is that existing knowledge which backs the inference is more or less activated. New knowledge is inferred once a cognitive search and evaluation of evidence is terminated. This occurs when the evidence considered is deemed sufficiently relevant by the subject. In other words, a parameter of *subjective relevance* defines how pertinent evidence E is to reaching conclusion C, depending on existing knowledge. The process is regulated by a motivational need for cognitive closure; a socio-cognitive bias that serves to truncate a search for alternatives that is potentially infinite, therefore cognitively costly for the individual. The need for cognitive closure serves to 'seize and freeze' relevant evidence, justifying action. Without cognitive closure, the individual is paralysed by a never-ending cognitive search for other, potentially superior alternatives. The endless search results in inaction. Once cognitive closure is achieved, however, the individual can proceed with action. The higher the need for closure in an individual, the stronger the motivation to terminate the cognitive search for alternatives once some available evidence has been deemed relevant to some determined conclusion.

Framed in this way, the need for cognitive closure fits with the notion of *satisficing*, which is the tendency to terminate a search for alternatives once a set of minimum requirements has been fulfilled (Simon, 1956); the notion of *motivated reasoning*, that is, the tendency to search for evidence confirming our pre-existing beliefs (Kunda, 1990); as well as with the notion of *naive realism*, that is, the tendency to consider evidence that matches our pre-existing beliefs as accurate and disconfirming evidence as biased (Ross & Ward, 1996). These socio-cognitive tendencies are also associated with cognitive dissonance, reviewed earlier. According to Kruglanski, when the need for cognitive closure is high in an individual, lack of closure is experienced as aversive and stressful. The individual is thus motivated to truncate the search for alternatives and to derive a relevant conclusion to ward off the discomfort (Kruglanski, Orehek, Dechesne & Pierro, 2010).

At the individual level, the need for closure affects one's attitudes and beliefs. At the interpersonal level, it affects one's communications with others. Studies have shown that individuals high in need of cognitive closure tend to resist persuasive appeals once they have formed a firm opinion about the topic, but are more susceptible to persuasion when they have not (Kruglanski, Webster & Klem, 1993). Moreover, high need for closure individuals tend to tailor their own messages to an audience less than low need for closure individuals, resulting in less effective communications (Richter & Kruglanski, 1999).

As we have seen, cognitive closure is achieved when the cognitive search for alternatives is terminated following the identification of evidence that is deemed pertinent to a conclusion. Kruglanski departs from dual process theories, which postulate rule-based-deliberative and automatic-heuristic processes, arguing for a unimodel assuming that all persuasion is rule-based (Kruglanski & Thompson, 1999). This suggests that what counts as relevant evidence to a conclusion is relative to a listener; it is a subjective undertaking. According to a dual process configuration, what counts as central (triggered by arguments) or peripheral evidence (triggered cues) is an objective feature of the persuasive message itself. Kruglanski goes one step further by arguing that what is evidence depends on the attending individual (be it tangible information or tangential cues) and judged on a continuum of subjective relevance. The bottom line is not whether a message feature triggers central or peripheral processing, but whether it is relevant to the listener to reach a conclusion or not considering his or her total situation of knowledge and motivation. What is a cue for an expert is rich information for a novice; what is noise for a novice is signal for an expert. And individuals rely on easy-to-process information when their need for cognitive closure is high, whilst they also entertain hard-to-process evidence when their need for cognitive closure is low and the information appears to be more relevant to the judgement task at hand. According to Kruglanski, it is the extent of information processing devoted to some evidence that determines attitude change, rather than objective features of the information itself; rich or poor stimulus information reflects the state of the beholder. Given ample cognitive resources (i.e., low need for closure), more relevant information results as more persuasive than less relevant information. When cognitive resources are limited (i.e., high need for closure), the easy-to-process information (which falls above the relevance threshold) has greater impact than hard-to-process information (Kruglanski, Orehek, Dechesne & Pierro, 2009).

According to the 'unimodel of persuasion', any type of information stands to exert influence if and when judged relevant by the situated subject (Kruglanski & Thompson, 1999). One type of evidence that individuals typically consider in a search for alternatives is other people's perspectives and position. Elsewhere we have identified this tendency as the *social check* (Asch, 1952) (see Chapter 5). In lay epistemic theory, other's opinions are judged as relevant, or otherwise, depending on the *epistemic authority* they command. This is akin to the notion of source credibility in the moderators to persuasion paradigm (Hovland & Weiss, 1951) (Box 7.1), or what classical rhetoric identified as Ethos. The epistemic authority assigned to some sources may be highly powerful to the point of overriding other forms of evidence and exerting a determinative influence on the individual. We have seen in Chapter 3 how prototypical members of a group command a disproportionate amount of influence relative to less prototypical members due to social identification processes; but to a community, prototypicality is relative. Any Imam might have this authority in his mosque, but it does not necessarily extend beyond, depending on his reputation. We have also seen in Chapter 6 how surprisingly high levels of obedience accrue when commands are conveyed by a legitimate and authoritative voice. Lay epistemic theory contends that knowledge is socially constructed and that other people's views bear a significant influence on our own frame of reference, particularly those provided by individuals we hold in high regard in our community.

Argumentation

We have seen how lay epistemic theory proposes that persuasion takes place as a result of inferential rules that are implicitly adopted by individuals when they consider the relevance of some piece of evidence for warranting a certain conclusion. One thing that we have not explicitly addressed so far is the mechanics of persuasion, that is, what is involved in successful instances of persuasion. We have alluded that the target for persuasion is not manifest behaviour, at least not directly. Unlike obedience, for instance, which aims at obtaining a certain behaviour regardless of the opinions and beliefs the subject holds with regards to the behaviour itself, persuasion works by precipitating an attitude change that is considered to be a pre-cursor to actual behaviour. The process has been systematised in the **theory of planned behaviour**, which contends that the influence attitudes exert on behaviour is moderated by behavioural intentions (Ajzen, 1985, 1991; Fishbein & Ajzen, 1975). Persuasion targets attitudes about behaviour that are used to form behavioural intentions, to eventually precipitate behavioural change. It follows that a successful persuasive appeal will change an underlying attitude that will, in turn, modify behavioural intentions and responses.

Attitudes can be broadly defined as evaluations of attitude objects. Consequently, attitudes provide a positive or negative inclination towards something based on images and beliefs. If I have a positive attitude towards smoking, I will be inclined to form behavioural intentions to smoke. If, through a persuasive appeal, my positive attitude towards smoking changes and becomes negative, then I will be inclined to *not* form intentions to smoke. A successful persuasive appeal is one that successfully alters an individual's underlying attitude towards something to make a certain behaviour more likely to follow. This represents the silver bullet approach to behavioural change. In other words, if you could string a persuasive appeal together using the right set of features that appeal to a particular individual, attitude change will follow as a function of the persuasive appeal. So, for instance, if you were after helping individuals to stop smoking and you found that fear appeals are more likely to be persuasive, then one could present fear-arousing messages to smokers (such as by portraying pictures of damaged lungs on cigarette packs) to change their attitude towards smoking from a positive to a negative one, such that this could subsequently alter intentions and actual behaviour in future. Persuasion, therefore, is a matter of presenting the right features to the right individuals to pre-cipitate attitude change, and the rest should follow.

Researchers working in the persuasion paradigm have long noted that individuals demonstrate tendencies to resist persuasive appeals, however. For instance, Brehm (1966) noted that when individuals suspect a nudge or targeted persuasive attempt they demonstrate *reactance*, that is, neg-ative attitude change that restores the individual's sense of agency in the face of constraints. Cialdini & Petty (1979) noted that *forewarning*, that is, prior knowledge of a persuasive intent, stimulates resistance to per-suasion. And McGuire (1964) showed that weak counter-attitudinal arguments provide *inoculation*, that is, they help build resistance to stronger arguments presented at a later point. The US Biotechnology Industry Association BIO campaigned explicitly to 'inoculate' the American public against arguments over genetically modified (GM) crops and foods drifting over from Europe, where there has been a moratorium on GM foods for human consumption since the mid-1990s (Bauer, 2015).

According to Billig (1987, 1991), many persuasive appeals fail due to the fact that the implicit model for attitude change underlying the persua-sion paradigm does not represent the full story. The theory of planned behaviour suggests that alongside attitudes, *perceived behavioural control* (i.e., the extent to which an individual believes they are able to alter their behaviour) and *subjective norms* (i.e., the extent to which an individual believes significant others approve of the behavioural change) also influ-ence *behavioural intentions*, such that attitude change on its own might not be sufficient to bring about behavioural change. Billig, however, further argues that the reliance on attitudes in precipitating behavioural changes misses two critical points: (a) that individuals are agentic, and (b) that attitudes include a social positioning dimension.

Billig argues that a well-designed persuasive appeal might not deliver due to the fact that for persuasion to actually occur, the thinking subject needs to be *persuaded*. In other words, the subject needs to emerge convinced about the *content* of the message, which might or might not have something to do with the form the persuasive appeal takes. According to Billig, the content of the persuasive argument itself might make all the difference. Billig recovers here the ancient notion of invention of argu-ments, or Logos. Consequently, no silver bullet to persuasion can ever be identified because persuasion involves a thinking subject coming to agree with the content of the appeal regardless of how this has been presented.

Let us go back to a fear-arousing appeal presented on a cigarette pack intended to alter positive attitudes towards smoking. However susceptible a given individual is to fear-arousing appeals, that individual needs to emerge convinced that smoking is actually wrong and undesirable. It will not do for an individual to become terrified of the prospect of smoking whilst maintaining that cigarette smoking is the most effective antidote to stress. If, in the individual's own experience, cigarette smoking is a coping strategy then the individual might subjectively disagree that smoking is bad overall, even if it kills, because its negative effects are compensated for by other benefits.

The process of agreeing or disagreeing with a particular clause, Billig proposes, is essentially a rhetorical exercise that involves the individual taking a stand for or against something. For the individual, the stand adopted must make sense regardless of how emotionally appealing the message is – the subject must come to agree with the content or argument of the appeal.

To put this another way, an individual may be sufficiently susceptible to a persuasive appeal to yield and adopt the suggested behaviour, for example, by consuming a certain chocolate bar. One could hardly expect, on the back of this sequence alone, that the same individual will yield to the same advertising features if the advert appeal was marketing something else, such as joining the marines and fighting for one's country. The individual could be yielding to one and resisting another for the simple fact that they agree that they know what chocolate is and that it is a good thing in the first instance, but they disagree that current wars being fought by one's country are legitimate. In other words, whether an individual yields to a persuasive appeal or otherwise depends also on the content of the message itself. For individuals to be persuaded, they must come to agree with the content of the message and this depends also on the social dimension of the individual's own beliefs.

This takes us to Billig's (1987, 1991) second point regarding the shortcomings of the persuasion paradigm. Like Kruglanski, Billig argues that individual attitudes have a social dimension; they are commonsensical relative to a communal frame of reference. Whilst persuasion seemingly occurs inside the individual mind through attitude change, the implications of attitude change demonstrate social bearing. This is due to the fact that attitudes position us relative to others on matters of controversy. Consequently, having a positive or a negative attitude towards something is not a neutral affair. It means that in the social realm, an individual will be positioned in agreement with some and in disagreement with others, and this bears consequences on one's *social identity*. It means that as a function of attitudes, individuals come to form part of one social group and become opposed to some others. Attitudes and attitude change are therefore consequential not only in terms of private behaviour alone, but also in forging alliances and opponents in wider networks. At the root of persuasion, therefore, lies the negotiation of the boundary between in-group and out-group. Attitude change is consequential in this regard.

Let us consider a recent example. In 2018, Nike ran an advertising campaign headlined by Colin Kaepernick. The caption used in the campaign read: 'Believe in something. Even if it means sacrificing everything'. A spokesman of the company said that this message was intended to introduce 'Just Do It', Nike's famous slogan, to a new generation. The campaign, however, backfired and Nike's share price fell in its wake. People resisted the message vociferously and many called for boycotting the brand altogether. The reason for the outcry was that Kaepernick, a San Francisco 49ers NFL player, had refused to stand for the national anthem, opting to kneel down instead to draw attention to police killings of African Americans in the United States. The public's reaction, in this case, clearly demonstrates that Nike consumers were not simply positively or negatively inclined to the product itself. Rather, their attitude was shaped by the social controversy surrounding the infamous NFL national anthem protests. Consumers of the brand understood that their choices positioned them on one side of the controversy.

For this reason, Billig (1987) goes on to call for studying the 'thinking society', arguing for a focus on argumentation and discourse that can help shed light on the positioning entailed in holding particular attitudes. He invites a concern with common sense that is held to underlie the taken-for-granted in persuasive appeals. In rhetorical terms (Bauer & Glăveanu, 2011), the argument (logos) and the appeal (pathos) are variables, but the third element (ethos), representing the common ground and frame of reference, is missing in the experimental persuasion paradigms due to it being taken for granted. In a sense, much persuasion research does take for granted and not make explicit its own conditions of possibility which lie in local common sense; the conclusions reached are therefore locally bound despite claims to scientific/universal validity. Consequently, persuasion research falls short in considering the question as to which arguments are possible and which not, given the common ground. Without such an understanding, it is difficult to comprehend how and why persuasive appeals succeed or fail. In other words, to understand persuasion one requires details of the social community that inheres in the act of holding and changing attitudes.

Billig's call has been addressed by social representations scholars that have elaborated a social marketing approach to persuasion (Lauri, 2008, 2015). This involves designing and delivering persuasive appeals following extensive study of social representations that are already in circulation. **Social representations** can be defined as systemic conceptions of relevant objects and events generated by social groups. They represent what a social group holds something to be. For instance, the common portrayal of Arab-Muslims as dangerous and close-minded is a prevalent social representation in many Western societies (Sammut, Jovchelovitch, Buhagiar, Veltri, Redd & Salvatore, 2017). Social representations are the social counterpart of individualised cognitions (beliefs, attitudes, stereotypes and opinions). They are to attitudes what language is to speech (Saussure, 1916). By virtue of social representations, individual attitudes are deemed meaningful in the social domain in the same way that a personal speech is meaningful to anyone who speaks the language.

The social marketing approach to persuasion relies on the prior study of social representations to design and deliver persuasive appeals in line with the social reality that prevails in the target group. In this approach, groups are more likely to be segmented on identity-based, rather than demographic, criteria. A social marketing approach aspires to present persuasive appeals that help individuals make good sense of what is offered. It is this sense-making process that is held to tip the balance in persuasion, rather than any objective feature of the appeal in itself.

In essence, the social marketing approach fulfils the critical components outlined in Lay Epistemic Theory (Kruglanski, 1989). The first step to a social marketing approach consists in establishing the parameters of evidence that is deemed relevant to justify a certain course of action in a given sociocultural context. In the second step, persuasive appeals are designed that present this evidence to segments in the target population. This is not dissimilar to targeted advertising using big data that rely on the user's own inclinations to formulate and pitch appeals, rather than any elements intrinsic to the appeal itself. Lauri & Lauri's (2005) study on organ donation (Box 7.3) exemplifies how the persuasion modality of social influence is rooted in a social context of collective beliefs and common sense.

Box 7.3 Social marketing

Lauri (2008, 2015; Lauri & Lauri, 2005) undertook a social marketing campaign in 1996 to promote organ donation in Malta, following the introduction of an organ donation register that saw limited uptake. The aim of the campaign was to increase registration. Focus group research undertaken prior to the campaign revealed diametrically opposed social representations concerning organ donation. On the one hand, organ donation was understood to foster the giving of life. Respondents, however, also harboured concerns about how the medical model promoted the exchange of body parts. During the focus groups, respondents were asked to identify pictures of whom they held to be a typical donor and non-donor. Prior to the campaign, donors were perceived to be young, sporty, caring and loving individuals whilst non-donors were perceived to be conservative, non-caring, fearful and uninformed people. The campaign was designed using findings from a social representations inquiry held prior to the campaign. It carried a slogan taken from actual respondent speech, that is, 'Give a new life'. The campaign addressed three overarching issues. In the first effort, models who represented ordinary people were selected to pitch the campaign's message, over high-profile public figures. This was due to the fact that descriptions of donors articulated in focus groups were unrealistically positive and in this sense, extraordinary. Ordinary models were selected to facilitate social identification. In the second effort, the campaign solicited the help of local bishops who issued pastoral letters promoting organ donation as charity. This was due to the fact that the normative context in Malta is highly Roman Catholic. Findings from the focus groups revealed concern about the extent to which Catholics believe they are at liberty to donate organs provided to them by God. In the third effort, doctors were recruited to detail the medical procedures involved. This was done due to the fact that focus group findings revealed concerns about the extent to which doctors would strive to save one's life over recycling one's organs with a wider range of organ recipients. In this way, epistemic authorities were recruited not by virtue of their inherent source credibility in some objective sense, but by virtue of domain-specific concerns (bishops with regards to faith concerns; doctors with regards to medical concerns). The campaign was highly effective, with a significant increase in donor card registrations that was maintained in the last survey undertaken thirty months after the campaign. Crucially, the campaign served to modify the social representations of donors and non-donors that enabled identification with the cause. In follow-up research, donors had come to be represented as ordinary people, manual workers, family people, educated, happy, generous and well-informed individuals. These attributes appealed to ordinary Maltese citizens more strongly than those in circulation prior to the campaign. Representations of non-donors also shifted, depicting them as older, uninformed, uneducated, vain and egocentric. The success of the campaign is attributed to the fact that it was designed to alter the representational grounds for social identification. This made organ donation both relevant and desirable for ordinary people.

Conclusion

In this chapter we have seen how the persuasion paradigm has investigated this modality of social influence by seeking to identify which features of a persuasive appeal maximise success. We have seen that a successful appeal is one where the subject determines that the evidence presented is relevant and warrants a certain conclusion. We have also seen how persuasion, unlike other modalities of influence, involves a change of attitudes in the subject. Rather than merely yielding to the force of the appeal, the subject cognitively processes the appeal and emerges argumentatively convinced; she comes to change her mind, not only behaviour. Finally, we have seen that there is no silver bullet to persuasion. No objective feature of source, message or audience stands to be persuasive all the time and in every scenario. Rather, which features hold persuasive potential depends on the social representations framing the interaction and the social positioning entailed in adopting a certain attitude. We have also seen how other people's opinions matter to us in terms of a balance of reciprocity in a constellation of attitudes that is systemically achieved in social interaction (see Figure 7.2). Persuasion accrues as a function of cognitive dissonance that arises in the subject when a misalignment of attitudes is experienced in social interaction. This motivates the subject to change some attitudes and restore systemic equilibrium.

In conclusion, it is worth noting that persuasion is not down to a magical box of tricks that can make any appeal persuasive; any trick box takes for granted the specific common sense base that is the precondition of its efficacy, what the ancients called Ethos. The subject, an agentic human being, needs to come to agree that the ends and means proposed are indeed desirable. Persuasion is thus a relational dynamic that needs to be considered in the ecological context in which it manifests. In the study we reviewed in Box 7.3, we saw how bishops and medics were relied upon by virtue of the epistemic authority, religious and secular, they command in subsections of society in which the social marketing intervention took place. This, in itself, is not directly transferable to other contexts in which bishops' statements are treated with scepticism, such as in secular society. Again, whether a particular voice commands epistemic authority or otherwise is down to social representations that inform subjects' sense-making processes. The understanding of persuasion has moved from cognitive mechanics in isolation to a recognition of common sense as the taken-for-granted frame of reference of communities providing the necessary context of possibility. The societal background that selects persuasive social interaction (i.e., ethos, logos and pathos) is critical in understanding how subjects make sense of appeals and how, when and why they emerge convinced (Howarth, et al., 2013). Research into persuasion, rather than being universal in its recipes, remains like cooking up a skilled and local effort, by gauging for a particular situation and considering the available means to sway a public audience (Aristotle; fourth century BCA). In the next chapter, we extend this discussion to mass media effects.

In Essence

In a given culture, certain characteristics of communicators, the messages they transmit and the audience receiving the message are more persuasive than other characteristics. Which characteristics are persuasive in a given situation depends also on how the message is cognitively processed by the recipient.

Cognitive dissonance arises from a mismatch between one's beliefs and one's behavioural inclinations. The psychological tension involved is resolved by changing one's attitudes or one's behaviour. Choice architecture relies on scenarios that induce cognitive dissonance to lure respondents to behave in a determined direction.

Ultimately, there is no silver bullet to persuasion as individual attitudes depend on the social positioning the individual assumes in their personal life. For persuasion to work, the individual must be persuaded to take a stand on the matter against any other – the persuasive appeal needs to make sense.

PART III

Necessary Extensions

The classical research paradigms on social influence have yielded innumerable insights, as shown in the previous sections. The exercise of social influence in everyday life, however, does not follow strict laboratory protocols. Perhaps for this reason, some clear concerns have been overlooked over the years despite repeated calls for their investigation. In this section, we aim to address this shortcoming. We thus extend our inquiry into mediated domains: the mass media on the one hand and artefact designs on the other. The coordination of human action in our contemporary world very rarely relies on word of mouth and verbal transmission of social influence in co-presence. The social media is a popular avenue for socialising, if not socialisation! It is also a gateway to coordinating protests and riots in real-time. Channelling the energy, however, requires more than a 'Like' – it requires barricades that separate anti-immigration protesters from pro-immigration protestors to avoid confrontation and the degeneration of social order. This section deals with these necessary extensions of social influence research that have become the cornerstone of social movements in our time.

We thus advance our vision of social influence into less common research territories, at least in social psychology. In Chapter 8, we examine different modalities of social influence under conditions of **mass mediation,** or what we call **mode 2:** the broadcasting of symbols and images which became a pervasive reality of modern life during the twentieth century. Here we bring to bear a parallel research tradition of media effect studies, as developed by psychologists in communication science, and link these to modalities of social influence. A key modality arising here is **agenda setting**. Chapter 9 takes this ambition even a step further, and considers social influence under conditions of **inter-objectivity** or what we call **mode 3**. Here we examine how influence is amplified by designed installations and technological gadgets and infrastructure; in this context we 'discover' the effect that resistance has against such machinations. In the light of mode 3, **resistance** becomes a modality of influence, paradoxically, by obstructing change, the projected innovation becomes sustainable.

CHAPTER 8

Agenda Setting, Framing and Mass Mediation

phase	modality	function for CS	Mode 2 symbolic
Order created 'out of Chaos', new beginnings			
Phase 1	norm formation	**Normalisation**	debate
	crowds		joint attention imitation
	prototyping		diegetic prototyping
	leadership		priming
Challenge from newcomers, homecomers, strangers or 'aliens'			
Phase 2	*fait accompli*	**Assimilation**	nudging
	majority		diffusion
	minority (elite)		spiral of silence
	persuasion		micro-target
	authority		Hi-Fi signal transfer
Sustained challenge by consistent dissenters			
Phase 3	persuasion	**Accomodation**	propagation
	minority (non dominant)		agenda setting framing
	resistance		propaganda
	?		?

Figure 8.1 A challenge and response model VII: mass mediation

In 1998, a young British doctor made observations that suggested a link between the triple MMR (measles, mumps and rubella) vaccination and the onset of autism. He and his team published an exploratory study (n = 12) making a causal claim in the *Lancet*, a key medical journal. At a press conference, it was suggested that MMR triple vaccinations was unsafe and should not be administered. What could have been a useful line of enquiry became a public health controversy of global proportion. The study was retracted in 2010, but the wide media attention, no least in anti-vaccination social media, to the causal claim MMR –> autism amplified vaccination hesitation and vaccination rates dropped in many places, and some years later (after 2008), the illnesses returned. The case illustrates many things, but for our purposes it shows that the persuasion and authority of a scientific claim is massively amplified by mass mediation that resonates in a confluence of concerns among parents about the number of vaccinations or a rise in autism.

If we think of modalities of social influence in the twenty-first century, we need to consider them under conditions of mass media technology, the mode of circulating symbols (mode 2 symbolic). Where would persuasion be without advertising images in cinemas, or political campaigning without TV time? Where would modern leaders be without their social media profiles or their Twitter presence? How does peer pressure arise with the parading of beauty ideals in magazines, TV, film and social media? Also, what kind of politics would we have without the relentlessly investigative newspapers, broadcasting or documentary films; mass media which are after all the fourth estate in a modern division of powers?

In 2020, when we talk of 'social influence' and mean social media, are we not mixing up means and ends, or structures and functions? It would appear that social influence is continuous, social media is just the latest technology. Historically, research on the effects of mass mediation started within a broad social psychology with research on war propaganda, radio audiences and agricultural extension linking farmers to agricultural research (Rogers, 1997). Professionalisation created the applied field of 'communication studies' which came to be located in agronomy or marketing. We find it unhelpful when textbooks of social psychology sideline mass mediation. Therefore, when considering mass media effects, we ask two questions: which modality of social influence is implied, and how is the modality enhanced by symbolic mediation? In doing so, we start from two working assumptions:

- Mass media do not define modalities of social influence; they enhance the functionality of existing modalities in particular ways.

- Different mass media are functionally equivalent; they create novel genres that enhance the existing functions of normalising, assimilating or accommodating common sense.

The range of mass communication models is large (Bonfadelli, 2004; Bryant & Zillman, 2002; McQuail & Windahl, 1996), thus our exercise is illustrative rather than exhaustive. Furthermore, the pace of change in media technology is fast and the media mix very diverse. Handwriting and parchment copying were displaced by printed book, magazines and newspapers, after this came moving images and broadcasting on radio and TV, video and CD, and lastly the Internet and social media arrived. With all these shifts, what is really new? (see Box 8.1). We feel at times the 'shock of the old' (Edgerton, 2006). Consider **joint attention:** what is really new when we compare the morning papers of 1890 and social media of 2015? The key function of mass media remains the creation of joint attention on issues, and establishing, defending and challenging the frames of public debate. The functions remain, the platforms come and go.

The argument of this chapter will unfold in three steps: first we examine how common sense, our structures of intersubjectivity, surround us under conditions of mass mediation as **social representations** (SR). We have already discussed SRs in Chapter 4 (norming) as the most generic concept of a frame of reference in an intergroup context. Second, we will see how concerns come and go in **issue cycles** resonating on **salience and credibility**. Some cycles are short, others longer, some topics resonate for years. Having established the logic of intersubjectivity under conditions of mass mediation, we examine the processes of *normalisation, assimilation* and *accommodation* of social representations. We will review models of media effects and order them according to their functions of social influence. This will all come together in a transversal overview of how social influence operates under conditions of mass mediation, and defines the symbolic mode 2 of social influence (see Chapter 10).

Social Representations: Formal and Informal Communication

We have already come across (see Chapter 4) the idea of 'social representations' as the most generic term for what is stabilised in society, defended and also shifted. In these representations, a social milieu 'mirrors' itself, not in the sense of faithful reproduction, but in the sense of making available information about itself that would otherwise not be accessible. This is well expressed by the old saying 'we do not see things as they are, but as we are'.

When sampling such 'collective selfies', we need to consider both face-to-face and formal communication (Bauer, 2015b; Bar-Tal, 2000; Bauer & Gaskell, 1999; Sammut et al., 2015). Everyday **common sense** is mobilised by mass mediation and produces social representations of world issues for the community. In normal circumstances of low tension, common sense and representations coincide. This overlap is dislocated in polarised societies of high tensions of tribal solidarity or authoritarian rule. Under such conditions tribal orientations prevail (echo chambers), and the reference to 'common sense' takes the function of an appeal to good sense and reason where common ground is lost (Lindenberg, 1987).

In a classical study Moscovici (2009 [1961]) held the mirror up to the fragmented French society of the 1950s, reflecting how it was thinking tribally about human psychology. The book systematised social representations of the 'psychoanalytic self' in the daily press and weekly magazines and in conversations with people of different walks of life. The study distinguished three *communication genres* considering their social milieu, the discursive contents, particular speaker–audience relations and their prototypical outcomes. The three genres produced different discourses of 'psychoanalysis' by familiarising the unfamiliar in common language relative to different milieus: (a) entertaining or instructing an audience among Liberals and Catholics, or mobilising for an alternative worldview among Communists. For this they were (b) cultivating opinions, attitudes and stereotypes, and (c) expressing joint intentionality by degrees of resistance towards psychoanalysis. The three genres were called *diffusion, propagation* and *propaganda* characteristic of three social milieus, the urban-liberal, Catholic and Communist Party community. According to Staerkle (2015), these genres more generally are capable of normalising political beliefs of legitimate order, producing consent by defending majority views, and offering minority influence for social change. Through the ritual of a morning newspaper, the opinions of millions are recruited by headlines, in more or less polarised debates. Nowadays, it is a Twitter feed and a Facebook post that does so.

How do formal and informal communication compare? The key feature of face-to-face conversation is co-presence in time and space. Mass mediation transcends this constraint. The presence of another allows for immediate responses, turn-taking and feedback; in mass mediation turn-taking is irregular and delayed (though social media have reduced the response time to 'write a comment'). In informal communication we face concrete others, while in formal settings we speak to a 'type', a rhetorically imagined audience, an imagination which is hit or miss. The formal settings privilege

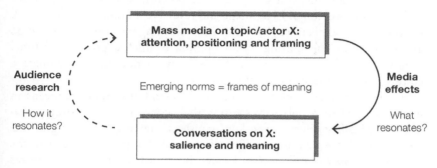

Figure 8.2   The resonating dual reality of everyday conversations and mass mediation

speakers/writers in broadcasting or for that matter on Twitter. Formal communication relies on complex technology for production and distribution of contents (see Box 8.1); a third-party platform is always involved. In social media, platform providers are not neutral but contribute their part, their algorithms feeding our searches and attention. These providers are not just tech companies, but mediators who curate though not yet produce, our content and therefore what we pay attention to.

Ultimately, mass media are a cultural form of creating **collective attention, a precondition of joint intentionality**. And, we are dealing with a dual reality, the individual stream of consciousness and the reality of streams of mass mediation. We need to understand how this duality fosters social representations and common sense in the community (see Figure 8.2). We must ask: how do conversations affect mass media content, and how does media content affect everyday conversations? What is driver, what is driven, what is **resonance**, that is, selecting the amplified presence of an issue in joint attention?

Resonance, Thematic Cycles and Mass Media Effects

The key term is **resonance**. In acoustics, resonance arises when two systems vibrate simultaneously; it describes the coupling between independent systems of similar Eigen-frequency. The two systems affect each other mutually; the resonance amplification is highest when the gap between Eigen-frequencies is smallest. This influence at a distance happens where there is existing communality. Under this analogy, we consider mass media effects as resonances between face-to-face and mediated communication which are independently active and potentially in synch. Resonance is the synchronisation of Eigen-logic and results in amplification (of news). Gamson & Modigliani (1989) show how meaning packages come and go and characterise the shifting public opinion of nuclear power over time. Benford & Snow (2000) claim that effective action frames resonate a culture and thus result in social mobilisation.

Frame resonance depends on salience and credibility. **Salience** means an issue is central to people's lives fitting their concerns and existing narratives. **Credibility** refers to speakers' consistent talking and acting in line with the evidence (i.e., no bullshit). Franzosi & Vicari (2013) refer to the list of *commonplaces* and *topoi* when advising on what potentially resonates in which rhetorical situation. Rosa (2016) builds a theory of modern society on resonance – in contrast to alienation – as modes of being-in-the-world (ibidem, 298): resonance characterises a triple relation between persons (PP), person and self (PS) and person and the world (PW) where all parts are self-active and relatively independent. Lack of resonance is diagnostic of malfunction and lead to social pathologies.

Resonance is manifest in intensification and amplification of joint attention. Many themes in mass media form issue cycles. We count the number of issue references per time unit, map their coming and going; the peak intensity is the resonance moment, when mass media and everyday conversations couple. Public opinion is unstable, it comes and goes depending on the convergence of media themes and fluid everyday concerns. Such cycles come with different extensions. And indeed, we recognise *short-term hype cycles* (van Lente et al., 2015), on novelties, technological yuk-factors and moral panics. The upswing of Internet coverage towards 2000 is full of such hype cycles, much of it recruits anxieties over 'Y2K' (year 2000) as a harbinger of disaster but also presents the Internet as investment opportunity – cyber security firms predicted worldwide meltdown when computer clocks would date switch from 19XX to 20XX; little happened beyond widespread fears and profitable advice. The NASDAC investment index and UK 'Internet' news are highly correlated, r = 0.97 between 1993 and 2007 (annual data; Bauer, 2015a, 120ff).

We might identify *mid-range issue cycles* on a topic such as BSE (Bovine Spongiform Encephalopathy or 'mad cow disease'). In the 1990s, an obscure disease destroyed British cattle, and led to fears of human infection and a worldwide ban on British beef. Environmental concerns are long term with three cycles of different intensity since the 1960s (see Figure 8.3). After water pollution, the 1960s and 1970s focus on populations and

---

Box 8.1 The place of media technology in communication

We need to put media technology into its place when understanding communication; our key witness here is Niklas Luhmann (1927–1998). On the autistic spectrum, he struggled in daily social interactions, painfully aware of the 'improbability of communication' (Luhmann, 1990). For most of us, communication simply unfolds like breathing, with the occasional hiccup. Luhmann faced additional difficulties. His theory of communication points to three difficulties in particular:

- *Utterance: how to put thoughts into words and make sense, when we all have are idiosyncratic memories?*
- *Attention: how to reach others when they are not here?*
- *Acceptance: even if you reach people, will they agree with you or not?*

Each of these issues complicates communication. The combined probability of success will stack up difficulties by multiplication. Let us consider the initial likelihood of a successful exchange, measured on the speaker's intention: for example, utterance $p = 0.30$, attention $p = 0.20$ and acceptance $p = 0.20$, the resulting likelihood is just 1 per cent $[0.3 \times 0.2 \times 0.2 = 0.012]$. But there is hope for 'getting through to others'; humans have developed cultural props.

First, I think X, you should think similarly. **Language** *allows two minds to resonate in common understanding; not perfectly, but it is better than nothing. Speaking the same language is better than gesticulating wildly. Grammatical language is a biological and cultural achievement, standardising exchanges and increasing the probability of making sense: with a common language, our utterance moves from 0.30 to 0.65 (for example).*

The second problem arises when listeners' attention wanders freely. Capturing attention is very unlikely, when physically elsewhere. Again, help is available in **technology***. You leave a written note; scripture is an old culture technique for keeping lists and to create memory across time and place. Modern circulation technology captures the attention of people distributed in time and space. Printed books, newspapers, radio and TV initially allowed few authors to reach many people; now social media make it easier for many people to reach many others. Thanks to technologies, attention is more likely, moving from 0.20 to 0.45 (for example).*

So, language helps, technology too, but insufficiently, because people can still dismiss you. Thus, thirdly, symbolic structures called GSCM (Generalised Symbolic Communication Media) come to the rescue. Systems or **codes of discourse** *are symbolic constraints on communication (e.g., the code 'money'). To capture somebody's imagination, you need to 'code', for example, talk money and profit making. Excluding other concerns, you are more likely to get through, you can even bridge a language problem with US dollars. Within a discursive constraint acceptance increases, it is clear what to say and what not.*[1] *If we talk*

---

[1] Unforgettably, one of us had his first job in the computer industry, before returning to university life. On my first day, they welcomed me with the following advice: 'you can do anything you like here. The only thing that counts at the end of the month is dollars'. So, this felt like enormous freedom, but it was a freedom along a single dimension, a code: money in the till.

> *business and profit, it helps; if we talk science on evidence, it helps; if we talk art on beauty, it helps; if we talk law about legality and (not) guilty before the law, it helps. But it confuses things to talk about money and beauty, unless there is business in beauty. A code is a single-minded concern that translates everything, as if it were a 'currency' (but now we use the 'money' code to understand 'translation': exchange rates on a currency market). Your getting-through might increase from 0.20 to 0.70 (for example) when clearly talking money and not morality. So your business talk coded on money in English via social media might increase your success rate from 1 per cent to 21 per cent [0.65 × 0.45 × 0.70 = 0.21]; and you do not want to muddy waters with lateral concerns; that you do privately on Sundays. Famously, the purpose of business is to increase shareholder value and not to do 'good', unless signalling responsibility (otherwise called CSR or 'Corporate Social Responsibility') increases shareholder value. This is still far from perfect and requires efforts on language, media mix and coded discourse. What sounds like a set of mundane solutions, is a defining feature of **modern society**; functionally differentiated into subsystems (money, power, law, science, art, education, love and morality, etc.) and operating on a set of codes fit for different purposes. That said, one cannot avoid the impression that the code 'money' rules supreme. There is however famously no post-modernity, only a modern post that accelerates the circulation of messages.*

Figure 8.3   Different cycles: hyperbole, issues and grand narratives

nuclear power: too many people strain resources and nuclear energy is unsafe. The depleting 'ozone layer' is the news in the 1980s leading into global warming (Kroll, 2001; Mazur & Lee, 1993). Finally, there are longer phases, the *grand narratives* or representations of 30–50 years. The long waves of representing science in modern society alternate in periods of lower and higher intensity of public discourse (Bauer, 2012). So, issues come and go, reflecting shifting resonances in public conversations and concerns. The Annales school of history (Long, 2005) talks here of symbolic mentalities that survive economic conjunctures which in turn span sequences of political events.

Mass media effect studies have often been sought to contain *moral panics* over media power with verifiable evidence. Children and vulnerable adults are seen at risk: powerful media bring moral decline, unreason and nefarious politics (Starker, 1989). Over 500 years, such allegations targeted books of fact and fiction, the press and its makers, cinema, comics, radio, TV and recently the Internet and social media, sometimes leading to censorship, famously in the twenty editions (1559–1966) of the *Index Librorum Prohibitorum* of the Vatican. These attacks endorsed an implicit model of media virally infecting or injecting content into people. In times of oversimplified and conspiratorial explanation, media effect studies seek to sober up the debate and to evaluate political campaigning and product advertising; in civic society, the focus is entertainment and education and on 'Begleitforschung' (Bonfadelli, 2004, 12ff). The field is torn between what Lazarsfeld (1941) called 'administrative', efficiency oriented towards fixed targets, and 'critical' research studies, oriented towards the unintended streams of 'false consciousness' or 'artificial horizons' (Kepplinger, 1995).

For the past seventy years, media studies have gathered pace. Beyond matters of media regulations and politics, the field assesses 'new media' and their unintended, short- and long-term impacts; on particular groups (children, consumers, voters, minorities, etc.); seeking effective interventions at different stages (pre-, during and post-communication); and distinguishing cognitive effects (worldview, beliefs, knowledge, opinion), attitudinal positioning (emotion, affect, motives) and behavioural dispositions (intentions, behaviour, habits and routines). The field oscillates between phases of 'strong effects' (1910–1945, 1980 to present) and of 'weak effects' (1945–1980) on audiences; weak effects suggest an active and autonomous audience. One driver may be political realignment: as party affiliation and political parties lose their role as ideology filters, the grip of media on public opinion increases (Bonfadelli, 2004, 27ff). The nefarious potential of social media for politics has lead to a recent revival of strong effects (e.g., in the 'Cambridge Analytica' scandal of 2017).

Normalisation under Conditions of Mass Mediation

In the following, we want to consider media effects as extensions of modalities of social influence under conditions of mass mediation. With the first set of effects we examine the function of normalisation, the establishment of a frame of reference set to last. We have identified this as the social representation that resonates the common sense of the community through the short and long cycles of concerns.

Normalisation by Diffusion of Ideas

An important media effect is the diffusion of innovations, for example, bringing new crops to farmers (Valente & Rogers, 1995). In the rural United States of the 1930s, economists worried about farmers adopting a new and more productive hybrid corn. This was modelled as **mass diffusion**: first farmers hear the radio or read newspapers, then they talk to each other and some take on the new crop. That is how it happened in Iowa: slowly at first, then faster, then slow again, until 100 per cent were blessed with hybrid corn (see stylised model in Figure 8.4). In Wisconsin, farmers took their time; in Kentucky even later and slower, never reaching 100 per cent. In Texas – there must be something wrong – they hardly took it on. What happened? And Alabama, later, and little uptake. These

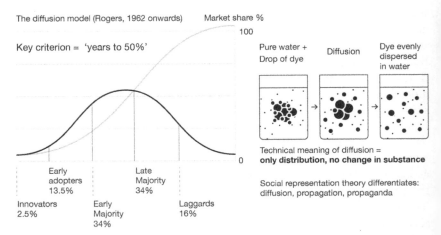

Figure 8.4   The logistical diffusion model and different types of adopters (left); the mechanical diffusion of mass across three mediums (right)

differentials on a uniform S-shaped curve became an index of resistance: delayed and slow uptake is a problem. But is it really?

Influential diffusion ideas have three basic elements (Rogers, 1996). Firstly, in a network of communication people emulate behaviour by contact as if 'infected by a virus'. Viral infection gives the mathematical model (see Box 8.2). Secondly, mass media and conversations have separate functions. Broadcasting raises awareness, conversations lead the emulation among neighbours. Thirdly, along the process, different people stack up: innovators, early adopters, late adopters or early majority, late majority and laggards. The task of research is to profile these types and to **micro-target messages** in a battle for their hearts and minds.

Diffusion seeks to establish the behavioural norm around new technology: **acceptance.** For this, it must make dubious assumptions. Diffusions arise from a single origin, when most innovations come about at several places simultaneously; adopters are deemed 'mindless emulators' and the common good is guaranteed a-priori when everybody adopts; the imperative is 'fast is better'. Innovations are only rejected temporarily, never finally; they are never dropped, and do not alter along the path of diffusion. Mass that is diffusing is not changing, only spreading until density is equal (see Figure 8.4). Thus, diffusion models are uncritically and unrealistically biased towards ready-made ideas.

When innovations become controversial, the diffusion path is dislocated. In history we find many instances of adaptation of novelty through public deliberation rather than acceptance of a ready-made by emulation. Consider nuclear power where emulation is rather the exception, even discouraged. Or take GM (genetically modified) crops: roll-out was to be an emulation process among farmers, but debates and controversies across Europe and Asia created a different realty in North and South America among exporters of soya beans (Bauer, 2015a, 30ff and 175ff). Diffusion only works in the absence of resistance (Bauer, 2017; also Chapter 9 on artefacts).

Normalisation with or without Knowledge Gaps

A paradox is often observed: more information in a social system does not level knowledge; the take-up is not homogenous. When information from a leading source flows along an issue cycle, better educated people have an advantage. Already more engaged in current affairs, the more efficient readers and viewers rely on more sources and pick up more. Thus, increasing information widens disparities, known as the **knowledge gap**

Box 8.2 On viral communication

Modelling communication on viral epidemiology is an old new idea. **Contagion** *was a model for imitating minds in the nineteenth century (see Chapter 3). Its vigour was renewed in concept such as memes (Dawkins, 1976; Lynch, 1996), representations (Sperber, 1990) and the* **stickiness** *of religious imagination (Atran & Norenzayan, 2004; Boyer, 2003). Kitcher (2003) raises the stakes for modelling communication on 'infection'. He looks at mathematical models and maps the analogy to see where it breaks down. A model of viral infection has the following basics: to entertain a new idea v ~ being infected by v, means*

- *virulence of the idea (stickiness)*
- *host susceptibility*
- *tipping point*
- *ecological milieu (herd immunity)*

What is actually being transmitted? It is claimed that after contact the object relations Y 'B being infected by virus v' is equal between two persons A and B; after contact, B is infected Y(bv), previously B's relation to virus v was opaque O(bv); after contact of A and B the relation Y is 'infected':

Before contact Y(av) O(bv) => Y(av) Y(bv) after contact.

However, ideas and attitudes are intentional in referring to something else; viruses are not intentional. In addition, humans have many relations to ideas, that is, propositional attitudes towards intentional content: being aware, believing, doubting, hating, rejecting, being certain about ideas, etc. What relation is being transmitted? Before and after transmission A to B, are in Y(bv) object v and object relation Y really identical? I carry a virus, have no symptoms, the virus might mutate, little more. However, when I hear that 'BREXIT is an historical mistake of epic proportion': I am now aware that you carry this claim (propositional attitude), but care little about it (the claim), or it changes my appreciation of you (I hate you for it); I might strongly object to this claim, which means I take the claim but form a different attitude; I might doubt that you really believe what you say but only entertain the claim ironically ... Me coming to the belief that 'BREXIT is a mistake' is only one among many possible post-contact relations with the idea, Y(bv). The quality of the relation changes in human communication, and so does the intentional object: a chain of infection believing claim1 => believing claim1 => believing claim1 is highly unlikely; more likely is a chain believing claim1 => doubting claim1.1 => disregarding claim1.2. It ultimately remains under-determined what object content v and what object relation Y is transmitted about BREXIT; human communication is less constrained than viral transmission literally speaking. Is fidelity of transmission on the object v, or on the object relations Y? Furthermore, viral communication has many unspecified epidemiological analogues: mutations, rate of recovery, immunity, competition, rate of reinfection after recovery, gestation time. If we were to be explicit with the virus idea, we would have to define all of these analogues in relation to 'BREXIT is a mistake'.

> *How far does the 'viral' analogy go? Not as far as the metaphor, it seems. We should remember Dr Pasteur, a pioneer of microbiology and public hygiene: **'the germ is nothing, the milieu is everything'**. Maybe the value of the virus model is not its semantic validity, but some pragmatic value. First, we need vigilance, contact avoidance and frequent mind cleansing against bad ideas. Second, to construct messages of high stickiness you need to destroy the herd immunity and undermine the natural resistance against your messages. Maybe, viral simply means spreading fast.*

hypothesis (McQuail & Windahl, 1993; 122ff). Empirically, this is demonstrated in the early stages of an issue cycle; repeated surveys measure domain knowledge (e.g., space exploration, the link between smoking and cancer, genetics) and increasing disparities; the educated gain new knowledge faster; those who already have, will be given more.

Three factors interfere in such gaps along the issue cycle: firstly, gaps naturally reduce with high intensity coverage. Secondly, controversy reduces gaps: as people of all backgrounds get sucked into the debate, the gap reduces. Bonfadelli (2005) demonstrated this on the great food debate over genetically modified varieties in 1990s Europe: after controversies, knowledge gaps on 'genetics' had reduced. Public controversies educate society and input policy. Thirdly, fragmentation of the mass media system hinders the closing of gaps. People in echo chambers encounter little debate, and gaps increase across education in each chamber (Tichenor et al., 1970).

Knowledge gap studies elaborate the diffusion ideas from a leading source; differential up-take models 'resistance', and controversy instructs and enfranchises the excluded. Along the issue cycle, the community updates its knowledge base; we see the use of gap models in the early storming phase before consensus is reached.

Normalisation by Cultivation: Mainstreaming of World Views

Over long-term exposure, media and minds resonate through cultivation. This paradigm emerges from research into TV broadcasting with a deep reach of the population. Despite market competition, TV channels compete for similar mass audiences with similar content and 'world views'. When consumed frequently, this cultivates beliefs about the world (see Box 8.3). The 'public message system' of media comprises intensity, sentiment, thematic fields and patterns of issues (Gerbner, 1969) which

---

Box 8.3 Cultivation of biotechnology into GREEN and RED revolutions

Cultivation can be demonstrated on the gene technology in Europe of the 1990s into the early 2000s. The analysis requires a media map on X, surveys of perceptions of X and measures of exposure plus controls. In the 1980s, it had been anticipated that a new 'life sciences' sector would arise from recombinant DNA techniques in a single Biotech revolution. By 2000, gene technology had split into two 'revolutions', GREEN for crops and food and controversial (at least in Europe, not the United States), and RED for human health and much less controversial (in Europe, not the United States). How did one become two? The 'dual revolution frame' that substituting the 'unity frame' was cultivated by the elite press in the 1995–2000 'great food debate' which pitted Europe against the United States and allowed the controversy to be contained; what resonated among a newspaper-reading public changed the strategic context. Pharma and chemical firms, initially seeking mergers, now rushed into separate 'revolutions' (Bauer, 2005b and 2015a). Cultivation and normalisation of a new representation of a technology is very much a long-term impact and reaches beyond the peak of an issue cycle; once the new frame is mainstreamed, the issue cycle recedes, as it did in this case by 2010. Cultivation bridges issue cycles and establishes a representation.

---

stabilise a representation that doubles up on reality with an artificial horizon. People who grow older with TV end up thinking like the TV. Documented on depicted violence, frequent viewers score higher on the 'mean world index' (Morgan et al., 2009, 35). Thus, media systems are able to stabilise a particular world view; partial correlations with exposure are around r = 0.09 (ibidem, 38). In 'mainstreaming' everybody converges on the TV world view in function of exposure; in 'resonance' frequent viewers diverge depending on whether their life experience is consistent with the TV world or not. Living in a rough neighbourhood, you might well think the world is a rough place. TV is a pervasive provider of world views, but not the only one (Morgan et al. 2009). Beyond exposure, motivation and ability to process information mediate these effects for individuals (Shrum, 2009).

Normalisation by Diegetic Prototyping

In science communication (Gregory & Miller, 1998), recently an interesting idea emerged. Universities and research laboratories increasingly take public communication into their own hands as a matter of course including lobbying governments on policy, creating a brand image to market their education and research services (Bucchi & Trench, 2014; Entradas &

Bauer, 2019). In this context, the film industry is part of the game. Kirby (2011) studied the relations of major US universities with Hollywood; universities make sure that their scientists are on the set as advisors. The effect is a format of science news, **diegetic prototypes**:

> [The]hese are stories of technology that only exist in fiction – what film scholars call the diegesis – but they exist as fully functional objects in that world. Diegetic prototypes foster public support for potential and emerging technologies by establishing the need, benevolence and viability of these technologies (ibidem, p18).

Kirby showed how doctors working on artificial hearts in the 1970s recognised the opportunity and engaged fictional film to dramatise 'artificial heart transplants' before it reached clinical trial; what in hindsight looks like docudrama was actually science fiction. Many new technologies, not least in the field of medicine, are morally challenging and thus face resistance. Movies can frame the new technology as necessary, normal and viable before any debate has started. Modern mass circulating movies are a new world of possibilities and necessity. Pre-product placement creates great expectations for what is not yet ready (ibidem, 196) by placing the moral challenge in a frame of necessity, viability and normalcy; it thus pre-empts controversy by familiarising any threat before it ever constitutes a problem. Thus fictional film paves the way for new science by promoting research agendas and conditioning public controversies (Kirby, 2014, 106).

Normalisation by Serial Reproduction in Echo Chambers

There is much current concern about rumours and echo chamber–linked information bias and 'fake news'. Take the vaccination controversy, which we mentioned at the start of this chapter. Bartlett (1932) conducted studies on remembering that became models for rumours. He asked participants to retell stories (or redraw picture sequences) at time intervals of increasing length. On the story 'war of ghosts' he observed that accurate recall was unlikely. Rather, retelling made the story more conventional by assimilating unfamiliar elements to familiar ones, by simplifying and by elaborating odd details (ibidem p93 and p268ff). Bartlett had discovered constructive memory correlated to cultural dispositions. Rather than recall from traces, people construct memory from schemata (ibidem, p275) and 'an active organisation of ... past experiences which must always be supposed to be operating any well-adapted organic response' (p. 201). This idea is consistent with the 'frame of reference' of Sherif and Asch, that is, a shared temporary framework to deal with uncertainty and to assimilate novelty.

Serial reproduction is a model of how modern social media propagate rumours and urban legends. Rumours are a genre of communication (Franks & Attia, 2011), a proposition is passed on by word of mouth, without standards of evidence. Rumours spread by serial retelling according to the law of rumour: $R \sim iXa$ (Allport & Postman, 1947). A rumour topic (X) is import (i) and ambiguous (a); all are required characteristics. Similarly, urban legends are contemporary stories with a traditional moral, and traceable to folk tales with supernatural protagonists. They vary easily the same old story. This can be tested in parallel chains of emails or lines of conversations like Chinese whispers. Wagner et al. (1995) showed, on a short text on human conception, how in reproduction basic relations between sperm and ovum were conventionalised to romantic relations and existing sex-role stereotypes: the sperm was male, dominant and active, and the ovum female, submissive and passive. Bangerter (2000) demonstrated anchoring and metaphorical objectification of human reproduction in chains of sequential email. How do we interpret these results: do we take the source text as the benchmark for a decay function on fidelity criteria or do we highlight the creative transformation into new meanings? Both Wagner and Bangerter recruit the decay model of fidelity, judging transformations against its scientific source, but this is not the only possibility.

This brings us to echo chambers and internet bubbles in political controversies. The moral panic over 'fake news' after 2016 following the BREXIT referendum in the United Kingdom (June 2016) and the American election of Trump as president (November 2016), highlighted the propaganda function of 'news' circulating, unchecked in echo chambers and internet bubbles and protected by motivated reasoning (Bessi et al., 2015). Because of much polemic over lost elections, moral panics and propaganda in cyberwarfare, it is difficult to see clearly. However, let us recall Tarde's observations of 100 years ago (see Chapter 3 on crowding): then as now, new media technology helps to focus joint attention on one topic at the expense of another, and this selectively dictates the political agenda. Secondly, notions such as 'echo chambers' and 'motivated reasoning' rediscover the phenomenon of 'social representations', that is, the fragmentation of production, framing and reception of news into different milieus, first described for France in the 1950s. Globally, with the Internet increasingly segmented, we are closing in on a tripartite world of Google, Yandex and Weibo search engines, where three different algorithms curate

Table 8.1 *Comparison of social representations and social media 'echo chambers'*

	Legacy media 'social representations'	Social media 'echo chambers'
Structures	Core – periphery elements of stories. Community specific elaboration. Argumentation along ideology.	Fragmented social media subnetworks; open access use focussed on 'likes', 'share' and 'comment'.
Processes	Familiarising the unfamiliar. Anchoring in given common ground objectification in metaphor transformation of meaning.	Circulating 'fake news'. Confirmation bias. Motivated reasoning. Decay of information.
Audience relations	Few to many networks – opinion leaders. Editorial leaders. Editorial rendering of news. Engagement with other audience.	Many to many subnetworks. Twitter stars (opinion leaders). Algorithms for searches (bubbling). Engagement with other, hardly.
Medium	'Legacy media'. Newspapers, magazines, radio, TV. Funded by paid content and adverts.	New social media Facebook, Twitter, YouTube, Google, Yandex, Weibo. Free content, selling user data.
Functions	Orientation, sense-making. Autonomy, independence. Resistance to interference.	Misinformation. Phatic communication. 'Black' propaganda, hidden source.
Social integration	Propaganda in solidarity. Propagation in communion. Diffusion in exchange, entertainment.	Mobilisation of movement. Manipulation of opinions.

information for a Western, Russian or Chinese sphere of influence. Table 8.1 compares social representations and echo chambers using old and new terms for similar phenomena.

Assimilation of Challenges to Existing Social Representations

Social representations of the world, once established as common sense in an intergroup context, face challenges from newcomers or from people who find reason to dissent. We have seen in previous chapters how different social influence modalities defend the status quo against such detractions. In the following we will examine how this task is achieved under conditions of mass mediation.

Assimilation into a Spiral of Silence

The **spiral of silence hypothesis** builds directly on conformity pressure (see Chapter 5). The current opinion climate affects the future expression of opinions: people in the 'majority' become louder, those in the 'minority' go quiet. A de facto minority position, emboldened by control of the media, can present itself as 'the silent majority'. This model of media influence shows how the media assimilate minorities into the mainstream. It makes two assumptions: first, we all fear social isolation and ostracism, an anthropological constant, and thus avoid becoming the odd one out. Second, unsure about the majority view in society, we take our own 'opinion samples' from cues in the mainstream media. To position themselves, people take the mass media mainstream as the frame of reference. Over time, and their views outside the mainstream, they more and more hesitate to express such views in public; as in the Asch experiments (see Chapter 4) they publicly admit majority views, while reserving a private opinion. As public opinion surveys only pick up public expressions, they record declining dissent from the norm opinion, which reinforces the apparent majority position. As people cave in and refuse to answer for real, more become 'silent' on the matter. Furthermore, non-responses and 'don't know' responses are often excluded from results, the silence becomes invisible and poll results are ever more incorrect proxies of real opinion.

Kepplinger (1995, 362) argued that German newspapers had painted an 'artificial horizon' (a trompe l'oeil) on nuclear power and genetics and its critical framing resonated more with professional journalists than anybody else. This opened a spiral of silence even before the Chernobyl disaster of 1986. Also, such silence is pertinent in times of war. Consider 9/11 (2001), when a terror attack on US soil created an imperative that brought the news media into the official line. Without debate and alternatives, the artificial 'majority view' constrains thinking: terrorism cannot be deserved nor homemade. Saddam Hussein became allied to Al-Qaida in Afghanistan by symbolic association (Rampton & Stauber, 2003). Similar things occurred post-BREXIT 2016 in the United Kingdom: the vociferous winners created a 'decisive majority' from what was in reality only 27 per cent of the population, or 33 per cent of the registered voters, brandishing 'Remainers' as traitors of the people who deserve no respect; such brandishing made it difficult to voice opposition and a spiral of silence set in, at least for some time.

The spiral of silence idea is thus an extension of conformity pressure. It shows how the duality of face-to-face and media reality allows for two possibilities: (a) an effective minority takes the majority posture in the media and turns the climate of opinion in their favour; (b) a real majority leads the dissenting minority back into the mainstream, albeit with persistent private dissent. We expect this effect to be strongest post-peak and towards the end of an issue cycle when the topic goes into hibernation and waits for an opportunity to revive.

Assimilation by HiFi Transmission from an Authority Voice

We must be able to expect a command to reach its target with high fidelity (HiFi) whatever the conditions of transmission. A prototypical model of communication is the wartime high-fidelity engineering of signal transfer (Shannon & Weaver, 1949): a sender encodes the message, sends a signal through a radio channel, this is received and decoded on reception, and enacted by those who understand the message. This model assumes four basic elements: sender, receiver, channels and code. It echoes in Lasswell's famous formula 'Who says what, in which channel, to whom, with what effect' (McQuail & Windahl, 1996, p13ff)), and rhymes with mediaeval forensics '*quis, quid, ubi, quibus auxiliis, cur, quomodo, quando*' (who, what, where, with what, why, how and when), merging into the 'Five Ws' of modern journalism (who, what, where, when and why). In addition, English language is rich in 'transport' or 'package' metaphors of communication: 'to put into words', 'to unpack a sentence', 'to get what was said', etc.; something is packed up and sent through a pipeline or post service, where on the other side it is unpacked and appreciated (Reddy, 1993). The focus on HiFi suggests that the authority of the sender is paramount. Three problems challenge this authority: (a) there is channel noise and the signal is difficult to receive, (b) sender and receiver operate on different channels and fail to transmit and (c) there are coding difficulties, either simple errors of encoding or decoding or working from different code lists. The model thus defines an ideal communication situation: sender and receiver perfectly share the code, they apply it error free and the receiver pays undivided attention. This is not a very realistic model of how we reach a common understanding among people; it works however, under conditions of command-and-control which obsesses with high fidelity in emergency situations.

Rothman (1990) examined how public opinion sometimes falls out of line with scientific authority. Authority is challenged when experts publicly disagree. When expert consensus is performed on a mass media platform, public opinion follows suit. However, when the scientific authority is challenged in reality, media organisations are often bound to an ethos of balancing opinions. However, on global warming, climate experts of the 99% do not want to share a stage with a '1% mad counter-experts'; this strains relations between scientists and journalists (Peters, 2014). Also, expert disagreement can be staged; counter-experts are mobilised by parties interested in undermining the consensus which bestows the authority of science; for example, on smoking and cancer or over chemical pollution and nuclear radiation risks.

We argue here that HiFi models extend the modality of obedience to authority under conditions of mass mediation, as Milgram himself examined when issuing his experimental instructions over the telephone. HiFi models obsess over fidelity of reproduction and seek to stem the decay function in transmission; they highlight the voice of authority and require undivided attention of the receivers; as such they seek compliance and obedience to established authority and hold at bay distraction and dissent.

Accommodating Social Representations to Challenges

We have seen how different influence modalities defend the status quo against detractions. However, this defence can reach its limits, and social representations adapt to the challenges posed by continuous dissent by shifting the frame of reference. In the following we will examine how social influence achieves accommodation under conditions of mass mediation; this might well involve an appeal to Common Sense from which social representations have diverted.

Accommodation by Agenda Setting

Agenda setting is widely recognised: the 'most prominent issue' becomes the 'most important issue' (McCombs, 2004, 5). Transfer of issues from media attention to personal attention is the initial stage of shifting public opinion. **Agenda setting** examined 'the rich, ever-changing mix of mass media content and public opinion' (McCombs & Reynolds, 2009, 6), and thus responds to our need for orientation in a complex world: among a multitude of issues, to which one should we give priority. Mass media are poor at telling us how to think, but good at telling us what to think about. People follow that guidance more easily on abstract issues which are remote from experience, such as national unity, pollution, energy policy. Issues closer to everyday life, inflation, crime, cost of living are less prone to easy agenda setting (McCombs, 2004, 61). Generally, educated citizens follow the media agenda more closely (ibidem, 41).

Empirical studies correlate media attention and perception data on the 'most important issues' for government action. This is done in several ways: (a) we rank the ratio of news articles across issues and match this with voters' priority ranking of government actions; (b) we measure the ratio of news articles across issues, and voters are asked to rank these issues; (c) we follow a single issue and correlate this to rising number of voters who consider it the 'most important'; and (d) we follow a single issue, pre- and post-exposure to experimental media coverage to examine mediators of such salience transfer.

A strong version of agenda setting claims that media attention, by mere quantity of coverage, elicits alarm attention to potential hazards (Mazur, 1981). News is often bad news, so the more there is on a topic, the stronger the alarm. Mazur had showed that as coverage of fluoridation increased, the higher risk people perceived. The same might be the case with vaccination. The more vaccination news, the more people worry about it. This points to an alert function: whatever the attention, it elicits worry. The effect is on 'negativity'. Gutteling (2005) challenged this claim in the European debates over genetically modified crops and food. As media coverage increased, risk perception should prevail. It did not, when controlling for exposure and the issue cycle. The implication of the 'quantity of coverage' hypothesis – avoid alarming a sleeping public – might itself be a risky strategy that backfires down the line. Biologically, attention avoids danger; but attention also hypes the future. However, media attention can alert, and this is more likely useful at the beginning of a technology cycle; at a later stage alarm is needed to counterbalance the growing hype.

Finally, if the media set the public agenda, we must ask: who sets the media agenda? This requires an assessment of the intermedia agenda (McCombs & Reynold, 2009, 11). Journalists read each other, but who leads whom? In many countries, there is a good understanding of the opinion leading source. National libraries used to hold the newspaper of record, the one a journalist closely reads in order not to miss a story. Recently, agenda setting among journalists has moved into social media to Twitter or Facebook are accentuating the risks of artificial storms in public opinion.

Accommodation by Issue Reframing and Priming

The crowning mass media effect is the design of perceptions: how can we shift the social representations of X when it is out of sync with common sense? **Frames** are the frontier of automatic text analysis (Franzosi &

Wang, 2018; Sagi et al, 2013) and the political science's Holy Grail to public opinion (Woolley, 2000). We recognise here the 'frame of reference', established and set to last (see Chapter 4). Mass media not only tell us what to think about, but they frame and suggest reframing a story that is likely to move things on. Reframing an issue has four functions (Entman, 1993; Scheufele, 1999): it names a problem, for example, in the United Kingdom, 'the NHS (National Health System) is failing' or 'the NHS is being destroyed'; it claims a cause 'the NHS is underfunded' and points to moral responsibility 'the NHS has been neglected by neo-liberal governments'. It finally calls to action: 'vote for the opposition'. An effective frame constructs a moral argument from cause to treatment; it is familiar and well understood, and resonates in the wider culture. Some frames are partial, for example, making moral attributions without clarifying causes. Frames more or less resonate in context. The 'underfunding frame' for the NHS might be better suited to guide the public debate than the 'efficiency frame' among a public full of admiration for the doctors and nurses who are far from lazy and wasteful of resources. The United Kingdom has a rich repertoire of arguments to discuss the NHS, which would make little sense in places where there is no such historical commitment to a unified health provision. On political issues, a choice of frame can shift public opinion. Abortion can be framed as a feminist 'women's choice' or as a religious issue of 'compassion'. The wider cultural resonance of 'compassion' allows a change of attitudes to abortion outside the feminist echo chamber (Ferree, 2003).

Related to framing is idea of **priming**, that is, a prior stimulus altering the response to a subsequent stimulus; thus earlier media exposure can alter later judgements temporarily (Roskos-Ewoldsen et al., 2009). Agenda setting distinguishes between setting the object of attention (first order) and highlighting object attributes for judgement (second order). The latter is consistent with priming; previous news conditions subsequent judgements. Particular stories highlight an issue, this issue becomes the criterion on which the government is evaluated. Much military news will suggest that the government should be evaluated on 'doing a good job on defence' (ibidem, 76f). Rock videos can prime gender stereotypes for the immediate judgement of women (ibidem, 79). It remains unclear whether stereotype priming is the same phenomenon as the temporary recruitment of exemplars for the evaluation of political actors; and many priming experiments fall foul of the replication crisis. However, 'priming' makes particular object attributes salient at the expense of others, and this can bias judgement of that object towards those attributes rather than other criteria.

An actor who wants to take control over being evaluated seeks to take control of potential primes.

Reframing and priming are ways by which active minorities can amplify their potential to reach conversion of the majority and reach long-term shifts in social representations under conditions of mass media. Tribal polarisation and dogmatic language dislocates from common sense in echo chambers and this allows for a reframing appeal to common sense to build bridges again across communities and effectively shift the frame of reference for this purpose (Lindenberg, 1987). And what in hindsight might look like a novel way of thinking and talking, is in matter of fact a subtle readjustment of previous ideas and images: the novel ways are emerging from the old and continuity is guaranteed (LeGoff, 2015). What within an existing framework appeared as unthinkable suddenly becomes thinkable, and increasingly the thinkable becomes possible, the possible becomes probable and finally taken for granted, no further questions asked. The mass mediation provides the record. Through minority influence under conditions of mass mediation, the minority escapes the tragedy of being forgotten.

Conclusion

In this chapter we examined the modalities of social influence under conditions of mass mediation. Mass media are a transversal mode of social influence, cutting across all modalities and enhancing the functions of normalisation, assimilation and accommodation of shared beliefs in society.

Circulation media such as print, broadcasting or Internet, significantly reduce the problem of attention, making it more likely that an audience can be reached beyond immediate time and space. As such media also make a contribution to social and cultural memory, because the record is fixed at least for some time and takes a documentary quality; systematically analysed as textual data they also pose a challenge for research methodology in text mining. This does not guarantee successful communication, but it helps.

In consequence, we have to consider a double reality of conversations and of mass mediation to analyse social representation resonating along issue cycles. Social influence, under conditions of mass mediation, models the coming together of informal and formal communication and their mutual resonance. Resonance is the key term here, because it avoids obsessing with causality and what drives what and focuses on the coupling

Table 8.2 *Summary of functions of media effect models in relation to issue cycle*

Informal interaction face-to-face	Formal communication Mass Media Effect	Relation to issue cycle
Normalisation of a frame of reference		
Crowding	Diffusion	Over full hype cycle
Leadership	Knowledge gaps	Early in the issue cycle
Norm formation	Cultivation analysis	Long wave representations
?	Diegetic prototyping	Early in the issue cycle
?	Rumors and echo chambers	Early in the issue cycle
Assimilation of challenges to existing social representations		
Peer pressure	Spiral of silence	Post peak in issue cycle
Obedience	HiFi transmission, consistency	Later in issue cycle
Accomodation of social representations to challenges		
Persuasion	Agenda setting	Early in hype or issue cycle
Conversion	Framing and priming	Early in long waves

of streams of independent activity. Resonance amplifies and enhances that which is already there. Thus, our concluding claim is: mediated social influence arises from resonance of formal and informal communication. Mass media effect models elaborate basic modalities of social influence along the issue cycle.

Table 8.2 orders various modalities of social influence across the three functions in relation to social representations, considers two types of communication and locates social influence in the issue cycles.

In all this we needed to consider empirically the facts of attention cycles. Mass media attention is no constant but comes in waves, short (hype), medium (issues) and long (grand narratives). Evidence for nested cycles is now easily at hand, as we can inspect mass media databases both retrospectively and monitor them into the future. These ingredients, doubling up reality of limited and unstable attention, help us to better understand the workings of social influence under conditions of symbolic mediation. They help us to recognise that mass media effects are derived from key functions of creating joint attention and joint intentionality across changing media technologies. At this level of abstraction, there is not much difference between a morning newspaper and Donald Trump's tweets.

This scheme should help us to link in a coherent way what hitherto was separated. Thus, different modalities of social influence enhanced by mass mediation establishes a frame of reference. Media are equally part of *assimilating* dissent into this given framework, and they are equally given to *accommodating* the frame of reference to the persistent challenges and dissent.

In the next chapter, we go even a step further and consider how social influence modalities operate under conditions of artefact installations in society. We ask: how do different modalities of social influence recruit designed environments beyond being mere carriers of signs and symbols?

In Essence

Mass media amplify the functionality of different influence modalities. They create genres of communication that inform and entertain, but function by assimilating novelty, accommodating challenges and normalising certain opinions and beliefs as common sense.

The mass media create mass attention to novel ideas/products. The mass media help the uptake m of issues in cycles. The diffusion path, however, may become dislocated. Mass media provide the feedback loop for revising novel ideas towards successful uptake.

The mass media serve thus in the battle for hearts and minds. What is initially cultivated and diegetically prototyped, is shored up by diffusion, HiFi transmission and spirals of silence; and ultimately adapted by agenda setting, framing and priming. In the process, the social representations acquire common-sense status as a matter of course (de facto).

CHAPTER 9

Designing and Resisting Artefacts

phase	modality	function for CS	Mode 3 artefact
Order created 'out of Chaos', new beginnings			
Phase 1	norm formation	**Normalisation**	installed affordances
	crowds		barricades
	prototyping		Beta-version
	leadership		monument
Challenge from newcomers, homecomers, strangers or 'aliens'			
Phase 2	*fait accompli*	**Assimilation**	installation (wall)
	majority		ready-made diffusion
	minority (elite)		nudge, boost, woop
	persuasion		algorithm
	authority		reliable, trusted system
Sustained challenge by consistent dissenters			
Phase 3	persuasion	**Accomodation**	re-design
	minority (non dominant)		innovation
	resistance		alternative design
	?		?

Figure 9.1   A challenge and response model VIII: designed artefacts

Imagine that you are the director of a place that hosts Hannibal Lecter (*Silence of the Lambs*; movie of 1991; books by Thomas Harris, 1988 and 1981). He is a man with a double life, by day a renowned forensic psychiatrist, at night a notorious psychopathic serial killer who cannibalises his victims. You want to prevent future killings by keeping Lecter in-house at night and by signing him up during the day to trace other serial killers. How will you go about this? Most likely *requesting* him to stay home will not work; neither does *dissuading* him from killing. He is agreeable to good arguments, but when it comes to it, he simply ignores the conclusions. Signing up friends to *pressure* him will also not work, he is too cunning and recognises no friends. You finally decide to construct an iron cage to lock him in. You use a **techno-fix** to create compliance. A prison confinement will enhance your authority and maybe later also persuasion. Here, the police can talk to him about other serial killers, but he himself is prevented from killing.

In Chapter 8, we considered modalities of social influence under conditions of mass mediation with books, newsprint, radio, TV and social media platforms. In this chapter, we generalise further: how do designed artefacts extend social influence? How do power stations, roads, cars, bicycles, washing machines, dishwashers or coffee machines extend social influence? Modern high-tech artefacts arise from techno-science at the frontiers of knowledge. So we ask, how does technoscience influence hearts, minds and behaviour? People often talk of a techno-fix, that is, providing a technical solution for a problem of social influence.

Why artefacts? A common answer is: because they are useful. A more considered answer focuses on civilisation; technology is a factor of progress (Mokyr, 1990). There are tangible benefits of enhancing human capabilities of perceiving, moving and reaching, eating, producing and reproducing: technology makes and takes lives (Gehlen, 1980) and enhances lives from beginning to end (Edgerton, 2006). From reproductive technologies, to medicines and armament, artefacts are stocks by which human societies are constituted (see Box 9.1).

Beyond the expected user benefits, everyday behaviour is made predictable by installations (Lahlou, 2017). The issue here is **inter-objectivity**: objects are designed by and in turn frame the relations between people. Very different from other apes, humans relate through accumulated clutter (see Chapter 3; Latour, 1996). We reach each other in cars, aeroplanes and on bicycles, meet in houses and eat by sitting on chairs around a table using cutlery (at least in Western style); the house shelters and the table apportions mutual distance between people; plates, spoons and forks enforce hygiene (no dirty hands on the food!)

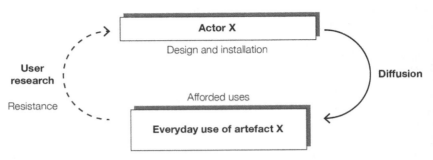

Figure 9.2   The duality of artefact-as-designed and artefact-in-use

and contain potential violence (behave yourself!); indeed, cutlery 'civi-lised' the roaming nomads (Elias, 1978). Morality is scripted into the inter-objectivity of artefacts.

We must treat artefacts as we considered mass mediation in Chapter 8, as a dual reality of artefact *as-designed* and *as-used* (see Figure 9.2). Artefacts induce behaviours, the scandals of artefacts, and everyday use changes the artefacts. Humans know how to make things, but finally they are ignorant of what they are doing because of the unintended consequences. So, how does stuff come about; how does it stabilise sociality; how does it assimilate dissent; and how do we adjust to challenges of artefacts? Social psychology has a limited voice here, dealing with stuff mainly as ready made for assimilation, as with Hannibal Lecter encaged. For actor–network theory (ANT), artefacts are 'actants', behaving like humans (note: artefacts behave, but do not act). In the inter-objective entanglement of people and stuff, it remains obscure what is causality and what is agency. 'Agency' and 'causality' are attributed in hindsight; the event has taken place and an account is given (Brey, 2005); somebody must be responsible. While 'responsible agency' is the moral reserve of humans, there are functional similarities between morality and 'stuffy actants': artefacts set standards for behaviour; they force our hands, scandalise, recruit minds and give plea-sure, and accommodate our resistances by shape shifting. We must deal with inter-objectivity as we treat intersubjectivity; these are parallel modes of social products (Sherif's term) which are established, defended against detractors and shape shifted by insisting dissent.

Box 9.1 Object relations

*When considering artefacts we must consider '**object relations**', which is a general problem of philosophy. Indeed, phenomenologists have laboured over this and recognised that we rarely relate to objects in the fullness of their sensory qualities. When listening we naturally hear a 'Harley Davidson', or the 'wind', and not the qualities of sound. To characterise the 'sound object' without naming the source requires a trained ear, bracketing off the preconceptions and misconstructions of the 'natural attitude'; this exercise is called **epoche** (Boehme, 2006; 58ff; Husserl, 1931, 59ff). Before any conceptual awareness, we are already entangled with being-with-others-in-the-sound; we can become aware of this **intersubjectively** in **inter-objectivity**; we relate to objects together with others.*

*Heidegger identified three layers of understanding an 'object' as a carrier of features: Firstly, '**things**' are simply there before any categorisation as stone, mountain, cloud or plant. Secondly, there is useful '**stuff**'; a flint stone used as an axe and a mountain as quarry have shifted status; most 'stuff' is thus designed and put into place and framed by a function, the flint stone to split, the quarry to carve building stuff; stuff is the world according to human machination which in turn entangles makers (homo faber) and users in utility. Thirdly, form is the key to '**art works**' as in sculpture, drama or music; here the engagement is less utility, but revealing a truth (Heidegger, 1977a and 1977b). For our purposes, we focus on stuff, on installing a world ('Gestell') like a plumber does (in Swiss German, an 'installateur' is a certified plumber, an expert in lining up pipes). Through machinations we discover the pulling power of a horse (horse power), or the energy of atoms (in tons TNT or gigawatts) or the changing climate (as in the Anthropocene). We now know how to change the climate; just heat up the planet by generating greenhouse gases.*

Normalisation of Behaviour by Artefacts

For modalities of social influence, normalisation is the function of establishing a frame of reference for thinking, feeling and behaving, of setting a standard to last. Let us consider processes by which 'artefacts' set standards with barricades in protests, infrastructure installations, fetishisation of things and monuments (see Box 9.2).

To the Barricades: Amplifying the Crowd Effect

The **barricade** is a glorious symbol of insurrection and a tragic passing point into a new dawn (Corbin & Mayeur, 1996; Hazan, 2015). This symbolic value arises from the barricades of Paris which were instrumental in the nineteenth-century crowd revolts that made new governments, and are still in use in the 2019 'Gilet Jaunes' protests across France.

The barricade is an improvised construction (from barrique = wine barrel). A city phenomenon; temporarily partitioning and claiming urban spaces; rebellious people defining a no-go area in their city by lining up vehicles or piling up stones, wood or sandbag. They are defensive obstacles against an advancing party, but little more than a temporary measure to challenge authorities. The barricade is also a stage, where rebels from high up can throw insult at police or soldiers and subvert their loyalty. Barricades are an effective part of crowd events; street violence and piling up rubble belong to the repertoire of social movements (Tilly, 2004). In 1866 Auguste Blanqui, a notorious ancestor of the urban guerrilla, published a manual of how to construct barricades to make a revolution. Where there are crowds there can be barricades to enhance their effect. This emblem of a city in turmoil and its effectiveness in politics gave crowd psychology its enduring undertone of anxiety (see Chapter 2).

Affordance: Installation and Inscription of Behaviour

Installation is a term used in the art world, referring to a three-dimensional set-up that induces an effect on the spectator who enters the space. They are powerful demonstrations of how a design works on a personal mindset; it reveals influence:

> entering an installation is experienced as being in a situation that has a momentum of its own: one feels naturally driven to what is appropriate. The components of the installation ... scaffold, produce and regulate a specific normative behavioural sequence ... installations operate as a behavioral attractor where the choices left to the subject are often minor (Lahlou, 2017, 14).

Large scale installations are called **infrastructures**. These arteries of modern life are a hidden basis of social progress, only visible when failing; we do not notice the sewage system unless it is blocked, overflowing and fetid. A comprehensive understanding of infrastructures spans not only public works and the physics of nature, but also the operating procedures, management and policies that respond or not to **societal demands**. The discussions on infrastructure include its public status, may be privately financed, run or maintained under public oversight. Infrastructure installations often build on existing structures, are networked and vulnerable to nefarious interference and thus a **security and safety concern**.

Box 9.2 Standardisation, accepted institutions and mediation

A feature of installations is **standardisation**, *that is, the specification of parts for easier recombination. There is a paradox in this rationalisation: reducing the flexibility of parts enhances the potential for recombination of parts. This is exemplified in the 'well-tempered tuning' of the twelve equal intervals in seventeenth-century Europe that brought forth European classical music (Barnett, 2002, 450). The mechanisation of tools involves the pressing, stamping and casting of parts, which once standardised become easily interchangeable between different installations (Giedion, 1975, 47ff). Current concerns about standardisation focus on computing and software developments and reflect on the tensions between standard and flexibility (Hanseth et al, 1996). Standards set the game for competition; a market for standards or path-dependency where latecomers follow a standard set earlier; the latter is faster but not best. The QWERTY keyboards still operate a manual typewriter to avoid jamming a mechanism, when there are no mechanics left to jam. People proposed better keyboards, but skills are embodied in the finger dexterity of millions of writers; retraining them would be too costly (David, 1985). Other standards are set by committees to opt-in; this is time consuming but better as in the 'metre' treaty (1875 Paris conference) or standard world times (1884 Meridian conference). Understanding how standards operate undermines* **technological determinism**, *it is not a question of TINA (there is no alternative). Technical standards are what is feasible under the circumstances; they translate interests, articulate and align actors.*

Another feature of installations is their **institutional buttress**. *Searle (2005) analysed the mode of existence of an institution. Designed stuff is a social institution when given a status so that we can say 'X counts as Y, in C'. For example 'copper formed into cables' (X) is an 'electricity grid' (function Y) in modern society (C) (Hindriks, 2003). This is only a reality in so far as people melt copper into cables for 'electricity grids', and this is an agreed status function. For this to work, it needs the* **joint intentionality** *of a shared vision and desire. Copper is* **assigned the function** *Y 'transmit electricity in our grid'; copper by itself could not care less. Community* **acceptance** *of this function is a defining feature of installations. This status function 'copper grid providing power' has deontic powers of rights and duties; enabling, empowerment or authorisation of things to happen. We are tied into an installation with* **duty, requirement and obligation**. *However, we act according to our own desire within the installation. Indeed, I may use my laptop as I see fit, but to do so I need the appropriate adapter. The laptop is my decision field, the grid is a requirement (not to speak of the installation 'laptop').*

A final characteristic of an installation is **mediation**. *This difference between 'means' and 'mediation' has been worked out by Latour (1994). 'Means' are tied into fixed ends, while 'mediation' involves the translating, drifting and shifting of ends on fixed means. Stuff might be designed for a purpose A, but users will translate its use and shift its function into new directions B, C or D. In reality, the ends are never fixed, the context of development does not determine the context of use.* **We are good at making things, but mostly we do not know what we are**

> **doing.** *For example, Edison's sound record was developed to minute business meetings (fixed purpose); it made the music industry for the next 100 years (use shifted goal). Condoms designed as contraceptive are distributed to prevent AIDS infections, and then used as elastics to fix machine tools in Africa (use shifted goal). Atomic bombs were built to create maximum destruction; they have now become an expensive posture to dissuade others from ever using them against us. The purpose has shifted from taking lives to signalling status (Cirincione, 2007, 47ff).*

Real-world installations combine affordances, skills and social regulation into pervasive and effective systems for channelling the flow of everyday behaviour. A modern traffic system for cars is such an installation that is massively efficient. Installed structures are set for duration, stability and resilience in the face of challenges:

> installations, because of their redundant threefold structure, have enough resilience and regulatory power to channel 'appropriate' behaviour even in novices or reluctant subjects (ibidem, 15).

Affordance is a concept credited to Gibson (1977), who showed how we perceive the world from an action tendency. On the move, we experience things affording this or that action: a thing to grasp, a handle to press, a lever to pull, a walkable surface, a picture to look at, a wall to climb, a fence to keep off; all preconscious, just happening. This logic is built into good design. Good stuff is functional, graspable, sustainable, hygienic, easily maintained and avoids mishandling errors; it feels and looks good (Norman, 2004; Sterling, 2005, 112).

So in principle, a designer creates affordances that make you do exactly what she wants you to do. A door announces 'here you leave the room!' If it does not achieve that, we have a dysfunctional door, maybe a hidden or a fake door. Thus, within the house, a door channels behaviour towards the exit/entry; somebody wants you and most people to move on this path. You could in principle leave through the wall or the window, but you rarely do so, as a major effort is required and you are institutionally dissuaded from doing so. The door has affordance. Thus, placing a door means we normalise people's behaviour: leave through here! This is how we do things around here, this is our frame of action.

Installations shape behaviour by *inscription*. Designs come with an instruction manual of how to operate; this manual is either printed for reading, or we mobilise our typified social knowledge or *know-how*. Social situations have a script of how to go about (Schank & Abelson, 1977), so do objects. When I buy a new gadget, I might read the user instruction, or I simply try it out to get started. The gadget urges you to do what the designer wants you to do in order to use it functionally. Like a ritual, a certain sequence of steps is required to get it started. In social learning we absorb these scripts and make them part of our action plans (Cranach & Valach, 1984). Hotels used to pin guest room keys to a bulky weight: too much to carry in your pocket. This is not to enhance the functionality of the key, but the morality of the house: 'Behave yourself, leave me at the reception'.

An interlock is a design that inscribes a particular sequence of actions: one action is required before another can take place. This is another way of establishing moral standards or supporting your memory: for example, a cash dispenser requires you to pull your card out before the money is dispensed. This gives the bank till a morality: 'you shall not forget your credit card'. With designs the banks avoid the nuisance of customers forgetting their cards and having to deal with it. Equally, a tobacco and alcohol vending machine can ask you for a valid ID card to prove your legal age before dispensing the goods. It thus enforces 'no sales to underage customers'. Similarly, you might have to breathe into a tube to check your alcohol level before your car responds to the ignition key. Again the message is clear: 'no drink driving'. We can see here that morality and standards of behaviour are easily embedded in designs (see Box 9.2).

The Fetish: The Magic Power of Objects

As installations take hold in society, they move from ideation to physical reality and back to ideation. We need to consider how we attribute status to objects, so they can influence us like a leader or an authority can. One such process is called 'making a **fetish** out of it' (Blandin, 2002, p. 255). We traditionally consider 'fetishisation' an aberration, but recent interpretations have rediscovered here another anthropological constant and the return of the repressed (Boehme, 2006; Ellen, 1988; Latour, 1993; see Box 9.3).

Consider for a moment a fashion item, a style icon, also an installation. Such a commodity is probably 5 per cent production and 95 per cent branding, or 10 per cent use and 90 per cent symbolic value. You are not buying a piece of leather in shoe or bag form and function, but the lifestyle and status of being a better person. To sustain this power over you, the production is small for an exclusive market. Luxury is never on sale and overproduction is destroyed. In 2018, *Burberry of London* destroyed luxury goods to the value of £28 million. Such industries have large budgets to cultivate the brand; holding the status of a product is a heavy investment.

Rhodes (1999, p22), on reviewing historical visions of technology, states that 'technology competes with the gods at miracle-making and the gods

---

Box 9.3 The fetish in modern society

A fetish is an object that bestows and holds power over us. Ellen (1988) reviews thinking about 'fetishism' and finds that a 'fetish' is a class of entities that arises from an escalation of basic human cognition in three phases (ibidem, 231):

- *Phase 1,* **making icons***: humans classify experience as percepts into categories, abstract as* **types** *and concrete as* **tokens***. By making concrete tokens of abstract types, we objectify a concept. By creating an iconic entity that in key features (prototypically) re-presents what is absent and desired; an icon is similar to the original. Parts can also re-present: a piece of clothing can be that 'obscure object of desire' and satisfy the sexual fetishist.*

- *Phase 2,* **animating icons***: we attribute features to the material icon; these features come by way of metaphorical transfer from plants, animals or humans culminating in personification. The thing is thus animated with specific potentials and propensities.*

- *Phase 3,* **conflating signifier and signified***: by considering inanimate objects to behave like animals (zoomorph), or like humans (anthropomorph), we tend to conflate the symbol and its referent. This stuff gains causal power over us, rather than merely signposting such causes. What is only a 'sign of evil' ('as if the devil'), becomes itself 'devil'.*

This opens up the ambivalence of control: by creating a fetish, we gain control over the unfamiliar; a fetish is here functionally similar to magic. We turn an unknown entity into a recognised utility, reserving the ability to destroy it if it does not serve. The fetish relationship is **ambivalent***, we seek it but worry about it. Paradoxically, the more power we attribute, the more we seek counter-control in order not to be overpowered. Mistaking the symbol for its referent creates anxieties of misplaced attention which erupt in iconoclastic destructions. 'Fetish' has been a missionary's battle to decry the futility of stones and wooden effigies which the ignorant flock is venerating. Also, holding to a fetish has been something that 'others' do, Catholics, the primitive, children, the mad, the poor, the pre-civilised. However, Ellen's reconstruction of the fetish relation is far from notions of regressive pathology and evolution, as in the Positivist (Comte) Progress from fetishism –> polytheism –> monotheism (ibidem, 214). Neither civilisation nor therapy need to displace what is normal human functioning. The discussion retains, however, a doubt about what is effective: is it the object itself, or the spirit that is put into the fetish? Frigg (2013) talks of 'clever fetishists', rejecting 'clever objects'. Asking whether an object can be 'clever', he seeks to expurgate any 'animism' that arises from such an attribution with Danto's formula of art: $I(o) = C$; the attribution of features to objects is an interpretation $I = C$; the object (o) is unaffected. But, what interpretations are available: scientific, artistic, magical, which are more or less effective, like any metaphor, to gain new insights or to persuade others? That is how even scientists fetishise, albeit with much restraint: they create models producing outcomes and risk conflating them with reality.*

> *Boehme (2006) and Latour (1993) rescue the maligned fetish from iconoclasts who take too literally the scriptural ban on 'graven images'. The history of monotheistic doctrine is in large part a balancing act between the ban on and popular demand for fetishes, defending their contribution as memory props and illustrations of the word (ibidem, 157ff). Boehme shows that the modern mentality is not so civilised and enlightened to the extent that all fetishes have gone. Rather than purifying the sphere of lives, us and them, and keeping the fetish locked up in 'them, the primitive', the contemporary fetish is on money and technology. The denunciation of the fetish has ended. Enlightenment is not defeated though, but has mollified as to what is humanly rational. This does not eradicate the ambivalence of fetishisation that alienates and distracts (attention on the icon rather than reality/ God). The quest is less for 'no fetish', but for an optimal number: what level of stardom, iconicity and branding does a technical installation need?*

take revenge: no wonder we're nervous about it'. Indeed, myth making and visioning is part of the resource mobilisation for new technology creating hype cycles (see Chapter 8; Bauer, 2015; Dierkes et al., 1996). Visioning focuses attention and provides a common reference for investment and recruitment of competences. Myth- and magic-making thus permeate technological installations as a modern triumph of irrationality (Stivers, 2001). Modern society is obsessed by efficiency (p. 39). The magical word appears in the discourse of administration, economics and science. All magic needs a 'set of words and practices that are believed to influence or effect a desired outcome' (ibidem, 42).

The myths and magic of installations are manifold: they bring fortunes and happiness, make babies and contentment, 'make lives healthier, easier and more comfortable' (the oldest survey item of public attitudes to science, asked since 1957) and defend the territory and keep evil forces at bay. Our relationship with installations can be considered to be premodern. We might be critical of fetishes but we nevertheless surround ourselves with them, because fetishes empower us to control the world; with their help we extend our reach and social influence. We endorse a fetish to impress other people with our extended capabilities.

Monuments: Memory, Leadership and Collective Identity

Swiss school books used to tell of Willhelm Tell, a mythical national hero: Count Gessler, representing the foreign occupiers, demanded that every passer-by greeted his hat, which was placed on top of a pole. Tell refused and was apprehended for 'lese majeste', insulting the authority. Among many other things, this story demonstrates the influence of objects: Gessler's hat was the authority of the land (though the story is about challenging this authority). We need to recognise that material set-ups buttress and extend authority in the community and instil awe and admiration. How is obedience enhanced when authority is buttressed by built **monuments**? According to Bellentani & Panico (2016), 'monuments are built forms to confer dominant meanings on space ... to remind people of important events and individuals' (28). Every nation has its landmarks. A nuclear power installation dominates the landscape as an emblem of national prowess: for example, '30% of the country's energy is produced here, that is impressive'. Scattered around urban spaces are effigies of national heroes. These are memory props, like the old knot in the handkerchief, to remind us of defining historical events. The gothic cathedrals that line Northern France are gigantic props; preaching monks and listening congregations find their memories buttressed by the gothic artwork. Mediaeval builders took their lead from ancient rhetoric: on important matters in life, memory works better with 'vivid images, beautiful, ugly or grotesque' (Ad Herennium book III, 37; see Yates, 1966). The stained-glass windows, the space and tympanum portals tell moral stories of light triumphing over darkness; Gnostic dualism held at bay. Such memory props have aesthetic as well as political functions. Indeed, the aesthetics of cathedrals, bridges and nuclear installations fill books of engineering and art history. For our purpose, we consider their cognitive, moral–emotional and political influence.

Monuments have epistemic value (Churchill was x, y, z), but more importantly they present our identity (we are ...), preserve our unity (united we stand) and guide our actions (keep calm and carry on; see Bar-Tal, 2000). After disasters and wars, monuments celebrate the spirit of sacrifice, resilience and reconstruction. Monuments are cultural memory of mythical times where the chronology is lost (Assmann, 2008, 111); one thinks here of the pyramids of Egypt or Mexico. A monument imparts knowledge; know-that has cognitive function. Necessarily selective, it cues passers-by to fill in the details: what did Churchill do, the daughter asks? By telling the story, we perform our shared beliefs and dominant discourse. But, in commemoration, we commit errors of commission and omission, thereby obliterating and obfuscating historical facts. Memory fades, but monuments last in wind and weather and memory props can revive memory. A 'cold' monument, lost in the urban landscape, can become 'hot' again and stir emotions and create controversy; it must be toppled or be reclaimed. A small alteration on Churchill's statue creates an art installation that provokes thinking: giving him a Mohican hairstyle by putting a slice of green grass on his head, or holding a word cloud to his mouth declaring 'a United Europe' reclaims Churchill as a non-conformist and pioneer of the European Union. Monuments depersonalise the leader of the nation; the token on the pedestal is made into a prototype in stone (or bronze). Churchill reminds us of the virtues of being British, one of us who led us against them: irreverent, determined and resilient we were united (see Chapter 3). DeGaulle on Champs d'Elysee in Paris reminds us that he is France (La France, c'est Moi); and in the inscription 'there is an eternal correlation between the Grandeur of France, and Liberty in the world' (DeGaulle was a tall man).

Other monuments are simply awe-inspiring. Dams, space rockets, factories, temples, cathedrals or towers are spacious, tall and take your breath away. They fix your gaze on high and into the deep, in awe and terror, carrying your spirit beyond. Large-scale technological installations, such as nuclear power plants or the MIR space station floating in space, exude trans-human qualities pointing to another world (Blumenberg, 2010). They elicit a sense of 'voluntary subjection', you yield to authority not by force, simply overwhelmed by what is your better and higher. In this way, installations resonate our spiritual potential, inspire feelings of awe (Keltner & Haidt, 2003) and elicit our small selves (Piff et al., 2015). In the face of installations, you do not raise questions, you obey as instructed. Court buildings are 'architectures of authority', often set on hills, and within the court room the judge resides above everybody else. Authority is embodied in height and volume. Thus monuments establish authority by cultivating awe. When *Notre Dame de Paris* was on fire (15 April 2019), many people were personally devastated, particularly if they had once been in that space and personally experienced the awe of something higher and better in that patrimony of humanity.

Assimilation Pressures of the Fait Accompli

Once our installations and monuments are built, and invested with the powers of a fetish, they remind us who we are, what we are capable of and how great our past and future will be, we have established the **inter-objectivity** around which to organise social life. We have argued that this not only makes our lives easier, healthier and more comfortable, but it is also heavily in-scripted with moral imperatives. *This is how we do things around here, take it or leave it.* Our beliefs, attitudes and norms of behaviour, in brief the intersubjectivity that underpins joint intentionality, is now buttressed by inter-objectivity. Human social life is stabilised by two pillars, norms and artefacts, and this as we argued earlier, is quite different from simians and other animals.

In this section, we will examine how installations also enhance the assimilation of social life; how deviations are reined in and conformity is enforced under conditions of installations. Here we examine assimilation by other means in mode 3: artefacts.

Diffusion as Fait Accompli and Ready-Made

A successful episode in the social sciences is the idea that artefacts roll out in society like mass diffusion between mediums of different density, mathematically modelled with the (sigmoid) curve of diffusion (Mahajan & Peterson, 1985). This reached the status of a paradigm (Valente & Rogers, 1995) until declared dead in the 1990s (Godin, 2005), but is enjoying a vivid afterlife in 'acceptance research', that is, defending installations without any questions asked. The linear model of design assumes that stuff emerges 'preformed' in scientific ideas; once invented, they become marketable products coached on by engineers and as the artefact enters the market, social scientists create the necessary attention and usher in social learning by contagion, obedience to authority and peer pressure (Payton Young, 2009). Indeed, **diffusion of innovation** assumes that in the early stages of the process, we accept novelty on the authority of innovators whom we believe are competent leaders in the 'world of innovation'. Later, early adopters emulate each other by way of viral contagion. After the tipping point, the majority puts pressure on late adopters and laggards to stop being silly and to see the light. Albeit modelled with impressive mathematics, this is a highly misleading account that fixates on ready-mades and ignores reinvention, redesign and creative use of objects (Edgerton, 1999). This 'fixedness' is a highly unrealistic assumption about moving designs, not describing reality but further pressurising potential adopters with an imperative of speed; diffusion graphs highlight speed after take-off, but are notoriously wrong on historical beginnings (Hannemyr, 2003). Diffusion of ready-mades is a very special case, as we argued in Chapter 8, of mindless imitation and lack of public deliberation guided by an irrational pro-innovation ideology (Godin & Vinck, 2017).

Rather than a description, diffusion itself is a negotiation technique, a red line in the sand. The stuff on offer is all there is; *TINA = there is no alternative*, accept it. Mothers know how to propose few options: fix the child on the chair to eat, then offer either broccoli or spinach. Eating time is not negotiable. Artefacts are ways of drawing red lines in the sand, and harnessing the normative power of the fact. Moral philosophers argue against the 'naturalistic fallacy': we cannot infer from 'is' what 'ought to be'; good cannot be defined by something being desirable, evolved or pleasant, this only applies the criterion 'good', and does not define it. Fact and values are independent. However, facts and artefacts gain staying power purely through the power of habit. The factual can become the new norm. In reverse, if 90 per cent of drivers violate the speed limit, the fact can challenge the regulation as it might look absurd, out of place and become too costly to enforce.

Social psychology knows of **acceptance after the fact** under the terms 'forced compliance' and 'cognitive dissonance' (Cooper, 2012; see Chapter 7). Festinger and colleagues studied a community who expected the world to flood and made preparations to leave the earth in a rescuing UFO, but nothing happened. How did they respond to this 'dissonance' between belief (the end is nigh) and reality (it did not end)? People coped in several ways with this discrepancy: (a) they updated their belief: the end has been postponed; and we were tested and passed because we 'seekers' obeyed the authority of the word; and (b) the 'seekers' went out proselytising new converts now strengthened in their belief. The theory of 'dissonance' claims that people are intolerant to contradictory beliefs or inconsistencies of mind and action (which might be cultural assumptions rather than universal): The presence of dissonance gives rise to pressures to reduce or eliminate dissonance. The strength of pressures . . . is a function of the magnitude of dissonance'; we are energised to set it straight (Festinger, 1957, 18). In laboratory experiments, people were put into situations that induced contradiction between behaviour and their attitudes, the forced compliance paradigm (see Chapter 7). Notoriously, people found a boring task afterwards more interesting, if they received no incentive for it. High returns gave people a reason to avoid 'dissonance': we prefer interesting tasks, we did this one only for the money, not because it is interesting. Those who did it without rewards, on the other hand, followed Mary Poppins: 'in every job that must be done, there is an element of fun'. It is only a matter of discovering it. Thus, extrinsic rewards can corrupt intrinsic motivation as rewards crowd out the fun of doing it.

New technologies even frame the way we think about ourselves. The computer is widely used as a metaphor for the mind. If we can make a computer think, we understand 'thinking'. Therefore, thinking is computing. Equally, we talk and think about 'self' no longer as the potentially neurotic confluence of unconscious energies (Freud), but as a computer program that needs debunking, updating and reprograming, with limited processing capacity and memory space (Turkle, 1984). In the presence of the Internet and social media, we come to believe that dialogical communication is what we do on social media, and that the self is parked on Facebook (Turkle, 2016). Not only do we easily adapt our beliefs and attitudes to stuff and artefacts we get entangled with, but we change the very manner in which we conceive of ourselves: we not only use computers, we become computers (if we are not careful); assimilation is so pervasive because of habituation and dissonance reduction in favour of the **fait accompli**.

Obedience and Trust in Reliable Systems

Humans not only trust others, but also confer trust to artefacts because of their capacity for delivery: I trust my blender not to explode on me in the morning as I mash fruits into juice, and I do so because I successfully mashed in the past, and the machine is a reputable brand make; they have tested it for reliability. However, trust and authority of artefacts and installations are of a particular nature: they are based on competent performance, thus entirely modern. While human authority retains atavistic elements of social hierarchy, kinship and tradition as sources of legitimacy, the authority of artefacts arises mainly from functional performance and the reputation of doing so; we trust artefacts because they are work (Luhmann, 1989, 59ff). Trusting a system can ignore varying motives; actants perform as required, cogs in the machine; they have the expertise and the restraint of keeping errors under control (ibidem, 64ff). Trusting a system comes with an awareness that these installations are designed to perform but could go otherwise; trust relieves us from the need to know more; we trust the system or have to undertake a risk assessment. Installations are like sausages, if we knew what makes them, we would not eat them. Under this veil of ignorance logic we confer authority to systems and we trust them and follow their requirements as scripted. I cross the bridge not because I tested its concrete, but because I trust the system that built it and the management procedures that maintain it. The modality of social influence, which we recognise as obedience to authority, is extended by reliable artefacts. In particular, the modern element of authority, the competence to deliver, is greatly enhanced by systems. This reaches the point where we trust systems and not persons because we think the latter will fail us. Thus, artefacts bias the constitution of authority in society towards competent performance, and devalue other sources of authority such as kinship, old age or charisma.

Persuasion by Algorithm: In This Opiated State I Stand Persuaded

Much is being talked about social media; how they create 'bubbles' and 'echo chambers' of confirmatory bias, polarization and reduced information, even 'fake news' and misinformation. It is difficult to disentangle moral panic about new media technology from the real phenomena.

The brave new world of social media seems to create a world of the Biblical 'Matthew Effect' from the parabel of talents: those who have will be given more of the same. We are increasingly provided with information similar to that which we have been searching before: 'people who buy X also look at Y' is the invitation from Amazon.com, Inc. Under the pretext of tailoring information for the user, we end up with more of the same within an echo chamber of homogeneity. We are subjected to efforts of persuasion, but this persuasion is not via good arguments in search for a better point, rather in the context of prepared circumstances. And these circumstances of persuasion are provided by algorithms.

An **algorithm** is originally a mathematical term that stands against heuristic. Both terms stand for procedures to solve problems. The algorithm guarantees a solution; the heuristic only brings you closer. Algorithm is therefore a list of computer commands that specify the solution including calculation, data analysis and automated reasoning. Algorithms are installations that have become much more, they are now capital to invest in and resources to make money. They mine large amounts of data and provide us with search results and choices that are tailored to us. This also allows companies, such as Cambridge Analytica, to create business models for information consultancy. Massive numbers of Facebook users are tested for their personality type (Big Five) and these types are linked to with what they 'liked' in the past (Hinds & Joinson, 2019). This allows the profiling of inclinations, and to create micro-tailored messages that are likely to persuade you under the circumstances of (a) the personality type that you are, and (b) the preferences that you have revealed in your social media footprint. Under these circumstances, you are more likely to be persuaded. You are persuaded because 'liking' mobilises bodily opiates in the 'hedonic hotspots' of the brain, and this gets you hooked on what you like by intense pleasure (Berridge, 2018). The Internet has become a massive manipulation machine shaping behaviour along the logic of operant conditioning on an intermittent reinforcement schedule of releasing your own opiates triggered by algorithms that curate stimulation. The installation makes us mindless. If viral communication implies reduced personal resistance, then algorithmic provision of what you like makes you vulnerable to contagion, indeed, it tampers with your immune system.

Figure 9.3   Delegating conformity pressure to a sign, a person or a road bump

Conformity Pressure by Moral Delegation

Once a moral behaviour is established and mandated, 'to be one of us, you must do X', there are ways of enforcing this intersubjective obligation (Latour, 1994). Let us take traffic speed limits as an example. There are good reasons to reduce traffic speed to 20 miles per hour in residential areas of cities; it reduces accidents, severity of accidents, noise emissions and saves fuel. But beyond good reasons, we want to enforce this rule of conduct. Firstly, we can simply sign post the situation. A 20 miles per hour sign indicates the valid speed limit (see Figure 9.3). Secondly, the speed limit can be enforced by an official watching and handing out speeding tickets to those who drive over the limit. Sometimes an effigy of an officer in uniform or police patrol car does the job. Thirdly, a live technical display indicating how much you need to reduce speed to stay within limits, or a well-placed camera threatening to take pictures of speeding cars does the job. Fourthly, and most efficiently, we simply build speed bumps, clearly marked as elevations on the road. If missed, the car violently shakes and forces the driver to take responsibility and apologise to fellow passengers. Speed bumps delegate the enforcement of community morality: we drive here at 20, to a techno-fix. Thus conformity is enforced and driving assimilated to local standards.

The Lock-Out and Lock-In to Defend the Moral Community

The most obvious technical fix to moral boundaries is the *lock-out* and the *lock-in*. A lock-out sets a moral boundary between those who are and those who are not entitled to be included: to enforce *you shall not trespass* and also *you shall not leave* (the prison), we build high walls that physically prevent people from passing.

We manage human interaction through fences, walls and linear barriers that line up along boundaries. The construction, maintenance and manning of watch walls (as in the Chinese wall) is a subject of historical research (Spring, 2015). Historical barriers were military constructions across Europe, Central and East Asia, mainly to keep out roaming nomads and 'uncivilised' barbarians that push from the North (Central Asian steps) and from the South (Sahara). Humans built walls mainly for defensive purposes (ibidem, p249ff). A barrier across a narrow land corridor prevented unwanted passage through a valley or over a mountain pass, as in the Gansu corridor into Western China. Walls policed the boundary between literate settlers and illiterate nomads. A barrier kept these people out, because it was difficult to negotiate formal treaties with illiterate people. Walls protected valuable land along large river valleys against raiding warriors from the hinterland, as in ancient Iraq and the Chinese river valleys. Equally, walls surrounded medieval cities, which we can still admire as monuments of national heritage. Aggressive barriers (ibidem, p. 258ff) sought to consolidate previous expansion and to prepare for further expansion, to facilitate communication and movement of troupes. Magnificent barriers impressed and dissuaded intruders; but they also impressed the home audience: grand communal efforts strengthen the ties of unification.

Walls continue to be part of international politics to the present day, though the boundaries between 'illiterate' and 'literate' parties is no longer so clear: US president Trump and his 'Great Wall' at the Mexican border comes to mind, paid for by Mexicans, it seeks to block immigration from Latin America and to unify the nation. A jointly built wall against common enemies (immigrants) is part of forming we-groups. Over-engineered walls can demonstrate power and become monuments for posterity. But wall building can overstretch resources, lock-ins reach the limits of toleration. Thus, the wall along the 'Iron Curtain' that separated Eastern and Western Europe 1946–1989, and from the early 1960s split Berlin into two parts, came crashing down in 1989. There are curious historical exceptions: there were no barriers in the Indus Valley, in the Portuguese and Spanish expansion and at the North American 'frontier' beyond temporary fortifications.

Barriers are also used for social segregation. In Padua, people erected a wall to separate out a housing block with mainly immigrants (reported in the *Herald Tribune*, 1 Sep 2006). Bridges on Long Island were built low, so that urban buses could not pass and bring poorer populations into the area. Bridges became part of social segregation by design, a techno-fix for a policy of apartheid (Campanella, 2017). More up-to-date techniques for segregation include machine checking of passwords, fingerprinting or iris-checks, and increasingly also facial recognition. Such high-tech ID checks replace the personal judgement of a porter with the 'incorruptible' machine. The 'Great Chinese Firewall' of cybersecurity, keeping unwanted contents and users off the Chinese Internet, is just a modern version of an old techno-fix to censor access and content.

Dependency: Behave or We Cut You Off

Modern life is locked into supply chains that make us dependent on their delivery; engaging with one design makes you dependent on another. Who has not experienced the quagmires of technological dependency? Take the small daily pleasure of making a coffee in the morning, if that is your habit. With modern amenities, you might use an 'espresso machine' of Italian design. This renders you dependent on electricity supply, on portioned coffee ready-grounded, and if the machine stops, on a technician ready to fix it. The same applies to your laptop or mobile phone and its software. Not to speak of just-in-time production systems, where industrial production uses the distributed storage of rolling transport and real-time delivery of parts for the assembling of cars, all optimally routed by computers. Modern life depends on the logistics of energy, transport and goods. Any object in use creates dependency on others. And once taken for granted, we cannot live without. Skills and capacities are lost, such as coffee making, or there is simply no space to store the parts. The most successful business models are based on engineered brand loyalty 'once X, forever X', tying customers into an activity stream with upgrades and accessories; brand loyalty succeeds when we are no longer able to do without; design before 'Dasein': having supervenes being. With inertia and lost capacities, we become vulnerable to blackmail: *Either you upgrade and buy our accessories, or we cut you off* (off your pleasures; off your files; off your friends, off your parts for car production). We comply because opt-out is too complicated.

Designing Decisions: Nudges, Boosts and Woops

A new form of social engineering has emerged in policy making under the heading of 'behavioural science': decision architects frame decisions while preserving individual choices (choice preserving interventions; see Chapters 1 and 7). A minority of 'enlightened' policymakers determine what is 'good behaviour' (behave yourselves!), and by designing the context, they shape our behaviour by designing how we make decisions. Policies can be based on tradition, preference or science. Evidence-based policies include fiscal incentives and mandating correct behaviour by law, considering the effects on behaviour targets. Recently, this tool box has expanded to include decision architecture; that is, setting features of the situation which direct decisions (**nudge**), enable better decisions (**boost**) or keep you on track (**woop**). These means-to-good-ends highlight human frailty, vices and deficiencies of reasoning and self-control, and harness peer pressure for shaping behaviour. Our individual rationality is jeopardised due to overconfidence, confirmatory information bias, loss aversion and status quo preference (resistance to change). Motivational vices include mindlessness, lack of self-control, inertia (resistance to change), procrastination and imitation and conformity to bad behaviour. This reasoning opened the door widely for psychology into economics (two Nobel prizes so far, Kahneman, 2002, and Thaler, 2017), or for economics to take over psychology. It was well put as 'all economics rests on some sort of implicit psychology. The only question is whether the implicit psychology in economics is good psychology or bad psychology' (Camerer & Loewenstein, 2002.

Now frequently found in urinals, a printed fly discretely directs boys to target their stream towards the point of least splash; they thus do so with increased hygiene; this is **nudging.** Frequently we order items from a menu that comes with a default, such as 'coffee, please' means 'coffee with sugar and milk', unless opting out of sugar and/or milk (such defaults are common in computer programs). On many websites, unless you tick the 'no, thanks' box, you will be flooded with 'additional information and special offers' by an opt-in default. Changing the default can change the mass outcome dramatically. Consider organ donations: if a minority of 42 per cent currently donates under an opt-out default (you need to be asked whether you want to donate), this can double to 82 per cent with an opt-in default unless otherwise requested (Johnson & Goldstein, 2003; see Chapter 7 on the deliberations needed to normalise a donation system on any default). As there is always a decision, inertia keeps us from bothering with alternatives, so we stay on default. Other nudging measures include information designs on disclosure requirements (on ingredients), warnings and labelling to make more people live healthier lives, recycle waste, save energy, put money into savings and pensions and invest for delayed gratification in economic affairs – not something people do easily when young, distracted and impulsive. But there a lots of actors who nudge to increase sales, and almost a century ago the Nazis nudged voters in the 1938 vote (see Figure 9.4) on the Anschluss of Austria to the German Reich with information design: the circle around the 'Yes' is (a) bigger than the circle around the 'No'; and (b) the name 'Adolf Hitler' looms large

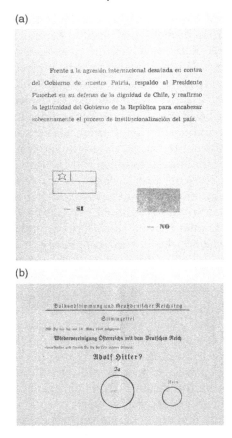

Figure 9.4   Nudging decision on voting paper. (a) For the referendum on the
Anschluss of Austria to the German Reich of 1938. Information design is nudging a Yes
for Adolf Hitler. (b) In the Chilean referendum of 1978 'Si' for Pinochet is
flagged five years after the 1973 military coup
(source: a. Museo de la Memoria y los Derechos Humanos, Chile; b. Wikimedia Commons)

over the 'Yes'. Similarly, Pinochet, who led the military coup in Chile in
1973, sought public support with a consultative vote in 1978 by flagging
the 'Si' vote and lowering the darkened 'No'. Well-intended, libertarian
paternalists seek better government, not bigger government, to maximise
welfare (Thaler & Sunstein, 2008 15). These nudges increase compliance
to norms set by authority, justified by paternalist arguments, the common
interest in mind and on proven efficiency (Hertwig, 2017). But what
about nudging sales or votes?

Boosting by contrast fosters decision-making capacities rather than suggesting particular directions. It competes with nudges on underlying theory by interpreting 'heuristics' not as deficits of rationality (as Kahnemann and Tversky do on 'biases', see Chapter 11) but as proven, fast and frugal decision rules that can be boosted in particular contexts (following Gigerenzer on heuristics). This leads to information designs that support correct statistical reasoning and offer risk information (Hertwig, 2017; Hertwig & Grune-Yanoff, 2017), thus avoiding paternalistic or coercive nudges. **Wooping** modulates control when implementing decisions already reached (see Oettinger, 2019 on http://woopmylife.org/further). Making a decision is one thing, sticking to it is another (rediscovered as 'will power' by Heckhausen following Caesar across the Rubicon; Cranach & Foppa, 1996). Practical mindsets tend to be open for deliberation of plans and goals; closed mindsets focused on implementing 'if-then' plans and the remaining concerns are timing and recognising if-conditions that trigger the planned action (Gollwitzer, 1990 and 1999; Gollwitzer & Sheeran, 2006). Through training, habits and mind skills, action control is cued up, externalised and set to sensory–motor control as in skills, thus liberating mind space. Contexts which avoid further thinking, keep attention and shield goals from distraction, keeping you on track with dieting or your fitness program, or larger projects: *we can do it* (President Obama's inaugural speech, 2008) or 'let's get on with it' (with BREXIT in 2020).

These now widespread tactics of social engineering, of directing, supporting and shielding decisions, are in continuation of an age old logic of social influence with two faces: we can set the agenda, or we choose within a given agenda (Bachrach & Baratz, 1962). Nudges and woops presume the authority of the agenda setters. But do they have a mandate of joint intentionality for this: who accepted the status function of any design 'X can do Y, under accepted conditions C'? And how did this acceptance come about? These questions now lead us to the problem of persistent challenges of artefactual installations, and how these are accommodated.

Accommodation of Objects to Challenges

On the accommodation of new technology set for permanence, Winston (1998) formulated two general laws on the empirical basis of 200 years of information technology from telegraph and telephone, to computers and social media. The **'law of supervening social necessity'** states that any prototype installation imagined for solving a problem A, gets shifted to solve a more important, supervening social problem B. For example, the

WWW (World Wide Web) was designed to liberate communication globally as an ideal public sphere, but it turned into a gigantic machine for social control and manipulating people while having fun in the process. Implied in this translation is the second **'law of suppression of radical potential'**. As the installation rolls out, all ambitions for radical changes are thwarted by business as usual, although with different means. As the new technology is incorporated we hear the pioneers complain that their 'baby' has been hijacked (e.g., Turkle, 2016; Weizenbaum, 1976). This forms dissent which will enable resistance and potentially redirect the installation (see next section).

Resistance and Re-framing the Installation

Diffusion of innovation seeks to assimilate users by reconfiguring hearts and minds, and considers resistance as a nuisance that shows in three ways, as in Figure 9.5. First, in a **ceiling effect** limiting the final penetration; under resistance, the artefact will reach only a part of the population. Second, resistance brings a **delayed onset** of acceptance. If we compare, one system takes off earlier than the others, while adoption speed and the ceiling are the same. Finally, resistance **slows the speed of adoption**, the slope is softer. All this celebrates being first and fast: speed is good. Furthermore, rejection in the system is only temporary, in time everybody

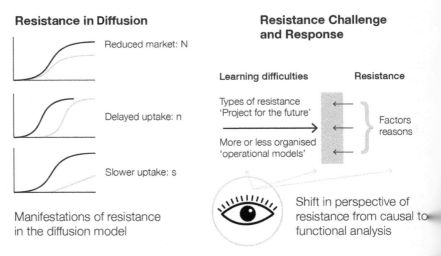

Figure 9.5   Left, manifestations of resistance in the diffusion model; on the right, the shift in perspective of resistance from causal to functional analysis

will 'see the light'. All this idolises innovations and directs social psychology to acceptance research and social assimilation (Bauer, 2017; Godin & Vinch, 2017).

Acceptance research considers resistance only as a dependent variable of design. Non-adopters and late adopters are socially profiled, their digital footprint is studied in search of better ways to target messages of persuasion, nudges, boosts or woops. The user is the problem. However, it is irrational and risky to exculpate and whitewash all designers and technology. Well-intended design does not guarantee functionality nor benevolence. One knows of beautiful and prizewinning buildings unsuitable for human habitation; marvellous shoes, unfit to walk in; technology aggravating problems it purports to solve (Tenner, 1997). This requires that we change acceptance level or resistance into an *independent variable*, and analyse the responses of innovators and how they respond to the challenges of resistance by redesigning the installation. Resistance monitors the innovation process, and thus is an influence on innovations (Bauer, 1991; Bauer, 2017).

A useful way of thinking here is to consider resistance in analogy of pain, a signal that something is wrong which recruits three immediate responses: (a) redirecting attention to where it is needed; (b) re-evaluating on-going designs; and (c) changing the designs. These are responses that we can observe among innovators, who are under the influence of resistance (see Figure 9.5). Resistance comes in many forms and motives; some are bloody-minded and self-interested, others are well informed and task oriented. When innovators are challenged, they can learn how to switch from a focus on 'deficits of users' and 'acceptance problems' to recognising issues with the installation (Oudshoorn & Pinch, 2003). They understand that dismissing resistance is risky, and learn to decode 'resistance' as evaluation of the design to accommodate concerns. So it comes that in time, most installations deviate from the initial plan; what becomes history as 'past future' is replaced by a 'new plan' and 'present future'. Thus, nuclear energy that was once 'too cheap to meter' and 'in everyone's backyard', is now concentrated in nuclear parks and an expensive energy afforded by a few countries. Genetic engineering has not merged farmers, bakers and butchers into a 'pharming' sector but has developed in separate paths of pharma and food. And the Internet is after all not the 'ideal public sphere' as envisaged in the 1990s, but now heavily weaponised by nefarious actors and colonised by state and commercial interests, threatening the very democratic rule which it was meant to enhance. The laws of 'supervening social necessity' and of 'suppression of radical potential' have taken grip and shapeshifted the World Wide Web. Resistance is needed to make things sustainable and future proof.

When we observe the accommodation of installations, we must consider resistance as one of its key drivers. Similar to active minority influence on social norms and attitudes, resistance to new technology succeeds, under circumstances that can be specified (Bauer, 2015), in challenging and altering the inter-objectivity of stuff as it is sent back to the drawing board.

Conclusion

In this chapter we extended the idea of intersubjectivity to inter-objectivity and examined the modalities of social influence under conditions of artefacts. Joint attention and joint intentionality have two outcomes: social norms and designed artefacts. The human ape is particularly well equipped for both, and also sustains tensions between artefact-as-designed and artefact-as-used. Thus, lasting technological installations become incorporated in modalities of social influence of normalising, assimilating and accommodating the frames of reference in modern society; here opinions, stuff, attitudes, artefacts, norms, monuments, beliefs and installations are happily entangled to establish standards of behaviour, to defend these in the face of detractors, and to respond to consistent challenges with necessary adjustments.

Artefacts are part of how we avoid violence and secure peace; but they are also key to warfare. One of the reasons that the bank till has glass between client and clerk is to avoid violence during the exchange of money: often this glass is also bulletproof. But besides all the fun, convenience and benefits that come with accumulating stuff and installations, we need to consider the scandals of artefacts, by which we mean the use of artefacts to influence individual inclinations in order to channel collective behaviour, and doing so by stealth, hidden and without the legitimacy of due procedure that secures acceptance. As we are aware but vigilant of social influence exerted by crowds, leading, peer pressure, authority, conversion or persuasion, we must strengthen awareness of how artefacts are deployed to buttress manipulation. So, what is scandalous about artefacts? By entangling us without consent, a techno-fix turns moral duties into functional requirements so that we adjust our bodies, pleasures (likes) and appetites (wants), accept the fait accompli, and follow the inscriptions blindly, fetishise the innovation, accept the dependencies and reconfigure our understanding of 'self and human nature'. We thus run the risk of happily falling prey to the natural fallacy: what works is right and proper.

Table 9.1 *Summary of functions of media effect models in relation to issue cycle*

Face-to-face equivalent	Design, Artefacts	Relation to life cycle
Normalisation		
Crowds	Barricades	Early in cycle
Norm formation	Installed affordances	Early in cycle
?	Fetishized icons	Mid-cycle
Leadership	Monuments	Mid-cycle
Assimilation		
Peer pressure	Algorithms	Early in cycle
Obedience	Diffusion of ready-mades	After cycle peak
Minority (elite)	Nudges, boosts, woops	Mid-cycle, before the peak
Obedience to authority	Reliable and trusted system	Early in cycle
Accomodation		
Conversion of majority	Alternative design	Early and late in the cycle

Without a platform to ask further questions in debate, *the scandal is TINA*: the perennial intimation that 'There Is No Alternative'.

In Table 9.1, we summarise our argument in this chapter. We have identified and named several ways of deploying artefacts in support of known modalities of social influence: barricades to support crowds, monuments to lead and affordances to norm behaviour and emotions. We have also sought to identify which stage of the artefact life cycles these modalities are best suited. Often fetishised, these artefacts ensure the normalisation of social life in society. Diffusion of fait accompli on the back of authority and peer pressure, algorithms to persuade and new elite tactics of nudging ensure the assimilation of social life in the face of challenges from dissidents. Finally, artefacts and installations accommodate to challenges by decoding the resistance and making designs future proof.

As 'artificial apes', we are all little cyborgs: mixtures of machine and human capacities. The fact that I wear glasses makes me a cyborg using a technical device that enhances my eyesight; the fact that I communicate via computer even more so. I need a computer even to lecture at a modern university using PowerPoint presentations and SKYPE, ZOOM or TEAM connections. Furthermore, I can have a chip implanted in my arm for organic monitoring and GPS location. We are already cyborgs by degree and ever more so. The key question arises: is the techno-fix desirable, benevolent and legitimate? And this question needs to be addressed in symmetry for both norms and artefacts. Who is nudging the nudgers, to whom do influencers answer? We tend to worry about new norms more than about novel artefacts, see norms as a matter for deliberation, and artefacts a mere matter of markets. Why this asymmetry, is not entirely clear. We must then challenge installations in the light of real consequences, in the same way that we challenge norms and attitudes as oppressive or liberating life in society. Resistance helps us monitor the normalisation process, stop the assimilation pressure, and shift the frame of reference for future collective activity.

In Essence

Like the mass media, artefacts amplify social influence through technological solutions that limit the behavioural choices open to individuals navigating a social space. The techno-fix is a way to obtain conformity through material designs involving interrelational networks comprised of subjects and objects.

Social engineering involves the installation of infrastructures that, designed by humans, are intended to frame relations between humans in inter-objective terms. Architectured designs induce particular behaviours that are scripted into the design as affordances. In this way, artefacts frame human action into compliance..

Resistance to prescribed designs urges innovators to respond through redesign that accommodates the challenge. The affordances of artefacts are relative, not given, and subject to counteraction. Resistance monitors the innovation and exerts a counter-influence. We must think of resistance in analogy to pain: it redirects attention to a problem, re-evaluates the design, and redesigns to accommodate the emergent concern in the service of sustainability.

PART IV

Theoretical Integration

We have charted a long course starting from how human beings co-ordinate social movements that achieve common projects. We have proceeded to consider several ways by which human beings exercise social influence on others towards pursuing their interests and bringing about their own aspirations. We then progressed to a consideration of unorthodox avenues by which social influence is exercised in our times more than ever. In what follows, we bring it all together and invite further scholarship. In essence, we explicitly address the thread running throughout this volume, that is: social influence is a collective and complicated (rather than complex) phenomenon involving a limited set of strategies and counter-strategies adopted by human agents who collaborate among some in order to compete more effectively with others.

In Chapter 10, we sum up the key tenets of our conceptualisation by outlining a **Periodic Table of Social Influence** (PTSI). We propose that social influence can be considered in terms of modalities, as detailed in the various chapters, and three modes including **face-to-face, mass mediated symbols and artefacts**. The confluence of three functions: **normalisation, assimilation and accommodation** of challenges gives rise to our **cyclone model**. With this model we offer a more encompassing vision of social influence than is typically the case. This will provide the researcher with novel questions, and the general reader with new insights into practical actions and events in everyday life. Finally, in Chapter 11, we address by way of excursions **four theoretical issues** raised by our model, each of which would have been unduly burdening in the various chapters. These four issues are: the challenges to common sense arising inside and outside the moral community, and with reference to common-sense; the controversy over dual or single processes models; the problem of 'objects' in psychology; and finally the question of authority in modern society.

CHAPTER 10

Common Sense
Normalisation, Assimilation and Accommodation

In 2017, the Nobel Prize for Economics went to Richard H. Thaler, for contributions to behavioural economics based on psychological insights concerning individual decision-making. Thaler & Sunstein (2008) had authored a widely acclaimed book on nudge theory. This theory proposes choice architecture as a method for redirecting human behaviour. Nudge theory suggests that certain human responses are more likely when stimuli are presented in a determinable fashion. The choice architect presents a configuration of environmental stimuli (a frame) that make desired behavioural responses for individuals less costly and more attractive than other alternatives, such that individual choices gravitate in the 'desired' direction; desired by the architect. In choice preserving designs, the individual is not deprived of choice, but the agenda is framed by the designer (see Chapter 9).

Nudge theorists adopted randomised control trial methodology (RCT), as in drug trial interventions, by which they determine the exact probabilistic effect of a particular nudge intervention against a comparator (i.e., odds comparisons). A nudge N [pX/y,z] selects an option pX by increasing its probability given the other options y, z. Ross & Nisbett (1991) had earlier termed similar strategies 'channel factors' (N,y,z → X). They argued that some systemic configurations either help or hinder the manifestation of particular behaviours. Consequently, predicting a certain behaviour requires a systemic analysis to determine which channel factors may be productive of that behaviour, and which others might be impediments. Rather than pursuing behavioural change by acting directly on the target behaviour with reinforcement or punishment, nudging relies on channels factors that, once in place, make the desired behaviour a more likely option among alternatives. For instance, the availability of separate rubbish bins in public places makes users more likely to recycle.

Even earlier, Lewin (1936) had suggested, in a series of experiments on feeding reluctant eaters, that behaviour was a function of the person-in-situation, i.e. $B = f(P,S)$, and in order to change behaviour, one had to rearrange the 'force field' that stabilised a particular direction of flow, so that the 'vector-combination of forces' pointed the resulting force into the desirable direction. Lewin and his colleagues developed stratagems to feed reluctant babies on spinach. One might call this a 'feeding the reluctant eater' paradigm (for a review, see Bauer, 1993; p. 188).

Choice architects harness innate dispositions to direct behaviour. Whilst human responses to stimuli are subject to individual differences (i.e., nudges will work better with some than with others; they are always reported probabilistically), nudging has attracted considerable interest as President Obama's (2009–2017) social engineering model. Famously, the British Cabinet Office set up a Behavioural Insights Team (or 'Nudge Unit') in 2010 tasked with applying nudging to government policy. Applied in this way, nudging raises serious ethical issues (Fischer, 2017; Sunstein, 2016) on how far one could/should manipulate humans in any direction. Such issues have haunted psychology since the time Pavlov, another Nobel laureate (1904), drew inferences about conditioning human behaviour from observing dogs salivating in reaction to ringing bells (Pavlov, 1902). Political propaganda, as Tchakhotine (1952) noted, has sharpened its tools on these insights.

Before turning our attention to ethical appraisals, let us consider two empirical issues: firstly, a potential enlightenment effect (Gergen, 1973) may further condition an individual's response to a nudging attempt. This effect would suggest (see Chapter 1) that knowledge of the logic of social influence enables counter-control, and allows one to resist such interventions. Admittedly, the contorted behaviours of avoiding a nudge for a service tip (see Box 10.1) feel rather ludicrous in hindsight. Yet, similar struggles in situations with restricted degrees of freedom have been documented in psychological research on attitude change. **Reactance** is a psychological response to actual or threatened loss of decision freedom that motivates individuals to engage in behaviours that are contrary to the influence attempt (Brehm, 1966). But, does knowledge about nudging neutralise its effect? Indeed, nudge researchers have shown that advanced warning of a default nudge weakens, but does not eradicate, the effect on medical care choices (Loewenstein et al., 2015). Nudges seem to work even with transparency. A second point worth noting is that nudge theory rests on the old conception of human vulnerability to social influence (see Chapter 2), akin to Tarde's somnambulant crowd. But the crowd is host to myriad other social influences that might well trump the gentle nudge. For instance, a crowd may resist influence under the spell of a charismatic

---

Box 10.1 Resisting a nudge

*The **enlightenment effect** enabling resistance to a nudge attempt can be illustrated on a real-life example of retrospection. Recently, one of the authors [GS] was subjected to a nudging attempt following a dining experience. After the diner asked for the bill and swiped the credit card, the EPOS unit was handed over to the diner for inputting the card's PIN (personal identification number) as per standard procedure. The EPOS unit automatically prompts a nudge asking the diner whether they would like to add a tip, equivalent to 10 per cent of the bill. Tipping behaviour varies cross-culturally (Fisher, 2009) and in Europe, the size of a tip is commonly at the discretion of the patron considering the quality of service received from waiting staff. The nudge short-circuits the calculation effort and facilitates automatisation. Resisting a nudge is costly in terms of effort involved. After declining the automatic request, the diner is prompted whether they would like to add a tip (amount unspecified) and in the event of an affirmative response, the diner is then prompted to enter the exact amount to add to their bill. In other words, a further two-step process follows the decline of the original nudge. The addition of an automatic tip is an opt-out nudge that increases the likelihood that patrons will tip by default the 'morally right' amount for services rendered. The nudge nudges patrons to behave in line with the restaurateur's own expectations. Yet, when one recognises a 'nudge' for what it is — a moral conformity demand in the mode of an artefact — one acquires the ability to respond to it on its own terms and thereby participate or challenge the social convention that is being enforced. In this event, the nudge was resisted on principle: routine nudging in everyday life changes the game and heightens the need for vigilance to avoid being taken for a ride unwittingly. In this case, the author resisted the original nudge but proceeded to give an equivalent tip through the two-step channel, resting in the satisfaction that a nudge had been resisted and an underhanded social influence attempt averted. Knowledge frees, and makes you feel free, indeed. Phew!*

---

leader (see Chapter 3), or endorse a new technology that enhances influences (see Chapter 9).

The critical point we wish to make in this final introduction is that nudging alone is as much of a silver bullet as any other social influence modality taken singly and in isolation. It might be more accurate to consider specific social influence modalities as effective relative to circumstances, and that effectiveness changes in the presence of other influences and over an event cycle. More likely than not, social influence is multifactorial, and we need to recognise these combinatorial pathways. In this book, we have travelled some distance over nine chapters on different modalities of social influence, covering crowds and crowding, leadership, norm formation, conformity, conversion, obedience, resistance and persuasion. We have considered these modalities escalating under conditions of face-to-face communication (mode 1), mass mediation (mode 2) and further enhanced by installed artefacts (mode 3). In this final chapter, we would like to present a scheme of ordering these social influences in a way that offers a coherent view on the matter and opens up avenues for novel research. For this, we briefly rehearse our basic assumptions about common sense in intersubjectivity and inter-objectivity; the three functions of social influence; the implied cyclone model; and the manifestations of social influence in three modes of communication, that is, face-to-face, mass mediation and implemented as designed artefact. These are the key building blocks for our final **Periodic Table of Social Influence [PTSI]**. We will close this chapter with implications for future research.

The Social Product Redefined: Common Sense, Intersubjectivity and Inter-objectivity

Imagine a time machine that takes you back in time. Imagine you find yourself in the same place you are now, several hundred years ago. It would certainly be a curious trip to take and, potentially, an illuminating one. Imagine how you would navigate the social world at the time.

You take a walk through the streets and you find, for instance, rampant child labour amongst the working people. You watch in disbelief as little children work hard, carrying goods from one place to another. In the absence of machinery, somebody needed to do the task. You are startled by a street seller. A merchant comes up to you flashing, not the latest smartphone package, but tries to sell you a sentient being – a slave! You walk on and turn a corner only to find two men crossing swords in a mortal duel. You might try to convince them to talk things through, but they insist they must fight to the death as a matter of personal honour. Imagine you proceed and happen upon a public execution – a heretic, earlier saved by the authorities from a lynch mob, has now been duly sentenced to death by the Holy Inquisition and is going to burn alive. Or a few years later, you come across a crowd cheering on the beheading by machine (a guillotine) of people considered to be reactionaries to the Revolution. Imagine if for entertainment you went further back in time, and entered the local arena and instead of watching your football team battling it out with the visiting team, you were treated to a spectacle of gladiators fighting each other to the death, with a couple of wild lions thrown in for good measure. Now imagine, how capable do you think you might be to join the cheering and enjoy the show?

Any student of distant history knows very well that practices our ancestors might have engaged in during their time, perhaps even with gusto, have fallen out of favour, or even a foul of the law. Many things have moved on and for good reason. To think that there was a time when humans could be purchased, owned and resold as commodities sanctioned by law; when disagreements were a matter of honour; when punishment for taking issue with prescribed dogma led to burning or beheading in public; when children were little more than household labour; all of these examples beggar belief nowadays. We find difficulty understanding why our forefathers lived in these cruel arrangements; why they engaged such drastic practices instead of the more humane alternatives we employ today. We find difficulty understanding how these and other practices made any sense at all; how the justified resentment amongst sufferers could have tolerated anything of the kind. Hindsight makes it easy for us to take the moral high ground; this is **common sense**! And we find difficulty understanding how our forebears failed to see that these practices created more harm than good, believing themselves to be right regardless of the consequences. It is hard for us today to understand practices that were commonsensical during a previous historical epoch but that no longer are today. This is due to the fact that the world we are socialised into, that we have internalised and nowadays take for granted relies on different construals of the configuration of elements than the ones that prevailed in a different era than ours (Ross & Nisbett, 1991). Asch (1952/1987) explains this very eloquently when noting how commonsensical knowledge frames our social attitudes:

> Only if the knowledge exists that there are germs and viruses that produce disease will it be meaningful to have an attitude about the right of the state to compel children to be vaccinated against smallpox regardless of the wishes of their parents. If, instead, the available data contain such entities as spirits and the belief that they produce illness, medical problems will be solved by medicine men and there will be different attitudes towards vaccination and hygiene. In order that the burning of witches make sense it is necessary to have as part of the intellectual climate the propositions that there are devils and that persons can be in league with them. In each of these instances a particular factual definition of the given situation is the necessary condition for conviction and action (p. 564).

For an action to be meaningful, it needs to make sense to others who observe it. It needs to make enough sense to invite or warrant a legitimate and anticipated reciprocal action; we need to have a common understanding of what we are doing. Indeed, it is a key distinction between behaviour and action, that the latter has social meaning (Cranach & Valach, 1983). The sense that is shared – common sense – enables routine interaction on an everyday basis, including recognising a behavioural movement as intended action. What we take for granted during the course of our social interactions is precisely the bedrock of common sense that frames our interactions (Daanen & Sammut, 2012). We are thus able to walk into a store, grab a sandwich from the shelf, take it to the counter, pay, exit the store and consume the sandwich – all without expressly needing to converse with the seller to communicate our intentions to purchase the sandwich for our personal consumption. This script is well shared and established. The act of a buyer in purchasing a sandwich goes hand in hand with the reciprocal act of a shopkeeper selling a sandwich, such that the interaction can take place without words – the intent, on both sides, is commonsensical. But you wouldn't see a person sitting at a table in the park and go ahead and grab a sandwich off their plate and hand them some money with the understanding that sandwiches are goods that are bought and sold. That would not make sense and if it did happen, it would invite a totally different, and equally commonsensical reciprocal act, such as an objection or a complaint (if not something even more severe, like a brawl).

Our social interactions are framed by the common sense that prevails during our time and in our cultural setting, and this common sense is a core focus of the social sciences (Haidt, 2012; Van Holthoon & Olson, 1987). Common sense becomes visible in moments of disruption, such as when a stranger visits who does not have access to the local stock of common sense and who is habituated to different routines framed by a discrepant common sense (Garfinkel, 1967). Such visibility arises when new technology reframes routine practice and in so doing leads to a revision of common sense. Think, for instance, about the consequences of plastic, cashless money transaction on our shopping habits. Or the use of smartphones in talking to friends, former friends or family. Think about intercultural relations and how the practices that prevail in other cultures might appear bizarre from our point of view. If you have spent time outside your comfort zone, coming home after some years, you might even perceive the familiar practices at home as bizarre.

Take as an example the common practice of bullfighting in Spain, which is objectionable to many visitors from outside; if you lived without it for years, you might start seeing it in a different light. What is commonsensical in one cultural setting may be totally nonsensical in another. In these encounters, merely a different outlook challenges prescribed common sense and can trigger 'innovations'. Innovations, whether they originate from within or from without, have the potential to disrupt the prevalent order and steer it in a different direction. Whether such changes really constitute innovations or just adoption of a practice that is elsewhere taken for granted is a complicated matter that needs careful examination of contexts. We argue that common sense is not monolithic as we might be inclined to believe, such as when we say that somebody we disagree with has no common sense. Rather, we contend that *common sense is plural and subject to change over time*, such that what is commonsensical today, has most likely been nonsensical in the past, and might be nonsensical again in future. We further argue that common sense moves along with the dynamics of social influence.

One of our key witnesses, Muzafer Sherif, set out to redefine the 'social product' (see Chapter 4), by which he meant the product of social interaction. Liberating thinking from the doctrine of suggestion, he elaborated the frame of reference that arises from social interactions to provide the basis for subsequent coordinated activity. Here common sense is specified as the frame of reference. Before we define the three functions of social influence, we need to clarify how functions link to common sense. One of our main propositions is therefore:

P1: The Functional Point of Reference of Social Influence
Is Common Sense

We observe common sense in joint attention, the capacity of perspective-taking, and in joint intentionality of we-intentions and we-feelings (see Chapter 4). Sloman & Fernbach (2017) rightly argue that the different bits of knowledge that a community has need to be integrated. They need to be compatible, as without common sense, the cognitive division of labour required to co-exist with others would fall apart. They argue that different subjects need not always agree, and in many cases they don't, but that they at least need to be *thinking* about the *same thing*. This sharing of *attention* and *intention* has been subject to intensive research on the foundation of culture looking at the continuum between human and non-human primates. Chimps (pan troglodytes), evolutionarily close to humans, show only rudimentary forms of intersubjectivity such as joint attention and gaze following, or very simple tool use or designed habitats as nests or shelters. Humans, however, excel in symbolic and material constructions which frame further joint activities. Human society is morally constituted both in statutory law as well as in transport infrastructures and urban landscapes. This shared inter-objectivity of stuff and texts requires the intersubjectivity of an accepting moral community (see Chapter 9). In modern society, technology requires 'acceptance in public consent' to be legitimate. Latour (1996) further showed how apish primates live in *complex* setups, while humans live *complicated* social lives. Complex means things can be at any moment totally otherwise; so much so that animals live in permanent uncertainty, where order is mainly guaranteed by a dominance hierarchy within the roaming group. The modern human world is thankfully less militant and complex, but somewhat complicated by enduring and risky arrangements. Human settings persist on a sense of past and future and an experience of change over time (temporality). This leads us to a second key proposition on the fact that common sense is manifested in two, mutually supporting, but different ways of setting some permanence:

P2: Common Sense Is Embodied in Intersubjectivity
As Well As Inter-objectivity

Joint attention and following the gaze of a conspecific, that is, taking the perspective of another mind, is only partially shared among chimps and humans; only human children reach the capacity for joint intentionality as a precondition of **intersubjectivity** (Tomasello, 2008; see also Chapter 4). Under evolutionarily upgrading, human sociality allows the calibration of minds and feelings to common standards of some persistence: humans operate on individual goals rooted in a common frame of reference of values and attitudes (Cranach & Valach, 1983). This permanence is further buttressed by **inter-objectivity**, the fact that humans, in contrast to chimps or other animals, accumulate artefacts in a built environment. No monkey ever used symbols or constructed a telegraph to link up with other conspecifics; by contrast humans gather and dance (in celebration) around artefacts that keep them unified and allow them to collaborate effectively. Human sociality is thus constituted both in norms, knowledge, beliefs, opinions and attitudes, and also in walls and buildings, gadgets of all kinds and installations of grand projects which are the pride of nations. Many of these artefacts are vested with high symbolic value. When the twelfth-century cathedral *Notre Dame de Paris* was partially destroyed by a fire in April 2019, far away commentaries deplored that this 'opening to transcendence', the invisible soul of humanity, had been touched, thus revealing residual religiosity in a secular world. This ancient pile of stones clearly means something else and more than a mere tourist attraction (Maffesoli, 2019).

Three Basic Functions: Normalisation, Assimilation and Accommodation

Our key image of moving common sense will be the **cyclone model**; common sense is like a cyclone. The whirlwind is the temporarily fossilised frame of reference that is prescriptive and, to some extent, determines our actions. Sandwiches on shelves in stores are for purchasing; sandwiches on plates at table are for consumption. And it is risky to act differently, as responses to deviant acts that go against the flow meet other acts that seek a restoration of order in line with the general direction. The cyclone's whirling on a path represents this general direction that bestows collective order. If you consume a sandwich at the supermarket and leave the packaging behind, you will need to answer to security and chances are you will be made to pay. If you take a sandwich off someone's plate and offer them money instead, you will likely be perceived as somebody looking for trouble. This brings a critical point immediately home: common sense, by means of its general and collective nature, seeks to **assimilate** deviance in an effort to preserve the prevailing order. Assimilation means that deviance is reduced and brought back to the prevailing norm again. The minority of one or few is called upon, reprimanded, pressurised and brought in line with the majority values, beliefs and attitudes. A second and related point is that changing common sense requires, in the first instance, deviance, that is, a point of view on the situation that is reasonable, and potentially sensible, but not yet common, that might end up as upgraded common sense.

Let us illustrate with an example. Assume that we lived in an age where human beings abducted from foreign lands could be traded as commodity – the era of slavery. The general direction of this practice is that this is perfectly doable as long as some commonsensical frame of reference (at the time) is fulfilled and adhered to, such as the necessary fees and permits need to be paid; merchants might require a license; some types of people might not be tradeable, and so on. Some people might have reservations about all of this, some others might readily object to it, but all are able to understand how it works as all are participative in the common sense that legitimates the practice. At some point, a challenge arises. A heckler or detractor decides that they want no part of it anymore because even if this is commonsensical, from their point of view, this is nevertheless wrong. **'Common-sense'** (in contrast to common sense) refers to the putative base of universal knowledge and ethos accessible to any reasonable person getting up in the morning, seeing the sun rise and not being echo-chambered and blinded by ideology and power. On this reference, a heckler can challenge the absurdity and the abuse (Lindenberg, 1987).

Initially, this deviant perspective is subject to assimilation pressures towards conformity: 'The deviant must be mad; society cannot function without slavery, obviously!' Interfering with this practice may be deemed a criminal act: 'you cannot set my slaves free because I formally own them and I have a certificate to prove it'. To the extent that the deviant subjects herself to the prevailing common sense and changes her own outlook to conform, the deviant view has been assimilated: 'We considered the possibility of abolishing slavery but concluded that it is not in society's best interests.' One could think of a number of modern day equivalents that, whilst reasonable, have not garnered sufficient influence to alter our contemporary common sense (e.g., bullfighting; whaling; animal rights, and others).

In certain instances, however, deviant perspectives are not quite so readily assimilated into common sense for a variety of reasons. A deviant person may be able to persuade like-minded others to action and gather around her, forming a deviant minority. We have seen in Chapter 5 how consistent minorities are able to influence the frame of reference of dominant majorities. In these instances, common sense alters to **accommodate** the challenge – slaves acquire human rights; laws are enacted against animal cruelty, in the name of Common-sense. In these instances, influence flows from the innovative minority to permeate and alter common sense for the majority.

It is worth noting at this point that influence processes working *within* the minority resemble closely the influence exercised by dominant majorities. That is, for a minority to succeed in precipitating conversion of a majority, it also needs to succeed, at the same time, in warding off challenges to its own innovation through internal conformity. This logic of active minority influence found historical systematisation in the discipline to which revolutionaries subscribe in order to achieve the 'Revolution' led by the 'Party' (as in Vladimir Lenin's Leninism or Sayyid Qutb's Islamism). That is, minority members must conform to the minority's creed in order to increase the likelihood of success. Yet, in society at large and to the extent that influence flows both ways, the minority's outlook is often accommodated in the majority and vice versa. This accommodation process is best understood as a sequence of shifts in the collective frame of reference (Gestalt-switches) that is empirically observable in the majority discourse as it moves from rejecting an absurd impossibility, through imagination and recognising a probability, to finally endorsing a novel taken-for-granted reality to act upon (maybe we are dealing here more with a shift in actuality than in reality; see Berger & Luckmann, 1966):

- Firstly, a thing, an idea or a practice is impossible and absurd; unimaginable and unthinkable, it beggars belief (*impossibility*)
- Secondly, what is unthinkable, might suddenly become imaginable (*imagination*)
- Thirdly, what was hitherto impossible is now possible to think of, but remains an uncertainty (*uncertain possibility*)
- Fourthly, through empirical enquiry the hypothetical possibility, may now become probable [p(E) > o], though still unlikely (*improbable possibility*)
- Fifthly, further shifts render what is now possible and probable also likely (*likelihood*)
- Finally, possible becomes a taken-for-granted reality, its origin is forgotten, the success of the minority remains without recognition and no further questions are asked until the cycle of challenges repeats again (*taken-for-granted*)

In this manner, a deviant minority outlook may, over time, alter common sense radically, by instituting itself as *the 'new' common sense*. Think about the fox-hunting ban that was introduced in the United Kingdom in 2004, making fox hunting with dogs illegal in law. Prior to the ban, fox hunting with dogs was considered somewhat of a traditional rural sport in England and many hunters would have both enjoyed and been proud of their trophies. Today, the practice is outlawed. At this point, therefore, the deviant perspective that has re-presented fox hunting with dogs as animal cruelty rather than sport, has prevailed and **normalised.** Over time, it has come to constitute the normative commonsensical order: that one cannot own human beings as slaves; that women are entitled to full political and labour market participation; that animals should not be killed for sport, and so on and so forth. In turn, this new common sense that has emerged becomes in itself the target of further deviant challenges that seek to revisit the established order for furthering their own particular interests. Fox hunters today have sought to replace dogs for birds of prey during the hunt, to keep their sport alive. The practice challenges the common sense behind the ban: that of abolishing the killing of animals for sport. Prevalent common sense will, therefore, seek to assimilate deviant outlooks and respond to rising challenges by seeking conformity – the same treatment it received when pitching its original challenge to the common practice of fox hunting with dogs. Or think about the possibility that at a future date slavery might be reintroduced. Although currently both immoral and illegal, in the case of future robots, both sentient and making autonomous decisions, how can such an entity be owned? 'Slavery' has solved this dilemma in the past, and such a vision is foreshadowed in our AI future (Hampton, 2015). The cyclone thus represents an inherent set of dynamics of evolving common sense that adapts as it charts a path through history.

The Cyclone Model of Social Influence

In light of these observations of a sequencing of normalisation, assimilation and accommodation of challenges towards a renormalisation, we propose our **cyclone model of social influence** (Figure 10.1). The cyclone is a moving structure of whirling winds. As far as a cyclone has a stable structure, we identify this structure as common sense and joint intentionality of a collective on the move in time and space. In the same way as the centre of

Normalisation

Figure 10.1   The Cyclone Model of Social Influence showing the confluence of three functions of normalisation, assimilation and accommodation

gravity of the cyclone is constantly on the move, so is the joint intentionality of coordinated action, in particular if we look at it over a longer period of time. We have also used terms such as **frame of reference**, **mindsets** or **social representations** to denote this moving centre of gravity of the cyclone.

Our initial idea was to model a 'cycle' of social influences, where an innovative idea that is originally deviant goes on to become mainstream and to come to be held as the new standard. Think about how absurd the idea of a female bank director or president was a mere 100 years ago, when women were still fighting for their right to vote. Though gender equality remains incomplete, it is no longer an unthinkable absurdity. We thought, however, that a cycle model conveys images of regularity and coherence in progressing from one state to another, with clear initial and terminal states. Think about the cycle image of human life, from birth, to childhood, to youth and adulthood and finally to old age and death. We are not modeling the rise and fall of civilizations.

Quite the contrary, initially, things might be rather mundane before an unexpected source of influence gains traction to alter, at times quite radically, a certain course of events. Think about the Arab Spring and the self-immolation of Mohammed Bouazizi in 2010, which led to the resignation of the Tunisian premier, Zine El Abidine Ben Ali, after twenty-three years in power. A cyclone model, in our view, represents the inherent volatility and messiness of social influence in real-life scenarios. Clearly, social interaction and its products do not demonstrate such an orderly, coherent and uniform progression from dust to dust; where it is even more difficult to ascertain a beginning or an end.

Secondly, the cycle would also tie us into a vision of the eternal return of the same, nothing new under the sun. By contrast, the image of the cyclone also represents the fact that the trajectory is not known in advance. In a cycle we know that it ends where we started, no surprise there. But much like the devastation trail charted by a cyclone, social influence involves powers that potentially supplant and radically transform a given state of affairs. The power involved may be soft and non-violent in nature (Nye, 1991; see Chapter 1), though hard power is residually active in the background to secure the playing field for social influences to flourish. It is worth noting that the soft/hard distinction says nothing about the stakes, high or low as the case may be. Consider the effects of social influence in negotiating a truce between two warring parties. Our cyclone model represents such a shift that in its dynamic nature charts a path for the evolution of common sense over time, and note progress is not necessarily an attribute of this path.

Thirdly, the cyclone model highlights the fact that its trajectory can only be verified empirically and in hindsight. Thus the cyclone of social influences has a path in history, and 'progress' on its trajectory is an aspirational ideal for the future, it can only be verified in hindsight evaluation. Needless to mention, 'progress' is itself a representation, a frame of reference which drives the cyclone on from within, either as normalised majority or as a challenging minority aspiration. Charting the trajectory of social influence is an intellectual challenge that brings us into the territory of historiography. In describing the transition from one common sense A to another common sense B, we account for the past by telling a moral story of either recovering a golden past or moving into a better future. Historical research reveals that such transitions are rarely discontinuous, rather the usual case is more or less long winded, and a more or less profound transformation of what we believe, value and find beautiful (LeGoff, 2015, 78). Two things are important for the historical perspective: turning points and points of no return, and thus significant events and internal renaissances. These outline the adaptive accommodation of challenges. Depending on hindsight, and this is itself controversial, the transition is either one from A to non-A = B (revolution), or more modest from A to A' (reform or renaissance of harking back to a real A). Such transitions are couched as moral stories and come as pre–post-narratives, as in before and after Christ, or with a three-step order, as in medieval, renaissance, modernity, or pre-modernity, modernity and post-modernity. We must recognise such narratives as part of the frame of reference and common sense that is normalised, assimilated and accommodated to challenges.

Fourthly, our image of a cyclone is consistent with the assumption that there is no silver bullet of social influence, but a multiplicity of factors at work in social change. This makes a cyclone model consistent with our ideas of multiple modalities. Thus a cyclone model of social influence can absorb key features such as volatility, an uncertain trajectory, aspirational 'progress' that is part of a moral story verifiable only in hindsight and a multiplicity of influences. Before we present the final ordering of things, let us briefly rehearse the distinction between modes and modalities of social influence.

Modes and Modalities of Social Influence

Social psychological research has prioritised the experimental method over other forms of enquiry, to compete with the natural sciences in providing valid analysis in the form of causal inferences from observations. Yet by its very nature, the experimental method controls for other influences when focussing on the effects of one that is isolated for the time being. In reality, multiple influences are involved in social relations that offer no degree of control. By and large, we can safely assume that multiple sources of influence are involved in any influence situation. We maintain, therefore, that a serious and realistic exploration of social influence requires consideration of a plurality of co-occurring influences serving particular projects for particular people at particular points in time. Experimental research into the mechanistic outcomes of social influence is certainly useful in understanding what to expect when considering real-life case studies, but it is by no means sufficient. It is no more sufficient than expecting a persuasive attempt to work invariably because a physically attractive face has been selected to pitch the message (Chaiken, 1979; see Chapter 7). It might work, and does work – under certain conditions and in certain circumstances. Then again, it might not – due to some other unknown feature, or due to other uncontrolled-for influences acting on the agent at the same time. To draw a conclusion: there is no silver bullet strategy that obtains successful social influence invariably.

For our purposes, it is important to recognise that modalities of social influence can operate in three different modes. Much research on social influence happens in *face-to-face interactions* (mode 1), as researched and demonstrated in laboratory experiments on peer pressure, obedience and persuasion (see Chapters 5, 6 and 7). In these demonstrations of *micro-genetic interactions* (Psaltis, 2015), face-to-face encounters involve the co-presence of interlocutors that provides an opportunity for immediate feedback in turn-taking interactive sequences. This mode of communication is immanent, reciprocal and more or less spontaneous. As we have seen in Chapter 7, persuasive attempts take place routinely in everyday life. We try to influence, as well as are influenced by, others' preferences and expectations of our behaviour in a way that satisfies our own interests. We often rely on direct communication to achieve this; the micro-genetic mode of influence is characteristically intersubjective involving, as it does, the interactive negotiation of meaning (Sammut, Bauer & Jovchelovitch, 2018).

But social influence can extend, change character and amplify in *mass mediation* (mode 2). Modern leaders use radio or TV to address the nation, or tweet their stream of thoughts at regular intervals to their supporters and massively spread their symbols in word or image format. Mass mediation comprises vast and technically efficient systems of circulating symbols across time and space. Mass-mediated influence bridges time and space through the use of technological and virtual platforms. This mode of influence serves to aggregate crowds, bringing disparate and unconnected actors together in adopting a certain point of view towards objects or events in social life. Think echo-chambers on Facebook, where interaction takes place mostly with others who share our views and 'like' the same stuff we do. Mass mediated forms of influence serve to create genres (e.g., what constitutes 'news'?) which, in their turn, advance particular versions of collective projects. Some forms of mass mediation, such as social media, allow a degree of reciprocation and spontaneity. In this way, this mode of influence can also be intersubjective. Generally, however, the degree of intersubjective potential is limited in favour of sharper and more popular messages that appeal to the masses over specific individuals. This mode of social influence does not permit nuanced interactions to the same extent that micro-genetic interactions do. The loss in specificity, however, is countered by an increase in reach that is achieved through the use of technology. Consequently, the mass-mediation mode is both intersubjective and inter-objective (Harré & Sammut, 2013).

Finally, social influence is exerted by placing ***designed artefacts*** and thus reminding and affording people to behave, feel and think in a particular way (mode 3). A wall is often more effective to remind people where not to go, or to separate those who are allowed from those who are not allowed into the game. These particular human structures are set to last, but only for relative permanence compared to the short-term arrangements in ape and animal societies. Social influence extended to architecture involves the built environment as an installation, that can be engineered to elicit determined responses that facilitate the achievement of a pre-conceived social order (Lahlou, 2015). This mode of influence is characteristically inter-objective (Sammut, Daanen & Moghaddam, 2013; Sammut, Daanen & Sartawi, 2010), but depends on intersubjectivity of consent to remain sustainable. These three modes of social influence – face-to-face, mediation and designed artefacts – come together in our cyclone image as further characteristics of the whirlwind.

The Periodic Table of Social Influence

So far, we have reviewed and typified various **modalities** of social influence in the chapters of this volume. This included the workings of crowds, leadership, norms, conformity, conversion, obedience, resistance and persuasion. We have considered their manifestation in the modes of face-to-face interaction, mass mediation and artefacts. Both modes and modalities of influence are open to dominant social groups seeking conformity in the preservation of social order and in the face of a challenge mounted by an active minority. They are equally available to non-dominant groups who resist, seeking conversion and the usurpation of common sense. In other words, the various modes and modalities of social influence are variably implicated in the cyclone of common sense negotiated by diverse actors across historical time (Sammut, Tsirogianni & Wagoner, 2012). At this point, we are able to bring together the various features in our discussion in the **Periodic Table of Social Influence [PTSI],** which provides a coherent overview.

Table 10.1 *Different 'language games' of social influence as lists of concepts and terms pertaining to a modality; in yellow are the notions that are most specific to a modality*

Crowds	Leadership	Norm formation	Conformity & conversion
hypnosis	leader	framing	self-monitoring
contagion	followers	common ground	conformity-bias
mass society	criteria	social construction	naive realism
herding	personality	inter-subjectivity	attachment
mad and bad crowd	charisma	inter-objectivity	majority influence
stock market crashes	transformational	frame of reference	imitation
mass behaviour	situational	dual product	emulation
law of mental unity	contingency	psychological reality	over-imitation
de-individuation	dictatorship	social product	social check
suggestion	social identity	judgement+uncertainty	inter-penetration of views
imagination	stereotypes	frame analysis	distributed cognition
leadership	prototypicality	common sense	conformity pressure
personality cult	social attraction	social movement	conversion
dissolution of responsibility	fundamental attr. error	social representation	minority influence
collective neurosis	personalistic	group decisions	deviance
somnambulance		inter-penetration of views	norms
effemination		group formation	
hylomorphism		stabilising the fact	
chemical analogy		thought collective	
crowd sourcing		thinking style	
public safety		swarming	
blame game		pack hunting	
opinion		joint intentionality	
conversation		joint attention	
joint attention		mind reading	
contempt of masses		we-intentions	
pure energy			

Table 10.1 (cont.)

Obedience	Persuasion	Medialisation	Artefact design
authority	strategic action	formal	installation
compliance	soft power	informal	inter-objectivity
obedience	persuasion	resonance	attitudes
command	moderators	thematic cycles	identity presentation
tyranny, despotism	hypodermic needle model	diffusion	tool use
autonomy	Lasswell formula	knowledge gaps	affordance
social roles	rhetorical trope	cultivation	actants
banality of evil	market segmentation	diegetic prototyping	standards
fundamental attr. error	ELM	echo chambers	barricades
scientific authority	HSM	rumors	inscription of behaviour
ecological validity	dual process models	spiral of silence	regulation
mediated violence	heuristic-systematic	HiFi transmission	joint intentionality
social identity	central-peripheral	agenda service	assigned function
self-interest	classical conditioning	issue priming	goal shifting
prototypicality	ecological rationality	framing	supervising necessity
need for cognitive closure	compliance tactics	technology	suppression of radical potential
installation	forced compliance	utterance	fetish
architecture of authority	balance of reciprocity	attention	myth
	cognitive dissonance	acceptance	magic
	nudge theory	language	monuments
	shaping	symbolic media	collective memory
	operant conditioning	codes of discourse	ready-mades
	lay epistemic theory	social representation	diffusion
	individual differences	serial reproduction	trust in systems
	unimodel of persuasion	hype cycles	algorithms
	need for cognitive closure	grand narratives	moral delegation
	motivated reasoning	viral communication	interlock
	naive realism	mainstreaming	lock-out and lock-in
	epistemic authority	schemata	barriers
	argumentation		dependency
	theory of planned behaviour		designing decisions
	reactance		nudging
	innoculation		boosting
	forewarning		whooping
	fear appeal		resistance
	rhetoric		reframing
	social identity		acceptance research
	social representation		
	taken-for-granted		
	common ground		
	social marketing		
	ethos		
	logos		
	pathos		

We make an attempt to order the language of social influence into different games, that is, lists of terms, concepts and notions pertaining to each modality of social influence as shown in Table 10.1. This helps construct a kind of dictionary of terms associated with each modality of social influence and might be a useful first step in clarifying the different modalities. However, this exercise also shows that terms are not consistently used and that there is considerable overlap in the vocabulary across columns. We recognise that this is a good starting point and an invitation for further research to specify each column by systematically ordering the relevant corpus of literature and extract the defining vocabulary (see Table 10.1). This task can be completed with current techniques of computerised text analysis and the scientometrics of keywords (Wyatt et al., 2017).

Our periodic table of social influence (see Table 10.2), however, aims to bring together the various features of social influence that we have traced along the discussions in this volume. The table demonstrates how particular **modalities** of influence are associated with certain **functions** in social interaction, along the cyclone model of normalisation, assimilation and accommodation. Each modality of influence achieves a particular **outcome**, which enables the function that is being served. Furthermore, each modality can be extended by **mass mediation**, symbols remaining part of the intersubjective world of common sense. Each modality extends, potentially but not necessarily, to **designed artefact**.

Let us take an example: crowding. We consider the crowd to be foremost a modality of normalisation, by which a new order is established; sometimes even new order out of chaos. Crowds in modern technology constitute echo-chambers, where ideas are shared by contagion, rumours and word of mouth. With the help of mass mediation, crowds focus joint attention across diverse locations and allow for imitation on a larger scale; sometimes, and maybe more prominently in history, crowd events are enhanced by barricades by which the forces of order are challenged and defeated. Crowd events are thus characterised by the collocation of concepts along the line of: crowds normalise through echo chamber with rumour contagion or joint attention or barricades.

We could go through another example: persuasion. This modality achieves both assimilation and accommodation through different features. Persuasion assimilates through compliance with a request or appeal. This is often extended to mass mediation via micro-targeting, and more recently also subject to AI installations called algorithms. Persuasion accommodates common sense by convincing with argumentation in the debate, extended

Table 10.2 *The Periodic Table of Social Influence [PTSI] ordering modalities of social influence by basic function and modes of operation in relation to intersubjectivity and inter-objectivity*

				Mode 1 face-to-face	Mode 2 symbolic	Mode 3 artefact
phase	modality	function for CS	outcome	inter-subjective		inter-objective
Order created 'out of Chaos' of interaction: social representations, common sense, joint intentionality						
Phase 1	Norm formation	Normalisation	frame of reference	deliberation, compromise	debate	installed affordances
	Crowds		echo chambers	contagion virality/rumor	joint attention imitation	barricades
	prototyping		action script	demonstration	diegetic prototyping	Beta-version
	leadership		atmosphere	social identification	priming	monument
Challenge from conflict, dissonance, controversy arising from newcomers, homecomers, strangers or 'aliens'						
Phase 2	*fait accompli*	Assimilation	affordance	dissonance, reduction	nudging	installation (wall)
	majority		conformity	peer pressure, ostracising	diffusion	ready-made diffusion
	minority (elite)		us & them gap	treason, ignorance	spiral of silence	nudge, boost, woop
	persuasion		compliance	request, appeal	micro-target	algorithm
	authority		obedience	command	Hi-Fi signal transfer	reliable, trusted system
Sustained challenge by consistent dissenters						
Phase 3	persuasion	Accomodation	conviction	argumentation	propagation	re-design
	minority (non dominant)		conversion	consistency	agenda setting framing	innovation
	resistance		attention, re-evaluation	rejection, objection	propaganda	alternative design
	?		?	?	?	?

to mass media as propagation of a considered point of view, and also in the deployment of redesigned artefacts that are being challenged.

Once again, we note that the periodic table of social influence should save us the quest of identifying which social influence modality is the most effective. The search for such answers has historically been a matter of fashion (see Chapter 1). We present here a ***challenge & response model***, as compared to a stimulus-response model. We are not looking for the perfect stimulus to elicit a desirable response, nor for the mediators that bring that about. In our table, the effectiveness of any particular modality depends on the wider context; it depends on the time it was deployed, whom it was targeting, what the particular issue was about, what influence attempts preceded, what reciprocal influence attempts it stimulated and so on. While for each of these modalities, social psychology and other social sciences have developed empirical research programmes with a variety of controversies, monopolistic claims and micro-models of operation, our Periodic Table [PTSI] attempts to integrate these disparate programmes into a unified model. We hope that this can renew scholarly interest in social influence such that we may better understand how this psychological mechanism contributes to the construction of social realities and the characteristic forms of social relations that ensue.

Furthermore, we capitalise on a coincidence of history. In 2019, the discipline of chemistry celebrated 150 years of its Periodic Table of Elements, credited to the Russian Dimitri Mendeleev, who charted a first version of it in 1869 (*Nature*, 31 Jan 2019, pp. 535, 551–565). Historians highlight three characteristics of this table, which we seek to inherit for our purposes. First, the Periodic Table has become an iconic image that is widely reproduced, and is offered as an analogue for all possible issues; it hangs in every school class where the sciences are curriculum. That is a high aspiration for social psychology, but creating an icon of systematicity is within the possibilities. Pratkanis (2007, 60ff) alluded to a periodic table, but desisted because it might give too static an image of the matter; an evolutionary map of common origins might be preferable. We consider these not mutually exclusive taxonomies. Secondly, a table ordering the modalities of social influence in a coherent manner provides educational value. Not only does it summarise the argument of many chapters of this book, it also serves as a memory prop to keep at hand the range of possibilities for any situation of urgency. Our overview avoids claims making, where the recent notion is supposed to replace all previous notions. The table also reflects our teaching experience along a course of eleven weeks of trying to construct a unity of what is a vast empirical, operational and discursive diversity. Thirdly and most importantly, the Period Table is a heuristic tool; it is an instrument of discovery, not of closing a dogma. The original periodic table of 1869 was a preliminary affair of ordering 60+ elements along a set of key features; current research traces element 119 and 120, but the heuristic structure persists. Similarly, we set out to review the classical seven key modalities of social influence and render them as distinct types – **crowds, leadership, norm formation, conformity, conversion, obedience and persuasion**. We then concluded that we can recognise at least three more: **prototyping, the fait accompli** and **resistance** (in capitals in Table 10.2). We 'discovered' these by working backwards from the literature on artefacts and mass mediation to basic face-to-face processes. Once you consider different modes towards the right, the cells multiply to cover an even wider field of distinct types. Thus, we expect other scholars to extend the Table within the heuristic logic of functions and modes of social influence; hence we left open spaces for new modalities marked by '???'.

A final issue of research on social influence, which we tried to address with our Period Table of Social Influence [PTSI], is the unstable flexibility of words, concepts and notions. It is unlikely that the social sciences will ever reach the level of standardisation of a technical vocabulary that characterises Chemistry's Periodic Table of Elements. This has many reasons beyond anybody's control; not least the innovation bias forcing young researchers to substitute new words for real novelty and to sell old wine in new bottles to gain attention in the knowledge economy (Godin & Vinch, 2017). We struggled to name the beasts, to develop a taxonomy and to find the adequate label for each cell. And we harbour no illusion that this is the final version. For example, we called the 'fait accompli' under conditions of mass mediation a 'nudge', but we believe this could equally be called an 'information design'. However, any labelling effort is a search for elegance mixed with trademark issues. We thus extend an open invitation to find the most adequate terms for the phenomena, not to speak of translations into other languages. In stabilising the relevant cells, however, we hope to have achieved an initial order.

A Novel Agenda for Social Influence Research

In June 2018, a public outcry took place in Malta when designs for a redeveloped square in the town of Paola were released. The public outcry concerned the fact that a number of trees lining the square needed uprooting to accommodate the new design. The protest was in line with recurring environmentalist objections to an aggressive development agenda pursued by the Maltese government. The architect of the project took to Facebook to address public expectations, listing a variety of reasons to justify uprooting the trees. Amongst others, the architect noted that the point for redeveloping the square was to incorporate a design that would make it uncomfortable for drivers who exceed the 30 km/h speed limit for built-up areas, forcing them to slow down.

This case is illustrative of the dynamics of social influence we have grappled with throughout this volume. On the one hand, the very communication of the redesigned plans is interpretable as an attempt on the government's side to influence voters' expectations, by presenting government as proactive in addressing citizens' demands. On the other hand, the outcry itself is interpretable as an attempt by lay citizens to challenge government – an attempt to quell its development agenda – in line with the pain model of resistance we reviewed in Chapter 9. And the redevelopment of the square is clearly an attempt to install an inter-objective structure to shape future driving habits, as the architect pointed out. How would we conceive of social influence in examining the present case? Whose influence attempts have succeeded? And whose have failed? Which influence modality met its target? And which influence modality could have been used to better effect?

The point we wish to make here is that the singular treatment of diverse modalities of influence in research programmes does not afford even a tentative answer to any of these questions. In everyday life, social influence attempts do not follow the serial and mechanistic conceptions of the laboratory experiment. We argue that whilst social influence research has yielded numerous insights, which indeed we systematise in our Periodic Table, it remains hampered by a restricted categorical focus. We argue that, given that social influence (a) emanates from diverse sources; (b) is exercised over diverse modes; and (c) manifests in diverse modalities, future research should follow the phenomenon in these features. We believe that the periodic table of social influence will be useful in this regard. Specifically, we can make some broad suggestions for future research.

Firstly, as we have noted numerous times in this volume, we should call off the search for a silver bullet to social influence. There is, and there can never be, a King's Way to social influence. What influences one person may well dissuade another (constraint: 'individual differences').

Secondly, it is more fruitful to query the conditions under which certain characteristic influences work in different publics. Such an attempt would call, in the first instance, for case studies focusing on specific events and documenting which influence modalities were deployed, in which mode, to what effectiveness and at which particular points in the debate (constraint: 'issue cycle' for mass mediation and artefacts). Every public sphere already has established discourses and a history of debates. For instance, the issue of gender equality has been on the agenda for over 100 years and in numerous countries. Over this time, this agenda has been served by crowds, charismatic leaders, persuasive appeals, positive discrimination in favour of the minority, as well as majority endorsements. We contend that comparative case studies, maybe of lesser historical extension than the gender issue, provide an opportunity to investigate interaction effects between modalities of influence in a given public.

Thirdly, case studies also afford a comparative focus that sheds new light on which conditions are required for certain modalities to work in certain publics (constraint: 'public sphere'). Comparing, for instance, the gender equality debate with the GMO debate, in the same public, could provide insights into which conditions facilitate success of specific modalities for certain publics at which state of the issue cycle.

Fourthly, a new focus for social influence research that stems from the Periodic Table of Social Influence is an investigation of interlinkages between modalities. One wonders not only which modalities are successful given the conditions of a certain public, but also which other modalities may provide effective complements and which others yet may provide effective antidotes in securing resistance. As noted, influence attempts on individuals can align vector combinations as well as push in opposite directions. A concern with interlinked effects between modalities may shed light on why, at times, some modalities work and others fail. Our Periodic Table of Social Influence suggests to compare real situations on portfolios of social influence modalities.

Fifthly, social influence research could benefit from an explicit articulation of power – both hard and soft. Considering that social influence serves in sustaining or supplanting prevalent common sense, it follows that social influence is intrinsically tied to the legitimation of collective projects. We hinted at this previously with regard to the problem of assessing 'progress' when this is part of the dominant discourse. The success, or otherwise, of any influence modality takes place in a context of power relations between interlocutors that secures the playing field and stacks the rules of the game for or against some actors. Consequently, the consideration of any influence modality in any case requires sensitivity to how power is involved, when social influence is both part of the game, but also a defining feature of the rules of the game. We hinted at this when considering the ethics of manipulation and social engineering (see Chapter 1).

Sixthly, we suggest that temporal analyses could be useful in understanding which collective characteristics provide adequate grounds for particular modalities. For instance, the characterisation of specific public spheres in terms of which modalities of influence prevailed during which historical period of that public sphere will facilitate our understanding of the fashion cycle of rise and fall of influence notions correlated with other issues such as freedom of expression, phases of democracy, rising costs of living, technological cycles and so on and so forth. This work might require the specification of a set of social influence indicators that could compare across (a) historical epochs, as well as (b) publics themselves.

These suggestions for further scholarship are all largely intended to query the conditions under which social influence is obtained. The ultimate aspiration is to acquire a good grasp of the portfolio of modalities in a particular public sphere to obtain specific functions. We would like to propose a three-tiered approach to update Lasswell's (1948) mediaeval formula of 'who says what to whom with what effect' for contemporary social influence research. Arising from our Periodic Table of Social Influence [PTSI], we argue that social influence research should address the following three questions for a conditional diagnostic: 'consider x, y, z to achieve F in condition P':

1   What is the state of the public sphere P?
2   What is the influence function F to be achieved?
3   Which portfolio x, y and z of influence modalities is best suited to obtain this function, given the circumstances?

To elaborate further, we believe that the starting point of any social influence inquiry is to query the circumstances in a given public – that is, to what extent does the public sphere demonstrate chaos, controversy, or relative stability? Even if the same objective is being pursued (e.g., equal wage for equal labour), the social influence modality which stands to succeed will differ for each of the circumstances noted. In a chaotic environment, a strong and charismatic leader might be needed to secure solidarity in the crowd. In a stable environment, a fait accompli might be equally successful.

Once the researcher has taken stock of circumstances, a second issue to enquire is what function is in focus – is the group striving for equal pay a dominant or non-dominant group? Is the group seeking assimilation of an equal wage proposal acting in an environment where gender equality is already established as common sense? Or is the social group a minority group seeking conversion of common sense? A minority seeking conversion does not have at its disposal the same influence modalities that a dominant group is able to rely on in preservation of its own sense, more common by virtue of its majoritarian status. Consequently, successful social influence tactics will follow function to accommodate the aspiration – fait accompli is not even an option.

Human relations are complicated rather than complex, and to good effect: not everything goes. The further narrowing of empirical focus enables a nuanced understanding of how social influence is manifest in particular circumstances. Real-world events, such as Donald Trump's presidential campaign in the United States in 2016; the UK Brexit referendum on leaving the EU the same year; how Jair Messias Bolsonaro, a marginal politician of thirty years, could win the Brazilian election in 2018 or how Xi Jinping revised the Chinese Constitution in 2017 to extend his chairmanship without limit – all of these events require an empirical focus that caters to a portfolio of social influences. We believe that it is high time that social psychological research extended its gaze to such real-world concerns, and we believe that the Periodic Table of Social Influences (PTSI) serves as a mental gateway and a catalyst to such inquiry.

Finally, and perhaps most interestingly, our Period Table of Social Influence [PTSI] will be useful in the search for missing elements. We have no ambition to have the last word, rather we hope for new beginnings. Our book is most probably full of oversights and omissions, to mend this in part we have relied on our students for the past years. We now turn to you – our reader – and end with a question: in your view, what modality of social influence might we have missed, what would you call it and where in the table would you put it?

In Essence

The study of social influence requires an exploration of co-occurring influences that act on social vectors at different times.

Social influence is exercised over three modes (face-to-face; symbolic; artefacts) and through various modalities that achieve changes in social relations without recourse to violence.

The use of social influence serves three basic functions: normalisation of belief to the point where it comes to be regarded as common sense, requiring no further justification; assimilation of deviant ideas into the prevalent common sense; and accommodation of the persisting challenge by alternative ideas while preserving a sense of continuity at the expense of a radical break with the past.

CHAPTER 11

Epilogue
Theoretical Issues and Challenges

Challenges to Common Sense, from Within and Without

A key feature of our model of social influence is the frame of reference, the common ground, common understanding or social representation arising in the community project. These standards of behaviour and experience are the product of past influence with relative permanence. Standards are normalised, and challengers are assimilated into it; and when this reaches its limits, accommodation shifts the common ground in subtle ways in favour of the challengers, and renormalises what in hindsight can be gauged as social change. That is our model in a nutshell.

Lindenberg (1987) argues that the consistency of Common-sense and common ground has two main challenges; they are dislocated by excessive solidarity and power hierarchies. Here we would like to examine briefly several challenges that arise from concerns for solidarity and threats to it. Disruptors of solidarity come from within or from without the boundaries of the established community. The reality of these challengers are topics of literary writing as well as scientific analysis. Both sources are rich in insight and well beyond our present purpose.

Challenges from Within

Let us consider four challenges to common sense that can arise from within any group project: there are children born into the community, dissident outsiders, homecomers and AI technology in the form of human-oid robots. These challenges arise from within the community, but carry categorical ambiguity of being insider or other.

Children, Newborn and Growing Up
Children are born into society from a woman's womb. Ideally, they are supported by an existing system of carers, often constituted as a family.

243

These newborns variously destabilise existing relations by demanding adjustments from carers in terms of time, attention and lifestyle. In turn considerable effort goes into 'socialising' these newcomers into routines of sleep and potty use of babies and toddlers, to more elaborate rituals of preschool and schooling, adolescence and early adulthood. At each stage children and young adults and their unruly behaviours question the ways of the family and also of society. The response is the pedagogical imperative, **'behave yourself!'** according to established rules and norms. At some stage, the child will ask 'why-questions' on everything including what is taken-for-granted, and because time is limited the parental answers become authoritative and final: 'because I say so . . .' (Bova & Arcidiacono, 2013). The literary genre of the coming-of-age novel (Bildungsroman) examines character formation in these clashes between personal quests and societal expectations from the point of view of the protagonists; developmental and educational psychology, and the sociology of socialisation systematise these dilemmas within a societal context. Modern tactics of 'nudging' seek to extend educational paternalism of 'legitimate' manipulation to the governance of society as a whole (see Chapters 8 and 9).

Dissident or Deviant Outsiders

Social science approaches the issue of deviant or dissident 'outsiders' in society under labelling theory (Becker, 1973). To talk of 'outsiders' one needs to consider three elements relative to an existing group: established rules, behaviour deviating from these rules and a judgement of deviance. Key to this is the act of labelling somebody as 'deviant' by moral entrepreneurs who champion these rules. Deviance is thus the result of an enterprise; rule makers and rule enforcers categorise a class of acts as deviant. Rules can be formal, a matter of law and police enforcement (e.g., do not steal), or informally a matter of tradition (no alcohol); some rules are enforced most of the time, others no longer. Labelling implies the possibility of category error when correct behaviour is labelled 'deviant' as in 'stop and search' policies (false positive), or when rule-breaking behaviour remains secret (false negative). Being labelled 'deviant', correctly or incorrectly, puts the actor in a situation which makes them less likely to continue with 'normal behaviour'; it pushes people into a career by defining the situation (what you are doing is a crime) and the person (you are a criminal). A deviance career has four stages: (1) break a rule purposefully and not arising from ignorance of the rule; (2) neutralise the act by rejecting responsibility, by justifying it as necessary in the circumstances, by minimising harm and by applying euphemism (not stealing but borrowing), attacking the accuser ad hominem as hypocrite and impelled by spite, by claiming to act on group loyalty; (3) developing a subculture and a self-justifying 'ideology' including a general repudiation of social conventions; (4) learning from other 'deviants' the stock of lore, how to avoid trouble and not to get caught.

The analysis of 'outsiders' involves the escalation of two equally valid perspectives: the moral entrepreneur defining the rules, and the 'deviant career' challenging these rules. Both act rationally, and we must understand how this looks from the actor's point of view. Extensive fieldwork in difficult-access territory is often needed to gain these insights, starting from common sense understandings of the acts. Becker's (1973) key examples are homosexuals or gays who successfully challenged societal norms, formal and informal, and moved from 'deviance' to 'normality' in many contexts; drug users, jazz musicians or the temperance movement who historically failed to challenge the common ground and convert the majority.

Homecomers

"The Homecomer" is the title of a famous essay by Alfred Schutz (1945) about returning soldiers who have served some years in foreign lands. They struggle to resettle in their old community because of an unbridgeable gap between their present experience and past memories. They have moved on, while their memories of the place and of its people are of the past. The same is true of the welcomers who stayed at home: they also have moved on, maybe to a lesser extent, and keep a frozen in the past memory of the homecomer. Both welcomer and homecomer know each other mainly as memory representations, their tacit common understanding has somewhat evaporated. Schutz concludes that homecomers as well as welcomers should be warned and prepared: their encounters will not be easy and they need to prepare for these gaps in memory and experience. This disorients the homecomers and challenges the welcomers.

In many contexts, homecomers are also received with suspicion. We learn of returning Russian prisoners of war being viewed as potential traitors during and after WWII because they have had contact with the class enemy. The homecomer also faces a dubious status in the context of migration: Niseis are second generation Japanese immigrants to Brazil; as homecomers to Japan (an estimated 300,000) they are called 'Dekasegi' and find it very difficult to be accepted (Tsuda, 2003).

'Nostos' is Greek for longing to return home. Nostalgia is the sickness to which homecoming seems the treatment. Without a concrete geographical place, the yearning becomes a metaphysical quest for an authentic existence. Nietzsche and Heidegger explored existential homelessness and the Gnostic feelings of being a prisoner in this world, longing to escape to somewhere totally else, also called nihilism or the counting of losses (Begout, 2014). This quest for exodus, overcoming metaphysical exile for a new homeland, contrasts the way of life of wondering nomads who express only contempt of cosy provincialism and the desire for rootedness (O'Donahoe, 2011, p. 4). In the poem 'Heimkunft' [Holderlin, 1802], Heidegger (2012 [1944]) recognises the continued disquiet even after returning: 'in coming home you have not reached your homeland' [ibidem, 13, author translation]; the existential homecoming is far from simply resettling in harmony; it is more likely a continued restlessness.

Plato's Allegory of the Cave (Republic, 514–520) turns homecoming (after having been educated) into an epistemic advantage. Having been out there gives one a better view of things; most people live in a cave observing shadowy illusions rather than reality. The homecomer has seen the sunlight and can recognise these shadows clearly as mere projections. This opens up the fundamental difference between appearances and reality; the homecomer has had access to 'real' reality and thus shares the privilege of the selected few called to unsettle the many.

Literature is a rich source of narratives on the one who left the fold and returns to find peace, to restore justice or to celebrate success. The typical format involves three acts (Campbell, 1949): (a) plucked up by courage, the protagonist leaves the safe space; (b) ventures into the unknown to face trials; with completed initiation and being homesick (nostalgic), yearns to return; (c) the homecomer has life-transforming experiences to share, and is warmly welcomed back. Beyond the welcome, Odysseus, the returning King of Ithaca, seeks to restore his right to former glory against the detractors, and he does so with the help of loyal supporters who, he being in disguise, only recognise him by a test of loyalty. The Bible tells the parable of the 'lost son' (Luke 15:11–32) who, upon returning, gets all the attention, including a celebration, which stirs the resentment among those who stayed home.

Homecoming is a defining theme of national literatures, not least the Swiss tradition. Keller's nineteenth-century *Green Henry* (1855) returns from a lengthy excursion to Germany; having discovered himself a patriot, he wants to support the fledgling Swiss nation. By contrast, his later *Martin Salander* (1886) returns from Brazil to find his lovely country in a deep moral crisis. The homecomer is thus an instrument of social diagnosis (vonMatt, 2012). In Durrenmatt's *Visit of the Old Lady* (1956), Clara Zachanassian demands justice for past inflicted pain in return for philanthropic generosity her violator, now an honourable member of the community, needs to be sacrificed. The community dithers, but comes around from refusing the unthinkable to doing what is sarcastically 'best for all of us'.

Vengeful homecomers, sometimes masking their own short comings, also appear in films. In the Spaghetti Western *Once Upon a Time in the West* (1968), the lynch mob is shot one by one by the former child witness; every time, Charles Bronson, now grown up, takes out his harmonica to announce with haunting sounds (Ennio Moricone) the impending justice. More recently in *Homeland* (US TV series 2011–2020, based on Israeli TV series *Hatufim* 2010–2012), a former prisoner of war returns as an undercover foreign agent; the focus is on good intentions, suspicion and paranoia among the welcomers in the context of the terrorist threat post 9/11. Music too adopts the trope, as in Beyoncé's recent show *Homecoming* celebrating her black roots (released in May 2019). The homecomer, herself disoriented, destabilises the common ground in many ways, both in reality and in fiction.

Robots

Finally, further challenges to common ground arise from technology in the form of artificial intelligence and robotics. Modern technology is itself an expression of not being at home in the world, needing to compensate for an incomplete biological niche and manifold organic deficiencies. Technological imagination can adopt the Gnostic mindset of being imprisoned in an alien world, not least by celebrating the dualism of hardware and software, body and soul of the machine (Begout, 2014; O'Donahue, 2011, p. 13).

Robots are designed within the community to help, to augment or to substitute for human drudgery. Are they adapting to human ways, or are they demanding that we adapt to their ways? There are many types of robotic installations, both real and anticipated: mobility robots promise autonomous cars, convoys of driverless trucks, and in many places, we have already driverless trains on tracks. Robots come as expert systems, that is, single purpose AI machines, that mimic a particular human expertise as in chess playing or in making a medical diagnosis. Production robots are already in use in the car industry imitating repetitive human actions precisely and efficiently. Maybe finally, there are sex robots which substitute for real sexual relations and rehearse on a rich canvas many male fantasies of female subservience.

There is a fundamental paradox involved in robotics: the more similar they are to humans, the more disturbing they become. This observation is known as the sudden 'uncanny valley' in the otherwise monotonous function of acceptance to human–machine similarity (Mori, 1970). The uncanny valley seems to show an inherent limitation of human–machine assimilation. Similar to literary homecomers, robots in reality become a mirror in which humans enhance self-understanding (Broadbent, 2017), and human strength and weaknesses are contrasted, recognised and highlighted.

Challenges from Without: Newcomers, Strangers-Foreigners, Aliens [from Outer Space]

The challenge from without is the favourite focus of populist politics engaging the anxieties of the people with anti-immigrant and xenophobic attention and polemic. This can take the form of deflecting the real cause of things towards a side show; what comes from inside is now conveniently located outside. The potential scapegoat 'foreigner' concentrates all bad forces and can be blamed for all ills of society. The label 'not one of us' has great powers to destabilise the common ground, not least because it points to the presence of alternative ways of life and thus an alternative view on things.

Newcomers

There is a considerable literature on newcomers in organisations (Louis, 1980), and the rituals of access into ongoing interactions (Phillet-Shore, 2010). Recruitment of new skills is a classical problem of the organisation. However, finding the right persons is not enough, they also have to be brought into the organisation and convinced to stay. This process is not without its problems. Assimilation is not painless, it has its struggles and crises. Recruitment is expensive, so retaining people is important to avoid costly turnovers. This may be defined as the newcomer problem. Organisational entry can be seen as matching expectations. If these are met, the person stays, otherwise they leave. These expectations are assumed to be fixed, and either met or not.

An alternative view considers a process of socialisation (Louis, 1980), of settling into the new situation through a series of phases. Initially, the potential recruit 'anticipates' the new job in a mix of images and expectations, tacit and explicit; they then move from outsider to newcomer and 'encounter' reality shocks while learning the ropes of the job. Finally, the 'adapted' newcomer turns insider once they are given broader responsibilities, autonomy of decision-making and are entrusted with privileged information.

All through this process, the newcomer will experience unfamiliar situations, surprise and confusion, that is, unmet anticipations, and struggle to make sense of it all. A key resource for sense making is a 'mentor' who serves as interpreter and informant being able to explain and justify the frame of reference of why 'we do things here the way we do'. Adequate activities on the job will depend on understanding the meaning of situations and knowing where to bring one's habits and skills to bear without being overbearing. Assimilation of newcomers maybe thus involve a series of steps, including moments of crisis in transition.

Studies on access rituals into ongoing interactions stress the 'conversational preserve', that is, the right to protect an ongoing huddle against overbearing others. Conversation analysis shows how pre-present parties control the entry of newcomers: the latter become a focus of bodily attention, and the update on interactions, so called 'previous activity formulations', is negotiated, including subtle hints to postpone the approach to avoid the pain of rejection. Conversational logic suggests that the burden of apology falls on the newcomer and rejection threatens their face (Phillet-Shore, 2010). The newcomer is thus the target of a balanced response, to actively welcome and to preserve the ongoing interactions from overbearing intrusion.

The Stranger-Foreigner

In a famous essay, Alfred Schutz (1944) examined the situation of a stranger, thus intellectualising his own emigration from Austria to the United States in the 1930s. Normal life in a social group is characterised by the 'the way we do things here'. Thinking as usual is full of assumptions which allow us to say 'of course', and tried and tested scripts to guide and interpret typical everyday events and actions. This common sense of group life includes received and shared knowledge to various degrees of thoroughness depending on relevance. Some matters we know very well and explicitly (knowledge about), others we are simply familiar with (have knowledge of), further notions we simply take on trust, but on most matters we are content to be in complete ignorance because they are irrelevant for the conduct of everyday life. The group defining feature of this common sense is the fact that is it taken-for-granted; no further questions are asked by the members of the group because they can assume that everybody is in on it.

The stranger, however, cannot share these assumptions without questioning them. The stranger brings his or her own taken-for-granted world to the situation, but needs to use it to observe the new environment and to make sense of it; engaging with the new situation in their own terms, the strangers will violate local assumptions and create disturbances. Their own meaning resources only lead them to prejudice, bias and misunderstandings of the local context. The stranger experiences a crisis of habitual behaviour, and this shock leads them to question the validity of thinking as usual; they cannot live as usual nor simply attempt a one-to-one translation of the schemes of interpretations because there is no common map between the locality and their own world; the stranger 'has to reckon with fundamental discrepancies in seeing things and handling situations' (ibidem, 504). What locals take for granted is for the stranger a problem, not a shelter from uncertainty but an adventure full of pitfalls, no matter of course, but instead of investigation, no instrument to deploy but the problem itself (ibidem, 506).

In consequence, the stranger is more objective and the focus of mistrust; the foreigner disturbs the unquestioned peace. Their heightened objectivity stems not from a particularly critical attitude aiming to debunk local myths, prejudices or biases, but from the experience of the limits of 'thinking as usual' which brings clear-sighted advantages over the locals, not least in moments of crisis. The stranger also must face suspicions of disloyalty, see their loyalty put to doubt. The stranger might be unable or unwilling to replace their own world with that of locals and therefore remains hybrid on the margins of two worlds. Locals may reproach them because they see them as ungrateful and rejecting the 'best of all worlds' as the taken-for-granted is proudly enacted locally. Assimilation then is the process by which strangers progressively move to adopt the local world by conforming to the local precepts and reconstructing their old worldviews until they blend in. Some never really assimilate, but simply comply with existing rules and do not adjust their mentality; these persons might end up as pariahs, bohemians and intellectuals or parvenus and nouveau riche (Arendt, 1951, chapter 3).

Milgram examined the idea of a 'familiar stranger' in overcrowded city life. The urbanite recognises many people in the street, as part of the daily commute, but one talks only to very few of these; and the longer we 'know' people only from seeing, the more difficult real contact becomes (Blass, 2004; p. 178). City life seems to immunise its common ground against being destabilised by strangers, by simply avoiding confrontation. One is reminded of an old rule of politeness: in the countryside you greet everybody, in the city only those whom you know.

The stranger is also a fictional character of novels, films and music exploring the situation of not-belonging-to-society, of being alienated from normal life. Most famously, Albert Camus' *L'Etranger* (1942, translated as 'the outsider') examines the character of Meursault who leads a meaningless life irritating others with his indifference and culminating in a random killing ('because the sun blinded me') for which he takes responsibility. Meursault is caught up in violence without a purpose; the absurdity of this experience puts established rules and norms into perspective, and renders any moral judgement arbitrary. The story is a philosophical examination of the absurd life as a cause for rebellion. Camus himself was a hybrid 'Pied-Noir', growing up as French in Algeria, and living as North African in France.

Exalted into metaphysics, being a stranger to this world is the defining obsession of ancient Gnostic religion (Jonas, 1963) and its current revivals in a generic mindset (Begout, 2014). According to dualist Gnosis, the world is an inhospitable place for the pure soul which is imprisoned and intoxicated by an impure material body. The world is utterly disqualified, and God, the Light, does not need to justify anything, no theodicy is needed, because the rotten world is the creation of a demiurge, the Force of Darkness. We need to liberate ourselves from this prison by initiating awareness (gnosis, manda), and by actively advancing destruction (apocalypse, revolution) to create a new beginning. As only the few will survive, being a stranger becomes a mark of excellence empowered by a metaphysical ideology that provides all ingredients to challenge the established common ground. The stranger feels exiled; some turn this into a lifestyle and a platform to challenge existing society.

Aliens – From Outer Space
The 'alien life, which stems from elsewhere and does not belong here', is the principle symbol of Gnosticism, both in terms of suffering and in terms of superiority that this confers (Jonas, 1963, p. 49). Maybe derived from this, the alien is also a narrative trope of science fiction. This species of imagination is able to destabilise the common ground despite all efforts of assimilation and anthropomorphising. Aliens are consistent with the idea that there are other planets that might support life (Kaplan, 2009), and the idea that life on earth originates elsewhere as claimed by British astronomer Fred Hoyle both in fact and fiction (Gregory, 2005, p. 94). But, aliens remain imaginary as no visits from other planets are historically recorded. The search for extraterrestrial life continues with high tech means at NASA and the SETI Institute (Search for Extraterrestrial Intelligence) in US-California, with the ambivalence on whether this should be passive–receiving of signals or an active–outgoing messaging (NZZ Folio, 2019, p. 44). Knowing of other life in the universe challenges human self-understanding.

There is a history to images of 'men on the Moon', on Mars and on various exoplanets. Aliens are the projection ground of anxieties, dreams and desires, often reflecting the flavours of the time, both different and similar to humans: insectoids, small green mannequins threatening women, shapeshifters, humanoid females in mini-skirts; Spock in *Star Trek* (1966) is an emotion-free logician; ET is a turtle-like galactic foundling extraterrestrial (1982); there are wise men like Yoda or horrific cyborgs in *Star Wars* (1977), or the good savage in *Avatar* (2009) (NZZ, 2019; p. 54; Seed, 2011, p. 27).

How would a community respond to an alien visitation? Defend the patch against 'invasion' or welcome the 'saviours'? The 'friend-or-foe' ambivalence is explored in Stanislav Lem's *His Master's Voice* (1968). A pulsating stream of neutrino radiation from a powerful extraterrestrial source is detected. The authorities suspect a super-intelligent message and commission two expert groups to decode the 'signal' with different briefs: friendly or a threat. But this all too human exercise of competitive semiotic decoding only confirms the starting assumptions, 'friend' or 'foe'; without common ground, understanding aliens is impossible and produces only projections. Attempts to message outer space must second-guess the capacities of extraterrestrial intelligence. Mathematical symbols play a special role as a putative universal language. With the *Lageos placette*, the *Arcebido messages*, *Voyager* and *Pioneer placettes*, space expeditions tell potential aliens about life on distant earth; back on earth this engendered a controversy over how to represent female genitals to aliens (NZZ, 2019; p. 42).

Potential communality with aliens is explored in HG Wells' *The War of the Worlds* (1898). Martians and earthlings share the need for survival in a cooling universe (nineteenth-century entropic pessimism) and the struggle for existence of conquer or be conquered, which makes carrying warfare to other planets an intelligible purpose (ibidem, p. 4). Hence, the alien encounter takes the form of an invasion unfolding in phases: initially, there is ignorance and obliviousness towards a looming existential threat; only 'the selected few' see clearly what is coming. Once aliens have landed, witness accounts are disbelieved, and followed by half-hearted responses to a still unknown threat; later events unfold into total panic and the collapse of the social order. Wells summarises the impact of alien invasion as the disruption of common places foreshadowing the total collapse of order:

> the most extraordinary thing . . . that happened that Friday, was the dovetailing of the common place habits of our social order with the beginnings of the series of events that was to topple that social order headlong (ibidem, p. 33).

The Earth is ultimately saved by the common flu; the Martians' immune system proves helpless against simple local microbes.

Alien is also a classical sci-fi horror movie with a female hero (1979). Giger's props are weird organic shapes reminiscent of sexual organs, and the movie reflects a mix of earthly ambivalence: fascination with and repulsion towards giving birth and the female body (Roberts, 2005, p. 282). It spawned an industry of cultural commentary including a large scale retrospective study of fan responses (Barker et al., 2016).

Aliens invade by substitution of locals, infection or takeover. They are a field of fake news as in the 'grey alien', constructed as a film prop and then presented as 'real' in a spoof-documentary (*Alien Autopsy* 1995; see NZZ, 2019). They also disturb through **conspiracy theories**. Firstly, authorities are accused of hiding evidence of their presence among us, often in conjunction with UFO cover-up stories (Seed, 2011, p. 40); and secondly, aliens are the ultimate shape-shifting reptilians already ruling us behind frontmen with familiar faces who are not what they seem. We are 'kept like mushrooms, kept in the dark and fed on shit' (a formulation often heard in focus group interviews), only very few 'enlightened' people like David Icke are able to see and tell you the 'truth', but for a fee (Butter, 2018; Byford, 2011). Aliens clearly destabilise life as usual.

Psychology Not Finding Its Objects

Bruno Latour (2000) argued that sociology had missed out on objects, because it misunderstood them either as fetishes to be smashed (iconoclasm) or as already accomplished facts (ready made by science and engineering). He coined the term 'factishes' to point out that things were neither given facts nor fetishes, but emerge in the 'progressive composition of a common world' (social constructivism; ibidem, p. 121). Inter-objectivity (Latour, 1996) thus highlights the processes by which objects come about and change shape. Psychology has had similar difficulties with material stuff, taking them for granted or leaving them to design experts in economics, engineering and architecture, the 'sciences of the artificial' (Simon, 1981). However, there were alternative voices. Gunter Anders (2002), a contemporary of Asch and Sherif, called as early as 1956 for a psychology of things:

> our everyday life is a world of objects where there are also human beings, and not a world of humans, where there are also objects; ... in order to understand how humans cope with this inversion ... we need a social psychology that studies our object relations (author translation and highlight, 60).

Anders was flabbergasted by the amount of common ground across Cold War front lines (1946–1989): the trust and ambition vested in technological systems is a universal 'taboo that is class and system neutral' (p. 63) and inhibits adequate thinking about this state of affairs. Asch and Sherif (see Chapter 4) recognised the dual products of inter-action, that is, social norms (intersubjectivity) and material artefacts (inter-objectivity); but both ignored artefacts beyond attitude 'objects'. Artefacts meant attitudes to 'imaginary objects' such as unicorns or the 'metallic metal act' (in opinion polling methodology). Therefore, inter-objectivity does not figure as prominently in psychological analysis as the normative intersubjectivity of beliefs, opinions and attitudes. Earlier in the 1920s, psychology had recognised an object as well as a subject-psychotechnics; the former morphed into Ergonomics/Human Factors with focus on tools and workbenches accommodating human capacities (adapting the tool to the worker), while the latter assimilated people to ready-made workbenches through testing, training and therapy (adapting the worker to the tool; 16; Geuter, 1988, 148; Lewin, 1920; Ulich, 2011). Social psychology remained exclusively intersubjectivity focused until ecological concerns (Stern, 2000) and the personal computer revolution foregrounded the designed environment (Norman, 1988, 1998 and 2004).

In all this, the defining manner of how psychology dealt with objects is ex-post-factum, as accomplished fact and ready-made. This entirely ignores the genesis, invention and construction of objects. We might recognise four different subject–object relations that are examined in this restricted way: developmental object constancy, opinions and attitudes (e.g., attitudes to nuclear power), possession (e.g., conspicuous consumption) and tool use.

From a **developmental** point of view, children mature into 'object constancy' on form, size, colour, brightness and sound. Initially a toy object is little more than a changing set of sensory impressions with little reality beyond immediate touch. If you hide the toy, the baby loses interest: out of sight, out of mind. However, the older toddler will look for what is now out of sight. Over time, babies stabilise an object across variable visual angles and illuminations; the emergent qualities will be more constant than the physical events impinging on the senses. Maturation thus stabilises the world of the senses in stable patterns, enhanced by language and categorical behaviour: having achieved colour constancy, the child can now learn to stop at a 'red light' assimilating many shades of 'red' to the identical response (Koffka, 1959, p. 299).

Attitudes are the classical problem of social psychological research. The term 'attitude' means we can position person X on a scale A in relation to an object Y (McGuire, 1986). So for example, people have an attitude to a nuclear power station in their neighbourhood, and we can report whether these attitudes are well informed or not, and their stratification, for example, women tend to be less favourable than men. 'Nuclear power' readily exists and interested people seek to change only attitudes through social influence. There is methodological concern that people opine on imagination rather than fact, such as the 'metallic metal act of 1973'; these factoids are then considered 'artefacts' of polling; people will answer any question, because they assume a genuine conversation. However, social psychologists hardly ever ask: how do attitudes bring about the object?

We are what we possess; we express our **identity** with fashion items, favourite things, souvenirs, status symbols and memorabilia. These objects are appropriated to create an image in the eye of others (Dittmar, 1992; Habermas, 1999). Again, the objects are ready-made; but we give them a new spin and gain some autonomy over stuff; banality becomes memorabilia, the stone from thirty years ago on a beach holiday with friends has little significance to anyone else.

Finally, **humans use tools**. Social psychology was mainly concerned with adjusting humans to ready-mades and their functionality. If you have never handled a heavy axe, you need to make adjustments; you need muscles to lift the axe and to target the wood to split. Sophisticated machinery requires mind training to use it properly. Psychology traditionally focused on **'reconfiguring the user'** to guarantee efficiency, training appropriate skills and cultivating acceptance, for example, training coding and treating computer phobia (Bauer, 1995).

In this fourfold sense, the emergence of inter-objectivity is largely absent from social psychology textbooks, despite it being the key frame of reference and a genuine product of social interaction.

Gestalt Patterns or Psychophysics – Single or Dual Process

We do not see things as they are, we see them as we are [Babylonian Talmud]

In this book, we came across **dual process ideas** centrally in crowd psychology and leadership (see Chapters 2 and 3), on norm formation (see Chapter 4), on slow and fast processes of persuasion (see Chapter 7) and on nudging techniques (see Chapter 9). These ideas develop on analogies between perceptual–cognitive processes and social processes. In order to understand present tension between **dual systems ideas** and **dynamic self-organisation of one system**, we might usefully examine a historical controversy that prefigures some of these controversies.

The autokinetic movement (Schiffmann, 1976, p. 266) allowed Sherif to demonstrate experimentally the stabilisation of a frame of reference in social interaction dealing with an uncertain situation (see Chapter 4). Gestalt psychologists were concerned with **self-organising foundations of experience**. In this note, we trace the origins of this debate over 'dual system' ideas in psychology to an earlier controversy between the Gestaltists' focus on perceptual patterns and the Introspectionists' focus on **sensations plus biased signification**. Gestaltists were concerned with the emergence of stable features in uncertain contexts, that is, the same stimulus leads to different experiences and the same experience can arise from different stimuli; while Introspectionists were concerned with the biasing of 'true but difficult to access sensations', obsessing with how constant sensory imprints lead to variable experiences.

When dualism assumes **primary and secondary processes,** we assume that basic input gains its 'meaning' through learned secondary associations. Perception is thus essentially true sensation 'biased' by interference of attention, knowledge, memory traces and attitude, that is, distortions that dress true, pre-conscious and automatic sensations in a secondary coat (Prinz, 2012). Perception is thus modelled as a linear regression of a constant function sensation $f(C)$ plus an inferential bias $f(Xi)$: $P = C + bXi$. Gestaltists and phenomenologists rejected this assumption polemically as the metaphysical **constancy hypothesis** (Graumann & Metraux, 1977; Gurwitch, 1964, p. 92; Koehler, 1947; Metzger, 1975, p. 74 and p. 134; Merleau-Ponty, 1962, p. 7; Sajama & Kamppinen, 1987; p. 20; Scheler, 1960, p. 319). This unprovable idea assumes that we can easily separate the constant C from the interference Xi.

By contrast, Gestaltists were interested in a different kind of stability: 'constant sensation under changing environmental conditions' (Metzger, 1975, p. 75), or why there are 'patterns in the clouds'. Phenomenal experience is not perception minus judgement, but constancy from fluctuating sensory inputs; stabilising an 'object' in the face of sensory ambiguity and uncertainty is a dynamic achievement of the organism: colour constancy under variable lighting, object size constancy with variable object distance, after-effects persist when the stimulus is terminated, stars group naturally into configurations in the night sky, the experience of movement from a sequence of discrete stills (Wertheimer, 1912) or the experience of pain in the absence of injury. None of this is an illusion or a bias. So how is it possible that for any 'object', physical conditions vary wildly and we have a constant experience of the 'object'? Common sense has it that this experienced constancy corresponds to the real-world constancies. What of this is learnt, what matures and what is framed by attitude? The argument is that this achievement depends on an oriented system, a moving organism. Perception is thus no linear-combination of a constant sensation plus irritating additives, but a relatively stable result of internal and external conditions. The resulting axiom states that all perception-action depends on a **'frame of reference'** (Metzger, 1975, p. 131): we perceive X only within such a context; meaning is construed on the spot; we compensate for dizzying uncertainty with a frame of reference to make a judgement. For social psychology, these 'frames of reference' are part of perception and arise in social interaction, temporarily fitting a changing situation. We capture this as the ***normalisation*** of a frame of reference in the face of uncertainty. We perceive the world of everyday life in socially normalised frames of references.

However, in a key book introducing the history and relevance of 'dual-process thinking', we read the following citation:

> if I say I see a book before me on my desk, I shall be criticised, because nobody can see a 'book' ... Even the character of being an 'object', or 'thing', which I have tacitly attributed to the experience I have called 'book' and 'desk' is improper in correct psychological description ... **we must learn to make the all-important distinction between sensation and perception**, between the bare sensory material actually given to us and the host of other items which since childhood have become associated with it. You cannot see a book, I am told, since this term involves some knowledge about a class of objects to which this specimen belongs, and about their use, etc. ... where in pure seeing such knowledge cannot enter ... Objects cannot exist for us before sensory experience has become imbued with meaning." (Wolfgang Koehler, 1930, pp. 54–55, as cited by Moskowitz, Skurnik and Galinsky, 1999, p. 12; highlight by us).

In their historical review, Moskowitz et al. (1999) invoke the leading Gestaltist Wolfgang Koehler as key witness in support of dual-process theories that separate sensation from perception, which they formulate as follows:

> [I]n the quotation above, Koehler asserts that even the simplest forms of knowing, such as knowing that the thing on the desk is a 'book', require the individual to make inferences that are not directly revealed by the properties of the things (book). Such inferences represent a leap beyond what is objectively revealed by the stimulus, and this inferential leap becomes far

more elaborate when the stimuli are social in nature – such as interpreting
what others are like (ibidem, 12).

Indeed, this idea that all experience is inferential is what Metzger (1975)
polemically called the **'Eleatic axiom'** (denigrating appearance against
reality, credited to ancient thinkers of Elea: Parmenides, Zeno and
Xenophanes): most things are not what they seem, need to be verified by
inferential judgement; the 'immediately given' is suspect. The Eleatics
originated this sceptical idea that most people are biased by their particular
views; they see what they want to see, that which they already believe to be
true. Certainly, this epistemological canon predates its exposition by
psychologists such as Koehler (1930)' (ibidem, p. 12). In citing and
interpreting Koehler, the authors make three claims:

(a) Perception of a 'book' is based on learned inferences from primary
    sense data;
(b) Inferences are more elaborate for social others than for physical
    objects;
(c) We are biased towards seeing a 'book' because we have learnt that a
    'pile of paper with ink spots' is a 'book', even before we learnt to call
    it a 'book', 'livre' or 'Buch'.

The question is whether these three claims form a package. While we
might happily agree with (c), we doubt that this necessarily implies (a) nor
(b). Rather this choice of citation and its interpretation is in itself an
example of (c), an interpretation in support of dual-process notions. What
if this reading of Koehler is wrong? Perception of an 'object' needs no
inferences, while to call it a 'book' does.

Let us look closer at Koehler's (1930 and 1947) original chapter 3
entitled 'a criticism of introspection' from which that long citation is taken.
Koehler explores the difference between Introspectionists and Gestaltists,
and while he defends the latter, he thinks the former are unscientific.
He states 'I propose to examine the way in which Introspectionists deal
with objective experience ... Surprisingly enough, the premises of their
work will prove to be quite similar to those of behaviourism' (1947, 42),
with which he took issue in the previous chapter. Koehler continues
explaining his scientific position, 'the very moment we try to observe
experience in an impartial fashion, we are bound to hear objections from
the Introspectionists. If I say that before me on my desk I see a book, the
criticism will be raised that nobody can see a book' (ibidem, p. 42). What
Moskowitz et al. (1999) cite as Koehler's support for inferential processes

is in matter of fact, the caricatured Introspectionist claim that 'we must learn to make the all important distinction between sensation and perception' (p. 43, as attributed to Koehler by Moskowitz).

In fact, Koehler critiques the idea of perception as **sensation + biased judgement;** this position considers all 'meaning' as secondary embellishment that needs to be carefully bracketed out by 'introspective methods'. He considers this an overgeneralisation of an obvious language feature: an acoustic sound or a Ngram is arbitrarily associated as signifier–signified; if animal is seen as a 'dog' in English, 'chien' in French, 'Hund' in German, the primary barking sensations are secondarily embellished as 'chien' or 'Hund', depending on our history. He defines this semiotic position as follows:

> In psychology, we must therefore try to ignore it [i.e., biographically learnt meaning that 'a book is on the table'] and to focus only on the mental sensations of shape, size and colour. The procedure by which this is achieved is called introspection ... The main question is, of course, according to what criteria some experiences are to be selected as genuine sensory facts [i.e., primary] while others are discarded as mere products of learning [i.e., secondary] (ibidem, p. 44).

Koehler's polemic is against a narrow take on 'sense making' as secondary and modelled on linguistic meaning; he seeks to recover subjective experience as key data. Note, Gestaltists take issue with 'introspection' of experience only in this very restrictive understanding of methods.

Koehler lists all classical examples of **perceptual constancies of size, shape and brightness** when sensory impressions vary wildly, as mentioned. We see people of constant height, or even recognise Sandra at a distance, even when the retinal imprint changes with every step we take; we see plates on the table as circular when they should be elliptical in geometric projection, and colours keep their brightness under widely variable illumination. And we see dramatic movement in the cinema, when we should only see a rapid sequence of stills. According to Introspectionists, we do so because we have learnt by experience to correct appearances: we actually see elliptic shapes (qua constant sensation; the empirical Major); because we know that plates with food are normally circular and on tables (the learnt Minor), these elliptic shapes must be round 'plates' (Conclusion). While this might be true for issues of linguistic meaning and classification; it is not the case for everyday experiences, except held as a metaphysical extension. Not all meaning is an association of signifier and signified.

This 'metaphysical' constancy hypothesis cannot be proven nor does it make sense in the light of living organisms. Scheler (1960, 323) called it paradoxical reasoning of an extreme case 'as if we were dead' (or maybe unconscious): while alive it is impossible to separate sensations from perception; when dead, we might have sensations (sensory mechanics), but no longer experiences (because dead). This unfortunate assumption reduces psychology to the study of spirited illusions and biased judgements compared to the 'true sensations' of a mechanical imprint of stimulus to sensation. But lived perceptual processes are mostly 'direct and constructive' and beyond the stimulus information (Prinz, 2012). There is no going back to a 'pure sensation' above a fixed threshold C, nor behaviour as a constant function b of physical stimuli Xi purified of centrally biased signification as in psycho-physics:

$$\mathbf{B_I = C + bXi,} \text{ if } b = 1, B_I = C + Xi$$

The alternative is a living person-in-situation, whose perceptions and behaviour arises from multitude of internal as well as external conditions; our brain is simultaneously activated by sensory input, and by motor activity, emotional activation and memory traces: $\mathbf{B_2 = f\,(Xe;\,Xi)}$. If the external conditions are kept constant, $B_2 = f(\text{constant}, Xi)$, this is very different from a linear combination $\mathbf{B_I = C + f(xi)}$. B_I and B_2 are qualitatively different experiences; B_I is at best a special case of B_2, and neither of them is particularly privileged and unbiased (Gurwitch, 1964, p. 95). These two very different ways of conceptualising the relation of environment and behaviour is illustrated in Figure 11.1.

For Koehler this unfortunately distracts from the real task of examining the actual 'plates on the table', rather than elliptic shapes that miraculously became plates, and from asking the key questions how plates are used (usage), and whether we like them or not (attitudes). Koehler continues:

> When I apply the introspectionist methods I often find the same experience as he does (the pure sensation). But I am far from attributing to such facts a rare value as though they were more 'true' than the facts of everyday experience. If common experience by introspection depends upon the attitude of introspection, one cannot show that they also exist in absence of this attitude (ibidem, 52).

Koehler thus claims that **pure sensations are an artefact of methods** (for Scheler, playing a 'dead body'). The very separation of 'primary' sensation (C) and 'secondary' appreciation (bXi) is the model that creates the separation. And if this attitude prevails, **psychologists will ignore the experiences of everyday life**. Koehler widely caricatured this 'empiricist-rationalist' metaphysics – empiricist focus on the 'sensation'; rationalist on the 'bias' – in search for a third way of direct experiences (ibidem, p. 51):

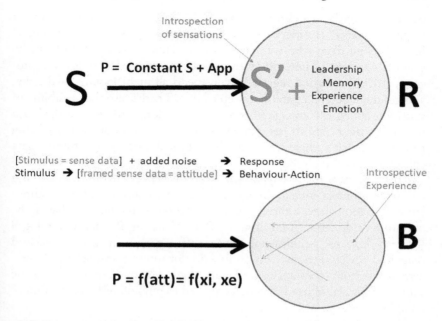

Figure 11.1   Two concepts of the relation between situation and behaviour. A linear combination with a constant 'stimulus-sensation'; or a function of multiple factors in the 'behavioural environment' of the person with a natural attitude

'Millions of people will never transform objects of their environment into true sensations, will always react to sizes, shapes, brightness and speeds as they find them, will like and dislike forms as they appear to them' and, If an empiricist-rationalist attitude would prevail, 'such experience as form the matrix of our whole life would never be seriously studied' (ibidem, p. 51).

So, rather than providing authoritative support for a dual-process notion – primary sensations + secondary bias – Koehler caricatures this distinction as implied metaphysics. Moskowitz et al. reproduce their own attitude: they assume to be true exactly what Koehler satirises. What if at the core of dual-process ideas lies this fundamental misunderstanding? Rather than dealing with a duality of direct sensation + biased elaboration, we are dealing with a single process of meaningful life experiences under conditions of variable external stimuli, bodily state and attitude?

In the nineteenth century, astronomers worried about the fact that when star gazing they see stars passing at different speeds. They would record slightly different passing times, and this became known as the

personal equation in chronometry. So how long does it take for Jupiter to pass a line? This variation created suspicions; astronomers were cheating, falsifying data; who was then correct? They tried to control this by training observers. Those doing the measurement need to follow a protocol, a strict observation regime. If you spend all night looking at the sky, you get tired. So you establish a sleep regime. There's also the possibility of statistics, taking the average of several observations and arguing the truth in close to the mean. At last, you automate, as you do not trust any living person, and that's where we are in observational astrophysics: robotic data collection (Schaffer, 1988).

This logic gave rise to **psycho-physics**. Sensory experience (psycho-) is a constant and proportional, though non-linear function of a physical stimulation (-physics) above a threshold. The function charts the bias, that is, the curvature or deviation from linearity: $P = kS^x$ **or** $\log P = \log k + x \log S$ (Stevens' law; see Schiffmann, 1976, 15ff): in the ear sense, perceived magnitude of loudness is a power function of sound pressure (S^x) above a certain threshold (constant k; see Figure 11.2). The question is: what is the source of this bias of psychological compared to physical ordering of stimuli? Sampling inadequacy or small N?

This metaphysical idea seems preserved in behavioural economics, which constructs a psycho-physics of value: what is the utility of some investment value? Prospect theory (Kahneman & Tversky, 1979) maps utility (psycho-) as a function of financial gains and losses (-physics). Utility is a non-linear and non-symmetrical function of the 'true value' of things (defined by economists = physics) as illustrated in Figure 11.2. The non-linear shape of the curve defines the deviation from 'rationality' and becomes predictable as biased judgement: **Util = value constancy + bias**. The question is whether this is a good start for assessing valuation. Is this the way to reduce the ambiguity of a situation, or a metaphysical assumption about how nearly dead people would apportion 'true' values?

These alternative considerations are all important in a world of ambiguity and uncertainty. The environment requires that human systems stabilise perceptions to guide activities. **This stabilisation of perception in an ambivalent environment is a human process of social influence.** But is this process one of biasing an 'initially true' judgement? Sherif made the point with his demonstrations: stabilisation is no bias, but rather the self-organising of a frame of reference for future activities.

Why is this important? There are dual process ideas in most of our previous chapters on social influence: with notions of system 1 and system 2, 'chaotic input' is given orderly shape by higher order processes; 'true

Magnitude estimation

Have subject rate (e.g., 1–10) some aspect of a stimulus (e.g., how bright it appears or how loud it sounds)..

Steven's power law

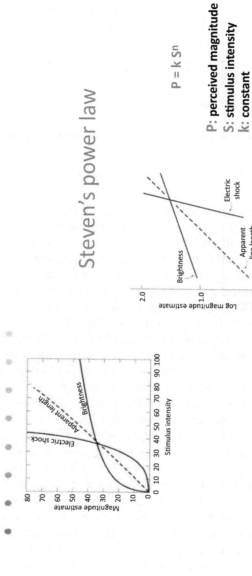

$$P = k\,S^n$$

P: perceived magnitude
S: stimulus intensity
k: constant

Relationship between intensity of stimulus and perception
of magnitude follows the same general equation in all senses

Figure 11.2 Psycho-physics illustrated in two classical cases: (left) Steven's Law of power functions between stimulus and estimates (Schiffmann, 1976); (right) the prospect theory utility function: utility value depends on loss/gain outcomes, non-linear and non-symmetrical, and a measure of 'human irrationality' of over- and underestimation compared to a linear function (Kahneman & Tversky, 1979)

The 'psycho-physics' of value-utility

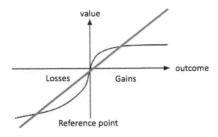

Loss aversion and benefit seeking are not symmetrical as they should be;
losses hurt more than gains feel good

Figure 11.2 (*cont.*)

input' is distorted by biases; unruly automatic emotional stimulus-response transductions, the behavioural path, are controlled by secondary processes, the cognitive path (Liebermann, 2007); or fast cuing information is moderated by more elaborate meditation. The commonality of these ideas inherits the old 'constancy hypothesis': an initial 'true' input is unconsciously 'deposited' and then secondarily processed into a 'biased response': **P1 = C + f(Xi)**. By avoiding the secondary bias (if Xi = 0), we can supposedly reach the initial 'true' stimulus: P1 = C.

Independent of any inherited metaphysical confusion, dual process theories are conceptually and empirically controversial (Evans & Stanovich, 2013; Keren & Schul, 2007; Kruglanski & Thompson, 1999). Dualities generally convey a rhetorical advantage through amplification of extreme cases (Godin, 1999); tables that juxtapose A with B on many features are appealing and popular in communication. Empirically, it remains unclear on which criteria and how strongly different systems are distinguishable (Keren, 2013); what duality is neurologically plausible in correlational structures (Liebermann, 2007); whether these are either/or systems or interacting pathways; whether the empirical evidence for duality is reducible to a common single process (Kruglanski & Gigerenzer, 2011); what is ultimately the advantage of dual system thinking beyond convenience?

The alternative is to embrace **single process ideas** which stipulate multiple factors of one process: the crowd is a self-organising process finding direction in and out of itself, without needing external leadership. Leadership is calibrated to the group by proto-typicality. Persuasion involves the calibration of messages to relevance and cognitive need; or, according to classical rhetoric, persuasion involves the optimal aligning of the logos of argument, the pathos of appeal and the ethos of credibility. This alternative meta-physics became known as 'autopoiesis'; focus on self-activity as found in physical, biological, social and psychological systems-in-context (Luhmann, 1984; Maturana & Varela, 1980). Social influence is thus at most a trigger event, stimulating the reorganisation of the social group, and 'pure sensation biased' is not the real thing, but at most one among many internal and external conditions of activity: $P_2 = f (X_e , X_i)$.

We started this excursion with a citation, apparently an old Talmudic truth: **'we do not see things as they are, we see them as we are'.** It seems that this age-old wisdom reflects the psychological fact that living is prior to perception, and a social affair of being-with-others. This tribal context of 'identity' provides not only for safety, conviviality and comfort, but also has epistemic relevance. The tribal frame of reference is the point of social influence, in normalising it, in assimilating the detractors and in accommodating the necessary changes to make the future sustainable for an ever wider community. How such a social group self-regulates with an 'orientation towards the truth', or by referring back to 'common sense' needs to be understood in terms of cultivating the challenges and responses.

The Authority of Science [As in Milgram's Experiment]

The problem of authority appears variously in relation to social influence. Authority appears in persuasion models as credibility of the source. It is central in obedience research; is 'obedience' irrational or a deliberate choice? The literature that replicates the obedience paradigm of Milgram (see Chapter 6) grapples with the nature of that authority.

- 'Obedience to authority' is a propensity that overrides the common morality 'thou shalt not hurt another human being'
- This propensity depends on 'legitimate authority' which defines the situation and takes away responsibility; what is a legitimate authority, what is illegitimate?
- Obedience is cultivated as a propensity in education: disobedience is a vice
- Obedience is conformity in the vertical dimension: comply with the orders of a higher status person [Asch paradigm = conformity to majority peers, horizontal dimension]

Milgram stages a lab situation where the authority is 'scientific', conducting a learning experiment and inviting the participants to be part of that collective effort. The experiment takes on the paraphernalia of science: lab environment at a leading university, lab coats, technical instrumentation, etc. The Milgram study is however cited in contexts other than scientific authority, such as military training or genocide studies, or administrative authorities (Blass, 2004). The question arises: how can we generalise to different types of authorities? Can we assume that a general situation covers all types of obedience?

Social psychology has a tendency to hail **anti-authoritarism** and **nonconformism** as values. In this light 'obedience' is a vice, and only irrational because people do things which they would not desire to do outside the particular situation; 'something about the situation subverts subjects' ability to do what they want to do' (Sabini & Silver, 1983, p. 151). This might be too simplistic, as authority is a precious resource in society to check violence and tyranny. Obedience can be autonomous as well as automatically blind. Also, in 'going beyond the call of duty', obedience turns into something else: sadism, gratuitous cruelty, autotelic violence, evil acts, arbitrary duress (Reemtsma, 2016).

We need to clarify what is 'authority' and, what is the 'authority of science' in Milgram's lab set-up. Key features of any authority are: being grounded outside power, and therefore able to speak truth to power; it occupies the middle ground between violence and endless debate, thus guarantees freedom; it establishes a hierarchy in a world without hierarchies; it is based on consent and reputation; accepting authority means deferring judgement; challenges to authority give rise to a sense of crisis.

Firstly, authority finds its **legitimation in sources outside of power** that is based on force and violence. This is its first characteristic. This source can be in natural law, or in traditions of 'sacred' rituals or in a mandate from heaven deposited in scripture. This provides the independence of authority and allows them to speak truth to power (Arendt, 1958).

Secondly, when authority is lost, individual freedom seems to gain. Russell identifies authority with group coercion and freedom with individual spontaneity, and suggests a natural trade-off between authority and freedom in society (Russell, 1949). However this might be a liberal-anarchic illusion. Hannah Arendt (1958) warned that the **absence of authority means tyranny, not freedom**. Only legitimate authority puts limits to power and guarantees freedom. Therefore, less authority can mean less freedom.

Thirdly, authority is historically a vertical relation A to B, establishing a hierarchy modelled on the familial education or military command; it speaks from 'upon high' like a mandate of heaven. In modern society, though, hierarchical stratification is superseded by functionally differentiated systems. Law operating on legality, the economy on profit, politics on power and techno-science on truth and efficiency (Luhmann, 1984). Modern **authority falls between these cracks**. Authority can only irritate across system boundaries; it cannot afford obedience, only calculated compliance. Business follows the profit motive, science seeks new efficient facts and complies with the rules as needed; the law bestows authority to judges only within the legal system. Herein lies a source of instability: modern authority is only sectorial.

Fifth, authority is the 'via media' between violence and argumentation to determine collective agency; putting a stop both to violence and endless debate. **Authority needs neither argument nor violence**. Any call for more debate poses a challenge to authority (Arendt, 1958). Public debate challenges the speakers: is the claim evidentially true, morally right and truthfully put forward. These three validity claims must be guaranteed by substantive arguments and not the external authority of the speaker (Habermas, 2001).

Sixth, authority goes with autonomous agency. In Roman rhetoric, authority makes us believe X, Y or Z. The speaker's authority rests in the aura of his or her character (ethos), more than in the strength of argument (logos). In court, the judge decides and thus **avoids long arguments**, reasons of justification will be provided by the clerks for the historical record. We might appeal, but this chain will end at the highest court (Eschenburg, 1965).

Seventh, authority involves a psychic act of acknowledgement. For Gadamer (1960), worrying about authoritative text interpretation, **authority is relational, A has authority over B**. But this is not a coercive subjugation of B by A nor an abdication of reason on the part of B; it is a reasonable acknowledgement by B that A has sharper insights or superior judgement. **Authority means autonomy** also on the side of those who obey (Kant's *'sapere aude'*, Latin for *dare to make use of your own judgement*). Rather than 'blind compliance', deferring to an authority is an act of freedom. It means accepting one's dependence on somebody else's judgement. Authority is thus accepted and acknowledged, and it can therefore be withheld by B and lost for A.

Eighth, authority thrives on images and representation, pomp and circumstances, on the one hand, and competent performance on the other.

Insignia of distinction inspire deference (Sennett, 1980). And effective performance put on pedestals provides prestige (e.g., Nobel Prizes, university rankings). Modern authority often includes a choice: reputation has it that B poses more of a risk of disappointment than A; C thus trusts A more than B to deliver the goods. By contrast, we need **confidence in situations without choice**. We confide in the police when they exercise a monopoly; in situations where the police compete with private security firms (as in Brazil) we trust either the police or the security firm to deliver safety (Luhmann, 1998). Fiduciary responsibility for public welfare, and the competence to deliver, are key features of reputation which convey public authority (Barber, 1990).

Finally, 'authority' becomes **an issue when no longer taken for granted**. Discussions of authority often invoke a 'moral panic' of decline in society, and a loss of freedom coming with it. Arendt (1958) raised the question 'what is authority?' and Eschenburg (1965) reviewed its protracted history during a crisis of post-war institutions in the 1950s and 1960s, and Milgram started his experiments in 1963/1964. In the 'events of 68', highly educated students, cheered on by some academics, made a front against 'authoritarian personalities' (Adorno et al., 1950), which had enabled the totalitarian tyrannies of the twentieth century.

We must credit the emergence of research on 'authority' to these challenges. Social researchers started to **observe 'perceived authorities' as an empirical matter**. In the United States, items on 'how much would you say you trust institution x' appeared in the General Social Survey (GSS) in 1974; in the United Kingdom, Ipsos-MORI publishes its 'veracity index' *(I believe that x is telling the truth)* since 1983. Authority is vested in public opinion and mentality as social capital. There is continued debate whether perception measures are sufficiently reliable: if they are unstable we cannot distinguish method variance from change over time (see Turner & Kraus, 1978) for indicators of value and well-being (Schwartz, 2011) and generalised trust (Lundmark et al. 2016) or science culture (Godin, 2012). Equally, the inclusion of 'science' among the actors for which we measure trust is itself a problem marker: the unproblematic needs no metrics (Muller, 2018).

We recognise the authority of science has many of these nine features. Speaking truth to power and autonomy to do so is high on the agenda for science in society. However, at the heart of an authority of science lies a contradiction. The history of science is full of stories of unshackling from false authorities of superstition, religion, ideology and state control. There is an anti-authoritarian streak running through scientific methodology.

captured in the seventeenth-century motto of the Royal Society '*nullius in verba*' (take nobody's word for it). The business of science is facts, demonstrated under the eyes of peers, and arguments from authority are rejected along with the whole of rhetoric (see Feyerabend, 2016). Thus, the attempt of science to seek an authority for this enterprise seems self-contradictory (Luhmann, 1996, 23). How can and why does an anti-authoritarian attitude seek authority? There is a similar paradox in law, which struggles to include a right to civil disobedience into the rule of law (Pottage, 2013). Another solution is offered by attempts to establish science as the only authority of modern society in substitute of all others (Shapin, 2008).

But modern society is characterised by competing authorities each with a different reach. With **legal authority**, we mean the authority bestowed by constituted law. The position is guaranteed by statute, but judges nevertheless worry about their reputation: 'doing justice and being seen to do justice'. By contrast, science tends not to enjoy such privileges, while its freedom of enquiry might be protected under the law and old universities inherit limited jurisdiction. In many countries there is a 'scientific advisor' to government (Bijker et al., 2009); or science has authority in court, when DNA evidence or psychological testing is granted status of 'objective evidence' (Brandmayr, 2017) with mixed consequences (Gauchat, 2012).

One might argue that such privileges lead to a loss of authority. With **social authority** we mean the fact that trust is confined to a subgroup in society, that is, tribal authority. The capacity for superior judgement is only recognised in a particular social milieu. While a speaker-actor might have authority in that group, he or she is not recognised or even rejected elsewhere. Typically, religious or scientific leaders have authority in their community, outside of which the person has no particular status. The Pope might have little tracking among non-Catholics, where the Church has lost its legal privileges.

With **cultural authority**, we mean the wider acknowledgement of authority well beyond a natural milieu. Institutions, such as the Royal Society or the Nobel Prize Committee, seek to project persons into society that deserve authority beyond their particular achievement. Scientists might take on the role of prophets in times of crisis (Walsh, 2013). In India, the **'scientific temper'** is a key dimension of secular nation-building on the subcontinent. This idea entails the aspiration of all Indians to bestow authority to science for peace and prosperity (see Raza in Bauer et al., 2019). Scientific temper is one of three constraints on public decisions after preferences and tradition, or it can be misused to buttress a technocratic regime with the aspiration that decisions should be confined to experts who restrict decision criteria to technical ones (Khilnany, 1997).

Cultural authority is an aspiration as much as it is an empirical fact in any society. Recent alarms over a 'Post-Truth Society' where 'fake news' rules the information diet of the public, signals concern for scientific authority on issues such as vaccination, global warming, crime rates or the economic prospects of the nation. What a leading British politician in 2016 announced on public TV, 'we have had enough of experts', strikes a sinister note on the state of scientific authority (Bauer, 2018; Bauer et al., 2019). The rate of obedience demonstrated in the Milgram paradigm in different places and at different times is thus an indicator of scientific authority, and its changes should be monitored with care (see Chapter 5; Blass, 2004), including a discussion of the desirable level of cultural authority of science, because it is our freedom that is at stake.

References

Abrams, D., & Hogg, M. A. (1990). Social identification, self-categorization and social influence. *European Review of Social Psychology*, 1, 195–228.

Abrams, D., & Levine, J. M. (2012). Norm formation: revisiting Sherif's auto-kinetic illusion study. In J. R. Smith & S. A. Haslam (eds.), *Social Psychology: Revisiting the Classical Studies*, (pp. 57–75). Los Angeles: Sage.

Adorno, T. W., Frenkel-Brunswik, E., Levinson, D. J. & Sanford, R. N. (1950). *The Authoritarian Personality*. New York: Harper and Row.

Ainsworth, M. D. S., Blehar, M. C., Waters, E. & Wall, S. (1978). *Patterns of Attachment: A Psychological Study of the Strange Situation*. Hillsdale, NJ: Erlbaum

Ajzen, I. (1985). From intentions to actions: a theory of planned behavior. In J. Kuhl & J. Beckmann (eds.), *Action Control: From Cognition to Behaviour* (pp. 11–39). New York: Springer-Verlag.

(1991). The theory of planned behaviour. *Organizational Behavior and Human Decision Processes*, 50(2), 179–211.

Allport, G. W., & Postman, L. (1947). *The Psychology of Rumor*. New York: Henry Holt & Co.

Allyn, J., & Festinger, L. (1961). The effectiveness of unanticipated persuasive communications. *Journal of Abnormal and Social Psychology*, 62(1), 35–40.

Anders, G. (2002). *Die Antiquiertheit des Menschen. Ueber die Seele im Zeitalter der zweiten Industriellen Revolution* (vol. 2). Munich: C. H. Beck Verlag.

Apfelbaum, E., & McGuire, G. R. (1986). Models of suggestive influence and the disqualification of the crowd. In C. F. Graumann & S. Moscovici (eds.), *Changing Conceptions of Crowd Mind and Behaviour* (pp. 27–50). New York: Springer Verlag.

Arendt, H. (1951). *The Origins of Totalitarianism*. New York: Schocken Books.

(1958/2012). *Was ist Autoritaet? Zwischen Vergangenheit und Zukunft, Uebungen im politischen Denken I*. Munchen: Piper.

(1963). *Eichmann in Jerusalem: A Report on the Banality of Evil*. New York: Viking Press.

Arnheim, R. (1974). *Art and Visual Perception: A Psychology of the Creative eye*. Berkeley: University of California Press.

Arnstein, S. R. (1969). A ladder of citizen participation. *Journal of the American Planning Association*, 35, 216–224.

271

Aron, A., Aron, E. N. & Smollan, D. (1992) Inclusion of other in the self scale and the structure of interpersonal closeness. *Journal of Personality and Social Psychology*, 63(4), 596–612.

Aronson, E., Wilson, T. D., Akert, R. M. & Sommers, S. R. (2017). *Social Psychology* (9th ed.). Harlow: Pearson.

Arrow, H., McGrath, J. E. & Berdahl, J. L. (2000). *Small Groups as Complex Systems: Formation, Coordination, Development, and Adaptation*. Thousand Oaks, CA: SAGE Publications.

Asch, S. E. (1951). Effects of group pressure on the modification and distortion of judgments. In H. Guetzkow (ed.), *Groups, Leadership and Men* (pp. 177–190). Pittsburgh, PA: Carnegie Press.

(1952/1987). *Social Psychology*. Oxford: Oxford University Press.

(1956). Studies of independence and conformity: a minority of one against a unanimous majority. *Psychological Monographs: General and Applied*, 70(9), 1–70

Assmann, J. (2008). Communicative and cultural memory. In A. Erll & A. Nunning (eds.), *Cultural Memory Studies: An International and Interdisciplinary Handbook* (pp. 109–118). Berlin: DeGruyter.

(2018). *Achsenzeit: Eine Archäologie der Moderne*. Munchen: CH Beck.

Atran, S., & Norenzayan, A. (2004). Religion's evolutionary landscape: counter-intuition, commitment, compassion, communion. *Behavioural and Brain Science*, 27, 713–770.

Austin, J. L. (1976). *How to Do Things with Words* (2nd ed.). Oxford: Oxford University Press.

Avolio, B. J., & Bass, B. M. (1988). Transformational leadership, charisma, and beyond. In J. G. Hunt, B. R. Baliga, H. P. Dachler & C. A. Schriesheim (eds.), *Emerging Leadership Vistas* (pp. 29–49). Lexington, MA: D. C. Heath.

Bachrach, P., & Baratz, M. S. (1962). Two faces of power. *American Political Science Review*, 56, 947–952.

Bales, R. F. (1950). *Interaction Process Analysis*. New York: Addison-Wesley.

Bangerter, A. (2000). Transformation between scientific and social representations of conception: the method of serial reproduction. *British Journal of Social Psychology*, 39, 521–535.

Bangerter, A. & Heath, C. (2004). The Mozart effect: tracking the evolution of a scientific legend. *British Journal of Social Psychology*, 43, 1–37.

Barber, B. (1993) *The Logic and Limits of Trust*. New Brunswick, NJ: Rutgers University Press.

Barker, M., Egan, K., Ralph, S. & Phillips, T. (2016). *Alien Audiences: Remembering and Evaluating a Classic Movie*. Basingstoke: Palgrave Macmillan.

Barley, R. S., & Kunda, G. (1992). Design and devotion: surges of rational and normative ideology of control in managerial discourse. *Administrative Science Quarterly*, 37(3), 363–399.

Barnett, B. (2002). Tonal organization in seventeenth-century music theory. In T. Christensen (ed.), *The Cambridge History of Western Music Theory* (pp. 407–455). Cambridge: Cambridge University Press.

Bar-Tal, D. (2000). *Shared Belief in a Society: A Social-Psychological Analysis.* London: Sage.

(2015). *Intractable Conflicts: Socio-Psychological Foundations and Dynamics.* Cambridge: Cambridge University Press.

Barthes, R. (1965/1988). The old rhetoric: an aid-memoire. In *The Semiotic Challenge* (pp. 11–94). Oxford: Basil Blackwell.

Bartlett, F. C. (1932). *Remembering: A Study in Experimental and Social Psychology.* Cambridge: Cambridge University Press.

Bass, B. M. (1985). *Leadership and Performance Beyond Expectations.* New York: Free Press.

Bauer, M. W. (1991). Resistance to change: a monitor of new technology? *Systems Practice,* 4(3), 181–196.

(1993). *Resistance to Change: A Functional Analysis of Responses to Technical Change in a Swiss Bank,* PhD Thesis, University of London.

(1994). A popularização da ciencia como immunização cultural: a funçáo de Resistencia das representaçóes sociais. In S. Jovchelovitch & P. Guareschi (eds.), *Textos em representaçóes sociais* (pp. 229–260). Petropolis: Vozes.

(1995). Towards a functional analysis of resistance. In M. W. Bauer (ed.), *Resistance to New Technology: Nuclear Power, Information Technology, Biotechnology* (pp. 393–418). Cambridge: Cambridge University Press.

(2005a). The mass media and the biotechnology controversy. *International Journal of Public Opinion Research,* 17(1), 5–22.

(2005b). Distinguishing red from green biotechnology: cultivation effects of the elite press. *International Journal of Public Opinion Research,* 17(1), 63–89.

(2006). The paradoxes of resistance in Brazil. In G. Gaskell & M. W. Bauer (eds.), *Genomic & Society: Legal, Ethical and Social Dimension,* (pp. 228–249). London: Earthscan.

(2012). Public attention to science 1820–2010: a 'longue duree' picture. In S. Rödder, M. Franzen & P. Weingart (eds.), *The Sciences' Media Connection – Public Communication and Its Repercussions* (Sociology of the Sciences Yearbook 28) (pp. 35–58). Dordrecht: Springer.

(2013). Social influence by artefacts: norms and objects as conflict zones. In G. Sammut, P. Daanen & F. M. Moghaddam (eds.), *Understanding Self and Others: Explorations in Intersubjectivity and Interobjectivity* (pp. 189–205). London: Routledge.

(2015a). *Atoms, Bytes and Genes: Public Resistance and Techno-Scientific Responses.* New York: Routledge.

(2015b). On (social) representations and the iconoclastic impetus. In G. Sammut, E. Andreouli, G. Gaskell & J. Valsiner (eds.), *The Cambridge Handbook of Social Representations,* Cambridge: Cambridge University Press.

(2017). Resistance as a latent factor of innovation. In B. Godin & D. Vinck (eds.), *Critical Studies of Innovation: Alternative Approaches to the Pro-innovation Bias* (pp. 159–181). Cheltenham: Elgar Publishers.

(2018). UK: trust in science after the BREXIT. In J. deMarec & B. Schiele (eds.), *Culture of Science* (pp. 95–102). Montreal: Acfas.

Bauer, M. W., & Gaskell, G. (1999). Towards a paradigm of research on social representations. *Journal for the Theory of Social Behaviour*, 29, 163–186.

(eds.). (2002). *Biotechnology: The Making of a Global Controversy*. Cambridge: Cambridge University Press.

(2008). Social representation theory: a progressive research programme for social psychology. *Journal for the Theory of Social Behaviour*, 38(4), 327–334.

Bauer, M. W., & Glăveanu, V. (2011). Communication as rhetoric and argumentation. In D. Hook, B. Franks & M. W. Bauer (eds.), *The Social Psychology of Communication* (pp. 209–228). Hampshire: Palgrave Macmillan.

Bauer, M. W., Gylstorff, S., Madsen, E. B. & Mejlgaard, N. (2019). The Fukushima accident and public perceptions about nuclear power around the globe: a challenge and response model. *Environmental Communication*, 13(4), 505–526.

Bauer, M. W., Harré, R. & Jensen, C. (eds.). (2013) *Resistance and the Practice of Rationality*. Newcastle upon Tyne: Cambridge Scholars Publishers.

Bauer, M. W., Pansegrau, P. & Shukla, R. (2019). *The Cultural Authority of Science: Comparing across Europe, Asia, Africa and the Americas* (Routledge Studies of Science: Technology & Society, Vol. 40). London: Routledge.

Bauer, R. A. (1964). The obstinate audience: the influence process from the point of view of social communication. *American Psychologist*, 19, 319–328.

Becker, H. S. (1973). *Outsiders: Studies in the Sociology of Deviance*. London: Collier Macmillan.

Begout, B. (2014). Le recidives de la gnose. *ESPRIT*, 403, March–April, 68–74.

Bellentani, F., & Panico, M. (2016). The meanings of monuments and memorials: toward a semiotic approach. *Punctum*, 2(1), 28–46.

Benford, R. D., & Snow, D. A. (2000). Framing processes and social movements: an overview and assessment. *Annual Review of Sociology*, 26, 611–639.

Bensaude-Vincent, B., & Blondel, C. (eds.). (2002) *Des Savants face à l'Occult 1870–1940*. Paris: Edition La Decouverte.

Berger, P., & Luckmann, T. (1966). *The Social Construction of Reality: A Treatise in the Sociology of Knowledge*. London: Penguin.

Berlonghi, A. E. (1995). Understanding and planning for different spectator crowds. *Safety Science*, 18(4), 239–247.

Bernsdorf, W. (1969). Autoritaet. In W. Bernsdorf (ed.) *Worterbuch der Soziologie*. Stuttgart: F. Enke Verlag.

Berridge, K. C. (2018). Evolving concepts of motion and motivation. *Frontiers of Psychology*. doi: 10.3389/fpsyg.2018.01647 7 September.

Bessi, A., Colletto, M., Davidescu, G. A., Scala, A., Caldarelli, G. & Quattrociocchi A. (2015). Science vs Conspiracy: collective narratives in the age of misinformation. *PLOS one*, doi:10.1371/journal.pone.0118093 23 February.

Bijker W. E., Bal, R., & Hendriks, R. (2009). *The Paradox of Scientific Authority: The Role of Scientific Advice in Democracies*. Cambridge, MA: MIT Press.

Billig, M. (1987). *Arguing and Thinking: A Rhetorical Approach to Social Psychology*. Cambridge: Cambridge University Press.

(1991). *Ideology and Opinions: Studies in Rhetorical Psychology*. London: Sage.

Blandin, B. (2002). *La construction du social par les objects*. Paris: Presses Universitaires de France.

Blass, T. (1999). The Milgram paradigm after 35 years: some things we now know about obedience to authority. *Journal of Applied Social Psychology*, 29 (5), 955–978.

(2004). *The Man Who Shocked the World: The Life and Legacy of Stanley Milgram*. New York, NY: Basic Books.

Blumenberg, H. (2010). "Lebenswelt und Technisierung under Aspekten der Phenomenologie." In *Theorie der Lebenswelt* (pp. 181–223). Berlin: Suhrkamp.

Boehme, H. (2006). *Fetischismus und Kultur*. Hamburg: Rowohlt Verlag.

Bond, R., & Smith, P. B. (1996). Culture and conformity: a meta-analysis of studies using Asch's (1952b, 1956) line judgement task. *Psychological Bulletin*, 119(1), 111–137.

Bonfadelli, H. (2004). *Medienwirkungsforschung I – Grundlagen* (3rd ed.). Konstanz: UVK-UTB

(2005). Mass media and biotechnology: knowledge gaps within and between European countries. *International Journal of Public Opinion Research*, 17(1), 42–62.

Bova, A., & Arcidiacono, F. (2013). Investigating children's why-questions: a study comparing argumentative and explanatory function. *Discourse Studies*, 15(6), 713–734.

Bowlby, J. (1969). *Attachment. Attachment and loss (Vol. 1: Loss)*. New York: Basic Books.

(1979). *The Making and Breaking of Affectional Bonds*. London: Tavistock Publications.

Boyd, R., & Richerson, P. (1985). *Culture and the Evolutionary Process*. Chicago: University of Chicago Press.

Boyer, P. (2003). *Cognitive Aspects of Religious Symbolism*. Cambridge: Cambridge University Press.

Brandmayr, F. (2017). How social scientists make causal claims in court: evidence from the Aquila trial. *Science, Technology and Human Values*, 42(3), 346–380.

Brehm, J. W. (1966). *A Theory of Psychological Reactance*. New York: Academic Press.

Brey, P. (2005). Artifacts as social agents. In H. Harbers (ed.), *Inside the Politics of Technology* (pp. 61–84). Amsterdam: Amsterdam University Press.

Briguglio, M. (2015). The bird hunting referendum in Malta. *Environmental Politics*, 24(5), 835–839.

Broadbent, W. (2017). Interactions with robots: the truth they reveal about ourselves. *Annual Review of Psychology*, 68, 627–652.

Brock, T. C. (1965). Communicator-recipient similarity and decision change. *Journal of Personality and Social Psychology*, 1(6), 650–654.

Bryant, J., & Zillman, D. (eds.). (2002). *Media Effects: Advances in Theory and Research* (2nd ed.). Hillsdale, NJ: LEA.

Bryant, J., & Oliver, M.B. (eds.). (2009) *Media Effects: Advances in Theory and Practice* (3rd ed.). New York: Routledge.

Bucchi, M. (2002). *Science in Society: An Introduction to Social Studies of Science.* London: Routledge.

Bucchi, M., & Trench, B. (eds.). (2014) *The Routledge Handbook of Public Communication of Science* (2nd ed.). London: Routledge.

Burger, J. M. (1986). Increasing compliance by improving the deal: the that's not-all technique. *Journal of Personality and Social Psychology,* 51(2), 227–283.

(1999). The foot-in-the-door compliance procedure: a multiple-process analysis and review. *Personality and Social Psychology Review,* 3(4), 303–325.

(2009). Replicating Milgram: would people still obey today? *American Psychologist,* 64(1), 1–11.

Buss, D. M. (2008). *Evolutionary Psychology: The New Science of the Mind* (5th ed.). Oxford: Routledge.

Butter, M. (2018). *Nichts ist, wie es scheint – Ueber Verschwoerungtheorien.* Berlin: Edition Suhrkamp.

Byford, J. (2011). *Conspiracy Theories: A Critical Introduction.* Basingstoke: Palgrave Macmillan.

Cacioppo, J. T., Petty, R. E. & Sidera, J. (1982). The effects of a salient self-schema on the evaluation of proattitudinal editorials: top-down versus bottom-up message processing. *Journal of Experimental Social Psychology,* 18(4), 324–338.

Calhoun, J. (1962). Population density and social pathology. *Scientific American,* 206, 139–148.

Calkins, S. D., & Williford, A. P. (2009). Taming the terrible twos: self-regulation and school readiness. In O. A. Barbarin & B. H. Wasik (eds.), *Handbook of Child Development and Early Education: Research to Practice* (pp. 172–198). New York: Guilford Press.

Camerer, C. F., & Lewenstein, G. (2002). Behavioural economics: past, present and future. In C. F. Camerer, G. Lewenstein & M. Rabin (eds.), *Advances in Behavioural Economics* (pp. 3–51). New York: Russel Sage.

Campanella, T. J. (2017). How low did he go? *City Lab,* 9 July. www.citylab.com/transportation/2017/07/how-low-did-he-go/533019 [accessed, 15 April 2019].

Campbell, J. (1949). *The Hero with a Thousand Faces.* Princeton, NJ: Princeton University Press.

Canetti, E. (1960/1973). *Crowds and Power.* London: Penguin.

Carey, J. (1992). *The Intellectuals and the Masses: Pride and Prejudice among the Literary Intelligentsia 1880–1939.* London: Faber & Faber.

Carr, E. H. (1961). *What Is History?* Harmondsworth: Penguin.

Chaiken, S. (1979). Communicator physical attractiveness and persuasion. *Journal of Personality and Social Psychology,* 37(8), 1387–1397.

Chemers, M. M. (2001). Leadership effectiveness: an integrative review. In M. A. Hogg & R. Scott Tindale (eds.), *The Blackwell Handbook of Social Psychology: Group Processes* (pp. 376–399). Malden, MA: Blackwell.

Chiantera-Stutte, P. (2018). Mob, people, crowds, and masses: mass psychology and populism. *The Tocqueville Review*, 39(1), 157–176.

Cialdini, R. B. (1984). *Influence: The Psychology of Persuasion*. New York: William Morrow.

Cialdini, R. B, & Goldstein, N. J. (2004). Social influence: compliance and conformity. *Annual Review of Psychology*, 55, 591–621.

Cialdini, R. B., & Petty, R. E. (1979). Anticipatory opinion effects. In R. E. Petty, T. M. Ostrom & T. C. Brock (eds.), *Cognitive Responses in Persuasion* (pp. 217–236). New York: Psychology Press.

Cialdini, R. B., Cacioppo, J. T., Bassett, R. & Miller, J. A. (1978). Low-balling procedure for producing compliance: commitment then cost. *Journal of Personality and Social Psychology*, 36(5), 463–476.

Cialdini, R. B., Vincent, J. E., Lewis, S. K., Catalan, J., Wheeler, D. & Darby, B. L. (1975). Reciprocal concessions procedure for inducing compliance: the door-in-the-face technique. *Journal of Personality and Social Psychology*, 31 (2), 206–215.

Cirincione, J. (2007). *Bomb Scare: The History and Future of Nuclear Weapons*. New York: Columbia University Press.

Clausewitz, C. von. (1832/1976). *On War*. Princeton, NJ: Princeton University Press.

Coch, L., & French, J. R. P. (1948). Overcoming resistance to change. *Human Relations*, 1, 512–532.

Cooper, J. (2012). Cognitive dissonance: revisiting Festinger's end of the world study. In J. R. Smith & S. A. Haslam (eds.), *Social Psychology: Revisiting the Classical Studies* (pp. 42–56). London: Sage.

Corbin, A., & Mayeur, J. M. (eds.). (1996). La Barricade. *Actes du colloque organisé, 17–19 May*. Paris: Publications de la Sorbonne.

Costa, P. T., Jr., & McCrae, R. R. (1992). *NEO Personality Inventory – Revised (NEO-PI-R) and NEO Five-Factor Inventory (NEO-FFI) Professional Manual*. Odessa, FL: Psychological Assessment Resources.

Cranach, M. von. (1986). Leadership as a function of group action. In C. F. Graumann & S. Moscovici (eds.), *Changing Conceptions of Leadership* (pp. 115–134). New York: Springer.

 (1996). Towards a theory of the acting group. In E. Witte & J. Davis (eds.), *Understanding Group Behaviour* (Vol 2: Small Group Processes and Personal Relations). Mahwah, NJ: Lawrence Erlbaum.

Cranach, M. von., & Foppa, K. (eds.). (1996). *Freiheit des Entscheidens and Handelns*. Heidelberg: Asanger.

Cranach, M. von., Ochsenbein, G. & Valach, L. (1986). The group as a self-active system. *European Journal of Social Psychology*, 16, 193–229.

Cranach, M. von. & Valach, L. (1983). Die soziale Dimension des zielgerichteten Handelns. *Schweizerische Zeitschrift fuer Psychologie*, 42, 160–177.

 (1984). The social dimension of goal-directed action. In H. Tajfel (ed.), *The Social Dimension* (vol. 1) (pp. 285–299). Cambridge: Cambridge University Press.

Daanen, P., & Sammut, G. (2012). G. H. Mead and knowing how to act: practical meaning, routine interaction and the theory of interobjectivity, *Theory and Psychology*, 22(5), 556–571.

David, P. A. (1985). Clio and the economics of QWERTY. *The American Economic Review*, 75(2), 332–337.

Dawkins, R. (1976). *The Selfish Gene*. New York: Oxford University Press.

De Dreu, C. K. W. (2007). Minority dissent, attitude change, and group performance. In A. R. Pratkanis (ed.), *The Science of Social Influence: Advances and Future Progress* (pp. 247–270). New York: Psychology Press.

Dierkes, M., Hoffman, U. & Marz, L. (1996). *Visions of Technology – Social and Institutional Factors Shaping the Development of New Technologies*. Frankfurt: Campus Verlag.

Dittmar, H. (1992). *The Social Psychology of Material Possessions: To Have Is to Be*. Hemel Hempstead: Harvester Wheatsheaf.

Douglas, M. (1990). Risk as a forensic resource. *Daedalus*, 119(4), 1–16.

Drury, J., & Reicher, S. (2009). Collective psychological empowerment as a model of social change: researching crowds and power. *Journal of Social Issues*, 65(4), 707–715.

Drury, J., & Stott, C. (2011). Contextualising the crowd in contemporary social science. *Contemporary Social Science*, 6(3), 275–288.

Eagly, A. H. & Chaiken, S. (1993). Process theories of attitude formation and change: the elaboration likelihood and heuristic-systematic models. In A. H. Eagly & S. Chaiken, (eds.), *The Psychology of Attitudes* (pp. 303–350). Orlando, FL: Harcourt Brace.

(1998) Attitude structure and function. In D. T. Gilbert, S. T. Fiske and G. Lindzey (eds.), *The Handbook of Social Psychology* (4th ed., Vol 1) (pp. 269–322). New York: McGrawHill.

Edgerton, D. (1999). From innovation to use: ten eclectic theses on the historiography of technology. *History and Technology*, 16, 111–136.

(2006). *The Shock of the Old – Technology and Global History since 1900*. London: Profile Books.

Ehrlich, P. (1968). *The Population Bomb*. New York: Ballantine Books.

Einsiedel, E. (2014). Publics and their participation in science and technology. In M. Bucchi & B. Trench (eds.), *The Routledge Handbook of Public Communication of Science and Technology* (2nd ed.) (pp. 125–139). Abingdon: Routledge.

Eisenberger, N. I., Lieberman, M. D., & Williams, K. D. (2003). Does rejection hurt? an fMRI study of social exclusion. *Science*, 302, 290–292.

Elias, N. (1936/1978). *The Civilizing Process: The History of Manners*. Oxford: Blackwell.

(1939/2000). *The Civilizing Process: Sociogenetic and Psychogenetic Investigations*. Oxford: Blackwell.

Entman, R. M. (1993). Framing: towards clarification of a fractured paradigm. *Journal of Communication*, 43, 51–58.

Entradas, M., & Bauer, M. W. (2019). Kommunikationsfunktionen im Mehrebenensystem Hochschule. In *Forschungsfeld Hochschulkommunikation* (pp. 97–121). Wiesbaden: Springer.

Eschenburg, T. (1965). *Ueber Autoritaet, 129.* Frankfurt: Suhrkamp.

Escobar, O. (2011). *Public Dialogue and Deliberation: A Communication Perspective for Public Engagement Practitioners.* Edinburgh: UK Beacons for Public Engagement.

Evans, S. S. B. T., & Stanovich, K. S. (2013). Dual-process theories of higher cognitions: advancing the debate. *Perspectives on Psychological Science,* 8(3), 223–241.

Farr, R. (1982). Interviewing: an introduction to the social psychology of the interview. In A. J. Chapman & A. Gale (eds.), *Psychology and People: A Tutorial Text* (pp. 287–305). London: Macmillan.

  (1987). Social representations: a French tradition of research. *Journal for the Theory of Social Behaviour,* 17(4), 343–370.

Ferguson, N. (2009). *The Ascent of Money: A Financial History of the World.* London: Penguin.

Ferree, M. M. (2003). Resonance and radicalism: feminist framing in the abortion debates of the United States and Germany. *American Journal of Sociology,* 109(2), 304–344.

Fessler, D. M. T., & Holbrook, C. (2016). Synchronised behaviour increases assessment of formidability and cohesion of coalition. *Evolution and Human Behaviour,* 37(6), 502–509.

Festinger, L. (1957). *A Theory of Cognitive Dissonance.* Evanston, IL: Row, Peterson and Company.

Festinger, L., & Carlsmith, J. M. (1959). Cognitive consequences of forced compliance. *Journal of Abnormal and Social Psychology,* 58(2), 203–210.

Feyerabend, P. (1981). Classical empiricism. In P. Feyerabend, *Problems of Empiricism: Philosophical Papers* (vol. 2)(pp. 34–51). Cambridge: Cambridge University Press.

  (2016). *Philosophy of Nature.* Cambridge: Polity Press.

Fiedler, F. E. (1965). A contingency model of leadership effectiveness. In L. Berkowitz (ed.), *Advances in Experimental Social Psychology* (vol. 1)(pp. 149–190). New York, NY: Academic Press.

Fischer, A. (2017). *Manipulation: zur Theorie und Ethik einer Form der Beeinflussung.* Frankfurt: Suhrkamp.

Fischhoff, B. (1998). Risk perception and communication unplugged: twenty years of process. *Risk Analysis,* 15(2), 137–145.

Fishbein, M., & Ajzen, I. (1975). *Belief, Attitude, Intention, and Behavior: An Introduction to Theory and Research.* Reading, MA: Addison-Wesley.

Fisher, D. (2009). Grid–group analysis and tourism: tipping as a cultural behaviour. *Journal of Tourism and Cultural Change,* 7(1), 34–47.

Fisher, K. (1997). Locating frames in the discursive universe. *Sociological Research Online,* 2(3); www.socresonline.org.uk/2/3/4.html.

Fleck, L. (1935/1979). *Genesis and Development of a Scientific Fact.* Chicago: University of Chicago Press.

Franks, B., & Attia, S. (2011). Rumours and gossip as genres of communication. In D. Hook, B. Franks & M. W. Bauer (eds.), *The Social Psychology of Communication* (pp. 169–186). London: Palgrave MacMillan.

Franks, B., Bangerter, A. & Bauer, M. W. (2013). Conspiracy theories as quasi-religious mentality: an integrated account from cognitive science, social representations theory, and frame theory. *Frontiers in Psychology*, 4, Article 424. doi: 10.3389/fpsyg.2013.00424.

Franzosi, R., & Vicari, S. (2013). What's in a text? answers from frame analysis and rhetoric for measuring meaning systems and argumentative structures. *Rhetorica*, 36(4), 394–429.

Franzosi, R., & Wang, R. (2018). From Words to Numbers: An Automatic Approach to Information Retrieval from Narrative Texts. Unpublished manuscript, July 2018.

Freelon, D. (2018). *The Filter Map: Media and the Pursuit of Truth and Legitimacy*. Miami: The Knight Foundation.

Freud, S. (1921/1985). Group psychology and the analysis of the ego. In S. Freud, *Collected Works: Civilisation, Society and Religion* (vol. 12). London: Penguin.

Friedkin, N. E. (2001). Norm formation in social influence networks. *Social Networks*, 23(3), 167–189.

Frigg, R. (2013). Clever fetishists. *Art History*, 36(3), 664–669.

Fuller, S. (2013). History of the psychology of science. In G .J. Feist & M. E. Gorman (eds.), *Handbook of the Psychology of Science* (pp. 21–47). New York: Springer Publishing Company.

Funk, C., & Kennedy, B. (2016). *The Politics of Climate*. Washington, DC: PEW Foundation.

Gadamer, H. G. (1960). *Wahrheit und Methode: Grundzuege einer philosophischen Hermeneutik*. Tubingen: JCB Mohr.

Gamson, W. A., & Modigliani, A. (1989). Media discourse and public opinion on nuclear power: a constructionist approach. *American Journal of Sociology*, 95, 1–37.

Garrett, R. K. (2009). Echo chambers online? politically motivated selective exposure among Internet news users. *Journal of Computer-Mediated Communication*, 14(2), 265–285. httcp://doi.org/10.1111/j.1083-6101 .2009.01440.x.

Gauchat, G. (2012). Politicization of science in the public sphere: A study of public trust in the United States, 1974 to 2010. *American Sociological Review*, 77(2), 167–187.

Gehlen, A. (1980). *Man in the Age of Technology*. New York: Columbia University Press.

Gerbner, G., Gross, L., Morgan, M., Signorelli, N. & Shanahan, J. (2002). Growing up with television: cultivation processes. In J. Bryant & D. Zillman (eds.), *Media Effects: Advances in Theory and Research* (pp. 43–67). Hillsdale, NJ: LEA.

Gerbner, G. (1969). Towards 'cultural indicators': the analysis of mass mediated public message systems. In G. Gerbner, O. Holsti, K. Krippendorff, W. I. Paisley & P. I. Stone (eds.), *The Analysis of Communication Content* (pp. 123–132). New York: John Wiley.

Gergen, K. J. (1973). Social psychology as history. *Journal of Personality and Social Psychology*, 26(2), 309–320.

Gersick, C. (1988). Time and transition in work teams: toward a new model of group development. *The Academy of Management Journal*, 31(1), 9–41.

Geuter, U. (1988). *Die Professionalisierung der deutschen Psychologie im Nationalsozialismus*. Frankfurt: Suhrkamp.

Gibson, J. J. (1977). The theory of affordances. In R. Shaw & J. Bransford (eds.), *Perceiving, Acting and Knowing: Toward an Ecological Psychology* (pp. 67–82). Hillsdale, NY: Lawrence Erlbaum Associates.

Gibson, S. (2013). Milgram's obedience experiments: a rhetorical analysis. *British Journal of Social Psychology*, 52(2), 290–309.

Giedion, S. (1975 [1948]). *Mechanization Takes Command: A Contribution to Anonymous History*. New York: WW Norton & Co.

Gildea, R. (2010). How to Understand the Dreyfus Affair. *New York Review of Books*, 10 June, 42–44.

Gillespie, A., & Cornish, F. (2009). Intersubjectivity: Towards a dialogical analysis. *Journal for the Theory of Social Behaviour*, 40(1), 19–46.

Ginneken, J. Van. (1992). *Crowds, Psychology and Politics, 1871–1899*. Cambridge: Cambridge University Press.

Girard, R. (2008). *Evolution and Conversion: Dialogues on the Origins of Culture*. London: Continuum.

Gladwell, M. (2000). *The Tipping Point: How Little Things Can Make a Big Difference*. New York,: Little, Brown and Company.

Godin, B. (1999). Argument from consequences and the urge to polarize. *Argumentation*, 13, 347–365.

(2005). *The Linear Model of Innovation: The Historical Construction of an Analytical Framework*. Project on the history and sociology of S&T statistics, Working paper no 30, Montreal.

(2012). On cultural indicators of science. In M. W. Bauer, R. Shukla & N. Allum (sds.), *The Culture of Science – How the Public Relates to Science across the Globe* (pp. 18–37). New York: Routledge.

Godin, B., & Vinck, D. (2017). Introduction: innovation: from the forbidden to the cliché. In B. Godin & D. Vinck (eds), *Critical Studies of Innovation: Alternative Approaches to the Pro-innovation Bias* (pp. 1–16). Cheltenham: Edward Elgar.

(eds.). (2017). *Reflexive Innovation: Alternative Approaches to the Pro-innovation Bias*. Cheltenham: Edward Elgar.

Goffmann, E. (1974). *Frame Analysis: An Essay on the Organisation of Experience*. Harmondsworth: Penguin.

Gollwitzer, P. M. (1990). Action phase and mind-sets. In E. T. Higgins & R. M. Sorrentino (eds.), *Handbook of Motivation and Cognition: Foundations of Social Behavior* (vol. 2)(pp. 53–92). New York: Guilford.

(1999). Implementation intentions: strong effects of simple plans. *American Psychologist*, 54, 493–503.

Gollwitzer, P. M., & Sheeran, P. (2006). Implementation intentions and goal achievement: a meta-analysis of effects and processes. *Advances in Experimental Social Psychology*, 38, 69–119.

Graumann, C. F., & Metraux, A. (1977). Die phanomenologische Orientierung in der Psychologie. In K. A. Schneewind (ed.), *Wissenschaftstheoretische Grundlagen der Psychologie* (pp. 27–54). Munich: Reinhardt.

Graumann, C. F., & Moscovici, S. (eds.). (1986). *Changing Conceptions of Leadership*. New York: Springer Verlag.

Gregory, J. (2005). *Fred Hoyle's Universe*. Oxford: Oxford University Press.

Gregory, L. W., Cialdini, R. B. & Carpenter, K. M. (1982). Self-relevant scenarios as mediators of likelihood estimates and compliance: does imagining make it so? *Journal of Personality and Social Psychology*, 43(1), 89–99.

Gregory, J., & Miller, S. (1998). *Science in Public: Communication, Culture and Credibility*. Cambridge: Perseus Publishers.

Gridley, M. C. (1978). *Jazz Styles*. Englewood Cliff, NJ: Prentice-Hall.

Groh, D. (1986). Collective behaviour from the seventeenth to the twentieth century: change of phenomenon, change of perception, or no change at all? Some preliminary reflections. In C. F. Graumann & S. Moscovici (eds.), *Changing Conceptions of Crowd, Mind and Behaviour* (pp. 143–162). New York: Springer Verlag.

Gross, A. G., & Walzer, A. E. (2000). *Aristotle's Rhetoric: A Guide to the Scholarship*. Carbondale: Southern Illinois University Press.

Gurwitch, A. (1957/1964). *The Field of Consciousness*. Pittsburgh, PA: Duquesne University Press.

Gutteling, J. M. (2005). Mazur's hypothesis on technology controversy and media. *International Journal of Public Opinion Research*, 17(1), 2–41.

Habermas, J. (1981/1994). *The Theory of Communicative Action* (vol 1: Reason and rationalisation of society; vol 2: Lifeworld and systems). Cambridge: Polity Press.

(1989). *The Structural Transformation of the Public Sphere: An Inquiry into a Category of Bourgeois Society*. Cambridge: Polity Press.

(1999). *Geliebte Objekte*. Frankfurt: Suhrkamp.

(2001). *Kommunikatives Handeln und detranszendentalisierte Vernunft*. Stuttgart: Reclam Jr.

Haidt, J. (2012). *The Righteous Mind: Why Good People Are Divided by Politics and Religion*. London: Penguin.

Hampton, G. J. (2015). *Imagining Slaves and Robots in Literature, Film and Popular Culture: Reinventing Yesterday's Slaves with Tomorrow's Robots*. Lanham, MD: Lexington Books.

Hannemyr, G. (2003). The Internet as hyperbole: a critical examination of adoption rates. *The Information Society*, 19(2), 111–121.

Hanseth, O., Monteiro, E. & Hatling, M. (1996). Developing information infrastructure: the tension between standardisation and flexibility. *Science Technology and Human Values*, 21(4), 407–426.

Hardt, M., & Negri, A. (2005). *Multitude: War and Democracy in the Age of Empire*. London: Penguin.

Harlow, H. F., & Zimmermann, R. R. (1958). The development of affective responsiveness in infant monkeys. *Proceedings of the American Philosophical Society*, 102, 501–509.

Harré, R., & Secord, P. F. (1973). *The Explanation of Social Behaviour*. Oxford: Blackwell.

Harré, R., & Sammut, G. (2013). What lies between? In G. Sammut, P. Daanen & F. M. Moghaddam (eds.), *Understanding the Self and Others: Explorations in Intersubjectivity and Interobjectivity* (pp. 15–30). London: Routledge.

Haslam, S. A., & Reicher, S. (2018). A truth that does not always speak its name: how Hollander and Turowetz's findings confirm and extend the engaged followership analysis of harm-doing in the Milgram paradigm. *British Journal of Social Psychology*, 57, 292–300.

Hazan, E. (2015). *A History of the Barricade*. London: Verso.

Heidegger, M. (1935/1977). Der Ursprung des Kunstwerks. In *Gesamtausgabe: Veroeffentlichte Schriften 1914–1970, Band 5 Holzwege*. Frankfurt: Klostermann.

(1944/2012) *Erlaeuterungen zu Holderlin's Dichtung*. Frankfurt: Klostermann.

(1954/1977). *The Question concerning Technology and Other Essays*. New York: Harper & Row.

Heider, F. (1958). *The Psychology of Interpersonal Relations*. New York: Wiley.

Helbling, D., Fakas, L. & Viscek, T. (2000). Simulating dynamical features of escape panic. *Nature*, 407, 28 September, 487–490.

Hertwig, R. (2017). When to consider boosting: some rules for policy makers. *Behavioural Public Policy*, 1(2), 143–161.

Hertwig, R., & Grune-Yanoff, T. (2017). Nudging and boosting: steering or empowering good decisions. *Perspectives on Psychological Science*, 12(6), 1–14.

Hilgartner, S., & Bock, C. L. (1988). The rise and fall of social problems: a public arenas model. *American Journal of Sociology*, 94, 53–78.

Hindriks, F. A. (2003). A new role for the constitutive rule. *American Journal of Economics and Sociology*, 62(1), 185–208.

Hinds, J., & Joinson, A. (2019). Human and computer personality predictions from digital footprints. *Current Directions in Psychological Science*, 28(2), 204–211.

Hingst, R. D. (2006). Tuckman's theory of group development in a call centre context: does it still work? In *Fifth Global Conference on Business & Economics Proceedings*. Global Conference on Business & Economics, 6–8 July 2006, Cambridge. *Access*: http://eprints.usq.edu.au.

Hofstaetter, P. R. (1957). *Gruppendynamik – Kritik der Massenpsychologie*. Hamburg: Rowolt Verlag.

Hogg, M. A. (2001). A social identity theory of leadership. *Personality and Social Psychology Review*, 5(3) 184–200.

Hogg, M. A., & Reid, S. A. (2006). Social identity, self-categorization, and the communication of group norms. *Communication Theory*, 16, 7–30

Hogg, M. A., & Vaughan, G. M. (2018). *Social Psychology* (8th ed.). Harlow: Pearson.

Hollander, M. M. (2015). The repertoire of resistance: non-compliance with directives in Milgram's obedience experiments. *British Journal of Social Psychology*, 54, 425–444.

House, R. J. (1977). A 1976 theory of charismatic leadership. In J. G. Hunt & L. L. Larson (eds.), *Leadership: The Cutting Edge* (pp. 189–207). Carbondale: Southern Illinois University Press.

House, R. J., & Howell, J. M. (1992). Personality and charismatic leadership. *Leadership Quarterly*, 3(2), 81–108.

Hovland, C. I, Janis, I. L. & Kelley, H. (1953). *Communication and Persuasion*. New Haven, CT: Yale University Press.

Hovland, C. I., Lumsdaine, A. A. & Sheffield, F. D. (1949). *Experiments in Mass Communication*. Princeton, NJ: Princeton University Press.

Hovland, C. I., & Mandell, W. (1952). An experimental comparison of conclusion-drawing by the communicator and by the audience. *Journal of Abnormal and Social Psychology*, 47(3), 581–588.

Hovland, C. I., & Weiss, W. (1951). The influence of source credibility on communication effectiveness. *Public Opinion Quarterly*, 15(4), 635–650.

Howarth, C. S, Campbell, C., Cornish, F., Franks, B., Garcia-Lorenzo, L., Gillespie, A., Gleibs, I. H., Goncalves-Portelinha, I., Jovchelovitch, S., Lahlou, S., Mannell, J. C., Reader, T. W. & Tennant, C. (2013). Insights from societal psychology: a contextual politics of societal change. *Journal of Social and Political Psychology*, 1(1), 364–384.

Howarth, C. S, Wagner, W., Magnusson, N. & Sammut, G. (2014). 'It's only other people who make me feel black': acculturation, identity and agency in a multicultural community. *Political Psychology*, 35(1), 81–95.

Howe, J. (2008). *Crowdsourcing: How the Power of the Crowd Is Driving the Future of Business*. London: Random House Business Books.

Husserl, E. (1931/2012). *Ideas*. London: Routledge.

Janis, I. L. (1954). Personality correlates of susceptibility to persuasion. *Journal of Personality*, 22(4), 504–518.

Jaspers, K. (1955). *Vom Ursprung und Ziel der Geschichte*. Frankfurt: Fischer Buecherei.

Jodelet, D. (1991). *Madness and Social Representation*. London: Harvester Wheatsheaf.

Johnson, E. J., & Goldstein, D. (2003). Do defaults save lives? *Science*, 302, 1138–1139.

Jonas, H. (2001). *The Gnostic Religion: The Message of the Alien God and the Beginnings of Christianity*. Boston: Beacon Press.

Jost, M. G. (2004). *Learning by Resistance: An Analysis of Resistance to Change As a Source of Organisational Learning*. Unpublished doctoral thesis, London School of Economics and Political Science.

Jovchelovitch, S. (2007). *Knowledge in Context: Representations, Community and Culture*. London: Routledge.

Jurdant, B. (1993). Popularisation as the autobiography of science. *Public Understanding of Science*, 2, 365–373.

Kahneman, D., & Tversky, A. (1979). Prospect theory: an analysis of decision under risk. *Econometrica*, 47(2), 263–291.

Kaplan, F. (2009). An alien concept. *Nature*, 461, 17 September, 345–346.

Kaplan, A., & Krueger, J. (1999). Compliance after threat: self-affirmation or self-presentation? *Current Research in Social Psychology*, 4(7), 178–197.

Kellerman, B. (2004). *Bad Leadership: What It Is, How It Happens, Why It Matters*. Boston: Harvard Business School Press.

Kelly, C., & Breinlinger, S. (1996). *The Social Psychology of Collective Action: Identity, Injustice and Gender*. London: Taylor & Francis.

Keltner, D., & Haidt, J. (2003). Approaching awe, a moral, spiritual and aesthetic emotion. *Cognition and Emotion*, 17(2), 197–314.

Kempe, M., Groh, D., & Mauelshagen, F. (eds). (2003). *Naturkatastrophen: Beitraege zu ihrer Deutung, Wahrnehmung und Darstellung von der Antike bis ins 20. Jahrhundert*. Tubingen: Narr.

Kennedy, G. A. (1998). *Comparative Rhetoric: A Historical and Cross-Cultural Introduction*. Oxford: Oxford University Press.

Kepplinger, H. M. (1995). Individual and institutional impacts upon press coverage of sciences: the case of nuclear power and genetic engineering in Germany. In M. W. Bauer (ed.), *Resistance to New Technology: Nuclear Power, Information Technology and Biotechnology* (pp. 357–378). Cambridge: Cambridge University Press.

Keren, G. (2013). A tale of two systems: a scientific advance or a theoretical stone soup? Commentary on Evans & Stonovich (2013). *Perspectives on Psychological Science*, 8(3), 257–262.

Keren, G., & Schul, Y. (2007). Two is not always better than one: a critical evaluation of two-system theories. *Perspectives on Psychological Science*, 4, 533–550.

Keupp, S., Behne, R. & Rakoczy, H. (2018). The rationality of (over)imitation. *Perspectives on Psychological Science*, 13(6), 678–687.

Khilnany, S. (1997). *The Idea of India*. London: Penguin.

Kim, H. S., & Markus, H. R. (1999). Deviance or uniqueness, harmony or conformity? a cultural analysis. *Journal of Personality and Social Psychology*, 77(4), 785–800.

Kinder, D. R. (1998). Opinion and action in the realm of politics. In D. T. Gilbert, S. T. Fiske & G. Lindzey (eds.), *The Handbook of Social Psychology* (vol. 2)(pp. 778–876). Boston: McGraw Hill.

Kirby, D. A. (2010). The future is now: diegetic prototyping and the role of popular film in generating real-world technological development. *Social Studies of Science*, 40(1), 41–70.

(2011). *Lab Coats in Hollywood: Science, Scientists and Cinema*. Cambridge, MA: MIT Press.

(2014). Science and technology in film: themes and representations. In M. Bucchi & B. Trench (eds.), *The Routledge Handbook of Public Communication of Science* (2nd ed.)(pp. 97–107). London: Routledge.

Kitcher, P. (2003). Infectious ideas: some preliminary explorations. In *In Mendel's Mirror: Philosophical Reflections on Biology* (pp. 213–232). Oxford: Oxford University Press.

Klein, H. K., & Kleinman, D. L. (2002). The social construction of technology: structural considerations. *Science, Technology and Human Values*, 27(1), 28–52.

Koehler, W. (1930/1975). *Gestalt Psychology: An Introduction to New Concepts in Modern Psychology*. New York: New American Library.

(1947). *Gestalt Psychology*. New York: New American Library.

Koffka, K. (1959). *The Growth of Mind: An Introduction to Child Psychology*. Paterson, NJ: Littlefield, Adams & Co.

Kracauer, S. (1977). Die Gruppe als Ideentraeger. In *Das Ornament der Masse* (pp. 123–156). Frankfurt: Suhrkamp.

Kroll, G. (2001). The silent springs of Rachel Carson: mass media and the origins of modern environmentalism. *Public Understanding of Science*, 10(4), 403–420.

Kruglanski, A. W. (1989). *Lay Epistemics and Human Knowledge: Cognitive and Motivational Bases*. New York: Plenum.

(2013). Only one? The default interventionist perspective as a unimodel. Commentary on Evans & Stonovich (2013), *Perspectives on Psychological Science*, 8(3), 242–247.

Kruglanski, A. W., & Gigerenzer, G. (2011). Intuitive and deliberative judgement are based on common principles. *Psychological Review*, 118, 97–109.

Kruglanski, A. W., & Thompson, E. P. (1999). Persuasion by a single route: a view from the unimodel. *Psychological Inquiry*, 10(2), 83–109.

Kruglanski, A. W., Orehek, E., Dechesne, M. & Pierro, A. (2010). Lay epistemic theory: the motivational, cognitive and social aspects of knowledge formation. *Social and Personality Psychology Compass*, 4(10), 939–950.

Kruglanski, A. W., Webster, D. W. & Klem, A. (1993). Motivated resistance and openness to persuasion in the presence or absence of prior information. *Journal of Personality and Social Psychology*, 65(5), 861–876.

Kruse, L. (1986). Conceptions of crowds and crowding. In C. F. Graumann & S. Moscovici (eds.), *Changing Conceptions of Crowd Mind and Behaviour* (pp. 117–142). New York: Springer Verlag.

Kuhn, T. S. (1962). *The Structure of Scientific Revolutions* (3rd ed.). Chicago: Chicago University Press.

(1987). *The Presence of the Past: Regaining, Portraying and Embodying*. Shearman Memorial Lecture, London, University College [manuscript], 23–25 November.

Kunda, Z. (1990). The case for motivated reasoning. *Psychological Bulletin*, 108 (3), 480–498.

Lachlan, R. F., Janik, V. M., & Slater, P. J. B. (2004). The evolution of conformity-enforcing behaviour in cultural communication systems. *Animal Behaviour*, 68(3), 561–570.

Lahlou, S. (2015). Social representations and social construction: the evolutionary perspective of installation theory. In G. Sammut, E. Andreouli, G. Gaskell

& J. Valsiner (eds.), *The Cambridge Handbook of Social Representations* (pp. 193–209). Cambridge: Cambridge University Press.

(2017). *Installation Theory: The Social Construction and Regulation of Behaviour.* Cambridge: Cambridge University Press.

Lasswell, H. D. (1948). The structure and function of communication in society. In L. Bryson (ed.), *The Communication of Ideas* (pp. 37–51). New York: The Institute for Religious and Social Studies.

Latour, B. (1993). *We Have Never Been Modern.* Cambridge, MA: Harvard University Press.

(1994). On technical mediation. *Common Knowledge*, 3, 29–64.

(1996). On interobjectivity. *Mind, Culture and Activity*, 3(4), 228–245.

(2000). When things strike back: a possible contribution of 'science studies' to the social sciences. *British Journal of Sociology*, 51(1), 107–123.

Laupa, M., & Turiel, E. (1986). Children's conceptions of adult and peer authority. *Child Development*, (2), 405–412.

Lauri, M. A. (2008). Changing public opinion towards organ donation: a social psychological approach to social marketing. In L. O. Pietriff & R. V. Miller (eds.), *Public Opinion Research Focus* (pp. 9–36). New York: Nova Science Publication.

(2015). Social change, social marketing and social representations. In G. Sammut, E. Andreouli, G. Gaskell & J. Valsiner (eds.), *The Cambridge Handbook of Social Representations* (pp. 397–410). Cambridge: Cambridge University Press.

Lauri, M. A., & Lauri, J. (2005), Social representations of organ donors and non-donors. *Journal of Community & Applied Social Psychology*, 15(2), 108–119.

Lawrence, P. (1954). How to overcome resistance to change. *Harvard Business Review*, 32(3), 49–57.

Lazarsfeld, P. F. (1941). Remarks on administrative and critical communication research. *Studies in Philosophy and Social Science*, 9, 2–16.

LeBon, G. (1895/1982). *The Crowd: A Study of the Popular Mind.* Atlanta: Cherokee Publishing Company.

Lefkowitz, M., Blake, R. R. & Mouton, J. (1955). Status factors in pedestrian violation of traffic signals. *Journal of Abnormal and Social Psychology*, 51(3), 704–706.

LeGoff, J. (2015). *Must We Divide History into Periods?* New York: Columbia University Press.

Lem, S. (1968). *His Master's Voice* (English, 1983). San Diego: Harcourt, Brace & Jovanovich.

Leventhal, H., Singer, R. & Jones, S. (1965). Effects of fear and specificity of recommendation upon attitudes and behavior. *Journal of Personality and Social Psychology*, 2(1), 20–29

Levitt, B., & March, M. G. (1988). Organisational learning. *Annual Review of Sociology*, 14, 319–40.

Lewin, K. (1920/1999) Socializing the taylor system. In M. Gold (ed.), *The Complete Social Scientist: A Kurt Lewin Reader.* Washington, DC: American Psychological Association.

(1936). *Principles of Topological Psychology*. New York: McGraw-Hill.

(1943). Forces behind food habits and methods of change. In *The Problem of Changing Food Habits*, (Bulletin no. 108 of the National Research Council), 35–65. Baltimore: Lord Baltimore Press.

(1948/1999) Group decision and social change. In M. Gold (ed.), *The Complete Social Scientist: A Kurt Lewin Reader*. Washington, DC: American Psychological Association.

(1952). *Field Theory in Social Science*. London: Tavistock Publications.

Lewin, K., Lippitt, R. & White, R. K. (1939). Patterns of aggressive behavior in experimentally created social climates. *Journal of Social Psychology*, 10(2), 271–301.

Lezaun, J., & Calvillo, N. (2013). In the political laboratory: Kurt Lewin's atmospheres. *Journal of Cultural Economy*, 7(4), 434–457.

Liebermann, M. D. (2007). Social cognitive neuroscience: a review of core processes. *Annual Review of Psychology*, 58, 259–289.

Lindenberg, S. (1987). Common sense and social structure: a sociological view. In Van Holthoon & D. R. Olson (eds.), *Common Sense: The Foundations for Social Science* (pp. 199–215). Lantham, MD: University of America Press.

Lippitt, R., & White, R. K. (1947/1965). An experimental study of leadership and group life. In H. Proshansky & B. Seidenberg (eds.), *Basic Studies in Social Psychology* (pp. 523–537). New York: Holt, Rinehart and Winston.

Loewenstein, G., Bryce, C., Hagmann, D. & Rajpal, S. (2015). Warning: you are about to be nuded. *Behavioural Science & Policy*, 1(1), 45–53.

Long, P. O. (2005). The annales and the history of technology. *Technology and Culture*, 46(1), 177–186.

Lopez, A. C., McDermott, R. & Bang Petersen, M. (2011). States in mind: evolution, coalitional psychology, and international politics. *International Security*, 36(2), 48–83.

Lorenz, K. (2005). *On Aggression*. London: Routledge.

Louis, M. R. (1980). Surprise and sense making: what newcomers experience in entering unfamiliar organizational settings. *Administrative Science Quarterly*, 25(2), 226–251.

Lowery, S. A., & DeFleur, M. L. (eds.). (1995) *Milestones in Mass Communication Research: Media Effects* (3rd ed.). London: Longman.

Luckmann, T. (2005). *On the Communicative Construction of Reality*. Lecture to the LSE Department of Information Systems, 2 February 2005.

Luhmann, N. (1984). *Sociale Systeme: Grundriss einer algemeinen Theorie*. Frankfurt: Suhrkamp.

(1989). *Vertrauen: ein Mechanismus der Reduktion von sozialer Komplexitaet*. Stuttgart: Enke Verlag.

(1990). The improbability of communication. In *Essays on Self-Reference* (pp. 86–98). New York: Columbia University Press

(1996). *Die neuzeitlichen Wissenschaften und die Phaenomenologie*. Wien: Picu Verlag.

(1998). Familiarity, confidence and trust: problems and alternatives. In D. Gambetta (ed.), *Trust: Making and Breaking Cooperative Relations* (pp. 94–107). Oxford: Basil Blackwell.

Lundmark, S., Gilljam, M. & Dahlberg, S. (2016). Measuring generalised trust: an examination of question wording and the number of scale points. *Public Opinion Quarterly*, 80(1), 26–43.

Lynch, A. (1996). *Thought Contagion: How Belief Spreads through Society: The New Science of Memes*. New York: Basic Books.

Maass, A., & Clark, R. D. (1984). Hidden impact of minorities: fifteen years of minority influence research. *Psychological Bulletin*, 9(3), 428–450.

Mackay, C. (1841/1980). *Extraordinary Popular Delusions and the Madness of the Crowds*. New York: Crown Publishers.

MacKenzie, N., & MacKenzie, J. (1977). *The First Fabians*. London: Quartet Books.

MacNeil, M. K., & Sherif, M. (1976). Norm change over subject generations as a function of arbitrariness of prescribed norms. *Journal of Personality and Social Psychology*, 34(5), 762–773.

Maffesoli, M. (2019). Transcendencia imanente. Caderno de Sabado, *Coreio de Pova* (Porto Alegre, BR), 20 April, p. 4.

Mahajan, V., & Peterson, R. A. (1985). *Models of Innovation Diffusion* (Series: quantitative applications in the social sciences no. 48). Beverly Hills, CA: Sage.

Malsin, J. (2015). *Why Western Media Overlooked a Massacre in Nigeria*; CJR, 2 February www.cjr.org/behind_the_news/nigeria_coverage.php#sthash .JnG8eNLJ.dpuf

Masterman, M. (1970). The nature of paradigm. In I. Lakotos & A. Musgrave (eds.), *Criticism and the Growth of Knowledge* (pp. 59–90). Cambridge: Cambridge University Press.

Maturana, H., & Varela, F. (1980). *Autopoiesis and Cognition: The Realization of the Living*. Dordrecht: D. Reidel Publishing.

Meyer, M. (2008). *Principia Rhetorica: une théorie générale de l'argumentation*. Paris: Fayard.

Mayo, E. (1933). *The Human Problems of an Industrial Civilization*. New York: Macmillan.

Mazur, A. (1981). Media coverage and public opinion on scientific controversies. *Journal of Communication*, 31(2), 106–115.

Mazur, A., & Lee, J. (1993). Sounding the global alarm: environmental issues in the US national news. *Social Studies of Science*, 23, 681–720

McCarthy, J. D., & Zald, M. N. (1987). Resource mobilization and social movements: a partial theory. In M. N. Zald & J. D. McCarthy (eds.), *Social Movement in an Organizational Society: Collected Essays* (pp. 15–48). New Brunswick, NJ: Transaction Books.

McCombs, M. (2004). *Setting the Agenda: The Mass Media and Public Opinion*. Cambridge: Polity Press.

McCombs, M., & Reynolds, A. (2009). How the news shapes our civic agenda. In J. Bryant & M. B. Oliver (eds.), *Media Effects: Advances in Theory and Practice* (pp. 1–16). New York: Routledge.

McGuire, W. J. (1964). Inducing resistance to persuasion. In L. Berkowitz (ed.), *Advances in Experimental Social Psychology* (vol. 1)(pp. 191–229). New York: Academic Press.

(1985). Attitudes and attitude change. In G. Lindzey & E. Aronson (eds.), *Handbook of Social Psychology* (3rd ed.)(pp. 233–346). New York: Random House.

(1986). The vicissitudes of attitudes and similar representational constructs in twentieth century psychology. *European Journal of Social Psychology*, 16, 89–130.

McQuail, D., & Windahl, S. (1996). *Communication Models for the Study of Mass Communication* (2nd ed.) London: Longman.

Meeus, W. H. J., & Raaijmakers, Q. A. W. (1995). Obedience in modern society: the Utrecht studies. *Journal of Social Issues*, 51(3), 155–175.

Mercier, H., & Sperber, D. (2017). *The Enigma of Reason*. Cambridge, MA: Harvard University Press.

Merleau-Ponty, M. (1945/1962). *Phenomenology of Perception*. London: Routledge & Kegan.

Metzger, W. (1940/1975). *Psychologie – Die Entwicklung ihrer Grundannahmen seit der Einfuehrung des Experiments* (5th ed.). Darmstadt: Steinkopff Verlag.

Milgram, S. (1963). Behavioral study of obedience. *The Journal of Abnormal and Social Psychology*, 67(4), 371–378.

(1974). *Obedience to Authority: An Experimental View*. London: Tavistock Publications.

Miller, J. M., Saunders, K. L. & Farhart C. E. (2015) Conspiracy endorsement as motivated reasoning: the moderating roles of political knowledge and trust. *American Journal of Political Science*, 60(4), 824–844.

Minsky, M. (1974/1992). A framework for representing knowledge. In A. Collins & E. E. Smith (eds.), *Cognitive Science*. Burlington, MA: Morgan-Kaufmann.

Moghaddam, F. M. (2003). Interobjectivity and culture. *Culture and Psychology*, 9(3), 221–232.

(2013). *The Psychology of Dictatorship*. Washington, DC: American Psychological Association.

(2016). *The Psychology of Democracy*. Washington, DC: American Psychological Association.

Mokyr, J. (1990). *The Levers of Riches: Technological Creativity and Economic Progress*. Oxford: Oxford University Press.

Monaco, J. (1981). *How to Read a Film: The Art, Technology, Language, History and Theory of Film and Media*. Oxford: Oxford University Press.

Morgan, M., Shanahan, J. & Signorelli, N. (2009). Growing up with television: cultivation processes. In J. Bryant & M. B. Oliver (eds.), *Media Effects: Advances in Theory and Practice* (pp. 34–59). New York: Routledge.

Mori, M. (1970). The uncanny valley. *Energy*, 7(4), 33–35.

Morris, D. B. (1991). *The Culture of Pain*. Berkeley: University of California Press.

Moscovici, S. (1961/2008). *Psychoanalysis: Its image and Its Public.* Cambridge: Polity.

(1985). *The Age of the Crowd – A Historical Treatise on Mass Psychology.* Cambridge: Cambridge University Press.

(1988). *La machine à faire des dieux.* Paris: Fayard.

Moscovici, S., & Doise, W. (1994). *Conflict and Consensus: A General Theory of Collective Decisions.* London: Sage.

Moscovici, S., Doise, W. & Dulong, R. (1972). Studies in group decision II: differences of positions, differences of opinion and group polarization. *European Journal of Social Psychology*, 2(4), 385–399.

Moscovici, S., Lage, E. & Naffrechoux, M. (1969). Influence of a consistent minority on the responses of a majority in a color perception task. *Sociometry*, 32(4), 365–380.

Moscovici, S., & Personnaz, B. (1980). Studies in social influence V: minority influence and conversion behavior in a perceptual task. *Journal of Experimental Social Psychology*, 16(3), 270–282.

Moskowitz, G. B., Skurnik, I. & Galinsky, A. D. (1999). The history of dual-process notions and the future of preconscious control. In S. Chaiken & Y. Trope (eds.), *Dual-Process Theories in Social Psychology* (pp. 12–36). New York: Guildford Press.

Muchnik, L., Aral, S. & Taylor, S. J. (2013). Social influence bias: a randomized experiment. *Science*, 341, 647–651. doi: http://dx.doi.org/10.1126/science.1240466

Mueller, J. W. (2016). *What Is Populism?* Philadelphia: University of Pennsylvania Press.

Mugny, G., & Papastamou, S. (1980). When rigidity does not fail: individuali-zation and psychologization as resistances to the diffusion of minority innovations. *European Journal of Social Psychology*, 10, 43–61.

Muller, J. Z. (2018). *The Tyranny of Metrics.* Princeton, NJ: Princeton University Press.

Nai, A., Coma, F. M. I. & Maier, J. (2019). Donald Trump, populism, and the age of extremes: comparing personality traits and campaigning styles of Trump and other leaders worldwide. *Presidential Studies Quarterly*, 49(3), 609–643.

Nature. (2019). Beyond the periodic table – the past, present and future of chemistry's iconic chart. *Nature*, 565, no. 7741, pp. 535 & 551–565.

Nisbet, M. C., & Myers, T. (2007). The polls – trends: twenty years of public opinion about global warming. *Public Opinion Quarterly*, 71(3), 444–470.

Nisbet, M. C., Scheufele, D. A., Shanahan, J., Moy, P., Brossard, D. & Lewenstein, B. V. (2002). Knowledge, reservations, or promise? A media effects model for public perception of science. *Communication Research*, 29(5), 585–608.

Nisbett, R. E., & Ross, L. (1980). *Human Inference: Strategies and Shortcomings of Social Judgment.* Englewood Cliffs, NJ: Prentice Hall.

Noelle-Neumann, E. (1974). The spiral of silence: a theory of public opinion. *Journal of Communication*, 1, 43–51.

Norman, D. A. (1988). *The Psychology of Everyday Things*. New York: Basic Books.
  (1998). *The Invisible Computer: Why Good Products Can Fail, the Personal Computer Is So Complex, and Information Appliances Are the Solution*. Cambridge, MA: MIT Press.
  (2004). *Emotional Design: Why We Love (or Hate) Everyday Things*. New York: Basic Books.

Nye, R. A. (1975). *The Origins of Crowd Psychology*. London: Sage.

Nye, J. S. (1991). *Bound to Lead: The Changing Nature of American Power*. New York: Basic Books.
  (2004). *Soft Power: The Means to Success in World Politics*. New York: Public Affairs.

Neue Zuercher Zeitung (NZZ). (2019). *Folio Magazin Thema 'Ausserirdische', no 336*, July. Zurich.

O'Donahoe, B. (2011). *The Poetics of Homecoming: Heidegger, Homelessness and Homecoming Venture*. Newcastle upon Tyne: Cambridge Scholars Publishers.

Ortega Y., & Gasset, J. (1930/1956). *Der Aufstand der Massen*. Hamburg: Rowolt Verlag.

Oudshoorn, N., & Pinch, T. (eds.). (2003) *How Users Matter: The Co-construction of Users and Technology*. Cambridge, MA: MIT Press.

Packer, D. J. (2008). Identifying systematic disobedience in Milgram's obedience experiments: a meta-analytic review. *Perspectives on Psychological Science*, 3, 301–304.

Paicheler, G. (1977). Norms and attitude change II: the phenomenon of bipolarization. *European Journal of Social Psychology*, 7, 5–14.
  (1988). *The Psychology of Social Influence*. Cambridge: Cambridge University Press.

Pakulski, J. (1993). Mass social movements and social class. *International Sociology*, 8, 131–158.

Parsons, T. (1963). On the concept of influence. *The Public Opinion Quarterly*, 1, 37–62.

Paulhus, D. L. (2014). Toward a taxonomy of dark personalities. *Current Directions in Psychological Science*, 23(6), 421–426.

Pavlov, I. P. (1897/1902). *The Work of the Digestive Glands*. London: Griffin.

Pellegrini, E. K., & Scandura, T. A. (2008). Paternalistic leadership: a review and agenda for future research. *Journal of Management*, 34(3), 566–593.

Perelman, C. (1982). *The Realm of Rhetoric*. Paris: University of Notre Dame Press.

Pérez, J. A., & Mugny, G. (1987). Paradoxical effects of categorization in minority influence: when being an out-group is an advantage. *European Journal of Social Psychology*, 17(2), 157–169.

Perloff, R. M. (2014). *The Dynamics of Persuasion: Communication and Attitudes in the 21st Century* (5th ed.). Abingdon: Routledge.

Peters, H. P. (2014). Scientists as public experts. In M. Bucchi & B. Trench (eds.), *The Routledge Handbook of Public Communication of Science* (2nd ed.) (pp. 70–82). London: Routledge.

Petty, R. E., & Cacioppo, J. T. (1986). *Communication and Persuasion: Central and Peripheral Routes to Attitude Change.* New York: Springer-Verlag.

Peyton Young, H. (2009). Innovation diffusion in heterogeneous populations: contagion, social influence and social learning. *American Economics Review*, 99(5), 1988–1924.

Phillet-Shore, D. (2010). Making way and making sense: including newcomers in interaction. *Social Psychology Quarterly*, 73(2), 152–175.

Piff, P. K., Dietze, P., Feinberg, M., Stancato, D. M. & Keltner, D. (2015). Awe, the small self and prosocial behaviour. *Journal of Personality and Social Psychology*, 108(6), 883–899.

Pinch, T., & Bijker, W. E. (1987). The social construction of facts and artefacts: or how the sociology of science and the sociology of technology might benefit each other. In T. Bijker, T. P. Hughes & T. J. Pinch (eds.), *The Social Construction of Technological Systems* (pp. 9–50). Cambridge, MA: MIT Press.

Pottage, A. (2013). Ius resistendi: resistance as reflexivity. In M. W. Bauer, R. Harré & C. Jensen (eds.), *Resistance and the Practice of Rationality* (pp. 262–281). Newcastle upon Tyne: Cambridge Scholars Publishers.

Pras, A., Schober, M. F. & Spiro, N. (2017). What about their performance do free jazz improvisers agree upon? a case study. *Frontiers of Psychology*, 8, 966. doi: 10.3389/fpsyg.2017.00966.

Pratkanis, A. R. (2007). Social influence analysis: an index of tactics. In A. R. Pratkanis (ed.), The Science of Social Influence: Advances and Future Progress (Frontiers of Social Psychology)(pp. 17–82). New York: Psychology Press.

Prinz, W. (2012). *Open Minds: The Social Making of Agency and Intentionality*: Cambridge MA: MIT Press.

Psaltis, C. (2015). Communication and the microgenetic construction of knowledge. In G. Sammut, E. Andreouli, G. Gaskell & J. Valsiner (eds.), *The Cambridge Handbook of Social Representations* (pp. 113–127). Cambridge: Cambridge University Press.

Radkau, J. (2011). *The Age of Ecology: A Global History.* Cambridge: Polity.

Rampton, S., & Stauber, J. (2003). *Weapons of Mass Deception.* New York: J. P. Tarcher-Penguin.

Rawls, J. (1972). *A Theory of Justice.* Oxford: Clarendon Press.

Reddy, M. J. (1993). The conduit metaphor: a case of frame conflict in our language about language. In E. Ortony (ed.), *Metaphor and Thought* (2nd ed.) (pp. 164–201). Cambridge: Cambridge University Press.

Reemtsma, J. P. (2016). *Gewalt als Lebensform.* Stuttgart: Reclam Verlag.

Reicher, S. (1984). The St Pauls riot: an explanation of the limits of crowd action in terms of a social identity model. *European Journal of Social Psychology*, 14, 1–21.

Reicher, S. (1996). The battle of Westminster: developing the social identity model of crowd behaviour in order to explain the initiation and development of collective conflict. *European Journal of Social Psychology*, 26, 115–134.

(1996). The crowd's century: reconciling practical success with theoretical failure. *British Journal of Social Psychology*, 35, 535–553.

(2011) Mass action and mundane reality: an argument for putting crowd analysis at the centre of the social sciences. *Contemporary Social Science*, 6 (3), 433–449.

Reicher, S., & Haslam, S. A. (2011). After shock? towards a social identity explanation of the Milgram obedience studies. *British Journal of Social Psychology*, 50(1), 163–169.

Rhodes, R. (1999). *Visions of Technology: A Century of Vital Debate about Machines, Systems and the Human World*. New York: Simon & Schuster.

Richter, L., & Kruglanski, A. W. (1999). Motivated search for common ground: need for closure effects on audience design in interpersonal communication. *Personality and Social Psychology Bulletin*, 25(9), 1101–1114.

Riesch, H., (2010). Theorizing boundary work as representation and identity. *Journal for the Theory of Social Behaviour*, 40(4), 452–473.

Roberts, A. (2005). *The History of Science Fiction*. Basingstoke: Palgrave Macmillan.

Rochat, F., & Modigliani, A. (1995). The ordinary quality of resistance: from Milgram's laboratory to the village of LeChambon. *Journal of Social Issues*, 51(3), 195–210.

Rock, I. (1990). The frame of reference. In I. Rock (ed.), *The Legacy of Solomon Asch* (pp. 243–270). Hillsdale, NJ: Lawrence Erlbaum.

Rogers, E. M. (1962/1996). *Diffusion of Innovation* (4th ed.). New York: Free Press.

(1997). *A History of Communication Study: A Biographical Approach*. New York: The Free Press.

Romeo, A., Tesio, V., Castelnuevo, G. & Castelli, L. (2017). Attachment style and chronic pain: towards an interpersonal model of pain. *Frontiers of Psychology*, 8, 284. doi: 10.3389/fpsyg.2017.00284.

Rosa, H. (2016). *Resonanz: eine Soziologie der Weltbeziehung*. Frankfurt: Suhrkamp.

Rosenthal, R., & Jacobson, L. (1968). *Pygmalion in the Classroom*. New York: Holt, Rinehart & Winston.

Roskos-Ewoldsen, D. R., Roskos-Ewoldsen, B. & Carpentier, F. D. (2009). Media priming: an updated synthesis. In J. Bryant & M. B. Oliver (eds.), *Media Effects: Advances in Theory and Practice* (pp. 75–93). New York: Routledge.

Ross, L. (1977). The intuitive psychologist and his shortcomings: distortions in the attribution process. In L. Berkowitz (ed.), *Advances in Experimental Psychology* (vol. 10) (pp. 173–220). New York: Academic Press.

Ross, L., & Nisbett, R. E. (1991). *The Person and the Situation: Perspectives of Social Psychology*. London: Pinter & Martin.

Ross, L., & Ward, A. (1996). Naive realism in everyday life: implications for social conflict and misunderstanding. In T. Brown, E. S. Reed & E. Turiel (eds.), *Values and Knowledge* (pp. 103–135). Hillsdale, NJ: Erlbaum.

Rothman, S. (1990). Journalists, broadcasters, scientific experts and public opinion. *Minerva*, 28(2), 117–133.

Runciman, D. (2019). *Where Power Stops: The Making and Unmaking of Presidents and Prime Ministers*. London: Profile Books.

Russell, B. (2010). *Authority and the Individual, BBC Reith Lecture of 1949*. London: Routledge Classics.

Sabini, J., & Silver, M. (1983). Dispositional vs situational interpretations of Milgram's obedience experiments: the fundamental attributional error. *Journal for the Theory of Social Behaviour*, 13(2), 147–154.

Sagi, E., Diermeier, D. & Kaufmann, S. (2013). Identifying issue frames in text. *PLoS One*, 8(7), e69185.

Sajama, S., & Kamppinen, M. (1987). *A Historical Introduction to Phenomenology*. London: Crome Helm.

Salomon, G. (ed.). (1993). *Distributed Cognitions: Psychological and Educational Considerations*. Cambridge: Cambridge University Press.

Sammut, G. (2011). Civic solidarity: the negotiation of identities in modern societies. *Papers on Social Representations*, 20(1), 4.1–4.24.

(2015). Attitudes, social representations and points of view. In G. Sammut, E. Andreouli, G. Gaskell & J. Valisner (eds), *The Cambridge Handbook of Social Representations* (pp. 96-112). Cambridge: Cambridge University Press.

Sammut, G., Andreouli, E., Gaskell, G. & Valsiner, J. (eds.). (2015) *The Cambridge Handbook of Social Representations*. Cambridge: Cambridge University Press.

Sammut, G., Bauer, M. & Jovchelovitch, S. (2018). Knowledge and experience: Interobjectivity, subjectivity and social relations. In A. Rosa & J. Valsiner (eds.), *The Cambridge Handbook of Sociocultural Psychology* (2nd ed.) (pp. 49–62). Cambridge: Cambridge University Press.

Sammut, G., Bezzina, F. & Sartawi, M. (2015). The spiral of conflict: naïve realism and the black sheep effect in attributions of knowledge and ignorance. *Peace and Conflict: Journal of Peace Psychology*, 21(2), 289–294.

Sammut, G., Daanen, P. & Moghaddam, F. M. (eds.). (2013) *Understanding the Self and Others: Explorations in Intersubjectivity and Interobjectivity*. London: Routledge.

Sammut, G., Daanen, P. & Sartawi, M. (2010). Interobjectivity: representations and artefacts in cultural psychology. *Culture & Psychology*, 16(4), 451–463.

Sammut, G., & Howarth, C. S. (2014). Social representations. In T. Teo (ed.), *Encyclopedia of Critical Psychology* (pp. 1799–1802). New York: Springer.

Sammut, G., Jovchelovitch, S., Buhagiar, L. J., Veltri, G. A., Redd, R. & Salvatore, S. (2018). Arabs in Europe: arguments for and against integration. *Peace and Conflict: Journal of Peace Psychology*, 24(4), 398–406.

Sammut, G., & Sartawi, M. (2012). Perspective-taking and the attribution of ignorance. *Journal for the Theory of Social Behavior*, 42(2), 181–200.

Sammut, G., Tsirogianni, S. & Moghaddam, F. M. (2013). Interobjective social values. In G. Sammut, P. Daanen & F. M. Moghaddam (eds.), *Understanding the Self and Others: Explorations in Intersubjectivity and Interobjectivity* (pp. 161–174). London: Routledge.

Sammut, G., Tsirogianni, S. & Wagoner, B. (2012). Representations from the past: social relations and the devolution of social representations. *Integrative Psychological and Behavioral Sciences*, 46(4), 493–511.

Sanders, C. (2007). Using social network analysis to explore social movements: a relational approach. *Social Movement Studies*, 6(3), 227–243.

Saussure de, F. (1915/1959). *Course in General Linguistics*. Glasgow: William Collins.

Schaffer, S. (1988). Astronomers mark time: discipline and the personal equation. *Science in Context*, 2(1), 115–145.

Schank, R. C., & Abelson, R. P. (1977). *Scripts, Plans, Goals and Understanding*. Hillsdale, NJ: Lawrence Erlbaum Associates.

Scheler, M. (1926/1960). *Die Wissensformen und die Gesellschaft*. Bern: Francke Verlag.

Scheufele, D. A. (1999). Framing as a theory of media effects. *Journal of Communication*, 49, 103–121.

Schiffmann, H. R. (1976). *Sensation and Perception: An Integrated Approach*. New York: John Wiley & Sons.

Schmidle, R. (2013). In the desert with Lawrence of Arabia. In G. Sammut, P. Daanen & F. M. Moghaddam (eds.), *Understanding the Self and Others: Explorations in Inter-subjectivity and Inter-objectivity* (pp. 175–189). London: Routledge.

Schopenhauer, A. (1830/2004). *The Art of Always Being Right: The 38 Subtle Ways to Win When You Are Defeated* (A. C. Grayling, ed.). London: Gibson Square Books.

Schutz, A. (1944). The stranger: an essay in social psychology. *American Journal of Sociology*, 49(6), 499–507.

  (1945). The homecomer. *American Journal of Sociology*, 50(5), 369–376.

Schwartz, S. H. (2011). Studying value: personal adventure, future directions. *Journal of Cross-Cultural Psychology*, 42(2), 307–319.

Scott, J. C. (1987). Resistance without protest and without organization: peasant opposition to the Islamic Zakat and the Christian Tithe. *Comparative Studies in Society and History*, 29, 417–453.

Searle, J. R. (1995). *The Construction of Social Reality*. London: Penguin.

  (2005). What is an institution? *Journal of Institutional Economics*, 1(1), 1–22.

Seed, D. (2011). *Science Fiction – A Very Short Introduction*. Oxford: Oxford University Press.

Sen, A. (2006). *The Argumentative Indian: Writings on Indian History, Culture and Identity*. London: Picador.

Sennett, R. (1980). *Authority*. New York: Knopf.

Shamir, B., & Howell, J. M. (1999). Organizational and contextual influences on the emergence and effectiveness of charismatic leadership. *Leadership Quarterly*, 10(2), 257–283.

Shamir, B., House, R. J. & Arthur, M. (1992). The motivational effects of charismatic leadership. *Organization Science*, 4(4), 577–594.

Shannon, C. E. & Weaver, W. (1949). *The Mathematical Theory of Communication*. Urbana: University of Illinois Press.

Shapin, S. (2008). Politics and publics. In E. J. Hackett, A. Amsterdamska, M. Lynch & J. Wajcman (eds.), *The Handbook of Science and Technology Studies* (3rd ed.)(pp. 433–448). Cambridge, MA: MIT Press.

Sherif, M. (1935). A study of some social factors in perception. *Archives of Psychology*, 27(187), 23–46.

(1936). *The Psychology of Social Norms*. New York: Octagon books.

(1937). An experimental approach to the study of attitudes. *Sociometry*, 1(1/2), 90–98.

Shrum, L. J. (2009). Media consumption and perception of social reality. In J. Bryant & M. B. Oliver (eds.), *Media Effects: Advances in Theory and Practice* (pp. 50–73). New York: Routledge.

Simon, B., & Klandermans, B. (2001). Politicized collective identity: a social psychological analysis. *American Psychologist*, 56(4), 319–331.

Simon, H. A. (1956). Rational choice and the structure of the environment. *Psychological Review*, 62(2), 129–138.

(1981). *The Sciences of the Artificial*. Cambridge, MA: MIT Press.

Skinner, B. F. (1953). *Science and Human Behavior*. Oxford: Macmillan.

Sloman, S., & Fernbach, P. (2017). *The Knowledge Illusion: Why We Never Think Alone*. New York: Riverhead Books.

Sloterdijk, P. (1985). *Der Zauberbaum*. Frankfurt: Suhrkamp.

(2000). *Die Verachtung der Massen: Versuch ueber Kulturkaempfe in der modernen Gesellschaft*. Frankfurt: Suhrkamp.

Smith, G. (2001). Group development: a review of the literature and a commentary on future research directions. *Group Facilitation*, 3(spring), 14–45.

Snyder, M. (1987). *Public Appearances, Private Realities*. New York: Freeman.

Sperber, D. (1990). The epidemiology of beliefs. In C. Fraser & G. Gaskell (eds.), *The Social Psychology of Widespread Beliefs* (pp. 25–44). Oxford: Clarendon Press.

Spring, P. (2015). *Great Walls and Linear Barriers*. Barnsley: Pen & Sword Military Books.

Staerkle, C. (2015). Social order and political legitimacy. In G. Sammut, E. Andreouli, G. Gaskell & J. Valsiner (eds.), *The Cambridge Handbook of Social Representations* (pp. 280–294). Cambridge: Cambridge University Press.

Starker, S. (1991). *Evil Influences: Crusades against the Mass Media*. New Brunswick, NJ: Transaction Publishers.

Steffen, W., Persson, A., Deutsch, L., Zalasiewicz, J., Williams, M., Richardson, K., Crumley, C., Crutzen, P., Folke, C., Gordon, L., Molina, M.,

Ramanthan, V., Rockstrom, J., Scheffer, M., Schellnhuber, H. J. & Svedin, U. (2011). The anthropocene: from global change to planetary stewardship. *AMBIO*, 40(7), 739–761. DOI 10.1007/s13280–011-0185-x.

Sterling, B. (2005). *Shaping Things*. Cambridge, MA: MIT Press.

Stern, P. (2000). Psychology and the science of human-environment interaction. *American Psychologist*, 55, 523–530.

Stivers, R. (2001). *Technology As Magic*. New York: The Continuum Publishing Company.

Stott, C., & Reicher, S. (1998). Crowd action as intergroup process: introducing the police perspective. *European Journal of Social Psychology*, 28, 509–529.

Strodthoff, G. G., Hawkins, R. P. & Schoenfeld, A. C. (1985). Media roles in a social movement: a model of ideology diffusion. *Journal of Communication*, 35, 134–153.

Suchmann, L., Trigg, R. & Blomberg, J. (2002). Working artefacts: ethno-methods of the prototype. *British Journal of Sociology*, 53(2), 163–179.

Sunstein, C. R. (2016). *The Ethics of Influence: Government in the Age of Behavioral Science*. Cambridge: Cambridge University Press.

Surowiecki, J. (2004). *The Wisdom of the Crowds: Why the Many Are Smarter than the Few*. London: Abacus.

Sztompka, P. (2007). Trust in science. *Journal of Classical Sociology*, 7(2), 211–220.

Tajfel, H., & Turner, J. C. (1979). An integrative theory of intergroup conflict. In W. G. Austin & S. Worchel (eds.), *The Social Psychology of Intergroup Relations* (pp. 33–47). Monterey, CA: Brooks/Cole.

Tarde, G. (1890/1962). *The Laws of Imitation*. Gloucester, MA: Peter Smith.
    (1901/2006). *L'opinion et la Foule*. Paris: Editions du Sandre.
    (2010). *On Communication and Social Influence: Selected Papers* [T. N. Clark ed.]. Cambridge: Cambridge University Press.

Tarrow, S. (1994). *Power in Movement: Social Movements, Collective Action and Politics*. Cambridge: Cambridge University Press.

Taylor, C. (2007). *A Secular Age*. Cambridge, MA: Belknap Press.

Taylor, T. (2012). *The Artificial Ape: How Technology Changed the Course of Human Evolution*. London: Palgrave.

Tchakhotine, S. (1952). *Le viol des foules par la propagande politique*. Paris: Gallimard.

Tenner, E. (1997). *Why Things Bite Back: Predicting the Problems of Progress*. London: Forth Estate.

Thaler, R. H., & Sunstein, C. R. (2008). *Nudge: Improving Decisions about Health, Wealth and Happiness*. New Haven, CT: Yale University Press.

Tichenor, P., Donohue, G. & Olen, C. (1970). Mass media flow and differential growth of knowledge. *Public Opinion Quarterly*, 34, 159–170.

Tie, X. (2011). *In the Name of the Masses: Conceptualisation and Representation of the Crowd in Early 20th Century China*. Humanities PhD, University of Chicago.

Tilly, C. (2004). *Social Movements, 1768–2004*. Boulder, CO: Paradigm.

Todd, P. M., & Gigerenzer, G. (2000). Précis of simple heuristics that make us smart. *Behavioral and Brain Sciences*, 23(5), 727–741.

Tomasello, M. (2008). *Origins of Human Communication*. Cambridge, MA: MIT Press.

(2009). *Why We Cooperate*. Cambridge, MA: MIT Press.

Tomasello, M., & Carpenter, M. (2007). Shared intentionality. *Developmental Science*, 10(1), 121–125.

Tsuda, T. (2003). *Strangers in the Ethnic Homeland: Japanese Brazilian Return Migration in Transnational Perspective*. New York: Columbia University Press.

Tuckman, B. (1965). Developmental sequence in small groups. *Psychological Bulletin*, 63(6), 384–399.

Tuckman, B., & Jensen, M. A. C. (1977). Stages of small-group development revisited. *Group & Organization Management*, 2(4), 419–427.

Tuomela, R. (2000). Collective and joint intention. *Mind & Society*, 2(1), 39–69.

Turkle, S. (1984). *The Second Self: Computers and the Human Spirit*. Cambridge, MA: MIT Press.

(2016). *Reclaiming Conversation: The Power of Talk in the Digital Age*. London: Penguin.

Turner, D. F. & Krauss, F. (1978). Fallible indicators of the subjective state of the nation. *American Psychologist*, 33, 456–470.

Ulich, E. (2011). *Arbeitspsychologie* (7th ed.). Stuttgart: Schaeffer-Poeschel.

Valente, T. W., & Rogers E. M. (1995). The origins and development of the diffusion of innovation paradigm as an example of scientific growth. *Science Communication*, 16(3), 242–273.

van Holthoon, F. L., & Olson, D. R. (eds.). (1987). *Common Sense: The Foundations for Social Science*. Lantham, MD: University of America Press.

van Lente, H., Spitters, C. & Peine, A. (2015). Comparing technological hype cycles: towards a theory. *Technological Forecasting & Social Change*, 80, 1615–1628.

VonMatt, P. (2012). Der Heimkehrer – eine Skizze. In das Kalb vor der Gotthardpost (ed.), *Zur Literatur und Politik der Schweiz* (pp. 273–276). Munchen: Hanser.

Wagner, W., Elejabarrieta, F. & Lahnsteiner, I. (1995). Objectification by metaphor in the social representation of conception. *European Journal of Social Psychology*, 25, 671–688.

Wagner, W., Sen, R., Permanadeli R. & Howarth, C. S. (2012). The veil and Muslim women's identity: cultural pressures and resistance to stereotyping. *Culture & Psychology*, 18(4), 521–541.

Wall, P. D. (1979). On the relation of injury to pain: the John J. Bonica Lecture *Pain*, 6, 253–264.

Walsh, L. (2013). *Scientists As Prophets: A Rhetorical Genealogy*. Oxford: Oxford University Press.

Walster, E., & Festinger, L. (1962). The effectiveness of 'overheard' persuasive communications. *Journal of Abnormal and Social Psychology*, 65(6), 395–402.

Ward, E., Ganis, G. & Bach, P. (2019). Spontaneous vicarious perception of the content of another's visual perspective. *Current Biology*. DOI: 10.1016/j.cub.2019.01.046.

Weber, M. (1968). The types of legitimate domination. In G. Roth & C. Wittich (eds.), *Economy and Society* (vol. 3) (pp. 212–216). New York: Bedminster. (1978/1922). *Economy and Society* (G. Roth & C. Wittich eds.). Berkeley: University of California Press.

Weinert, B. (2002). Integrating models of diffusion of innovation: a conceptual framework. *Annual Review of Sociology*, 28, 297–326.

Weizenbaum, J. (1976). *Computer Power and Human Reason: From Judgement to Calculation*. San Francisco: WH Freeman & Co.

Wells, H. G. (1898/2005). *The War of the Worlds*. London: Penguin.

Wertheimer, M. (1912). Experimentelle Studien ueber das Sehen von Bewegung. *Zeitschrift fuer Psychologie*, 61, 161–265.

Whiten, A., Horner, V., & de Waal, F. B. M. (2005). Conformity to cultural norms of tool use in chimpanzees. *Nature*, 437, 737–740.

Williams, K. D., & Nida, S. A. (2011). Ostracism: consequences and coping. *Current Directions in Psychological Science*, 20(2), 71–75.

Winston, B. (1998). *Media Technology and Society: A History from the Telegraph to the Internet*. London: Routledge.

Wood, W., Lundgren, S., Ouellette, J. A., Busceme, S. & Blackstone, T. (1994). Minority influence: a meta-analytic review of social influence processes. *Psychological Bulletin*, 115(3), 323–345.

Woolley, J. T. (2000). Using media-based data in studies of politics. *American Journal of Politics*, 44(1), 156–173.

Wyatt, S., Milojević, S., Park, H. W. & Leydesdorff, L. (2017). The intellectual and practical contributions of scientometrics to STS. In U. Felt, R. Fouché, C. Miller & L. Smith-Doerr (eds.), *Handbook of Science and Technology Studies* (4th ed.)(pp. 87–112). Boston: MIT Press.

Yardi, S., & Boyd, D. (2010). Dynamic debates: an analysis of group polarization over time on Twitter. *Bulletin of Science, Technology & Society*, 30(5), 316–327. http://doi.org/10.1177/0270467610380011.

Yates, F. (1966). *The Art of Memory*. London: Pimlico Press.

Zaller, J. R. (1992). *The Nature and Origin of Mass Opinion*. Cambridge: Cambridge University Press.

Zomeren, M., Potmes, T. & Spears, R. (2008). Towards an integrative social identity model of collective action: a quantitative research synthesis of three socio-psychological perspectives. *Psychological Bulletin*, 134, 504–535.

Zubek, J. (ed.). (1969). *Sensory Deprivation: Fifteen Years of Research*. New York: Appleton Century Crofts.

Zuckerman, E. (2015). *Media coverage of Charlie Hebdo and the Baga massacre: a study in contrasts*. MIT Centre for Civic Media [internet note published 13 January 2015, 8.38pm GMT].

Index

Abelson, R. P., 194, 296
Abrams, D., 80, 132, 271
acceptance, 6, 21, 108, 123, 135, 169, 173, 193, 200–201, 209–212, 224, 248, 255
accommodation, 2, 12, 22–23, 94–95, 109, 134, 138, 165, 182, 185, 209, 212, 215, 226, 228, 230, 235, 243
actants, 190, 202
Adorno, T. W., 48, 268, 271
affordances, 1, 194, 213, 281
agenda setting, 11, 23, 161, 182–183
Ainsworth, M. D. S., 99–100, 271
Ajzen, I., 153, 271, 279
algorithms, 167, 178, 203, 213, 235
Allport, G. W., 178, 271
Allyn, J., 141, 271
Anders, G., 253, 271
Andreouli, E., 273, 286–287, 293, 295, 297
animal magnetism, 29, 31, 38–39
Apfelbaum, E., 39, 41, 271
architecture of authority, 134
Arcidiacono, F., 244, 275
Arendt, H., 63, 122–123, 133, 250, 266–268, 271
argumentation, 12, 17, 108, 114, 139, 156, 235, 267, 289
Arnstein, S. R., 86, 271
Aronson, E., 3, 272, 290
Arrow, H., 89, 272
Arthur, M., 58, 297
Asch, S. E., 2, 31–32, 77–78, 86, 89, 95, 103–108, 110, 112–114, 117–118, 123, 131, 135, 152, 177, 180, 221, 253, 265, 272, 275, 294
assimilation, 2, 12, 22–23, 89, 94–95, 98, 135, 138, 165, 185, 200, 213–215, 226, 228, 235, 241, 250
Assmann, J., 18, 198, 272
Atran, S., 174, 272
attachment, 100, 113, 271

attention, 1, 15, 35–36, 80, 139, 143, 156, 167, 169, 181–182, 184–186, 196–197, 209, 211, 244, 256
Attia, S., 178, 279
attitudes, 14–16, 78, 81, 84, 88, 90, 108–109, 139, 145, 148–149, 151, 153–157, 159, 174, 199, 201–202, 221, 255
Austin, J. L., 130, 272
authority, 7, 54, 61, 63–64, 69, 72, 118–122, 124–125, 129–135, 181–182, 265–270
autonomy, 81, 84, 111, 248, 255, 267–268
Avolio, B. J., 58, 272
axial time, 18

Bach, P., 118, 300
Bachrach, P., 209, 272
Bal, R., 274
balance of reciprocity, 145, 147, 159
Bales, R. F., 89, 272
banality of evil, 63, 123, 135, 271
Bang Petersen, M., 114, 288
Bangerter, A., 73, 178, 272, 280
Baratz, M. S., 209, 272
Barber, B., 268, 272
Barker, M., 253, 272
Barley, R. S., 58, 272
Barnett, B., 193, 272
barricades, 11, 161, 191–192, 213, 235
barriers, 204–205, 297
Bar-Tal, D., 166, 198, 273
Barthes, R., 139, 273
Bartlett, F. C., 177, 273
Bass, B. M., 58, 272–273
Bassett, R., 147, 277
Bauer, M. W., 73, 77, 84, 86, 88, 94, 130, 139, 154, 156, 166, 168, 173, 176, 197, 211–212, 218, 231, 255, 269, 273–274, 278–281, 285, 293, 295
Becker, H. S., 244–245, 274
Begout, B., 246–247, 251, 274

301

Giedion, S., 193
Gigerenzer, G., 144, 209, 264, 286, 299
Gildea, R., 35, 281
Gillespie, A., 87, 281, 284
Ginneken, J van., 38, 281
Girard, R., 7, 281
Glăveanu, V., 139, 156, 274
Godin, B., 200, 211, 238, 264, 268, 273, 281
Goldstein, D., 147, 207, 277, 284
Gollwitzer, P. M., 209, 281–282
Goncalves-Portelinha, I., 284
grand narratives, 170, 186
Graumann, C. F., 48, 70, 256, 271, 277, 282, 286
Gregory, J., 141, 176, 251, 282
Gridley, M. C., 88, 282
Groh, D., 38, 282, 285
Gross, A. G., 18, 280, 282
group decision, 288
group formation, 88–89
Grune-Yanoff, T., 209, 283
Gurwitch, A., 87, 256, 260, 282
Gutteling, J. M., 183, 282

Habermas, J., 6, 11, 17–19, 138, 255, 267, 282
Haidt, J., 199, 222, 282, 285
Hampton, G. J., 228, 282
Hannemyr, G., 200, 282
Hanseth, O., 193, 282
hard power, 5, 7, 19, 21, 61, 63, 137, 229
Hardt, M., 43, 49, 282
Harlow, H. F., 99–100, 272, 283
Harré, R., 102–103, 142, 232, 274, 283, 293
Haslam, S. A., 130, 271, 277, 283, 294
Hazan, E., 191, 283
Heidegger, M., 49, 90, 191, 246, 283, 292
Heider, F., 145–147, 283
Helbling, D., 45, 283
herding, 45, 47
Hertwig, R., 208, 283
Heuristic-Systematic Model [HSM], 142
HiFi transmission, 181
Hindriks, F. A., 193, 283
Hinds, J., 203, 283
Hingst, R. D., 89, 283
Hogg, M. A., 3, 60, 64, 132, 271, 276, 283
Hollander, M. M., 135, 283–284
Horner, V., 101–102, 131, 300
House, R. J., 57–58, 284, 290, 297
Hovland, C. I., 140, 144, 152, 284
Howarth, C. S., 64, 66, 115, 133, 150, 160, 284, 295, 299
Howe, J., 44, 284
Howell, J. M., 57–59, 284, 296
Husserl, E., 191, 284
hylomorphism, 41
hype cycles, 168, 197, 299

hypnosis, 38
hypodermic needle model, 140

identity, 40, 42–43, 45, 47, 58, 64–67, 77–78, 87, 130–131, 133, 156–157, 198, 255, 265, 283–285, 293, 297, 299–300
imagination, 33–34, 38, 40, 49, 81, 83, 166, 169, 174, 226–227, 247, 251, 255
imitation, 32–33, 36, 99, 101, 113, 200, 207, 235, 285
individual differences, 15, 20–21, 57, 66, 69, 105, 119, 129, 139, 150, 218, 239
informal, 166
inoculation, 154
Inscription of Behaviour, 192
installation, 10, 192–195, 197, 199, 203, 209, 211, 232, 286
interlocked, 12
inter-objectivity, 15–16, 23, 89, 95, 161, 189–190, 199, 212, 220, 223–224, 254–255, 296
interpenetration of views, 86
intersubjectivity, 15–16, 81, 86–87, 94–95, 165, 190, 199, 212, 220, 223–224, 232, 254, 296
issue cycle, 173, 175–176, 181, 183, 186, 213, 240

Janik, V., 117, 286
Janis, I. L., 140–141, 284
Jaspers, K., 18, 284
Jensen, M. A. C., 89, 274, 293, 299
Jodelet, D., 84, 284
Johnson, E. J., 52, 56, 207, 284
Joinson, A., 203, 283
joint attention, 15, 35–37, 94–95, 165, 167–168, 178, 186, 212, 223, 235
joint intentionality, 16, 36, 94–95, 102, 109, 114–115, 138, 166–167, 186, 193, 199, 209, 212, 223–224, 228
Jonas, H., 48, 251, 284
Jones, S., 28, 141, 287
Jovchelovitch, S., 17, 84, 130, 157, 231, 273, 284, 295
Jurdant, B., 92, 284

Kahneman, D., 80, 207, 262–263, 285
Kamppinen, M., 256, 295
Kaplan, A., 141, 251, 285
Kaufmann, S., 290, 295
Kellerman, B., 55, 285
Kelley, H., 140, 284
Kelly, C., 42, 285
Keltner, D., 199, 285, 293
Kempe, M., 45, 285
Kennedy, G. A., 18, 93, 280, 285
Kepplinger, H. M., 171, 180, 285

Lightning Source UK Ltd.
Milton Keynes UK
UKHW020148161021
392307UK00020B/231